THE NAZIS

A WARNING FROM HISTORY

Laurence Rees wrote and produced the BBC Television series *The Nazis: A Warning from History*. He is also Creative Director of BBC History Programmes, as well as a former Editor of *Timewatch*, BBC TV's historical documentary series. Under his editorship *Timewatch* won three Emmy awards in three years. *The Times* has described him as 'Britain's most distinguished producer of historical documentaries'.

He has won many awards for his four series on World War II – *The Nazis: A Warning from History*, *War of the Century* (about the Hitler/Stalin war), *Horror in the East* (examining the wartime actions of the Japanese) and *Auschwitz: The Nazis and the 'Final Solution'* – including a BAFTA, an International Documentary Association Award and a Broadcasting Press Guild Award.

His other previous credits as a writer and producer of historical documentaries include a controversial investigation into alleged British war crimes at the end of World War II, *A British Betrayal*, and the acclaimed film *Goebbels: Master of Propaganda*. In 2005 he wrote and presented an analysis of his work – *Inside the Nazi State* – for UKTV History and was also awarded an Honorary Doctorate by the University of Sheffield for his contribution towards historical understanding.

He was educated at Solihull School and Oxford University.

For Oliver, Camilla and Benedict

THE NAZIS

A WARNING FROM HISTORY

LAURENCE REES

BBC
BOOKS

Other books by Laurence Rees

Non-fiction
Selling Politics (BBC Books 1992)
War of the Century (BBC Books 1999)
Horror in the East (BBC Books 2001)
Auschwitz: The Nazis and the 'Final Solution' (BBC Books 2005)

Fiction
Electric Beach (Weidenfeld & Nicolson 1990)

Copyright © Laurence Rees 2005
The moral right of the author has been asserted.
First published in hardback 1997. First published in paperback 1998
This paperback edition first published in 2005 by BBC Books, an imprint
of Ebury Publishing. A Random House Group Company

The Random House Group Limited Reg. No. 954009
Addresses for companies within the Random House Group can be found
at www.randomhouse.co.uk

Commissioning editor: Martin Redfern
Project editor: Eleanor Maxfield. Designer: Martin Hendry
Picture researcher: Joanne King. Production: Peter Hunt

Printed and bound in Great Britain by Clays Ltd, St Ives plc

ISBN 978 0 563 49333 4
20 19 18 17 16

CONTENTS

INTRODUCTION 7

Chapter 1
HELPED INTO POWER 13

Chapter 2
CHAOS AND CONSENT 45

Chapter 3
THE WRONG WAR 79

Chapter 4
THE WILD EAST 111

Chapter 5
HIGH HOPES 143

Chapter 6
A DIFFERENT KIND OF WAR 195

Chapter 7
THE TIDE TURNS 233

Chapter 8
THE ROAD TO TREBLINKA 287

Chapter 9
REAPING THE WHIRLWIND 327

NOTES 361   **NOTES ON EYEWITNESSES** 371

ACKNOWLEDGEMENTS 389   **INDEX** 392

PICTURE CREDITS 400

If you gaze for long into an abyss,
the abyss gazes also into you.

FRIEDRICH NIETZSCHE, Jenseits von Gut und Böse

INTRODUCTION

IT'S ONLY BY LOOKING BACK THAT LIFE TAKES ON A PATTERN. That's as true of our own individual lives as it is of the great events of history. I never thought, for example, when I embarked on *Nazis: A Warning from History* in the early 1990s that it would be the start of such a long journey. For it was only whilst making *Warning from History* that I fully realised the wealth of new historical material that the fall of the Berlin Wall had just made available in Eastern Europe. It was that, plus the growing realization that it was almost impossible to overemphasize the importance of the Hitler/Stalin war in any attempt to understand the mentality of the Nazis, that led me to move straight onto another project. I spent several more years writing, producing and directing *War of the Century* about the epic struggle between Nazism and Communism.

The pattern of all this work seems clear to me only now, in a way that it never was at the time, which is why I'm so grateful to BBC Books for reissuing here, not just the original *Nazis: A Warning from History*, but for allowing me to incorporate within it the majority of the *War of the Century* book. For I think the material in *War of the Century* – particularly the chapter 'A Different Kind of War' – vividly demonstrates the practical consequences of Nazism. Certainly travelling around Russia, Belarus and the Ukraine, and hearing stories about the Nazi occupation, allowed me personally to gain a greater insight into the essential nature of Hitler's world view: a bleak landscape where pity is outlawed and life is reduced to a Darwinian struggle in which the weak deserve to suffer because it is their destiny.

Of course there are potential problems in slotting one book inside another. Some are easy to rectify – the danger of repetition, for example – and I've done my best to re-edit the text to avoid going over the same ground twice. I've also updated the content in places where my thinking has changed since writing the original words – that's particularly the case with the section on the origins of the Nazis' 'Final Solution'. But there remains the real danger that, by focusing chiefly on the War in the East and hearing the extensive stories of Russian veterans, an impression is created that somehow the war in the West 'didn't matter'. So I need to emphasize here that nothing could be further from my own belief. I grew up on the heroic stories of the sacrifice of British and American servicemen during World War II. My father flew in the RAF and my uncle was torpedoed and killed whilst serving on the Atlantic convoys. It was because I wanted to see the full story of the Western Allies' fight against Nazism told to the widest possible audience that I devised television series such as *Battle of the Atlantic* and *D-Day to Berlin*, and then editorially oversaw their construction.

But the book you are holding in your hand is about something different. What I have tried to do here is to penetrate as deeply as I can the essential nature of Nazism. It's not a history of World War II or an account of all the significant military decisions of the conflict, but an attempt to see how far it is possible to understand why the Germans and their allies did what they did. It is in pursuit of that aim – and that aim alone – that I thought it important to include the material from *War of the Century*.

As I look back on this work now, I also see another

aspect of it that I didn't fully recognize at the time. These books, and the television series that went with them, were based on approximately 100 unique interviews – many with former members of the Nazi Party. I had the chance to meet and question people who adored Hitler, worked for Himmler, fought on the Eastern Front and committed atrocities whilst members of the SS. This is now an opportunity that is no longer available to anyone else who comes after me – for the simple reason that most of the people we interviewed have since died. In the heat of the production process, focused as I was on a forthcoming transmission or publication date, it didn't really occur to me that we were making something of value for future generations.

Of course, as the number of survivors diminishes, attitudes to Nazism and World War II will also change. For my generation the only way of understanding the world we grew up in was to know what happened during World War II: a divided Germany, the Cold War, the Soviet domination of Eastern Europe – the consequences of the conflict were all around us. But for today's schoolchildren it is all very different. I remember the daughter of a friend asking me, when she was seven years old: 'What came first, Adolf Hitler or the Battle of Hastings?' To her generation Nazism is just another bit of history, part of an enormous jigsaw that has to be fitted in along with the Romans, the Normans and Henry VIII.

You won't be surprised to hear, I guess, that I don't think that the Third Reich is 'just another bit of history'. I believe that a study of Nazism still offers us a level of insight into the human condition that is different from the benefits of understanding some other periods of the past. To start with, obviously, the Nazis walked the earth not so very long ago. They came from a civilized country at a time when, in the wake of World War I, a whole series of positive values and beliefs about democracy and human rights were prevalent in

Europe. They smashed all that away, having gained power as a result of a series of elections that demonstrated that a majority of Germans – in voting for either the Communists or the Nazis – had chosen to vote out democracy. Given that today there are so many fledgling democracies in the world, it's a stark warning.

Then there's something even more significant that I think we ought to take from this history. I'd expected when I embarked upon this task all these years ago to meet countless former Nazis who would say, 'I only committed war crimes because I was acting under orders.' However, when a former Nazi perpetrator was pressed on why he did what he did, his most likely response was: 'I thought it was the right thing to do at the time.' It was a much more terrifying answer than the trite and self-serving one I'd been expecting. These former Nazis believed that their support of Hitler had essentially been a rational response to the situation around them. They told of how they had felt humiliated by the Versailles Treaty at the end of World War I, and then had to endure the revolutions and hyper-inflation of the immediate post-war years, followed by the mass unemployment and bankruptcies of the early 1930s. They craved a 'strong man' who would restore national pride and defeat the growing threat of Communism.

As the years went by and I met more and more former Nazis, I came also to believe that there was another dimension to their support for the Third Reich that wasn't 'rational' at all. Instead, it was emotional and based on faith. The quasi-religious dimension to Nazism is obvious, of course, and I discuss this at greater length in the first chapter of the book. But we also have to recognize that Hitler as an individual provided something for these Germans that other political leaders didn't. Hitler scarcely ever mentioned anything so dull as 'policies'. Instead he offered a leadership couched in visions and dreams. In doing so he touched something deep within the human psyche. As George Orwell put it in his famous review of Hitler's *Mein Kampf*: 'human beings don't only want comfort, safety, short working-hours, hygiene, birth control and, in general, common sense; they also, at least intermittently, want struggle and self-sacrifice, not to mention drums, flags, and loyalty parades'. Many people also, Orwell might have added, like being told they are 'superior' to others merely by virtue of their birth, and that recent catastrophic events in their country's history were nothing to do with them, but the result of some shady 'international conspiracy'.

I think in many ways I was naïve about human motivation before I started on this project. I used to think that people made important decisions about their lives based on rational, intellectual criteria. Instead, the decision to follow Hitler and support him through bad times as well as good was to a large extent an emotional one. And we mustn't think of this as some kind of uniquely 'German' trait. Look at your own life and ask yourself how many of the decisions you make in your life are actually 'rational'. Was it a 'rational' decision you made to buy the house or car you did? Do you like certain people and dislike others for 'rational' reasons or 'emotional' ones?

And despite all of the work conducted over recent years by structuralist historians who seek to emphasize the circumstances that created Nazism, we still have to face the uncomfortable fact that Adolf Hitler was an extraordinary person who successfully played on the emotions of the German people. Of course you already had to be predisposed to believe in what he was saying to be affected by him – many testimonies contained in this book make that clear – and it needed an economic crisis over which he had no control to catapult him from obscurity to power. But the essential truth remains that for a number of people, even in the early years, meeting Hitler was a life-changing event. Albert Speer memorably said that after meeting Hitler he felt like he was living his life on 'high voltage', and he was not the only highly intelligent individual who felt compelled to subordinate himself to the will of the Austrian corporal. Charisma is, we learn from this history, a quality that we should treat with suspicion. More worryingly still, we also learn that we should harbour similar scepticism about those who follow political leaders out of 'faith'.

Ultimately, there is one overarching reason why I think this history remains of worth. As I wrote at the end of the short introduction to *War of the Century* nearly six years ago: 'This is not a happy story and it offers little comfort. But it should be taught in our schools and remembered. For this is what human beings were capable of in the twentieth century.'

Laurence Rees
London, October 2005

1

HELPED INTO POWER

NEAR WHAT WAS THE EAST PRUSSIAN TOWN OF RASTENBURG AND is now the Polish town of Ketrzyn lies a tangled mass of reinforced concrete hidden in a forest. Today, in this remote part of eastern Poland near the border with Russia, it is hard to imagine a place more distant from the heart of power. But if you had stood on this spot in the autumn of 1941 you would have been inside the command centre of one of the most powerful men in history – Adolf Hitler. His soldiers stood on the beaches of Brittany and in the wheat-fields of Ukraine. More than 100 million Europeans, who only months previously had lived in sovereign states, were now under his rule. In Poland one of the most bestial ethnic rearrangements of all time was in full swing. And, tran-scending all of this in evil, Hitler was just about to conspire with Heinrich Himmler to order the elimination of an entire people – the Jews. The decisions Hitler took in this now-ruined concrete city touched all our lives and shaped the course of the second half of the twentieth century – all for the worse.

How was it possible that a cultured nation at the heart of Europe ever allowed this man and the Nazi Party he led to come to power? Knowing as we do the suffering and destruction the Nazis were to bring to the world, the idea that Adolf Hitler could have become Chancellor of Germany in 1933 by constitutional means seems almost incomprehensible.

One popular way of explaining the Nazis' rise to power is through the character of Hitler. No human being's personality has been more discussed; there are more than twice as many biographies of Hitler than of Churchill. The Nazis themselves pursued this biographical route to extremes in their own search for an explanation of their success. Hitler's own disciples in the Nazi Party concluded that he was not a mere mortal but a superman. 'Hitler is lonely. So is God. Hitler is like God,'[1] said Hans Frank, Reich Minister of Justice, in 1936. Julius Streicher, a Nazi with a particular fondness for hyperbole, went further: 'It is only on one or two exceptional points that Christ and Hitler stand comparison, for Hitler is far too big a man to be compared with one so petty.'[2] A new prayer was read in German kindergartens in the 1930s: 'Dear Führer, we love you like our fathers and mothers. Just as we belong to them so we belong to you. Take unto yourself our love and trust, O Führer!'[3]

This is also the explanation of the Nazi rise to power that Josef Goebbels, the Nazi propaganda minister, wanted the whole world to have. (He himself asked of Hitler after reading *Mein Kampf* (My Struggle): 'Who is this man? half plebeian, half god! Truly Christ, or only St John?')[4] In the Nazi version of history, Hitler, the man of destiny, came to power in Germany in much the same way as Christ came to save the world two thousand years ago. In both cases their careers were predetermined by their superhuman destiny. This reasoning, although seldom taken to this extreme, is still popular in some quarters today as an explanation of how the Nazis came to power. It fits with the desire many people have to understand the past simply in terms of the story of 'great men' who carve the world to their will regardless of the circumstances around them. There is just one problem with this as an answer to the question 'How did the Nazis come to power?' – it's wrong.

The Nazi Party took part in the German general election of May 1928. Hitler had then been leader of the party for nearly seven years. The German people had by now had ample opportunity to witness his superhuman qualities and to fall under his hypnotic spell. In that election the Nazi Party polled precisely 2.6 per cent of the popular vote. In a secret Reich report of 1927 there is, in the context of the time, a sensible judgement on the Nazis; the Nazi Party has, according to this document, 'no noticeable influence on the great masses of the population'.[5] Thus the idea of Hitler having hypnotic or quasi-divine influence on the Germans regardless of circumstance is nonsense. Of course, Hitler was an extraordinary individual and his impact on events should not be underestimated, but the content of his character is not a sufficient explanation either for how the Nazis came to exist or for how they went on to gain power. The reality is that Hitler and the Nazis were just as much trapped in the circumstances of their time as we all are. Regardless of who Hitler was, only with the collaboration, weakness, miscalculation and tolerance of others could the Nazis come to power. Indeed, without a crisis that shook the world, the Nazi Party would not even have been born in the first place.

When Germany surrendered and World War I ended in November 1918, there were those in the German Army who couldn't understand why this disaster had happened. 'We did wonder,' says German war veteran Herbert Richter, 'because we didn't feel beaten at all. The front-line troops didn't feel themselves beaten, and we were wondering why the armistice was happening so quickly, and why we had to vacate all our positions in such a hurry, because we were still standing on enemy territory and we thought all this was strange.' Herbert Richter's memory of how he and his friends felt about the surrender is still vivid: 'We were angry because we did not feel we had come to the end of our strength.' This anger was to have dangerous consequences. Those who felt it quickly looked around to blame someone for the sudden and, to them, suspicious circumstances of the armistice. The myth of the 'stab in the back' grew – the idea that while German soldiers had been laying down their lives, others, behind the lines, back in the Fatherland, were betraying them. Who were these 'others'? They were the politicians of the Left who had agreed to the humiliating armistice in November 1918 – the so-called 'November criminals'. Germany had turned to democracy for the first time in its history at the end of 1918, and to the politicians it was obvious that continuing the war was pointless – Germany must lose. But many soldiers saw it differently; to them the circumstances of Germany's defeat in November 1918 brought only shame and dishonour.

In Bavaria, part of southern Germany, this feeling of betrayal was keenly felt among many of the returning soldiers and civilians on the right of the political spectrum. Munich, the capital of Bavaria, was in political chaos in 1919. The socialist politician Kurt Eisner was assassinated in February and this led to the Räterepublik (the councils republic), eventually a Communist government of Bavaria, in April 1919. In the violence and disorder of that spring the military forces of the Right, in part consisting of Freikorps troops (armed mercenaries supported by the government) brutally suppressed the Communists in Munich on 1 and 2 May. The very existence of this final, Communist-led, government of Munich made it plain to many in this traditionally conservative part of Germany that their fear of Communism was well founded. 'Long Live the World Revolution!' ends one of the pamphlets from this period by the Communist Party of Germany – just one of the many pieces of propaganda that fed the Right's paranoia and created an atmosphere in which radical parties opposed to the Communists could flourish.

There was another, more sinister, reason why the Munich Räterepublik was to have a lasting effect on the consciousness of the Right. The majority of the leaders of this left-wing coup were Jewish. This served to reinforce the prejudice that the Jews were behind all that was wrong in Germany. Rumours spread of how Jews had shirked their war service and of how it had been a Jew in the government – Walther Rathenau – who had deviously inspired the humiliating armistice. Even now, so the lies continued, German Jews were selling the country out as part of a worldwide conspiracy organized by international Jewry.

These lies were effective partly, and ironically, because there were surprisingly few Jews actually living in Germany. In June 1933 they numbered only 503,000, a mere 0.76 per cent of the population, and, unlike the Jewish populations of other European countries, such as Poland, they were relatively assimilated into the general population. Paradoxically, this worked in the German anti-Semites' favour, for in the absence of large numbers of flesh-and-blood Jews, a fantasy image of Jewishness could be spread in which the Jews became symbolic of everything the Right disliked about post-war Germany. 'Politically it was very easy for lots of people to focus upon the Jew,' says Professor Christopher Browning. 'The Jew became a symbol for left-wing politics, for exploitative capitalism, for avant-garde cultural kinds of experimentation, for secularization, all the things that were disturbing a fairly large sector of the conservative part of the political spectrum. The Jew was the ideal political buzz-word.'

German Jews had been the victims of prejudice for hundreds of years and banned from many walks of life. Not until the latter half of the nineteenth century were they free even to own land and farm it. Germany after World War I was a country in which anti-Semitism was still common. Eugene Leviné, a German Jew brought up in Berlin in the 1920s,

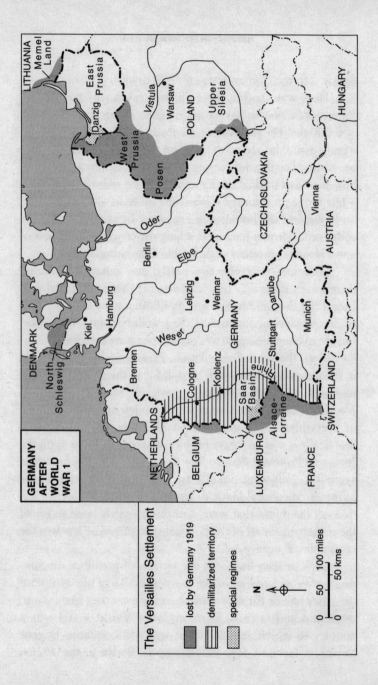

GERMANY AFTER WORLD WAR 1

LITHUANIA
Memel Land
East Prussia
Danzig
West Prussia
Posen
Vistula
Warsaw
POLAND
Upper Silesia
Oder
CZECHOSLOVAKIA
Vienna
HUNGARY
AUSTRIA
Berlin
Elbe
Leipzig
Weimar
Danube
Munich
Weser
Hamburg
Kiel
Bremen
DENMARK
North Schleswig
Cologne
Koblenz
Saar Basin
Rhine
Stuttgart
Alsace-Lorraine
GERMANY
NETHERLANDS
BELGIUM
LUXEMBURG
FRANCE
SWITZERLAND

The Versailles Settlement

lost by Germany 1919
demilitarized territory
special regimes

N

0   50   100 miles
0   50   100 kms

suffered as a child simply because he was Jewish. Until he was
four or five he used to play with other, non-Jewish children;
then, when their older brothers came home, they began to
say, 'Dirty little Jew, you can't play here, you've got to go.'
'The other children were quite sad,' says Eugene Leviné, 'but
these boys were already full of anti-Semitism. Once, one of
the bigger boys beat me up, and as a six-year-old you're not
much match for a fourteen-year-old.' Other than that brutal
experience, the anti-Semitism he experienced had a bizarre
ritual to it: 'In any new school in the first mid-morning break
somebody would pick on you because you were a Jew and see
what you were made of, and you'd have a fight. And if you
could fight back – you didn't even have to win – but if you
could fight back adequately, they'd leave you alone.'

Yet one must be careful not to be guilty of overstatement. As everyone knows the reality of Auschwitz, it is all
too simple to leap to the conclusion that at this time
Germany was a uniquely anti-Semitic country. It wasn't.
While anti-Semitism existed, it was generally, in the words of
Eugene Leviné, 'not the kind of anti-Semitism that would get
people to burn synagogues'. Tragically, given what was to
happen in Germany under the Nazis, a number of Jews fled
from Poland and Russia to Germany after World War I
partly in order to *escape* anti-Semitism at home. These 'eastern Jews' tended to be less assimilated than other German
Jews, and so attracted more anti-Semitism. Bernd Linn, who
later became an SS officer, grew up in Germany in the early
1920s and his anti-Semitism was fed by what he perceived as
the 'foreign' behaviour of the 'eastern Jews' in his father's
shop: 'We had many Jewish customers. They took so many
liberties. After all, they were our guests and they didn't
behave as such. The difference was obvious between them
and the long-settled Jews with whom we did have a good
relationship. But all those eastern Jews that came in, they

didn't get along at all with the western Jews, the settled ones. And how they behaved in the shop, that increased my antagonism all the more.' Bernd Linn happily confessed to us that as a child he threw fireworks at the Jews in the school playground and, in one trick which was a personal favourite, he and his schoolmates would post pretend one-way tickets to Jerusalem through Jewish letterboxes.

Fridolin von Spaun was old enough, immediately after World War I, to have joined one of the Freikorps. Like Bernd Linn, he too was to support the Nazi Party and he too had a personal problem with Jews. 'If the Jews had brought us something beautiful, that would have been OK,' he says. 'But they cheated us. When they make a fortune they go bankrupt and disappear with their pockets full. So I find it very natural that a generally anti-Jewish attitude became widespread.' Fridolin von Spaun goes on to add, without irony: 'Throughout my life I've had a lot to do with Jews, even as a child, and I must make this personal reproach to the Jews: among all those people whom I have met, not one has become my friend. Why? Not because of me. I had nothing against them. I always noticed they only want to use me. And that annoyed me. That is, I am not anti-Semitic. They are simply not my cup of tea.'

Eugene Leviné's reaction to all this is straightforward: 'I can't be very outraged by something that is so pointlessly unreasonable. To say it's unjust is to give it too much pride. It's a form of ignorance, isn't it? If two people have the same fault, then if it's a Jew they say, "Well typical – what would you expect. Bloody Jews." And if it's an Englishman, you say, "That's odd, that's not the English way of behaving." There are, after all, a hundred stories about this very attitude. About how the anti-Semite says, "This is another outrage by the Jews, and quite apart from that you Jews sank the *Titanic*." And the Jew says, "But excuse me, that's ridiculous, the *Titanic* was sunk by an iceberg." And he says, "Iceberg,

Greenberg, Goldberg, you Jews are all the same."'

Against this background, on 12 September 1919, a 30-year-old German Army corporal called Adolf Hitler walked into a meeting of the German Workers' Party in the Veterans' Hall of the Sterneckerbräu beer hall in Munich. Hitler had been sent to observe the party by Captain Mayr, head of press and propaganda in the Bavarian section of the army. At the meeting Hitler turned on one speaker who was calling for the secession of Bavaria from Germany and, showing an immediate rhetorical gift, demolished his arguments. Anton Drexler, a locksmith, who had founded the right-wing party only nine months previously, immediately asked Hitler to join.

Who was this man who walked into history that night at the Sterneckerbräu? Nothing in his first thirty years had marked him out as anything more than an oddball. A failure at school, a failure in Vienna where he had been rejected by the Academy of Graphic Arts, his only success in life had been as a soldier in World War I where his bravery had won him an Iron Cross First Class.

Sources for Hitler's life before that meeting in the Sterneckerbräu are sketchy. One of the chief ones is Hitler's own writing, dating from 1924, in *Mein Kampf*. Here he writes how, as he travelled through Vienna before World War I, 'I began to see Jews, and the more I saw the more sharply they became distinguished in my eyes from the rest of humanity...Was there any form of filth or profligacy, particularly in cultural life, without at least one Jew involved in it?' These familiar words confirm the idea Hitler wanted us to have – that here was a human being who had been set in his anti-Semitic views from the first. But is it true? Some of the most intriguing new work on Hitler's time in Vienna has recently been completed by Dr Brigitte Hamann. She set herself the task of minutely checking the registration details of the people with whom Hitler had come into contact at the Viennese men's hostel where he lodged. This led her to a startling conclusion: 'The picture which Hitler gives of Vienna in *Mein Kampf* is not correct. He says he became an anti-Semite in Vienna, but if you check the contemporary sources closely, you see that, on the contrary, he was very good friends with very many, extraordinarily many Jews, both in the men's hostel and through his contact with the dealers who sold his pictures.' She found that none of those many Jews with whom Hitler had good relations during his time in Vienna said that he was an anti-Semite in the period before 1913. Indeed, says Dr Hamann, Hitler 'preferred' selling his paintings to Jewish dealers 'because they took risks'.[6]

This is an important discovery. It demonstrates that Hitler, far from being the certain, quasi-divine individual he wanted us to think he was, had actually been buffeted around by circumstances as much as anyone else. In Vienna, according to Dr Hamann, Hitler 'didn't harm anybody, he was law-abiding, he painted fairly good paintings to make ends meet. He was an innocuous person.' The events that turned this 'innocuous person' into the Hitler that history was to know were the same events that traumatized the rest of Germany – World War I and its immediate aftermath. After his time in Vienna, in order to make sense of the new circumstances around him, Hitler, according to Dr Hamann, remembered the prophecies of the rabid Austrian anti-Semites and began spouting them himself.

A common thread in almost all of Hitler's political philosophy is theft. Most often he simply stole his arguments from others. But perhaps he knew that a 'great man' does not steal ideas, something that led him to place the origins of his vicious anti-Semitism in Vienna rather than in the commonplace feelings of betrayal and hatred felt by millions in 1918 and 1919.

Hitler falsified his own early history in other ways. Once he became famous, he was eager to show that he had been one of the earliest members of the German Workers' Party – member number seven. The fact that Hitler had been party member number seven was expressed to us by a number of former Nazis, proud of the fact that the Führer had been in at the start, shaping the fledgling Nazi Party from the very beginning. But it's not true. Anton Drexler wrote a letter of complaint to Hitler in January 1940: 'Nobody knows better than yourself, my Führer, that you were never the seventh member of the party, but at best the seventh member of the committee when I asked you to step in as propaganda representative. A few years ago I was forced to complain about this at a party meeting, that your first German Workers' Front card which carried Shüssler's and my own signature had been falsified, whereby the number 555 had been deleted and the number seven inserted...How much better and more valuable it would be for posterity if the course of history had been portrayed as it really had happened.'[7]

However, during 1919 Hitler discovered he did have one genuine and original talent – a gift for public speaking. So effective was he at the kind of rabble-rousing speeches then necessary to distinguish one far-right party from another that the German Workers' Party began to grow in membership. One of the earliest to join was Ernst Röhm, a Reichswehr (German Army) captain, who rapidly came to recognize the crowd-pulling attraction of Hitler's personality. Röhm was a man who liked action. 'Since I am an immature and wicked man,' he said, 'war and unrest appeal to me more than good bourgeois order.'[8] The party Hitler wanted could use a thug like Röhm. 'Brutality is respected,' Röhm once stated. 'The people need wholesome fear. They want to fear something. They want someone to frighten them and make them shudderingly submissive.'[9]

Within two years of joining the German Workers' Party Hitler had become its most valuable asset. His speeches attracted new members and his personality began to shape its growth. After a power struggle within the party in August 1921, Hitler emerged victorious, confirmed as the absolute ruler of the renamed National Socialist German Workers' Party, or Nazis for short (a change of name made in February 1920 in an attempt to appeal both to nationalists and socialists). From the first this was a party that traded less in detailed political manifestos than emotional commitment, rejecting democracy, preaching revolution. 'I joined the party because I was a revolutionary,' Hermann Göring was later to say, 'not because of any ideological nonsense.'[10] The mission of the party was and would remain plain – to right the wrongs done to Germany at the end of World War I, to punish those responsible and to 'annihilate the Marxist world view'.

In terms of this general policy there was little to distinguish the embryonic Nazi Party from the host of other small, extreme right-wing groups that flourished in the turmoil of post-World War I politics in southern Germany. The first party programme, presented on 24 February 1920, was a mish-mash of vague economic promises intended to protect the middle class and small businesses, coupled with a clear commitment to exclude Jews from full German citizenship. In none of this was the party unusual. Indeed, in its published programme of action it did not go as far as some other right-wing groups of the time. In the *Marktbreiter Wochenblatt*, the party newspaper of the German Protection and Defiance League, there appeared the following statement: 'It is absolutely necessary to kill the Jews.'[11] Another pamphlet read: 'What shall we do with the Jews? Don't be afraid of the slogan "No violent anti-Semitism" because only through violence can the Jews be driven away.'[12]

The symbols of the young Nazi Party were as unoriginal as its ideas. The swastika was already popular with other German right-wing groups before it was adopted by the Nazis.

The skull and crossbones, which would become infamous on the caps of the SS, had been used by the German cavalry. Even the stiff-armed Roman salute was taken from the greeting used by Mussolini's Fascists.

In one respect, however, the Nazi Party was different. Though these were violent times, this was, from the first, an exceptionally violent movement. In 1921 'Storm Detachments' were formed from the innocuously named 'Gymnastic and Sports Section' of the party to protect Nazi meetings and to disrupt the gatherings of rival parties. Battles between Nazi Storm Troopers and the followers of other political parties would be a common feature of German political life until 1933.

Since the Nazis were preaching that they were the 'salvation' to Germany's problems, it followed that their own fortunes would depend on the extent of the difficulties the country faced. The party had been born out of the trauma following the end of World War I and could flourish only in an atmosphere of political instability. Thus the Nazis benefited when a new crisis occurred involving the French. Angry at Germany's failure to keep up with reparation repayments, France sent troops to occupy the Ruhr at the beginning of 1923. For a nation already dismayed by the loss of honour that accompanied the armistice of November 1918 and the harsh terms of the Versailles peace treaty this was a grave humiliation. The German sense of shame was further increased by the behaviour of the French Army of occupation. 'That was when we found out that the French ruled with an iron hand,' says Jutta Rüdiger, the woman who was later to head the BDM, the female equivalent of the Hitler Youth. 'Perhaps they simply wanted their revenge. Revenge is an emotion I do not know at all.' Frau Rüdiger then adds the following assessment of the French; more than ironic given what the Nazis were later to do, but none the less revealing: 'But the French have a slightly different character, don't they? Perhaps there is a tiny bit of sadism there.'

Bernd Linn was five years old when he witnessed the French occupation of the Ruhr. As the French soldiers marched past, he stood on the pavement by his grandfather's house, wearing a child's army uniform and carrying a toy gun: 'I turned round and then a Frenchman came and he disarmed me – apparently he needed this for his children. And I felt very hurt.' Bernd Linn, the little boy from whom the French took a child's pop gun, later became a colonel in the SS (Schutzstaffeln – originally the personal bodyguard of Hitler in 1920s) .

The Ruhr crisis coincided with Germany's massive economic problems – most notoriously, runaway inflation. 'I once paid 4 billion marks for a sausagemeat roll,' says Emil Klein, who attended his first Hitler meeting in 1920. 'And this collapse naturally supported the Hitler movement and helped it grow, because people said, "It can't go on like this!" And then slowly emerged the discussion about the need for a strong man. And this stuff about a strong man grew more and more because democracy achieved nothing.'

In the political crisis caused both by the French occupation and Germany's economic difficulties, the right-wing Bavarian authorities clashed with the government of Gustav Stresemann in Berlin. The central government in Berlin tried to make the Bavarian authorities censor attacks by the Nazi paper, the *Völkischer Beobachter,* on Stresemann and his government. Kahr, the newly appointed state commissioner of Bavaria, refused, as did General von Lossow, the local military commander. In this atmosphere of internal conflict, Hitler attempted to hijack a meeting at the Bürgerbräukeller in Munich at which both Kahr and von Lossow were speaking. Hitler called for a Putsch (national revolution) to overthrow the central government. The Putschists began a march the next morning, intending to press on to Berlin. Emil Klein took part in that Nazi march through Munich; alongside him were Hitler, Göring and Himmler. 'We shone as marchers that day,' he recalls with fervour. 'But then we turned on to the Maximilianstrasse and as I came to the corner of the Residence [the palace of the former kings of Bavaria] we heard the shots ahead. What's going on?'

When confronted with the choice of cooperating in armed revolution or supporting the Bavarian authorities the police made a clear decision; they rejected the Nazis and shots were fired (it is unclear who fired the first shot – the marchers or the police). Thus, the Putschists' march through Munich came to a violent end. 'You asked me what emotions I felt,' says Emil Klein. 'I'd like to say that actually those were the first political emotions that I ever had. The way things can go wrong. That in itself was a blow to me and to many of my comrades. That such a thing could happen.' Hitler, too, was to learn from this experience. From now on the Nazis tried to gain power from within the democratic system.

Hitler, meanwhile, was arrested and his trial began on 26 February 1924. He was charged with high treason and the evidence against him was damning; not only had the Nazis committed armed robbery during the Putsch, but the violent confrontation had resulted in the death of three policemen. But unlike the others implicated in the failed Putsch, such as the World War I hero General Ludendorff, Hitler stood up and took full responsibility for his actions. His speeches to the judges made him known throughout Germany and he became, for the first time, a national figure. 'Gentlemen,' Hitler told the court, 'it is not you who pronounce judgment upon us, it is the eternal court of history which will make its pronounce-ment upon the charge which is brought against us...You may pronounce us guilty a thousand times, but the goddess who presides over the eternal court of history will with a smile tear in pieces the charge of the Public Prosecutor and the verdict of this court. For she acquits us.'[13] Brave words, but based upon deceit. What the vast majority of Germans did not know at the time was that as Hitler gave that speech he had every reason to suppose that he would be treated extremely leniently by the court, and a man is not courageous when he knows there is virtually no risk. For the judge who presided at the Putsch trial, Georg Neithardt, was the same judge who had sat at another lesser-known trial in January 1922. On that occasion the defendants had been accused of violently breaking up a meeting in the Löwenbräu cellar the previous September. They had been charged with the minimum possible offence, breach of the peace, then given the minimum possible sentence, three months in prison. Yet Georg Neithardt wrote to the superior court, saying that he wanted the sentence to be even more lenient, believing that the 'purpose of the imprisonment could be achieved by the imposition of a fine'. One of the defendants at that trial was Adolf Hitler. Judge Neithardt was so taken with him that he managed to press his superiors to allow Hitler's sentence of three months in prison to be commuted to one month in prison with a period on probation. Hitler was standing in front of this self-same judge during the Putsch trial, a man he knew to be extremely sympathetic to his cause. It was in the courtroom of Georg Neithardt that Hitler made his impassioned speech to the 'eternal court of history'. It is hardly surprising then, that after they came to power the Nazis seized almost all the documents relating to this first trial and burnt them. The sentence in the second, famous case was therefore predictable: five years' imprisonment – the minimum possible – but with the assumption that Hitler would soon be out on probation.

The Bavarian government have a great deal to account for. The Nazi Party had been banned in most German states in 1922, but not in Bavaria: there the Nazis were tacitly encouraged. After his conviction for high treason, Hitler was imprisoned in relative comfort at Landsberg Prison, near Munich, where he occupied himself by working on *Mein Kampf*.

While Hitler was in Landsberg, the Nazi Party split into factions. It was only after his release in December 1924 (after serving less than nine months of his five-year sentence) that the party could be put back together again. The Bavarian authorities acted true to form and allowed the party to be refounded on 27 February 1925 at the Bürgerbräukeller in Munich. But by now events in Germany were against the Nazis. The hyper-inflation was over and the future appeared full of hope. The middle years of the 1920s were the Weimar Republic's so-called 'golden' period. But this new prosperity was financed on credit; the German government used borrowed money to pay the Allies their reparations. Still, at the time, everything looked idyllic. The Nazis could never flourish in such sunlight and they were reduced to a tiny rump of fanatical support. Without a crisis to feed on, they were lost. Until the end of the 1920s they were active only at the margins of German political life.

Yet it was during these quiet years that the party evolved structurally into the Nazi Party which was eventually to govern much of Europe. Hitler's position became increasingly secure. He easily brushed away a small internal challenge to his absolute authority in 1926 by a simple appeal to loyalty. The collapse of the party during his absence in prison had demonstrated that it was only his presence as leader that held the movement together.

The Nazis were not a political party in the sense that we today understand the concept. Little in the way of detailed Nazi policy was ever published. A commitment to the Führer (as Hitler became known around this time) and a general belief in the aims of the movement was enough to prove one's loyalty. This was a party not of talk but of action, not of policy but of emotion. As a philosophy, this appealed particularly to the young; research shows that during this period the average age of those joining the party was less than thirty. One young man who joined at the age of twenty-five was a failed novelist called Josef Goebbels. Looking back fondly on the 1920s, after the Nazis had come to power, he spoke emotionally to a group of young people about these years of struggle: 'Then there were young people who wrote the word "Reich" on their banners, against a world of hatred and calumny and malice. They were convinced that a lost war was not enough to push a people into permanent servitude.'

'It was exciting,' says Wolfgang Teubert, who joined the Nazi Storm Troopers in the 1920s. 'There was the comradeship, the being-there-for-each-other, that's for a young man something outstanding – at least it was then.' Something else the party offered a man like Teubert, who wore the Storm Trooper's brown shirt with pride, was a sense of importance. In that shirt he may have been young, but he was still a somebody: 'We marched behind the swastika flag, marching through the towns. Outside working hours there was nothing but the Storm Troopers.' And then there was the factor that perhaps appealed most to these youths – fighting. 'There was the danger, the threats from other people. Night after night we increasingly provided protection at hall meetings not just in our town but in many other towns to strengthen the Storm Troopers there. We had no weapons, the most we could do was defend ourselves with our fists and only work the enemy over with our fists – where it was necessary. And it was necessary more often than not!' Teubert and his friends in the Bochum Storm Troopers would regularly fight the youths of the Communist Party. 'Breaking up the chairs in the hall and then fighting with the chair legs, that happened quite a lot.' Teubert smiles at the memory. 'Both sides did that, each as much as the other.'

Bruno Hähnel came into the Nazi Party at the same time via another popular route – from the Wandervogel, a 'folklorical' group which sought a return to nature and its values. At weekends, as a young Wandervogel, Herr Hähnel would wander with friends through the countryside. He dates his decision to join the Nazi Party to a discussion evening held in a youth hostel in 1927: 'There was one about the subject of internationalism and among other things it was said that one had to reach the point of being able to marry a Negress. And I found that thought very uncomfortable.' In so far as other reasons influenced Herr Hähnel in his decision to join the Nazi Party, they were the usual negative feelings about Versailles and the 'November criminals' of 1918. As a result, he had a strong 'resistance' to any international movement such as Communism. 'Many of us said simply, "We are Germans first",' says Herr Hähnel, 'and now there was a group who said "Germany first". They shouted, "Germany awake!"'

Recruits like Herr Hähnel were not concerned that they were joining an anti-Semitic party: 'I still remember those statements which frequently occurred, that 50 per cent of all Berlin doctors were Jews, 50 per cent of all Berlin lawyers, that the whole press in Berlin and in Germany was in the hands of the Jews and this had to be done away with.' While tacitly supporting this anti-Semitic idea in principle, Herr Hähnel had no problem in reconciling it with the realities of his own family life: 'I had relatives who were Jews and we would meet at family gatherings. I had a very warm relationship with two cousins who were Jewish. It didn't stop me from agreeing with the other things which the party demanded.'

For other young people at the time, such as Alois Pfaller, this anti-Semitic attitude proved a barrier to joining the Nazis: 'That was something very strange,' he says, 'this extreme anti-Semitism, the Jews being held responsible for everything. I knew Jews and I had friends with whom I used to spend time and I absolutely didn't understand what difference there was supposed to be – we're all humans...I have always stood up for justice – what is just and reasonable, that was my problem, and also fighting injustice, that was my problem, and not somehow persecuting other races or other people.' Alois Pfaller turned his back on the Storm Troopers, but, still looking for a radical solution to the country's problems, he joined the German Communist Party.

Hitler saw his personality as the Nazi Party's greatest strength; he cultivated 'great man' mannerisms, such as staring straight into the eyes of whoever was speaking to him. Fridolin von Spaun remembers just such an encounter with the Führer at a party dinner: 'Suddenly I noticed Hitler's eyes resting on me. So I looked up. And that was one of the most curious moments in my life. He didn't look at me suspiciously, but I felt that he is searching me somehow…It was hard for me to sustain this look for so long. But I thought: I mustn't avert my eyes, otherwise he may think I've something to hide. And then something happened which only psychologists can judge. The gaze, which at first rested completely on me, suddenly went straight through me into the unknown distance. It was so unusual. And the long gaze which he had given me convinced me completely that he was a man with honourable intentions. Most people nowadays would not believe this. They'd say I am getting old and childish, but that's untrue. He was a wonderful phenomenon.'

Hitler had a similar effect on many others. Herbert Richter watched him in 1921 when he walked into a student café behind the university in Munich: 'He was wearing an open-necked shirt and he was accompanied by guards or followers. And I noticed how the people with whom he arrived – there were about three or four of them – how their eyes were fixed on Hitler. For many people there must have been something fascinating about him.' But whatever it was that these others found so entrancing had no effect on Herbert Richter. 'He started to speak and I immediately disliked him. Of course I did not know then what he would later become. I found him rather comical, with his funny little moustache. I was not at all impressed by him.' Nor did Hitler's speaking style have the desired effect: 'He had a kind of scratchy voice,' remembers Herr Richter. 'And he shouted so much. He was shouting in this small room. And what he was saying was really simple. You couldn't say much against it. He mostly criticized the Versailles Treaty – how it had to be set aside.'

Aldous Huxley wrote, 'The propagandist is a man who canalizes an existing stream. In a land where there is no water he digs in vain.' Hitler was no exception to this rule. To those like Herbert Richter, who were sophisticated in their political judgements, he seemed a comical character who spoke the obvious. To those who were predisposed to believe in such solutions, he was a 'wonderful phenomenon'. It is all too easy in retrospect for Hitler's charisma and speaking talents to be used as an excuse. 'He hypnotized a nation' it has often been suggested. No, he didn't. A hypnotist does not make speeches which convince only those who like what they hear, as Hitler did.

The Nazis prided themselves on the fact that their party lacked democratic principles. (After all, had democracy not been brought in by the 'November criminals' and produced Versailles?) Towering over the structure of the party was the figure of Adolf Hitler. Unlike other political organizations, which relied on committees or policy discussions, in the Nazi Party only Hitler could arbitrate – he was the only man capable of making a final decision. Even in embryonic form, a dictator-led party like this should have collapsed under the weight of work the leader had to shoulder. Yet not only was Hitler not deluged with the burden of decision-making but, paradoxically, he seems scarcely to have been stretched by administrative tasks at all. An understanding of the reason for this apparent paradox gives an insight into not just how the Nazi Party was structured, but why it was so attractive to the young. For Hitler relied heavily on his own interpretation of the work of one dead Englishman to tell him how to govern the party – Charles Darwin.

'The idea of struggle is as old as life itself,' Hitler said in a speech at Kulmbach on 5 February 1928. 'In this struggle the stronger, the more able, win while the less able, the weak, lose. Struggle is the father of all things…It is not by the principles of humanity that man lives or is able to preserve himself above the animal world, but solely by means of the most brutal struggle.' Hitler sought to apply the Darwinian theory of the survival of the fittest to human action. 'God does not act differently,' he said over dinner on 23 September 1941. 'He suddenly hurls the masses of humanity on to the earth and he leaves it to each one to work out his own salvation. Men dispossess one another, and one perceives that, at the end of it all, it is always the stronger who triumphs. Is not that the most reasonable order of things? If it were otherwise, nothing good would ever have existed. If we did not respect the laws of nature, imposing our will by the right of the stronger, a day would come when the wild animals would once again devour us – then the insects would eat the wild animals and finally nothing would exist on the earth but microbes.'[14]

It should be no surprise, then, to learn that Hitler ran the Nazi Party according to pseudo-Darwinian theory. When Gustav Seifert wrote to Nazi Party HQ and asked to be reappointed as leader of its Hanover branch, he received this reply, dated 27 October 1925, from Max Amann, editor of the Nazi paper the *Völkischer Beobachter*: 'Herr Hitler takes the view on principle that it is not the job of the party leadership to "appoint" party leaders. Herr Hitler is today more than ever convinced that the most effective fighter in the National Socialist movement is the man who wins respect for himself as leader through his own achievements. You yourself say in your letter that almost all the members follow you.

Then why don't you take over the leadership of the branch?'
Why don't you '*take over*'? What command could be more
exciting to a young man? If you don't like it, change it, don't
come to us for orders, if you are stronger than your enemies,
you'll win. Equally, if you aren't stronger than your enemies
and you lose, then that's simply the way it should be. Such a
mindset helps to explain the bizarre utterings of Hitler
towards the end of the war when he remarked that Germany
'deserved' her fate at the hands of the Soviet Union.

When the Nazis came to power, Goebbels' film propaganda hammered the same point home – the fittest should
thrive and the weak should perish. In one of his later propaganda films, scientists are shown filming an experiment in
which two stag beetles are fighting each other. The laboratory
technician expresses some doubts about what she sees. 'It is a
shame really,' she says to her professor, 'to catch these beautiful, strong animals for a fight between life and death. And to
think back in the forest they could have a quiet life.' 'But my
dear,' the professor tells her, 'there is no such thing as a quiet
life anywhere in nature…They all live in a constant struggle,
in the course of which the weak perish. We regard this struggle as completely natural, but we would think it unnatural if
a cat lived peacefully with a mouse or a fox with a hare.'

In any attempt to understand the ideology of Nazism the
significance of such views can scarcely be understated. Nazi
ideology placed man as an animal with an animal's values.
The bully who wins *ought* to win if he is stronger. The child
who dies *ought* to die if he is weak. If one country is stronger
than another, it *ought* to conquer its neighbour. Traditional
values, like compassion and respect for the law, are nothing
but man-made shields behind which the weak can cower and
protect themselves from the fate that is naturally theirs. (It
was no accident that the two professions Hitler hated above
all others were lawyers and priests.) The Nazis were first and

foremost a racist party who believed that nation states, just like individuals, were locked in a permanent amoral struggle to see who should govern the largest portion of the Earth.

However, if Hitler had been applying his Darwinian theory to the Nazi Party in 1928, he should have despaired, for in the general election of that year the Nazis polled only 2.6 per cent of the vote. Germany did not want them because it saw no need for them – yet. Shortly after the election, the economic and political situation in Germany radically changed. First an agricultural depression hit home and then the Wall Street Crash triggered the most serious economic crisis ever encountered in Germany, as the United States called in its loans.

Unemployment started to grow and the effects were deep and bitter. 'In those days,' remembers Bruno Hähnel, 'our unemployed would stand in huge queues in front of the labour exchange every Friday, and they would receive 5 marks at the counter. This was a new and different situation – there were many who simply didn't have the means to buy food.' 'It was a hopeless business,' recalls Alois Pfaller. 'People walked around with spoons in their pockets because they got a meal for 1 mark [from the charity soup kitchens].'

The suffering hit middle-class families, such as Jutta Rüdiger's: 'My father did not become unemployed but he was told he had to agree to work for a lower salary.' Jutta Rüdiger thought she would have to 'kiss goodbye' to the chance of going to university, until a kindly uncle stepped in and gave her an allowance. A family experience like the Rüdigers' would not have appeared on any unemployment statistic, yet they suffered and feared further suffering. As German unemployment grew in the early 1930s to over 5 million, the longing for a radical solution to the nation's economic troubles was not confined to the unemployed – it also extended to millions of middle-class families like the Rüdigers.

The election of September 1930 was a breakthrough for the Nazi Party: their share of the vote increased to 18.3 per cent. Just as worrying for those looking for a life without conflict was the increase in the German Communist Party's vote from 10.6 per cent to 13.1 per cent. Germany seemed to be splitting towards the extremes. With a Reichstag (Parliament) in which the Nazis and Communists were now heavily represented, the German Chancellor, Heinrich Brüning, began to bypass it and issue emergency decrees, signed by President Hindenburg under Article 48 of the Constitution, in order to govern Germany. German democracy did not suddenly die with the arrival of Hitler; it began its slow death under Brüning.

Social unrest grew along with unemployment. 'You had to sign on every day at the dole office,' remembers Alois Pfaller. 'Everybody met there, the Nazi people, the SPD [German Socialist Party], the Communists – and then the discussions would start and the fights.' Gabriele Winckler gives a young woman's perspective: 'You felt uneasy when you crossed the road, you felt uneasy when you were alone in the woods and so on. The unemployed lay in the ditches and played cards.' In this atmosphere of danger and despair Jutta Rüdiger heard Hitler speak for the first time: 'There was a huge crowd and you got the feeling that he was aiming for electrifying tension. Today, I can probably only explain it with the poverty the people had been suffering and were suffering...In that context Hitler with his statements seemed to be the bringer of salvation. He said, "I will get you out of this misery, but you all have to join in." And everybody understood that.'

During this period the Nazis developed new forms of propaganda to push their message across – famously the 'Hitler over Germany' presidential campaign of April 1932, which saw Hitler speak to twenty-one meetings in seven days, travelling between them by light aircraft. But the importance of Nazi propaganda should not be overstated. Academic research conducted by Dr Richard Bessel shows that in the district of Neidenburg in East Prussia, where the Nazi Party did not build a firm organizational base until 1931, the Nazi vote nonetheless increased over the three years leading up to that time. In May 1928 the Nazis received only 360 votes (2.3 per cent) but this increased to 3831 (25.8 per cent) in September 1930. The voters of Neidenburg did not vote Nazi because they were entranced by Hitler or swamped with Nazi propaganda; they supported the Nazis because they wanted fundamental change.

Hitler was open about the nature of the change the Nazis intended to bring to German political life once they gained power. In a speech he gave on 27 July 1932 at Eberswalde in Brandenburg he openly wallowed in his contempt for democracy: 'The workers have their own parties,' he said, 'and not just one, that wouldn't be enough. There have to be at least three or four. The bourgeoisie, which is more intelligent, needs even more parties. The middle classes have to have their party. The economy has its party, the farmer his own party, and here again three or four of them. And the house-owners also have to have their particular political and philosophical interests represented by a party. And the tenants can't stay behind, of course. And the Catholics too, their own party, and even the Württembergers have a special party – thirty-four in one little land. And this at a time when before us lie the greatest tasks, which can only be undertaken if the strength of the whole nation is put together. The enemy accuses us National Socialists, and me in particular, of being intolerant and quarrelsome. They say that we do not want to work with other parties...So is it typically German to have thirty parties? I have to admit one thing: the gentlemen are quite right. We are intolerant. I have given myself one aim: to sweep the thirty parties out of Germany.'

This speech illustrates a crucial point – Hitler and the Nazis wanted a revolution in Germany and they were open in saying what they planned. In this the Nazis had common cause with the German Communist Party; both thought that democracy had failed. Democracy, after all, was relatively new in Germany; its arrival had virtually coincided with the disastrous peace settlement of Versailles, and in the early 1930s democracy appeared to many to be responsible both for the continuing crippling reparation payments and for massive unemployment. Incredible as it may seem to us today, by 1932 the majority of the German people, in supporting either the Communists or the Nazis, were voting for political parties openly committed to the overthrow of German democracy. Most of them, having seen what democracy had delivered, felt that it was time not just for another party to be given a chance, but for another *system*.

On 30 May 1932 Brüning resigned as Chancellor after losing President Hindenburg's support. The aristocratic Franz von Papen was appointed Chancellor on 1 June, but his government immediately ran into problems; at the Reichstag elections held on 31 July the Nazis gained 37.4 per cent of the vote and won 230 seats. They were now the biggest party in the Reichstag. Hitler claimed the right to be Chancellor and saw Hindenburg to press his claim on 13 August 1932. Otto Meissner, chief of the Reich Chancellery, described what happened: 'Hindenburg declared that he recognized Hitler's patriotic conviction and selfless intentions, but given the atmosphere of tension and his responsibility before God and the German people, he could not bring himself to give government power to a single party which did not represent the majority of the electorate, and which, furthermore, was intolerant, lacking in discipline and frequently even appeared violent. In foreign affairs, it was of the utmost importance to proceed extremely cautiously and to allow matters to mature. We should at all cost avoid conflicts with other states. As far as domestic affairs were concerned, any widening of the chasm between the opposing sides must be prevented and all powers should be concentrated in order to alleviate economic disaster.'[15]

Given what we know happened once Hitler did gain power, Hindenburg's concerns about him and the Nazis have a prophetic ring to them. Such sentiments clearly show that the aged President knew the dangers Germany faced under Hitler's Chancellorship. So that should have been that; Hitler's political demands had been crushingly rejected. Yet five months later, and at a time when the Nazi Party, wracked by internal crisis, had lost many votes in the November Reichstag election, Hitler was made Chancellor by the self-same President Hindenburg. Why? The Nazi Party's popularity appeared to have peaked in the summer of 1932. Its support was inherently unstable, the party held together more by emotion and notions of its leader's charisma than by any coherent manifesto of concrete policy. Its rapid growth in popularity owed much to the crisis in which Germany found herself and over which the Nazis had no control. If the German economy began to pick up, success could vanish as rapidly as it had appeared, and the signs were that the economy *was* about to improve given the political agreement at the Lausanne conference in June 1932 that effectively ended German reparation payments.

At the elections in November 1932 the Nazi Party vote dropped from 37 per cent to 33 per cent. Goebbels had seen the danger to the party when he wrote in his diary the previous April: 'We must come to power in the foreseeable future. Otherwise we'll win ourselves to death in elections.' (This failure in the November elections of 1932 was, as Dr Bessel points out, despite a massive propaganda effort – yet more evidence that the 'party's fortunes were not determined primarily by its propaganda'.)[16] The party was in financial trouble, the seemingly endless round of elections having shaken its finances. Worse, Gregor Strasser, leader of the north German wing of the Nazis, resigned amid emotional scenes on 7 December 1932. Strasser had been offered the Vice-Chancellorship by the new Chancellor, General von Schleicher (who had succeeded von Papen on 2 December 1932), but Hitler had insisted he turn the offer down. Strasser did so but quit politics after delivering a stinging indictment of Hitler's intransigence in holding out for the chancellorship. It appeared that Hitler might lose control of a Nazi Party that was nervy and on edge. (Hitler never forgave Strasser for his 'treachery' and he was murdered on the 'Night of the Long Knives' on 30 June 1934.)

In parallel with these developments was a series of events that persuaded the aged President Hindenburg to change his mind and appoint Hitler. In November 1932 Hjalmar Schacht, the former head of the Reichsbank, was one of a number of financiers and industrialists (though few apart from Schacht were prominent figures) who signed a petition to President Hindenburg asking him to appoint Hitler as Chancellor. The letter was respectful but clearly influenced by the fact that the November 1932 elections showed another increase in the Communist vote; many of Germany's industrial élite may have disliked the Nazis but they feared the Communists more. Equally, it was obvious that the aristocratic cabinet of von Papen commanded little public support. 'It is clear,' said the letter, 'that the oft-repeated dissolution of the Reichstag, with the growing number of elections that exacerbate the party struggle, has had a bad effect, not only political, but also on economic calm and stability. But it is also clear that any constitutional change which is not supported by the broadest popular currents will have even worse political, economic and spiritual consequences.' The letter went on to call for the transfer of the political leadership of the Reich to 'the leader of the largest national group'. This was Hitler. Such a course of action 'will arouse the millions of people who today stand at the margins, making of them an affirmative and approving force'.

Hitler had not been a figure whom these people had wanted to embrace in the past, but the economic crisis and huge popular support for the Nazi movement now made them feel that an accommodation must be reached. Key figures on the conservative Right also wanted an authoritarian solution to Germany's problems, and without Hitler no proposal they could initiate would have a base of mass-support. Johannes Zahn, the distinguished German banker, says that since young people at the time were joining either the Storm Troopers or the Communists, those in business preferred the Nazis because of their 'discipline and order'. In addition, 'At the beginning,' he says, 'you really have to say this today, at the beginning, you couldn't tell whether National Socialism was something good with a few bad side-effects, or something evil with a few good side-effects, you couldn't tell.' There was talk of a strategy of 'taming' Hitler. Such a policy was to be enthusiastically proposed by von Papen once he had been forced to step down as Chancellor in favour of General von Schleicher on 2 December 1932.

Then, more worrying news came to Hindenburg. The results of an army war-game, 'Planspiel Ott', were discussed at a cabinet meeting at the start of December 1932. The Armed Forces had examined a number of hypothetical scenarios of civil unrest in an attempt to gauge their ability to respond if called upon during a state of emergency. Major Ott presented their conclusion: '...all preparations have been made to be able to introduce an immediate state of emergency, if ordered. But after careful consideration, it has been shown that the forces of order of the Reich and the Länder [German states] are in no way sufficient to maintain constitutional order against National Socialists and Communists and to protect the borders.'[17] The army was effectively saying it could not control the country if there was a civil war between the Nazis and the Communists. General von Schleicher tried to make the best of it at the cabinet meeting but to no avail: 'Even when Schleicher tried to dampen the effect of what was said at the end by stating that a war-game would always have to be based on a worst-case scenario, and that one would not always have to expect such a worst-case scenario to happen, the deep impression that Ott's discourse made on the cabinet, even on the Chancellor who kept on wiping his eyes during the talk, was unmistakable.'[18]

On 4 January 1933 von Papen and Hitler met at the house of the Cologne banker Kurt von Schröder to discuss the way forward. It was the first in a series of meetings that led to von Papen agreeing that he would push for Hitler's appointment as Chancellor, but only on condition that he, von Papen, was made Vice-Chancellor and there were only two other Nazis in the cabinet apart from Hitler (Göring as Minister without Portfolio and acting Prussian Minister of the Interior, and Wilhelm Frick as Reich Minister of the Interior). Hitler agreed. As a result, on 30 January 1933, following these intrigues, and once von Papen's influence on President Hindenburg had finally opened the door, Hitler was appointed Chancellor of Germany.

Bruno Hähnel, a committed Nazi, describes his reaction to the news as 'elation'. But the reaction from the Nazis' political opponents was less straightforward. Josef Felder, a German Socialist Party (SPD) MP at the time, tells how the SPD believed that since Hitler was now the legally chosen Chancellor, then they were the legal opposition; the SPD could carry on as if in a normal, stable democracy. 'We hadn't fully realized what it would mean,' says Herr Felder. 'We believed that we could still control him through Parliament – total lunacy!'

When Eugene Leviné heard the news that Hitler was Chancellor he was concerned less because he was Jewish than because he was a Communist. He remembers that 'there were quite a few Storm Troopers who had Jewish girlfriends and therefore a lot of Germans just thought, "Oh well, it's not going to be so bad – they have Jewish girlfriends, they can't hate us all."' He also had personal reasons to suppose that the Nazis were capable of exercising their anti-Semitism with a degree of restraint: 'At one of the schools I was in there was a Nazi and he said to me, "You really should be one of us." I said, "Look, I can't, I'm a Jew," and he would say, "We don't mean you, decent chaps like you will be perfectly all right in the new Germany."'

As for the Communist Party, their attitude to the news of Hitler's Chancellorship was scarcely a call to world revolution: 'It all happened so fast in those days, after one had seen it coming gradually,' says Eugene Leviné. 'The Communist Party line, to which I still belonged, was that it didn't matter if Hitler gets to power. That's good. He'll soon have proved himself incompetent and then it's our turn…For some extraordinary reason they didn't realize that he was going to change the law once he came to power.'

To Alois Pfaller the lesson of Hitler's appointment is clear: 'The danger is always here, when crises are happening, that people come who say they have the wisdom and the answer, and they can bring salvation to everybody.'

Adolf Hitler had come to power legally within the existing constitutional system. Now he was to keep his promise and sweep democracy away.

2

CHAOS AND CONSENT –
THE NAZI RULE IN GERMANY

IN POPULAR MYTHOLOGY THERE IS ONE QUALITY ABOVE ALL OTHERS that the Germans possess – efficiency. Their cars are sold by advertisements that trumpet it ('If only everything in life was as reliable as a Volkswagen'). Their national football team performs with it ('There go the Germans with typical efficiency'). Hardly surprising then, that this one attribute, more than any other, is ascribed to the Nazis. Since efficiency is the one quality that Fascists are popularly supposed to have (Mussolini is alleged to have 'made the trains run on time'), a combination of being German and Fascist ought, so the logic goes, to have produced the most efficient state of all time. The propaganda images of Nazi parades, most famously in Leni Riefenstahl's film *Triumph of the Will* (1936), certainly support this idea. The propaganda confirms that German society, under Nazi rule, was run with clarity and order. But it wasn't.

'The Führer marches alone along the front,' says Dr Günter Lohse, a former Foreign Office official and member of the Nazi Party, talking of these *Triumph of the Will*-type images. 'This is propaganda and it is impressive. They're all standing in one line! But one simply mustn't look behind the scenes. There was no order there – it was total chaos.' Dr Lohse had to deal with liaison between the Foreign Office and other government departments during the 1930s. He estimates that at least 20 per cent of his day was spent fighting the other departments over jurisdiction. One former Foreign Office official, he claims, estimated that 60 per cent of his day was wasted in this way. Many words can be used to describe the Nazi rule of Germany in the 1930s, but 'efficient' isn't one of them.

In the first seventeen months of Hitler's Chancellorship there were plenty of opportunities to see the radical, chaotic and destructive nature of Nazi rule. Once in power, Hitler quickly called new elections, but made it clear that they were simply a vote of confidence; neither the cabinet nor the government would change as a result of them. (Even with bans imposed on newspapers and public meetings attacking the new state, and with thousands of political opponents already rounded up, the Nazis gained only 43.9 per cent of the vote in March 1933 and failed to acquire the absolute majority they had hoped for.) After the Reichstag had been set on fire on the night of 27 February (almost certainly by the Communist sympathizer, Marinus van der Lubbe), there were mass arrests of Communists the next day, and the Reichstag Fire Decree was inaugurated, which suspended indefinitely all personal rights and freedoms. Under its provisions, political prisoners could be held indefinitely in 'protective custody'. In March the Reichstag passed an Enabling Act, which gave Hitler absolute power. Outside on the streets, according to one Nazi Storm Trooper, there was chaos: 'Everyone is arresting everyone else, avoiding the prescribed official channels, everyone is threatening everyone else with protective custody, everyone is threatening everyone else with Dachau...Every little street cleaner today feels he is responsible for matters which he has never understood.'[1]

In those first months of power the chaotic terror was directed mainly at the Nazis' former political opponents. Josef Felder was an SPD member of the Reichstag who was picked up by the Nazis and taken to the newly established concentration camp at Dachau, outside Munich. He was thrown into a cell and chained to an iron ring, and his Nazi jailers removed the straw palliasse which was lying on the concrete floor, saying: 'You won't be needing this because you'll only be leaving here as a corpse.' The abuse continued as the guard took a rope and demonstrated the best way Felder could use it to hang himself. Felder told him, 'I have a family. I'm not going to do that. You'll have to do it yourselves!' He was eventually released after more than eighteen months in Dachau, having contracted a lung disease.

The pragmatists among the Nazis' political opponents either escaped Germany or tried to conform to the wishes of the new regime; only the exceptional, like Alois Pfaller, tried to resist. In 1934 he tried to restart his old Communist youth group. It was a heroic act but, against a ruthless regime that singled out Communists as a particular enemy, failure was inevitable. Pfaller was betrayed by a double agent – a woman who worked for both the Communist Party and the Gestapo. He was arrested, taken to a police station and brutally interrogated; his nose was broken and he was beaten unconscious with leather belts: 'And when I came to again, they did it a second time, again unconscious, the fourth time, again unconscious, then they stopped because I hadn't said anything.' Now the interrogation tactics changed. One man sat at a typewriter to take down Pfaller's 'confession', while the other smashed his fist into Pfaller's face every time he failed to answer a question. The interrogation grew worse after the violent policeman sprained his right hand and began using his left. Now he hit Pfaller on the side of the head and split his ear-drum. 'Then I heard an incredible racket,' says Pfaller. 'It was a roaring, as if your head was on the sea-bed, an incredible roaring.' Pfaller resolved to kill the man who was beating him, even though it would also mean his own certain death. He had learnt judo when he was young and he intended to stretch out and stick his fingers into his interrogator's eyes. But just as he decided on this course of action, he haemorrhaged. The interrogation stopped and Pfaller was given a bucket and cloth and ordered to clean his own blood off the floor. Then he was taken to a cell for the night and subsequently transferred to a concentration camp. He was not released until 1945.

In a period of history rich in stories of collaboration and weakness, Alois Pfaller's own personal history is uplifting. Here is a man who was tortured to betray his comrades and refused: 'It's a question of honour,' he says. 'I'd have let them beat me to death but I never would have betrayed anyone. I would rather have died miserably.'

Most Germans did not confront the regime. More common was the experience of Manfred Freiherr von Schröder, a banker's son from Hamburg, who welcomed the new regime and joined the Nazi Party in 1933. He thought himself an idealist and believed that 1933 was the beginning of a wonderful new period for Germany: 'Everything was in order again, and clean. There was a feeling of national liberation, a new start.' Like most Germans, von Schröder knew that Socialists and Communists were imprisoned in concentration camps, but he dismisses this as unimportant in the context of history: 'You have never had anything of this kind since Cromwell in England. Closest is the French Revolution, isn't it? To be a French nobleman in the Bastille was not so agreeable, was it? So people said, "Well, this is a revolution; it is an astonishing, peaceful revolution but it is a revolution." There were the concentration camps, but everybody said at that time, "Oh, the English invented them in South Africa with the Boers."' Although these remarks are unacceptably dismissive of the horror of Nazi concentration camps, it should be remembered that the camps which sprang up in 1933 were, for all their horror, not identical to the extermination camps of the Holocaust which were to emerge in during the war. If you were imprisoned in Dachau during the early 1930s, it was probable that you would be released after a brutal stay of about a year. (Alois Pfaller's experience is unusual for a political opponent arrested in 1934, in that he had to endure eleven years in a concentration camp.) On release, former inmates were compelled to sign a paper agreeing never to talk about the experience, on pain of immediate re-entry to the camp. Thus it was possible for Germans to believe, if they wanted to, that concentration camps were 'merely' places designed to shock opponents of the regime into conforming. Since the terror was mostly confined to the Nazis' political opponents, or to Jews, the majority of Germans could watch what Göring called the 'settling of scores' with equanimity, if not pleasure.

On 6 July 1933 Hitler announced that he wanted an end to arbitrary violence on the streets. 'Revolution is not a permanent state,' he declared. He realized that the Storm Troopers posed a threat to the stability of the new Germany. One group of powerful Germans agreed with him wholeheartedly – the army. The professional soldier Johann-Adolf Graf von Kielmansegg remembers: 'One rejected the Storm Troopers because of their behaviour, the way they looked, the way they were...they were hated by most soldiers.' Von Kielmansegg confirms that the regular army believed that Ernst Röhm, leader of the Storm Troopers, was trying to take over the armed forces of Germany. They thought he wanted to integrate the Nazi Storm Troopers into the regular army and become supreme commander of them all. This was not in the interests of either the army or of Hitler.

Von Kielmansegg emphasizes the importance of making a distinction between support for the Nazis and support for Hitler himself. He maintains that the Nazis were 'rejected' by professional soldiers like him, but that Hitler, the individual, wasn't. Given that Hitler epitomized his party in a way that few political leaders have ever done, such a distinction seems tenuous today. It was also a distinction Hitler adamantly denied, declaring: 'The Führer is the party and the party is the Führer.' Notwithstanding this, von Kielmansegg's separation of Hitler from the Nazis was a distinction some officers clearly felt able to make at the time. To the uncharitable mind, it can be seen as one way in which professional soldiers could reconcile any disquiet they might have felt about the abuses committed by rampaging Storm Trooper thugs, with their own approval of Hitler's rearmament programme.

Hitler himself soon felt compelled to act against the Storm Troopers. In addition to learning of the concerns of the Armed Forces, he also spotted what he took to be a deterioration in Röhm's behaviour. Röhm had talked of a 'second revolution' so that the Storm Troopers could receive the rewards they felt had been denied them. For Hitler, this was not to be countenanced. Heinrich Himmler seized the moment and made up a story about Röhm – that he was planning a coup – and Hitler believed him. Himmler, whose SS were still technically under the umbrella of the Storm Troopers, moved his men against Röhm on 30 June 1934 – the 'Night of the Long Knives'. Hitler also used this occasion to settle old scores against Gregor Strasser (who had quit the Nazi Party in December 1932) and General von Schleicher (the former German Chancellor) who both lost their lives. In all, around eighty-five people were killed.

General von Blomberg, the Minister of Defence, was delighted at the news, so much so that he ensured the army publicly thanked Hitler for the action. Only a few weeks later (after Hindenburg's death on 2 August 1934) he arranged for all soldiers to swear an oath of allegiance to Hitler personally. All the soldiers we interviewed from that time emphasized the importance of this oath in the context of what was to happen;

for this was an oath sworn not to an office-holder but to a man – Adolf Hitler. Karl Boehm-Tettelbach took the oath in 1934 as a young Luftwaffe officer. For him, like many others, the oath was sacred and accompanied him to the very end of the war. He felt, and still feels, that if he had broken the oath, he might have had to 'commit suicide'. For Boehm-Tettelbach this was to have clear consequences when he was at Hitler's headquarters in East Prussia, the Wolfsschanze (the 'Wolf's Lair') in 1944 and witnessed the results of Count von Stauffenberg's attempt to blow up Hitler. Boehm-Tettelbach had not been approached to take part in the bomb plot himself, but had he been he would have refused. He would never break his oath.

Karl Boehm-Tettelbach served as an attaché to the Minister of Defence, General von Blomberg, who was 'like a father' to him. 'Blomberg was a good soldier,' says Boehm-Tettelbach, 'but he also saw good things for the army in Hitler.' In 1933, Blomberg later said, he had been given three things as a result of Hitler's appointment as Chancellor: faith, veneration for a man and complete dedication to an idea. A kind remark from Hitler could bring tears to Blomberg's eyes and he used to say that a friendly handshake from the Führer could cure him of colds. Boehm-Tettelbach witnessed how much Blomberg venerated Hitler when he regularly drove him back from his audiences with the Führer: 'There was hardly a trip back when he didn't praise him, and said that he had a good idea.'[2]

Once Hitler had removed Röhm, become head of state as well as Chancellor (on Hindenburg's death) and been the subject of a solemn oath of allegiance from the army, his hold on power was secure. He and his Nazi Party were masters of Germany. Now he pursued one simple policy – rearmament. As for the day-to-day domestic considerations that weigh heavily on most political leaders, Hitler either delegated or abnegated them. Chaos may have disappeared from the streets but it became rampant inside the Nazi administration and government.

Fritz Wiedemann, one of Hitler's adjutants, wrote that Hitler 'disliked the study of documents. I have sometimes secured decisions from him, even ones about important matters, without his ever asking to see the relevant files. He took the view that many things sorted themselves out on their own if one did not interfere.' The result was, in the words of Otto Dietrich, Hitler's press chief, that 'in the twelve years of his rule in Germany Hitler produced the biggest confusion in government that has ever existed in a civilized state.'

Nor does Hitler's daily routine at this time sound like that of a political workaholic. Fritz Wiedemann wrote, 'Hitler would appear shortly before lunch, read through the press cuttings prepared by Reich press chief Dietrich, and then go into lunch. When Hitler stayed at the Obersalzberg [the mountain in southern Bavaria on whose slopes Hitler built his house – the Berghof], it was even worse. There he never left his room before 2.00 p.m. Then he went to lunch. He spent most afternoons taking a walk; in the evening straight after dinner, there were films.'

Albert Speer, the architect who was to become the Nazi armaments minister, tells how, when Hitler was staying in Munich, there would be only 'an hour or two' a day available for conferences: 'Most of his time he spent marching about building sites, relaxing in studios, cafés and restaurants, or hurling long monologues at his associates, who were already amply familiar with the un-changing themes and painfully tried to conceal their boredom.'[3] The fact that Hitler 'squandered' his working time was anathema to Speer, a man who threw himself into his work. 'When,' Speer often asked himself, 'did he really work?' The conclusion was inescapable: 'In the eyes of the people Hitler was the leader who watched over the nation day and night. This was hardly so.'[4]

Hitler was not a dictator like Stalin who sent countless letters and orders interfering with policy, yet he exercised as much or more ultimate authority over the state and was at least as secure as a dictator. How was this possible? How could a modern state function with a leader who spent a great deal of time in his bedroom or in a café? One answer has been provided by Professor Ian Kershaw in a careful study of a seemingly unimportant speech given by Werner Willikens, State Secretary in the Ministry of Food, on 21 February 1934. Willikens said: 'Everyone who has the opportunity to observe it knows that the Führer can hardly dictate from above everything he intends to realize sooner or later. On the contrary, up till now everyone with a post in the new Germany has worked best when he has, so to speak, worked towards the Führer...in fact it is the duty of everybody to try to work towards the Führer along the lines he would wish. Anyone who makes mistakes will notice it soon enough. But anyone who really works towards the Führer along his lines and towards his goal will certainly both now and in the future one day have the finest reward in the form of the sudden legal confirmation of his work.'[5]

'Working towards the Führer' suggests a strange kind of political structure. Not one in which those in power issue orders but one in which those at the lower end of the hierarchy initiate policies themselves within what they take to be the spirit of the regime and carry on implementing them until corrected. Perhaps the nearest example we have in British history occurred when Henry II is supposed to have said, 'Who will rid me of this turbulent priest?' and the barons rushed to Canterbury to murder Thomas à Becket. No direct order was given, but the courtiers sensed what would please their liege lord.

Professor Kershaw believes that the practice of 'working towards the Führer' is a key insight into understanding how the Nazi state functioned, not just in the 1930s, but also during the war, and is particularly relevant when examining the provenance of many of the administrative decisions taken in the occupied territories. It gives the lie to the excuse offered by some Nazis that they were just 'acting under orders'. Often, in fact, they were creating their own orders within the spirit of what they believed was required of them. Nor does the idea of 'working towards the Führer' excuse Hitler from blame. The reason Nazi functionaries acted as they did was because they were trying to make an informed judgement about what Hitler wanted of them and, more often than not, the substance of their actions was retrospectively legitimized. The system could not have functioned without Hitler or without those subordinates who initiated what they believed were desired policies.

'Working towards the Führer' can be used to explain the decision-making process in many of those areas of domestic policy that Hitler, through temperament, neglected. Most political parties, for example, have a carefully conceived economic policy at the core of their manifesto. The Nazis did not. Indeed, one academic joked to me that the question, 'What was Hitler's economic policy?' was easy to answer – 'He hadn't got one.' Perhaps that is unfair in one respect, for despite a lack of policy, Hitler always had economic *aims*. He promised to rid Germany of unemployment, and, less publicly trumpeted but, in his eyes, more important, to bring about rearmament. Initially he had only one idea how to achieve this and that was to ask Hjalmar Schacht, a former president of the Reichsbank and a brilliant economist, to 'sort it out' (see Chapter Three). Apart from rearmament and strengthening the army, Hitler had little detailed interest in domestic policies.

Surprisingly, for those who believe that a successful economy has to be guided by a political leader, in the short term Hitler's delegation of the economy to Schacht seemed to work. Schacht pursued a policy of reflation financed on credit, and alongside this implemented a work-creation programme based on compulsory work service for the unemployed. For average citizens, unless they were among the regime's racial or political enemies, life began to improve. They knew little of the economic theory behind the reflation of the economy. Nor did they suspect Hitler of indolence when it came to details of domestic policy. Instead they looked around and saw with their own eyes what the regime had done – and most liked what they saw. Almost everyone we talked to emphasized the Nazi achievement of reducing unemployment and clearing the streets of the desolate-looking jobless. (Unemployment, with some massaging of the figures, dropped from a high of 6 million in January 1932 to 2.4 million by July 1934.) The programme of public works – particularly the high-profile building of the autobahns – was seen as proof of Germany's new dynamism. 'Everybody was now happy,' says Karl Boehm-Tettelbach (in what is plainly an exaggeration). 'People now said, "My wife and all my daughters can walk through the park in darkness and not be molested." Today it's really dangerous again but at that time it was safe and this made them happy.'

Unlike most officers, Boehm-Tettelbach had the opportunity in the 1930s of getting to know the top Nazis. As Field-Marshal von Blomberg's aide, he sat alongside them at dinner parties and was impressed with what he saw. Göring was admired as a man who knew how to speak to pilots thanks to his exploits in the Richthofen fighter squadron during World War I. Goebbels had a 'pleasant' manner and would enquire, while drinking a glass of champagne, what films the Field-Marshal had seen so that he could then recommend his own favourites, such as *Gone with the Wind* (a film Goebbels was obsessed with). But it was another Nazi leader for whom Boehm-Tettelbach has the kindest words – Heinrich Himmler, head of the SS and by 1936 chief of the political and criminal police throughout Germany: 'He was a very nice and agreeable guest because he always involved younger people like me and would enquire about the air force, how I was getting along, how long I would be with Blomberg, if I liked it, what I had seen the last trip to Hungary and things like that.' All these people, Boehm-Tettelbach thought, were good at their jobs. When, much later, he learned of the horrors Himmler perpetrated, he found them hard to reconcile with the considerate man he had met across the dinner table. Unpalatable as it may be to accept today, it was not just the Nazi regime that was popular during the 1930s, but also many of the Nazi élite, whose names were later to become synonyms for evil.[6]

Erna Kranz was a teenager in the 1930s and is now a grandmother living just outside Munich. She remembers the early years of Nazi rule, around 1934, as offering a 'glimmer of hope…not just for the unemployed but for everybody because we all knew that we were downtrodden'. She looked at the effect of Nazi policies on her own family and approved: salaries increased and Germany seemed to have regained its sense of purpose. 'I can only speak for myself,' she emphasized a number of times during our interview, conscious no doubt that her views were not politically correct. 'I thought it was a good time. I liked it. We weren't living in affluence like today but there was order and discipline.' Ask Erna Kranz to compare life today with life in the 1930s under the Nazis and she says, 'I thought it was a better time then. To say this is, of course, taking a risk. But I'll say it anyway.'

Erna Kranz speaks fondly of the amusements the Nazis organized for young people, such as pageants and celebrations.

One of the most famous 'artistic' processions was the 'Night of the Amazons' held in Munich each year for four years, starting in 1936. Surviving colour film of this extraordinary event shows topless German maidens on horseback. The semi-naked young women were arranged to represent historical tableaux, including hunting scenes from Greek myths. Erna Kranz took part in the parade, not as one of the topless girls, but as a Madame Pompadour with a hooped skirt and a plunging neckline. She did not see the event as pornographic – far from it: 'The girls were there the way God created them, but the real purpose was, I think, a feast for the eyes and the edification and joy of the people who went there.' After all, she points out, 'In the Sistine Chapel, they're all naked, aren't they?'

There was more to an event like the 'Night of the Amazons' than a pageant designed to fulfil the fantasies of the watching Nazi leaders. According to Erna Kranz, the purpose of events like this was to present the Germans as an élite: 'People had the conceit to say that a German is special, that the German people should become a thoroughbred people, should stand above the others.' This idea was contagious: 'You used to say that if you tell a young person every day, "You are something special," then in the end they will believe you.'

Knowing as we do the unique horrors perpetrated by this regime, people who claim to have been happier under Nazi rule than they are today are, at best, likely to attract ridicule. But it is vital that people like Erna Kranz speak out, for without their testimony an easier, less troublesome view of Nazism might prevail – that the regime oppressed the German population from the very beginning. Academic research shows that Erna Kranz is not unusual in her rosy view of the regime during this period. Over 40 per cent of Germans questioned in a research project after the war said they remembered the

1930s as 'good times'. As this survey was conducted in 1951, when the Germans knew the full reality of the wartime extermination camps, it is a telling statistic.

All this may seem incomprehensible now, or perhaps only comprehensible by relying on a cultural view of the Germans as a uniquely odd people peculiarly susceptible to a crazed authority figure. But there is another explanation, and to grasp it fully one must try to imagine oneself in the same position as Erna Kranz and her family in 1934. What did they have to look back on over the previous twenty years? A war that had drained the country of young men and resulted in national shame; a peace treaty that had economically crippled the country and taken away much of its territory; raging inflation that had destroyed people's savings; a plethora of political parties who appeared to bicker constantly with each other; street fights between the paramilitary supporters of rival political parties; unemployment on a scale never seen before. Is it surprising that the apparent stability of the Nazi regime from 1934 onwards was welcomed?

Unexpected as it may be to discover that many Germans were content during the 1930s, this news is as nothing compared to recent revelations about the infamous Nazi secret police – the Gestapo. In popular myth the Gestapo have a secure and terrifying role as the all-powerful, all-seeing instrument of terror that oppressed an unwilling population. But this is far from the truth. To uncover the real story you have to travel to the town of Würzburg in southwest Germany. Würzburg is a German town much like any other, except for one special attribute: it is one of only three towns in Europe where Gestapo records were not destroyed by the Nazis at the end of the war. Resting in the Würzburg archive are around 18,000 Gestapo files, which exist more by luck than design; the Gestapo were in the process of burning them as the American troops arrived. They had begun to burn them alphabetically, so there are relatively few A–D files left; otherwise the files are complete.

Professor Robert Gellately of Ontario was the first person to uncover the secrets of the files. As he started work on them, an old German man saw what he was studying and said to him, 'Perhaps you'd like to interview me, because I lived here during that time and I know a lot about it.' Professor Gellately talked to him over a cup of coffee and asked him how many Gestapo officials there had been in this part of Germany. 'They were everywhere,' the old man replied, confirming the conventional view of the Gestapo.[7]

Yet after studying the files, Professor Gellately discovered that the Gestapo simply couldn't have been 'everywhere'. Würzburg lies in the administrative area of Lower Franconia, a district covering around a million people. For that whole area there were precisely twenty-eight Gestapo officials. Twenty-two were allocated to Würzburg, and almost half of those were involved only in administrative work. The idea that the Gestapo itself was constantly spying on the population is demonstrably a myth. So how was it possible that so few people exercised such control? The simple answer is because the Gestapo received enormous help from ordinary Germans. Like all modern policing systems, the Gestapo was only as good or bad as the cooperation it received – and the files reveal that it received a high level of cooperation, making it a very good secret police force indeed. Only around 10 per cent of political crimes committed between 1933 and 1945 were actually discovered by the Gestapo; another 10 per cent of cases were passed on to the Gestapo by the regular police or the Nazi Party. This means that around 80 per cent of all political crime was discovered by ordinary citizens who turned the information over to the police or the Gestapo. The files also show that most of this unpaid cooperation came from people who were not members of the Nazi Party

– they were 'ordinary' citizens. Yet there was never a duty to denounce or inform. The mass of files in the Würzburg archive came into being because some non-party member voluntarily denounced a fellow German. Far from being a proactive organization that resolutely sought out its political enemies itself, the Gestapo's main job was sorting out the voluntary denunciations it received.

The files teem with stories that do not reflect well on the motives of those who did the denouncing. One file tells of a Jewish wine-dealer from Würzburg who was having an affair with a non-Jewish woman who had been a widow since 1928. He had been staying overnight with her since 1930 and they had declared their intention of getting married. The file demonstrates how Hitler's becoming Chancellor coincided with the widow's neighbours starting to voice objections to the presence of the Jewish man and confronting him on the communal stairs. As a result, he stopped staying overnight with the widow, but continued to help her out financially and to eat with her. Then, a 56-year-old woman who lived in the same house sent a denunciation to the Gestapo. Her main complaint was that she objected to the widow having a relationship with a Jew, although it was not then an offence. From correspondence between the party and the police it becomes clear that she and a male neighbour pressurized the party into taking action. The local Nazi Party then put pressure on the SS, who, in August 1933, marched the Jewish man to the police station with a placard around his neck. The placard, with its despicable message painted in blood red, is still carefully preserved in the file. In neatly stencilled letters it reads, 'This is a Jewish male, Mr Müller. I have been living in sin with a German woman.' Herr Müller was then kept in jail for several weeks before leaving Germany altogether in 1934. He had broken no German law.

Denunciations became a way in which Germans could

make their voices heard in a system that had turned away from democracy; you see somebody who should be in the army but is not – you denounce them; you hear somebody tell a joke about Hitler – you denounce them as well. Denunciations could also be used for personal gain; you want the flat an old Jewish lady lives in – you denounce her; your neighbours irritate you – you denounce them too.

During his many months of research in the Würzburg archive Professor Gellately struggled hard to find a 'hero' – someone who had stood up to the regime, an antidote, if you like, to the bleak aspect that the study of the Gestapo files casts on human nature. He believed he had found just such a person in Ilse Sonja Totzke, who went to Würzburg as a music student in the 1930s. Her Gestapo file reveals that she became an object of suspicion for those around her. The first person to denounce her was a distant relative, who said that she was inclined to be too friendly to Jews and that she knew too much about things that should be of no concern to women, such as military matters. This relative said that he felt driven to tell the Gestapo this because he was a reserve officer (though there was nothing in being a reserve officer that required him to do so). Totzke was put under general surveillance by the Gestapo, but this surveillance took a strange form: it consisted of the Gestapo asking her neighbours to keep an eye on her. There follows in the file a mass of contradictory evidence supplied by her neighbours. Sometimes Totzke gave the 'Hitler greeting' (Heil Hitler) and sometimes she didn't, but overall she made it clear that she was not going to avoid socializing with Jews (something which at this point was not a crime). One anonymous denouncer even hinted that Totzke might be a lesbian ('Miss Totzke doesn't seem to have normal predispositions'). But there is no concrete evidence that she had committed any offence. Nonetheless, it was enough for the Gestapo to bring her in for questioning. The account of her interrogation in the file shows that she was bluntly warned about her attitude, but the Gestapo clearly didn't think she was a spy, or guilty of any of the outlandish accusations made against her. She was simply unconventional. The denunciations, however, kept coming in, and eventually the file landed on the desk of one of the most bloodthirsty Gestapo officials in Würzburg – Gormosky of Branch 2B, which dealt with Jews.

On 28 October 1941 Totzke was summoned for an interrogation. The Gestapo kept an immaculate record of what was said. Totzke acknowledged that, 'If I have anything to do with Jews any more, I know that I can reckon on a concentration camp.' But despite this, she still kept up her friendship with Jews and was ordered once more to report to the Gestapo. She took flight with a friend and tried to cross the border into Switzerland, but the Swiss customs officials turned her over to the German authorities. In the course of a long interrogation conducted in southwest Germany, she said: 'I, for one, find the Nuremberg Laws and Nazi anti-Semitism to be totally unacceptable. I find it intolerable that such a country as Germany exists and I do not want to live here any longer.' Eventually, after another lengthy interrogation in Würzburg, Totzke was sent to the women's concentration camp at Ravensbrück, from which we have no reason to believe she ever returned. Her courage cost her her life.

We decided to follow up Professor Gellately's research with this file by trying to find living witnesses to Totzke's denunciation. Eventually we traced Maria Kraus, who had lived with her parents less than a hundred metres from Totzke. At the time we interviewed her, she was 76 years old and no different in appearance from any of the respectable elderly ladies one sees on the streets of Würzburg, itself a solid, respectable town. But lying in Totzke's Gestapo file there is a denunciation signed by a 20-year-old Maria Kraus on 29 July 1940. The statement begins: 'Maria Theresia Kraus, born 19.5.20, appeared in the morning at the Secret State Police.' During our own interview with her we read her the statement, which includes the section: 'Ilse Sonja Totzke is a resident next door to us in a garden cottage. I noticed the above-named because she is of Jewish appearance...I should like to mention that Miss Totzke never responds to the German greeting [Heil Hitler]. I gathered from what she was saying that her attitude was anti-German. On the contrary she always favoured France and the Jews. Among other things, she told me that the German Army was not as well equipped as the French...Now and then a woman of about 36 years old comes and she is of Jewish appearance...To my mind, Miss Totzke is behaving suspiciously. I thought she might be engaged in some kind of activity which is harmful to the German Reich.' The signature 'Resi Kraus' is under the statement. We asked Frau Kraus if it was her signature. She agreed that it was but said that she did not understand how the document could exist. She denies having given the statement and has no recollection of ever visiting the Gestapo. 'I do not know,' she told us. 'The address is correct. My signature is correct. But where it comes from I do not know.' Whether Resi Kraus's amnesia was genuine or merely diplomatic is impossible to say. Of course, it is scarcely in anyone's interests today to confess to having denounced one's neighbour to the Gestapo. In a telling remark at the end of our brief interview with her she said: 'I was talking to a friend of mine and she said "Good God! To think that they rake it all up again fifty years later"...I mean I did not kill anyone. I did not murder anyone.'

I still have the image in my mind of Frau Kraus as we left her, after the interview, standing in the cobbled town square of Würzburg; a profoundly unexceptional figure and thus a deeply troubling one. If you want to believe there is a difference in kind between those who may have aided the Nazi regime and those who definitely did not, then a meeting with Frau Kraus is a shocking one, for in all respects, other than the denunciation signed with her name that lies in the Gestapo file, she appears an ordinary, decent woman – someone who kindly enquired how old my children were and where we planned to go for our holidays.

If Frau Kraus is the sort of person who signed a denunciation (which she cannot now remember), what does this say about the Gestapo itself? On examination, it transpires that just as the notion that the Gestapo were 'everywhere' is a myth, so is the idea that Gestapo officials themselves were fanatical SS members who, when the Nazi regime began, managed to oust decent law-abiding officers from the police and substitute themselves. What actually happened was that most of the police remained in their posts when the Nazi regime began, but they did not have to carry on as usual; they were now off the leash. Under the Nazis, the German police could act in ways that, for many of them, must have been liberating – disregarding the rights of suspects and pursuing what in their view was a strong law-and-order policy.

Heinrich Müller, the notorious head of the Gestapo from 1939, was no exception to this rule. He had been a policeman before the Nazis came to power, working in the political department, where he concentrated on left-wing parties. Indeed, Müller was so far from appearing to be a committed Nazi that the local party headquarters recommended that he should not be promoted in 1937 because he had done nothing of merit for the Nazi cause. Their appraisal, referring to his actions against left-wing groups before the Nazis came to power, contains the words: 'It must be acknowledged that he proceeded against these movements with great severity, in fact partially even ignoring the legal regulations and norms. It is not less clear, however, that

Müller, had it been his task, would have proceeded just the same against the right.' The report goes on to contain a chilling insight into Müller's motivation for serving the Nazis: 'With his vast ambition and relentless drive, he would have done everything to win the appreciation of whoever might happen to be his boss in a given system.' Despite this negative evaluation, Müller still won promotion. His superiors, Heinrich Himmler and Reinhard Heydrich, must have felt that it was more important to give the job to someone ruthless, ambitious and qualified rather than to someone who was merely politically correct.[8]

Most Germans, of course, would never have come into contact with the Gestapo. If you were law-abiding (in Nazi eyes), you were safe. The terror was rarely arbitrary, unless you had the misfortune to belong to one of the regime's target groups – beggars, social misfits, Communists or Jews.

The chaotic nature of the Nazi administration of Germany was one factor that meant that Nazi anti-Semitic policy, until the start of World War II, was less consistent than one might have expected from a party committed to hating Jews. The basic anti-Semitism, particularly among the hardline Nazis, never changed, but the nature of the persecution varied wildly.

There were a series of uncoordinated attacks against Jews immediately after the election of March 1933. We have already seen one form this took in Würzburg – the public humiliation and imprisonment of a Jewish man for having an affair with a non-Jew (something, it bears repeating, that was not then against the law). But unofficial anti-Semitic action could be even more violent. Arnon Tamir was a fifteen-year-old Jewish boy when Hitler became Chancellor, and was told by a friend that, shortly after Hitler gained power, Storm Troopers from outside his village came in and thrashed all the Jews so badly that they were 'unable to sit down for weeks'.

Elsewhere in Germany there were reports of Jews being subjected to a variety of humiliating measures, such as having their beards shorn or being forced to drink castor oil.

Rudi Bamber and his family, part of the Jewish community in Nuremberg, quickly learned about the arbitrary way in which Nazi Storm Troopers could act against Jews: 'In 1933 the Storm Troopers came and took my father away, and together with many other Jews in Nuremberg, they were taken to a sports stadium where there was a lot of grass and they were made to cut the grass with their teeth by sort of eating it...It was to humiliate them, to show them that they were the lowest of the low and simply to make a gesture.'

None of these actions was formally ordered by Hitler, though he must have sympathized with the motives of those involved. On 1 April he authorized a boycott of all Jewish shops and businesses. When it was planned, the boycott was intended to be indefinite but, after pressure from Hindenburg and others (concerned about the danger of foreign trade reprisals), it was limited to one day. Nonetheless, for the Jewish population of Germany it was a day of great symbolic importance. Arnon Tamir saw Storm Troopers daub paint on Jewish shop windows and then stand intimidatingly outside to enforce the boycott. The Storm Troopers shouted slogans such as, 'Germans do not buy in Jewish shops' and 'The Jews are our misfortune'. He saw one or two brave Germans force their way into Jewish shops but witnessing their bravery only showed him how desperate the position of Jews in Germany had become. 'I felt like I was falling into a deep hole,' he says. 'That was when I intuitively realized for the first time that the existing law did not apply to Jews...you could do with Jews whatever you liked...a Jew was an outlaw.' From that moment on he resolved to try to distance himself from non-Jewish Germans. In a sense, he reacted as the Storm Troopers hoped all Jews might. The Nazis wanted the Jews to separate themselves from other Germans, creating their own Jewish state within Germany. Jews consequently formed their own schools, their own youth clubs, their own sports clubs – they began voluntarily to segregate themselves. This was all the more tragic given that so many Jews in Germany had taken such pains to integrate themselves into the population as a whole. Even though they remained physically within Germany's borders, they felt expelled.

There were still Jews, Arnon Tamir's parents and their friends among them, who clung to the hope that the boycott was directed not against them – loyal German citizens – but against 'international' Jewry. Indeed, with the segregation of Jews and the announcement of the Nuremberg Laws in the autumn of 1935, which codified the extent of Jewish exclusion from normal German life (including stripping them of Reich citizenship and banning them from marrying 'Aryans'), many Jews thought the regime had finally controlled its hatred. A combination of pressure from Hjalmar Schacht, Minister of Economics and President of the Reichsbank, over the economic consequences of persecuting Jews and the necessity of presenting Germany in a good light for the Olympic Games of 1936 meant that 1936 and 1937 were relatively quiet years for German Jews. This is not to say that the persecution disappeared – merely that compared with the harassment meted out in earlier years, life was not quite so bad.

However, there was still great suffering. The 'Aryanization' programme – the forced exclusion of Jews from the owning of businesses – meant that many Jews were deprived of a livelihood. Even those in businesses not initially forbidden to Jews could face ruin. Shortly after the boycott of 1 April 1933, Arnon Tamir's father experienced problems in running his small cigarette factory. The town's cigarette dealers, with whom his father had previously had very good relations, told him one after the other that they were 'sorry' but that since he was known to be a Jew they were no longer able to sell his cigarettes. Within one or two months of this unofficial 'boycott', he was forced to close down his factory. 'That came as a heavy blow to him,' says Arnon Tamir, 'because after the war and after the inflation, this was the third time that he had lost the basis of his livelihood. After that he lay on the sofa for weeks staring into space.'

Thousands of other Jews lost their livelihood not through an unofficial boycott, like Arnon Tamir's father, but through the raft of legislation in the 1930s that prohibited Jews from certain professions, like the Civil Service. Thousands more were so desperate that they fled the country.

Karl Boehm-Tettelbach accepts that it was wrong that many Jews felt forced to leave Germany, but says he 'understood' why the Nazis felt as they did, given their claim that '90 per cent' of lawyers in Berlin were Jews. Former banker Johannes Zahn puts it this way: 'The general opinion was that the Jews had gone too far in Germany,' and he too mentions the perceived problem that certain professions (such as the law) were dominated by Jews. These are significant remarks since it is easy to assume, given where this anti-Semitism was to lead, that Nazi anti-Semitic policy was pushed through against the wishes of the majority. From the variety of different witnesses we talked to it is clear that many Germans at the time supported the restrictions the Nazis placed on Jews.

Of course, the reason why Jews were concentrated in certain professions was the legacy of hundreds of years of exclusion from other areas of employment. 'The Jews were actually pushed into a particular sector,' says Arnon Tamir. 'Until 200 years ago they were not allowed to be farmers or craftsmen.' But logical explanation does not prevail over prejudice.

For non-Jews it was easy to look the other way. I asked Karl Boehm-Tettelbach how it was possible in the 1930s that someone could respect Hitler and what he was doing for Germany when Jews were forced to lose their jobs and leave the country. In his reply he spoke, I believe, for millions of other Germans: 'That never came up. Everybody thought the same, that you were in a big team and you didn't separate from the group. You were infected. That explains it a little bit.' Thinking back to his own enjoyable experiences in the Luftwaffe in the 1930s, he says: 'A young pilot flying all day long, he didn't want to discuss these problems and they never came up in the officer's mess. We came home, had a nice dinner and then went to bed or went out dancing.'

Arnon Tamir suffered as he grew to adulthood in this atmosphere of 'infectious' anti-Semitism. He would look into the mirror and stare at his nose – was it too big? And his lower lip – did it protrude too much? As for his attitude to non-Jewish German girls, 'The mere idea of becoming friendly, or more, with a German girl was poisoned right from the start by those horrible cartoons and headlines which claimed that the Jews were contaminating them.' Arnon Tamir discovered that, to the committed Nazi, the Jews weren't just different, they were diabolical. When he was at work on a construction site he listened in horror as a young Storm Trooper told a story, in all seriousness, about a Jewish woman in his village who was a sorceress. He claimed she had been able to turn into a foal and then change back again. One day the blacksmith caught her while she was still a foal and shod her with horseshoes so that she stayed a foal. 'I was deeply dismayed,' says Arnon Tamir, 'that it was possible he believed something like this.' The ludicrous prejudice of this Storm Trooper could more easily flourish in a society where there were very few Jews – remember that only 0.76 per cent of the German population was Jewish. It is sometimes easier to be frightened of an unseen, almost supernatural enemy, than the ordinary neighbour who lives next door.

After escalating throughout the summer and autumn of 1938 in a third big wave of anti-Semitic outrages to follow those of spring 1933 and summer 1935, violence against the German Jews exploded in an unprecedented manner on the night of 9 November – Kristallnacht, the night of broken glass. Two days earlier, Ernst vom Rath, a German diplomat in Paris, had been shot by Herschel Grynszpan, a Polish Jew angry at the Nazi treatment of Jews, particularly his own family, who had been among those recently deported with great brutality across the Polish border. Josef Goebbels heard the news of vom Rath's death and, when the Nazi hierarchy met in Munich to commemorate the anniversary of the Putsch, asked Hitler to let loose the Nazi Storm Troopers. Hitler agreed.

The first Rudi Bamber and his family knew about Kristallnacht was when their front door crashed open: 'In the early hours of the morning they sort of broke the front door down and started to smash the place up – the Storm Troopers. We had two lots: one lot just concentrated on smashing things up and left, but then the second lot arrived.' He tried to ring the police but saw that the people perpetrating the violence were in uniform themselves. 'We had three elderly ladies who were living on the first floor with us. One was dragged out and beaten up, for no reason except she probably got in the way or something. And I was knocked about and finally ended up in the cellar which was where the kitchens were...Then I was arrested and put under a guard outside the front door while they finished off what they were doing inside.' In a typical example of their arbitrary behaviour, the Storm Troopers suddenly changed their mind and decided not to detain Rudi Bamber: 'A great many people were arrested that night and it was obviously their intention to arrest me as well. But after a while they found that the leader of the group had gone home. He had obviously had enough and they were very irritated by this. They weren't going to waste any more time, so they gave me a swift kick and said 'Push off,' or words to that effect, and they walked out and left me to it.' But a terrible sight awaited Rudi Bamber when he re-entered the house: 'I went upstairs and found my father dying, dead. I tried as far as I could to give artificial respiration but I don't think I was very good at it and in any case I think it was too late for that…I was absolutely in shock. I couldn't understand how this situation had arisen…uncalled-for violence against a people they didn't know.'

For Germans like Erna Kranz, Kristallnacht 'was a shock because from that moment on you thought about things more. You see, at first you let yourself be carried along by a wave of hope; we had it better then, we had order and security in the country. Then you really started to think.' We asked her if she therefore became an opponent of the regime. 'No, no,' she replied hastily, 'that, no. When the masses were shouting "Heil", what could the individual person do? You went along. We went along. We were the followers. That's how it was. We were the followers.'

The reaction of ordinary Germans to Kristallnacht varied. Many were shocked, disgusted or stunned by the violence and destruction. Often the extent of the material damage was criticized. Sometimes people felt ashamed that a cultured nation could stoop to this. Sometimes expressions of human sympathy, albeit muted, could be heard. Most people, however, appear to have approved of ridding Germany of Jews. The Jews were friendless.

The morning after Kristallnacht, in Nuremberg, local Germans demonstrated what they felt about the suffering Rudi Bamber and his family had experienced: they threw stones at the windows of their house.

There is no reliable record of how many Jews were murdered as a result of Kristallnacht, nor how much property was destroyed. Recent research by Professor Meier Schwarz (a biologist from Tel Aviv, whose own father was killed by the Nazis) suggests that more than a thousand synagogues were destroyed and at least four hundred German Jews died.

The circumstances of Kristallnacht demonstrate once again how momentous events could occur within Nazi Germany with little advanced planning, and how violence, always near the surface, could explode once Hitler gave the nod. Hitler's own reputation suffered little as a result of Kristallnacht. He never spoke openly about the affair and, for those Germans who wanted to, it remained possible to believe that such violence could once again be laid at the door of Goebbels and the party's rabble.

In 1938, the same year as Kristallnacht, a grand new Chancellery was built (to a design by Albert Speer) to symbolize the power and authority of Nazi rule. But within its walls Hitler's style of government could still only lead to chaos. According to Dr Günter Lohse, of the German Foreign Office, the basic problem was that Hitler would appoint two people in two separate departments to do relatively similar tasks without making it clear who was working for whom. Then they would fight between themselves. Alternatively, Hitler would issue an instruction and then 'everyone made an institution out of the instruction'. When it came to resolving the inevitable disputes, Hitler rarely made a decision as to the merits of a case or said who was right. He would say to his ministers, 'Now you should sit down together and when you've made up, you can come and see me.'

In this spirit of competition Hitler's working life within the Chancellery was organized not by one private office but by *five*. There was the office of the Reich Chancellery under Hans-Heinrich Lammers; the office of the Chancellery of the

Führer under Philipp Bouhler; the office of the Presidential Chancellery under Otto Meissner; the office of Hitler's personal adjutant under Wilhelm Brückner; and the office of the Führer's deputy under Martin Bormann. Since all these people claimed to represent Hitler, much of their time was spent fighting with each other over jurisdiction. All of them looked for ways of pleasing their Führer as a means of increasing their influence. The result was a system in which chance events could provoke radical policies. The most chilling example of how this could happen within the Chancellery is the origin of one of the most repugnant policies of the Third Reich – the Children's 'Euthanasia' Programme.[9]

Sometime in late 1938 or early 1939 the father of a deformed child wrote a petition to Hitler, one of hundreds received by the Chancellery of the Führer every week. (In a system that lacked democratic representation, writing to the Führer, like offering a petition to the King in medieval times, became one of the few ways individuals could try to influence their fate.) This father wrote that his child had been born blind, appeared to be an idiot and was also lacking a leg and part of an arm. He wanted the child to be 'put down'. Officials in the Chancellery of the Führer, under the ambitious Philipp Bouhler, now decided that this should be one of the few petitions that they actually put in front of Hitler rather than responded to themselves or passed to other government departments. (The process of selecting letters always involved 'working towards the Führer', namely deciding in advance which of the petitions would be most likely to please Hitler.) Knowing Hitler's obsessive pseudo-Darwinian views, it must have been obvious that this particular petition would feed his prejudice (laws had already been passed by the Nazis which ordered the compulsory sterilization of the mentally ill). Hitler read the petition and then asked his own physician Dr Karl Brandt to go and examine the child and, if the father's statement proved to be correct, to kill the child. According to the post-war testimony of Dr Hans Hefelmann, a leading functionary in the Chancellery of the Führer, the Knauer case, as it became known, prompted Hitler to authorize Brandt and Bouhler to deal with similar cases in the same way.

There then followed a period in which doctors and other medical officials drew up detailed criteria for children who were to be 'referred for treatment' under the new policy. Diseases that had to be referred included 'idiocy and mongolism…deformities of every kind, in particular the absence of limbs, spina bifida, etc.' Forms were returned to a Reich committee, from whence they were sent to three paediatricians who acted as assessors. They marked each form with a plus sign if the child were to die, or a minus sign if the child were to survive. None of the three doctors who made the judgement saw any of the children: they decided on the information of the forms alone.

Gerda Bernhardt's family was one of the thousands to suffer once the 'euthanasia' policy was in full swing in the early years of the war. Her younger brother, Manfred, had always been retarded. When he was ten he was still speaking like a three-year-old. He could say 'Mama' and 'Papa' but little else except 'Heil Hitler' – something he was pathetically proud of being able to pronounce. Some unpleasant neighbours in their block of flats said that it would be for the best if the boy was 'put away', but Manfred's mother always tried to resist the idea. Eventually, though, her husband convinced her that their son should be sent to a nearby children's hospital in Dortmund called Aplerbeck. Manfred was twelve years old now and becoming a strain for all the family. There was a farm at Aplerbeck and Herr Bernhardt comforted his wife with the thought that Manfred would be able to spend time around animals.

Manfred was duly admitted to the hospital and his parents went to visit him once a fortnight – all the regulations would allow. Gerda also visited her brother as often as she could, taking him little gifts of food. Then, around Christmas of Manfred's first year in Aplerbeck, Gerda noticed a change in him. He was brought into the anteroom where they normally met dressed only in his underpants and he seemed apathetic and weak. Gerda hugged him goodbye. That was the last time she saw him alive.

The hospital authorities said that Manfred had died a natural death of measles, but Gerda Bernhardt noticed that a lot of children were dying at Aplerbeck around this time. She asked to see the body of her brother and in one room saw the bodies of fifteen little children all wrapped in white sheets. The nurse asked her as they moved from one body to another, 'Is this your brother?' and at each body Gerda said, 'No.' Manfred's body was not one of these fifteen corpses, but lay in another room on a hospital trolley.

After the burial his father said to the family, 'They killed our son,' but he had no evidence to prove it. Only in the last few years has it been possible to piece the true story together and to be able to say with certainty that staff at Aplerbeck murdered children who were put into their care.

Paul Eggert was a patient at Aplerbeck around the time Manfred was there. His father was a violent drunkard and he was one of twelve children. With this family history, classed by the Nazis as 'delinquent', Paul Eggert was forcibly sterilized at a hospital in Bielefeld when he was 11 years old and then sent to Aplerbeck for 'assessment'. As he was not mentally disabled, he was given odd jobs to do, such as fetching clean linen or pushing trolleys containing dirty washing. Once he thought the trolley he was pushing felt unusually heavy, so when no one was looking, he pulled back the washing and saw the bodies of two girls and a boy.

The similarity between life at Aplerbeck and a horror story continued in the nightmare world that was the children's evening meal. Dr Weiner Sengenhof, one of the senior doctors at Aplerbeck, would come into the dining-room with a nurse. They would then select the children who had to go to the doctor's consultation room in the morning for 'immunization' injections; the children, however, had noticed that those selected for such 'immunization' in the past were never seen again. Outside the consultation room, a child hung on to Paul Eggert screaming for help as the nurse tugged him away. Paul Eggert told us, 'These pictures would swim in front of my eyes when I lay in bed at night and they are still before my eyes today.'

Assembling the historical evidence for what happened at a hospital like Aplerbeck has been extremely difficult. Almost all the papers that could have established clear proof about what went on there were burned in the last months of the war. After 1945 nothing was said by those who had perpetrated or witnessed these terrible acts. Dr Theo Niebel, the doctor who had been in charge of the Special Children's Unit at Aplerbeck under the Nazi regime, still worked there as a doctor until his retirement in the 1960s. According to local historian Uwe Bitzel, 'It became possible to uncover something only when the direct participants were no longer at the hospital.' To Herr Bitzel this compounds the crime: 'I do find it totally awful that after 1945 none of these people stood up and said: "I have done terrible things. I recognize that we have all done them." But they all remained silent, denied it and lied – trivialized it in some cases.'

Uwe Bitzel took us down into the dusty basement of Aplerbeck and showed us the few remaining records from which he has pieced together the true story of Aplerbeck. The official record of deaths at the hospital shows a large number of children dying from inconspicuous diseases such as measles or 'general weakness'. On the same day Manfred Bernhardt met his death, two other children died. In the previous week eleven children lost their lives. In the following week nine children died. As Uwe Bitzel concludes, 'This is such a high death rate that it can be ruled out that all these children died of natural causes.' The cause of measles or 'general weakness' at Aplerbeck turned out to be either a massive overdose of luminal (a powerful sedative) or morphine.

The origin and practice of child euthanasia in the Third Reich is not just abhorrent, it is instructive. As we have seen, it originated not just out of Nazi racist ideology, but from the chaotic manner in which decisions were taken in the Third Reich. A chance letter to the Führer on a subject dear to his heart resulted eventually in the deaths of more than five thousand children. By the time Manfred Bernhardt met his death, two years after the policy was instigated, doctors in homes such as Aplerbeck did not have to fill in Bouhler's form. In a typical example of how policies could spiral out of control, staff independently selected the children they wanted to kill. The chaotic radicalism inherent in the Nazi system meant that, unlike in the Fascist states of Italy and Spain, German Fascism could never settle to a status quo, however dreadful or repulsive. Any idea, given a leader who spoke in visions and enthusiastic supporters anxious to please, could grow radically to an extreme in almost an instant. The consequences, not just for Germany but for the rest of the world, would be enormous.

Of course, in 1939 the vast majority of Germans would have known nothing of the evil policy of child euthanasia. Nor would they have realized the chaotic structure of Nazi government and the reasons for it. Nor would they have understood just why the Gestapo was so effective. What they chose to see was a dynamic country on the move – and they were part of it.

Neither a study of the documents nor the opinions of academics enabled me to understand how it was possible, before World War II, to actually *like* living in Nazi Germany. But after listening to witness after witness, not hardline committed Nazis, tell us how positive their experiences had been, a glimmer of understanding emerged. If you have lived through times of chaos and humiliation, you welcome order and security. If the price of that is 'a little evil', then you put up with it. Except there is no such thing as a 'little' evil. I am reminded of the old joke about the man who says to a woman, 'Will you sleep with me for ten million pounds?' The woman says, 'Yes.' The man replies, 'Now we have established the principle, let's negotiate the price.'

For the people of Germany the price of putting up with 'a little evil' would be very high indeed.

3

THE WRONG WAR

AT THE BERGHOF, HIS HOUSE IN THE SHADOWS OF THE MOUNTAINS of Bavaria, Hitler would relax by watching feature films. One of his favourites was a 1930s Hollywood epic of adventure and conquest, *The Bengal Lancers*, which contained a message of which Hitler approved: it demonstrated how one 'Aryan' nation had subjugated another more numerous but 'inferior' race.

'Let's learn from the English,' Hitler said over dinner on 27 July 1941, 'who with 250,000 men in all, including 50,000 soldiers, govern 400 million Indians.'[1] Here, according to Hitler, was clear evidence of the superiority of the 'Aryan' race: the English could rule India with a relatively tiny force because of their better blood. 'What India was for England,' said Hitler in 1941, 'the territories of Russia will be for us. If only I could make the German people understand what this space means for our future!'[2]

When he became Chancellor in 1933, Hitler wanted close friendship with England (by which he meant Great Britain). Dr Günter Lohse of the German Foreign Office says, 'He wanted England as an ally, a real ally.' Other diplomats agree; Herbert Richter confirms that Hitler saw the English as fellow members of the very select 'master race' club.

Yet in 1939, Hitler ended up at war with Great Britain, the one country in the world he wanted as an ally, while Germany allied herself to the Soviet Union, the one country, as we shall see, he most believed he risked conflict with. This war was not planned. But the combination of Hitler's character, the international tensions of the time and the institutional structures of the Nazi state made a war of some kind inevitable. It was just that the war of 1939 was, from Hitler's initial point of view, the wrong one. How could he, a man often praised for his political acumen, make such a mess of his own foreign policy?

When he came to power in January 1933 Hitler told the world he wanted to rid Germany of the shackles of the Versailles Treaty in order to make her strong once more. To accomplish this goal the country needed massive rearmament. His reply in February 1933 to a proposal from the Reich Ministry of Transport to build a reservoir demonstrates the extent to which, in his eyes, the policy of rearmament came before anything else: 'The next five years in Germany had to be devoted to rendering the German people again capable of bearing arms. Every publicly sponsored measure to create employment had to be considered from the point of view of whether it was necessary with respect to rendering the German people again capable of bearing arms for military service.'[3]

Rearmament could only be possible if the German economy provided the funds. But Hitler knew next to nothing about economic theory. 'The Nazi movement was really quite primitive,' confirms the banker Johannes Zahn, who knew Hjalmar Schacht, the man who was to be responsible for getting the German economy on its feet in the 1930s. Hitler may have known nothing about how to run an economy but Schacht thought he knew everything. 'It is clear, obviously,' says Zahn discreetly, 'that Schacht was very self-confident.' In 1923, at the age of 46, Schacht was made Reich Currency

Commissioner and told to stabilize the economy in the face of runaway inflation; later that year he became head of the Reichsbank. In 1930 he resigned in protest at the Young Plan, a regime of reparation payments to the victors of World War I to which the German government had agreed. He turned to Hitler and the Nazis for the solution to Germany's problems. 'I desire a great and strong Germany,' he said, 'and to achieve it I would enter an alliance with the devil.'[4]

Hitler appointed Schacht as Minister of Economics in 1934 and passed a law giving him dictatorial powers over the economy. Unemployment had already started to fall sharply as a result of huge work-creation schemes, such as the auto-bahn construction programme, and the economy as a whole was beginning to recover from the effects of the Great Depression. Schacht managed to pay for rearmament via the 'Mefo bills' – a form of deficit financing that had two advan-tages: it allowed the risky early stages of rearmament to be kept relatively secret and meant the Nazis could pay for it on credit. The regime also benefited from an upturn in the world economy and the effective cancellation of reparation pay-ments that had been negotiated by Chancellor Brüning at the Lausanne conference in 1932.

For Hitler this turnaround in the economy must have seemed like magic – simply another exercise of his will. He certainly wasn't concerned with *how* Schacht was working this miracle. He said in August 1942: 'I have never had a conference with Schacht to find out what means were at our disposal. I restricted myself to saying, "This is what I require and this is what I must have."'[5]

The army could not have been more positive about Hitler's actions. He was finally ridding Germany of the 'ignominy' of disarmament. 'This was absolutely welcomed,' says Graf von Kielmansegg, an army officer at the time, 'and he didn't ask about the cost at all. At last, an army was to be formed which, everyone agreed, was truly capable of defending Germany. The Reichswehr [German Armed Forces] were not capable of doing this with their 100,000 men. And don't forget, Germany was surrounded by its main enemies from World War I.' For many of the soldiers we talked to, rearmament also had a symbolic, almost spiritual importance; it was the means by which the country regained its potency. Others thought that if the newly rearmed forces were used to threaten Germany's neighbours so that some of the wrongs of Versailles could be righted, then well and good. Nobody we talked to believed during the 1930s that they were engaged in the preparations for a world war of conquest. Yet in 1924, Hitler had outlined in *Mein Kampf* some clear foreign policy objectives: 'We are taking up where we left off six hundred years ago. We are putting an end to the perpetual German march towards the south and west of Europe and turning our eyes towards the east…However, when we speak of new land in Europe today, we must principally bear in mind Russia and the border states subject to her. Destiny itself seems to wish to point the way for us here.'[6] And how was Germany going to gain this new land? The answer is clear: 'At the present time, there are on this Earth immense areas of unused soil only waiting for the men to till them. However, it is equally true that Nature as such has not reserved this soil for the future possession of any particular nation or race. On the contrary, this soil exists for the people which possesses the force to take it and the industry to cultivate it.'[7]

Few people, however, had read *Mein Kampf*, or if they had read it, they had dismissed it. 'Nobody believed *Mein Kampf* was of any importance,' says diplomat Manfred Freiherr von Schröder. 'What would politicians think today of what they have written twenty years ago?'

'But let me digress a little,' says Johannes Zahn. 'If you take Christianity, for example, the demands of the Bible, the demands of the catechisms, do you know anybody who fulfils the demands of Christianity 100 per cent, or even pretends to fulfil them 100 per cent? And one thought the same way about *Mein Kampf* – these are demands, these are ideas, but nobody thought that they were to be taken literally.' Herbert Richter, who worked in the Foreign Office, says, 'I too am to blame. I read the first fifty pages and found it so crazy that I did not read any more of it.'

Had these gentlemen taken seriously what they read in *Mein Kampf*, they would have learnt that Hitler believed Germany lacked *Lebensraum* (living space). If life was a struggle between the fittest races, then in order to triumph the Germans needed the right balance between population numbers and agricultural land. But Germany, according to Hitler's analysis, lacked the land it needed to support a strong population. Germans were thus a 'people without space'.

Hitler looked around and saw one nation that had solved the problem of lack of living space – England. In the early years of Hitler's Chancellorship he pursued the dream of an alliance with England, something that also fitted his desire to deal with European nations one by one rather than through the collective League of Nations.

In parallel with the policy of friendship with England, Hitler attempted to shake off the restraints of Versailles. Germany withdrew from the League of Nations and a disarmament conference in October 1933 after agreement had not been reached on a revision of the Versailles Treaty as it applied to German armaments. Now, Hitler tried to reach an agreement separately with England. At this point in the story one of the oddest Nazis makes his entrance – Joachim von Ribbentrop. Hitler was so impressed by this former wine merchant, who had married into money and society, that he made him his personal emissary and sent him to London to float the question of a non-aggression pact between the two nations. The unspoken idea behind the attempted friendship was, as former diplomat Reinhard Spitzy says, 'that Britain and Germany should practically rule the world. Britain should rule the waves and Germany should rule from the Rhine to the Urals.'

In 1935 the strategy of wooing Britain appeared to work. After meetings between Sir John Simon, the British Foreign Secretary, Anthony Eden, the Under-Secretary, and Hitler and Ribbentrop a naval agreement was signed that allowed Germany to rebuild her navy to 35 per cent of the British surface fleet and 100 per cent of her submarine fleet. An important factor in the British decision to sign the naval agreement was the view that Germany had been punished too much by Versailles and that a reasonable accommodation should be reached with Adolf Hitler.

In March 1935 Germany had announced that it had no further intention of observing the defence limits in the Versailles Treaty. In April the League of Nations had passed a motion of censure against the Germans. The British, by their naval agreement, showed what little store they placed in the League of Nation's collective response to German military expansion. Hitler described hearing news of the naval agreement as the 'happiest day of his life'.[8]

The following year, Ribbentrop was appointed German ambassador to Britain. He did not make a good first impression. When he presented his letters of accreditation to the King, he raised his right arm in a Hitler salute. The British press ridiculed him for it, but having done it once, he felt compelled to do it every time he met the King or he would lose face. Dr Lohse, who worked with Ribbentrop, believes that 'he couldn't and wouldn't forgive the English for his own mistake'.

The atmosphere in the London embassy was not a happy one. According to Reinhard Spitzy, who served there,

Ribbentrop was almost impossible to work for, continually postponing appointments; he was 'pompous, conceited and not too intelligent'. More seriously for his reputation, Ribbentrop also mistreated British tradesmen. He would keep tailors waiting for hours, not realizing that they would tell their other aristocratic clients about his thoughtless behaviour. 'He behaved very stupidly and very pompously,' says Spitzy, 'and the British don't like pompous people.'

Ribbentrop was intensely disliked by many who crossed his path. Goebbels said, 'He bought his name, he married his money and he swindled his way into office.'[9] Count Ciano, the Italian Foreign Minister, remarked that, 'The Duce says you only have to look at his head to see that he has a small brain.'[10] His was the one name guaranteed to raise a negative response from our interviewees. Herbert Richter thought he was 'lazy and worthless' and Manfred von Schröder believed him to be 'vain and ambitious'. No other Nazi was so hated by his colleagues.

Hitler was well aware of the low opinion in which Ribbentrop was held. According to Herr Spitzy, Göring told Hitler that Ribbentrop was a 'stupid ass'. Hitler replied, 'But after all, he knows quite a lot of important people in England.' Göring retorted, 'Mein Führer, that may be right, but the bad thing is, they know him.'

So why did Hitler support Ribbentrop? In essence the answer is simple. Because Ribbentrop knew how to handle Hitler. At one level he was merely a sycophant: 'Ribbentrop didn't understand anything about foreign policy,' says Herbert Richter. 'His sole wish was to please Hitler. To have good relations with Hitler, that was his policy.' In pursuit of this policy Ribbentrop used every device he could think of, including informants. He would ask people who had had lunch with Hitler to report back to him on what Hitler had said. Then, the next day, he would tell Hitler the same opinions but pretend they were his own. Hitler, not surprisingly, felt Ribbentrop had fine judgement. But there is another, more sophisticated, reason why Ribbentrop was so favoured by Hitler during this period. As Reinhard Spitzy puts it: 'When Hitler said, "Grey," Ribbentrop said, "Black, black, black." He always said it three times more, and he was always more radical. I listened to what Hitler said one day when Ribbentrop wasn't present: "With Ribbentrop it is so easy, he is always so radical. Meanwhile, all the other people I have, they come here, they have problems, they are afraid, they think we should take care and then I have to blow them up, to get strong. And Ribbentrop was blowing the whole day and I had to do nothing. I had to brake – much better."'

Thus, despite his obvious faults, Ribbentrop had found the key to ingratiating himself with Hitler, something that was lost on his more obviously gifted colleagues; he realized that the Führer always smiled kindly on a radical solution. This fact alone meant that Nazi foreign policy must lead to crisis. To Hitler, the most exciting solution to any problem was always the most radical. It did not matter whether the radical solution was adopted – the mere fact of suggesting it proved the true National Socialist credentials of its proposer. The corollary of this was that qualities of intelligence and ability in subordinates were not valued by Hitler as much as loyalty and radicalism, a truth that Hjalmar Schacht, the most intelligent of all the leading figures in the Nazi government, was about to discover.

'The Nazis turned towards the obvious ills,' says Johannes Zahn. 'These were unemployment and disarmament and these things are not really economic questions.' Talking of Schacht's actions during 1933–5, Zahn says: 'The Nazis had solved the problem simply by increasing the circulation of banknotes without having a real understanding of the concept of inflation.' The difficulty with the Nazi policies of rearmament and road-building was that, as Herr Zahn puts it, 'A motorway doesn't sit in a shop window, a motorway cannot be sold, though the purchasing power remains. Rearmament cannot be sold, though the purchasing power remains.' As an economist Zahn knew what Hitler didn't – money is purchasing power and only at your peril do you create purchasing power without having goods to sell.

According to Zahn, Schacht was very clear about the destabilizing and inflationary pressure that had been injected into the German economy by his short-term solution to the problem of financing rearmament. Schacht knew that unless industry soon made goods that people could buy in the shops, or which could be exported for foreign currency, Germany was heading inexorably towards ruin. He made this reality clear in a speech in November 1938 in which he echoed Herr Zahn's point that the economy was creating a demand from those with money to spend which could not be satisfied. Schacht's conclusion was simple: 'The standard of living and the extent of armament production are in inverse ratio.'[11]

Johannes Zahn reveals that by 1938 Schacht was not alone in thinking that Nazi economic policies must fail: 'But we all, me included, we all underestimated what you could achieve with state power through pay freezes, exchange controls and concentration camps.'

Once this deficit financing had been running for several years (rather than the initial 'pump priming' process that trained economists would have favoured, in which deficit financing was used just to start the stalled economy), Schacht must have been asking himself the question – how can Germany get out of this mess? The answer, at least to Herr Zahn, was frighteningly clear: 'One day the Nazi regime would have collapsed economically and Hitler thought, to put it crudely, what I do not get voluntarily I will try and take through war. So the war broke out and was lost.'

Documents show that while Hitler was aware of the economic problems caused by the financing of rearmament, he saw any domestic difficulties palling beside the overwhelming foreign policy problem Germany faced and which only rearmament could solve. In a memo written at Berchtesgaden in 1936, Hitler said: 'Germany will, as always, have to be regarded as the focus of the Western world against the attacks of Bolshevism. I do not regard this as an agreeable mission but as a serious handicap and burden for our national life...The extent of the military development of our resources cannot be too large, nor is its pace too swift...If we do not succeed in bringing the German Army as rapidly as possible to the ranks of premier army in the world so far as its training, raising of units, armaments and above all spiritual education is concerned, then Germany will be lost!' To Hitler it was ludicrous that he must concern himself with the petty realities of economic theory in face of the need to arm the country against the perceived Bolshevik threat. 'Hence all other desires without exception must come second to this task [of rearmament]. For this task involves life and the preservation of life, and all other desires – however understandable at other junctures – are unimportant or even mortally dangerous and are therefore to be rejected.'[12]

At the same time as Hitler wrote this memo, justifying the introduction of the Four-Year Plan, he decided that Schacht should be sidelined and the drive to maximize armaments production be directed by someone interested less in the complexities of economic theory than in the crude philosophy of Nazism – Hermann Göring. Schacht had no further future in Hitler's administration. He finally resigned and left office as Minister of Economics on 26 November 1937.

Schacht is symbolic of those Nazi supporters who saw the new regime as a welcome change from the insecurities and failures of the Weimar period and who were striving for stability in government. They wanted a strong and prosperous Germany. If that could be accomplished only in a dictatorship, then so be it. Germany's brief experience of democracy had not served it well. But Schacht clearly grew uneasy as Hitler's regime progressed, gradually realizing the true realities of Nazism. He believed that rearmament of itself was not something to be opposed. In fact, to some degree it was clearly desirable to help revitalize the eco-nomy and to set aside the shame of the Versailles Treaty, which had presented Germany to the world as a neutered nation. But Hitler now appeared to have no other goal, and he was ready to pay any price so long as Germany was prepared for war.

During the course of making the television series on which this book is based I met many men who had the same awakening as Schacht, although in most cases their awakening came later. Many thought Nazism would bring good things to Germany and, as they surveyed the initial years of the regime, culminating in the Berlin Olympics of 1936, they were well satisfied with what they saw. Many of these people now try to make sense of their own experience by referring to 'several' Hitlers. There was the Hitler of the 1930s (the 'good' Hitler), the Hitler of the initial war years (the 'warlike' Hitler) and there was the Hitler of the Holocaust (the 'evil' Hitler). It's an understandable attitude, since few people want to believe they were part of something rotten from the first; but they were. The 'Night of the Long Knives', Dachau and the other concentration camps, the racism and anti-Semitism at the core of Nazi ideology – all were present from the early years. I thought more than once after talking to these people that their travels through Nazism had been like a rocket ride. They had started on the journey because they wanted an exciting new experience. Then, when the rocket went up through the clouds, they grew uneasy. 'That was fun, but now it's time to return,' they would have said. But the rocket did

not return. It went on and on into the dark, a bleak and horrible place. 'But I only asked for a rocket ride,' they said at
the end of the whole horrific journey. I never wanted to go
into the dark.' But the rocket was always going into the dark
if only they had looked ahead.

Many others were to suffer the same fate as Schacht
before the outbreak of war, for this was a regime that could not
'settle down'. Leaving aside Hitler's own visionary desires as
outlined in *Mein Kampf*, his own sense of power and prestige
relied on continual success. After some of the major foreign
policy coups – leaving the League of Nations (1933), the
reoccupation of the Rhineland (1936) and the Anschluss (unification) with Austria (1938) – Hitler held a plebiscite to gauge
public approval for his actions and support was predictably
huge. Though not a conventional politician who worried about
re-election, Hitler was nonetheless continually anxious lest the
regime and the country as a whole lack excitement and movement. 'Instead of increase, sterility was setting in,' he said in
November 1937, 'and in its train, disorders of a social character must arise in course of time.'

Did this mean that during the 1930s Hitler planned the
war? No single question about the Nazi state in the 1930s has
been more debated. Much of that debate centres on one document, known as the 'Hossbach Memorandum'. Colonel
Friedrich Hossbach was Hitler's Wehrmacht adjutant and took
notes of a meeting at the Reich Chancellery on 5 November
1937 attended by the Commanders of the Air Force (Göring),
Army (Fritsch) and Navy (Raeder), the Reich War Minister
(Blomberg) and the Foreign Minister (Neurath).

According to Hossbach's notes, the meeting started with
Hitler at his most portentous: 'The Führer began by stating
that the subject of the present conference was of such importance that its discussion would, in other countries, be a matter
for a full Cabinet meeting, but he, the Führer, had rejected the

idea of making it a subject of discussion before the wider circle of the Reich Cabinet just because of the importance of the matter. His exposition to follow was the fruit of thorough deliberation and the experiences of his four-and-a-half years in power. He wished to explain to the gentlemen present his basic ideas concerning the opportunities for the development of our position in the field of foreign affairs and its requirements, and he asked, in the interest of a long-term German policy, that his exposition be regarded, in the event of his death, as his last will and testament.'[13]

Even in these few brief lines, one experiences the authentic sense of Hitler's political character – his distrust of cabinet meetings, his fear of an early death that would cheat him of glory and his own belief in himself as a major figure in world history.

According to Hossbach, Hitler went on to outline how he believed it was impossible for Germany to maintain self-sufficiency 'in regard both to food and the economy as a whole' within her current borders. Germany should now seek *Lebensraum* within Europe. There was, however, no mention of a campaign against Russia. Instead, he proposed that by 1943–5 at the latest, Germany should move against Czechoslovakia and achieve unification with Austria even at the risk of war with the Western powers, since after that date Germany's relative strength could only diminish.

At the Nuremberg Trials the Hossbach Memorandum was presented as evidence that a complete blueprint existed of Hitler's expansionist plans. It has proved hard to sustain this position, not least because there is no mention of Russia in the document. Some argue that this omission was deliberate 'in order not to alarm his audience'.[14] On the other hand, the historian A.J.P. Taylor wrote that the Hossbach Memorandum was essentially 'day-dreaming, unrelated to what followed in real life'.[15] The memo should be treated, in his words, as a 'hot potato'. Yet recent study of material not available to Taylor (such as the complete run of Goebbels' diaries) indicates clearly that Hitler knew he could not get what he wanted without conflict. But even to read just the full text of the Hossbach Memorandum is scarcely to learn the intentions of a mere day-dreamer. There could be no clearer statements than: 'The aim of German policy was to make secure and preserve the racial community and to enlarge it. It was therefore a question of space...The question for Germany was where could she achieve the greatest gain at the lowest cost?...Germany's problem could be solved only by the use of force, and this was never without attendant risk.' The Hossbach Memorandum may not be a 'complete blueprint' for war but it is a clear statement of expansionist intention. It is evidence of a foreign policy that would offer the rest of the world a simple choice as to how it could react – capitulate or fight.

One other policy decision is clear from the Hossbach Memorandum: the love affair with Britain was over. Throughout the meeting, Britain was lumped with France as a potential enemy whose possible reaction to Germany's aggression should be carefully analysed. Ribbentrop had begun to influence Hitler against Britain, and would continue to do so. He wrote Hitler a note in January 1938: 'I have worked for years for friendship with England and nothing would make me happier than if it could be achieved. When I asked the Führer to send me to London, I was sceptical whether it would work. However, in view of Edward VIII, a final attempt seemed appropriate. Today I no longer believe in an understanding. England does not want a powerful Germany nearby which would pose a permanent threat to its islands.'[16]

British coolness towards Germany had also been reported to Hitler from other sources. Karl Boehm-Tettelbach accompanied Field Marshal von Blomberg to London in 1937 for the coronation of King George VI. The German delegation took the opportunity to have talks with senior British politicians. Blomberg told his aide how disappointed he had been with the results of his discussions with Baldwin, Chamberlain and Eden – especially with Eden, whom Blomberg described as 'unfriendly'. But the Royal Family were nicer, even without the presence of the newly abdicated Edward VIII, whose friendliness to the new German regime is infamous. At the coronation dinner in Buckingham Palace Blomberg was honoured to be asked to sit at the King and Queen's table, gaining the impression that the Royal Family wanted to be friends with the new Germany. Unfortunately for the Germans, the politicians appeared not to be so agreeable and this was the news Blomberg reported to Hitler at Berchtesgaden. Boehm-Tettelbach followed behind Hitler and Blomberg on a long walk in the mountains as the bad news was broken to the Führer. On the way back to Berlin, Boehm-Tettelbach asked Blomberg what Hitler had said about the news. 'Nothing,' replied Blomberg. But shortly afterwards more resources still were planned for the army, something which Boehm-Tettelbach believes 'was the answer and reaction from the coronation'.

Blomberg, of course, was also one of the key participants at the Hossbach meeting. Hossbach, in his memoirs, writes that neither Blomberg nor Fritsch, the commander of the army, appeared overenthusiastic after they heard Hitler explain his plans: 'the behaviour of Blomberg and Fritsch must have made it clear to the Führer that his political ideas had simply produced sober and objective counter-arguments instead of applause and approval. And he knew very well that the two generals rejected any involvement in a war provoked by us.'[17]

These two leading army officers were not behaving as Hitler would have liked. There could be no greater contrast than between their sober pragmatism and Ribbentrop's aggressive radicalism. Unfortunately for them, Hitler much preferred the latter's approach. According to diplomat Reinhard Spitzy, Hitler once said, 'My generals should be like bull terriers on chains, and they should want war, war, war. And I should have to put brakes on the whole thing. But what happens now? I want to go ahead with my strong politics and the generals try to stop me. That's a false situation.'

Within a few months of the Hossbach meeting, those senior military officers who had not leapt enthusiastically to support Hitler's plans were removed. Blomberg and Fritsch were forced to resign and Neurath, the Foreign Minister, was also disposed of, appointed to the powerless job of 'president' of a Reich secret cabinet. The linkage of these events to the Hossbach meeting seems obvious, and there is a strong temptation to make the link appear a simple one of cause and effect – as though Hitler had decided that since these men now displeased him, they should be removed. But that is not how it happened. An understanding of the true circumstances surrounding the removal of Blomberg and Fritsch reveals how Hitler and the Nazi élite worked as politicians; for rather than having a preconceived plan, they seized the moment.

Blomberg announced his intention of marrying a commoner called Erna Gruhn. Hitler gladly gave his permission for the match: he liked the idea that an ordinary German girl would marry the grand Blomberg. The marriage was conducted quietly on 12 January 1938, with Hitler and Göring as witnesses. Karl Boehm-Tettelbach, Blomberg's aide, was upset that the wedding was such a small affair and that he himself hadn't been invited: 'I called my other adjutants and said, "Now look, isn't that strange? He's going to marry tomorrow and we don't even get a glass of champagne! Isn't that strange?"' Immediately after the wedding, following pressure from his fellow officers, Blomberg permitted a small wedding announcement to be placed in the newspaper. The next morning the paper was read by a policeman who recognized the bride's name and, checking his files, found that this same woman had posed for pornographic pictures, some of which were even in the file. The file was passed to the chief of Berlin's police, Count von Helldorf. He rang Karl Boehm-Tettelbach and made an appointment to see Blomberg at once, entering the ministry discreetly through a back entrance. After the meeting he said to Boehm-Tettelbach, 'Well young boy, you'd better look for a new job.'

On the afternoon of 26 January 1938 Hitler accepted Blomberg's resignation. Blomberg had no alternative but to quit, living as he did by the strict honour code of the German officer corps. Blomberg returned to the Ministry of Defence, entered Boehm-Tettelbach's room and asked him to open the safe. 'Here is the last will of Hitler,' Blomberg told him. 'Take that and give it tomorrow to Hitler with my field marshal's baton.' Then, shaking and crying, he said, 'Goodbye, my friend,' and embraced him. To Boehm-Tettelbach 'the world broke down because I believed in him and saw that he had made a big mistake in marrying someone not decent for a field marshal.' Blomberg's decision to hand back his baton is significant because a field marshal usually keeps it into retirement. Perhaps the shame was simply too great.

Hitler could not have predicted these events, but once they occurred, he and his hardline subordinates exploited them. Days after Blomberg's removal, Fritsch was forced to resign after Himmler and Göring instigated a trumped-up charge of homosexuality against him, even hiring a false witness. In addition, sixteen older generals were retired and forty-four transferred. At the same time as Hitler made these changes, he also replaced Neurath with Ribbentrop as minister of foreign affairs.[18]

This radical clearing-out of any restraining element on Hitler stemmed entirely from the resignation of Blomberg –

something that could not have been anticipated. But one of Hitler's strengths as a politician was an ability to exploit a situation when it occurred. He hinted at his attitude in July 1924 when he explained, 'The theoretician must always preach the pure idea and have it always before his eyes: the politician, however, must not only think of the great objective but also the way that leads to it.' One reason why so many contradictions appear in German foreign policy during this period is that Hitler was always keen to exploit the immediate situation, sometimes (as in the alliance with the Soviet Union) at the short-term expense of the long-term 'theoretical' goal. One day during a lunch at which Reinhard Spitzy was present, Hitler said, 'If someone is burning a little fire, I would put there my pot with soup and heat it for the good German people, and blow a little bit in the fire.' To Spitzy it was clear he meant that 'he wanted to take the occasions as they came, he wasn't fixed'.

Without, as he saw it, the shackles of the old guard, Hitler now began to pursue a more radical foreign policy, and Austria was his first target. General Alfred Jodl noted in his diary on 31 January 1938: 'Führer wants to divert the spotlights from the Wehrmacht. Keep Europe gasping and by replacements in various posts not awaken the impression of an element of weakness but of a concentration of forces. Schuschnigg is not to take heart, but to tremble.'[19] Kurt von Schuschnigg, the Chancellor of Austria, had been bravely resisting Nazi influence in his country. In 1936 an agreement had been signed in which Austria acknowledged herself to be a German state, but was nonetheless free to run her own domestic affairs. Hitler put pressure on the Austrians for still greater ties with Germany only days after the Cabinet meeting at which the changes following Blomberg's departure had been announced. In January 1938 Franz von Papen, now ambassador to Austria, passed on to Schuschnigg Hitler's

A Freikorps detachment marches into Munich in 1919. Even though the Nazi Party was not yet in existence, many wear swastikas on their arms – a traditional right-wing emblem that pre-dated the Nazis.

Left A formal portrait of Hitler by Heinrich Hoffmann from the mid-1920s. Many supporters remarked on the power of Hitler's stare, a trick he attempts to pull on the camera here.

Below Hitler and President Hindenburg shortly after Hitler became Chancellor. A rare picture of Hitler smiling, but then, unlike Hindenburg, he had a lot to smile about.

Opposite A clear illustration of the split in German politics in the early 1930s with swastika banners flying from the same block of flats as the Communists' hammer and sickle. The only policy both Communists and Nazis had in common was their commitment to end democracy in Germany.

Top Prisoners at the newly opened concentration camp at Dachau outside Munich in 1933.
Above Nazi Storm Troopers enjoy themselves by shaving a young Communist's hair, March 1933.
Opposite 1 April 1933: the Nazis organize a boycott of Jewish shops and the Storm Troopers fix hate-filled slogans on shop windows.

Right Hitler and Röhm in the summer of 1933. One year later Röhm would be dead, murdered on the orders of the man standing next to him.
Below right Field Marshal Werner von Blomberg, German Minister of Defence, and Hitler in September 1937; less than six months later Blomberg resigned.
Below left Karl Boehm-Tettelbach as a young Luftwaffe officer.
Opposite German troops march in Nuremberg in September 1937. Hitler would shortly reveal why he wanted this new army.

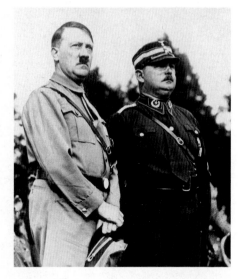

Above Jubilant crowds greet Hitler at the Party Congress in Nuremberg in 1938.

Right Ribbentrop (left) and Himmler at Nuremberg in 1938. Himmler was one of the few leading Nazis not to despise Ribbentrop openly. At least they shared a sense of radicalism.

invitation to meet him at Berchtesgaden. The meeting revealed Hitler at his most bullying. Dr Otto Pirkham was a member of the Austrian delegation and recalls how 'on the staircase Schuschnigg was already seized by Hitler and taken to his rooms'. Hitler demanded the appointment of the Austrian Nazi, Arthur Seyss-Inquart, as Austrian Minister of Interior and the integration of Austrian economic and foreign policy with Germany's. Schuschnigg was clearly shocked by these demands. At lunch that day, where Hitler played the amiable host and talked about trivial matters, Schuschnigg sat completely silent. At the end of the day, when Schuschnigg had been bullied into giving Hitler what he wanted, he was even more depressed and silent. 'His silence,' says Dr Otto Pirkham, 'was due to the fact that what he had learned at the meeting with Hitler would not have been very agreeable.'

Shortly after the Berchtesgaden meeting, Jutta Rüdiger learnt Hitler's own opinion of Schuschnigg. She was attending an official Nazi dinner in her capacity as a senior figure in the BDM (the Nazi league of young women) when Hitler joined her table and the talk turned to the character of the Austrian Chancellor. 'Hitler said that he reminded him of a butterfly collector and only the botanist's vasculum [collecting case] was missing.' Hitler then described the metaphor he had used to illustrate why Austria and Germany must be together. 'I have told him that we had always said, "a good engine alone is no good. It has to have a good chassis too, but the good chassis on its own won't do either."'

Chancellor Schuschnigg still tried to resist what he knew was the eventual Nazi goal – the subjugation of his whole country. On 8 March 1938 he announced that there would be a plebiscite on 13 March so that Austrians could vote on whether or not they wished to be part of the German Reich. Schuschnigg was forced to drop the planned plebiscite after German pressure, but despite this, Hitler decided to increase the tension still further. He had learnt from Ribbentrop that England would not fight over Austria and now moved to neutralize any adverse reaction from his neighbour, Italy.

On 10 March Hitler sent Prince Philip of Hesse to Rome with a letter that explained that the Italians had nothing to fear from any action the Germans might take against Austria; Hitler would always regard the Brenner Pass as the border with Italy. The following day Mussolini's view on the potential invasion of Austria by Germany was conveyed to Hitler in a telephone call from Prince Philip of Hesse:

'I have just come from the Palazzo Venezia. The Duce accepted the whole thing in a very friendly manner. He sends you his regards.'[20]

'Then please tell Mussolini I will never forget him for this,' said Hitler. 'Never, never, never, whatever happens. As soon as the Austrian affair is settled, I shall be ready to go with him, through thick and thin, no matter what happens.'

The tone of Hitler's response shows how anxious he was during the crisis, and perhaps also explains why he remained loyal to Mussolini until the end of the war. The historian Joachim Fest describes 'the mood of hysteria and indecision' that characterized the atmosphere around Hitler during this crisis: 'All reports from members of Hitler's entourage speak of the extraordinary chaos surrounding the decision, the panicky confusion that overtook Hitler on the verge of this first expansionist action of his career. A multitude of over-hasty mistaken decisions, choleric outbursts, senseless telephone calls, orders and cancellation of orders, followed in quick succession during the few hours between Schuschnigg's call for a plebiscite and March 12...Keitel [Chief of Staff of the High Command] later spoke of the period as a "martyrdom".'[21]

This is not a familiar portrait of Hitler. In popular myth (and, indeed, in Nazi myth) one of Hitler's defining characteristics is decisiveness. Yet it was Göring, not Hitler, who coolly called for the most radical action – invasion – and who actually issued the order for the troops to invade. Göring was behaving as Hitler believed a general should, as a 'bull terrier'. (Göring's decisiveness may also have been self-serving; it was in his own interests to keep the German Army distracted by an invasion of Austria from pursuing any investigation into the Fritsch affair and his own role in it.)

On 12 March 1938 Hitler drove in triumph into Austria, the land of his birth. Film footage captured the wild emotional response of the Austrians. They weep, they scream, they chant: 'One Reich, One People, One Führer!' German troops are pelted with flowers and showered in kisses. To watch this raw footage, without commentary, but accompanied by the sounds of ecstatic Austrians, is still to be affected by the emotions of the time. For the Germans who were the objects of such veneration it was overwhelming. 'It was the nicest day of my life when we entered Austria,' says Reinhard Spitzy. 'I entered with Hitler in the sixth car. I had tears in my eyes.'

For Austrians such as Susi Seitz, the sight of Hitler caused an outpouring of a simple desire: 'All the people were answering Hitler in one way – "Get us to the German country, get us to Germany, let us be with you." And it was as if Hitler really got from all the people the answer to a question he was himself not thinking to have asked, because at that time we knew very well Hitler didn't want to take Austria in.' What we now know is that Hitler, too, was profoundly moved by what he saw – so moved that he altered his plans regarding Austria's political fate. Before entering Austria his only firm plan had been to put a puppet government in place. Now, as he experienced an enthusiastic reception in his former home town of Linz, he simply changed his mind. He decided that Austria deserved not to be a puppet state but a full member of the Reich; Germany and Austria should unite.

It is hard for us today to comprehend the ecstasy with which so many Austrians greeted the Nazis in general and Hitler in particular. In fact, the cause of their joy was clear – the Germans were righting a wrong done to them by the post-World War I settlement. Only twenty years earlier Austria had been a world power wallowing in the grandeur of the Austro-Hungarian Empire, but defeat in the war had reduced the country to the status of Switzerland. Now the Austrians felt they could recover their own greatness in a Germanic Reich.

After the triumphal Linz rally in March 1938, the fourteen-year-old Susi Seitz managed to shake Hitler's hand, and has never forgotten the moment: 'He came. Everything got quiet. And we were so excited, I felt my heart up here in the throat. And when he came to me I nearly forgot to give him my hand; I just looked at him and I saw good eyes. And in my heart I promised him, "I always will be faithful to you because you are a good man…." That was a dream-like time. And later I kept my promise. All my free time, besides school, I gave to the work because he had called us: "You all," he said to us, "you all shall help me build up my empire to be a good empire with happy people who are thinking and promising to be good people."'

But this was to be a brutal act of union. Hitler had been met on his entry into Austria by Heinrich Himmler, who had crossed the border the night before in order to start 'cleansing' the country of any elements of opposition. Austrian Jews suffered immediately. Walter Kammerling was then a fifteen-year-old Jew living in Vienna: 'We hear the noises from the streets coming in, the whole Viennese population, that is obviously the non-Jewish population, in jubilation and enjoyment. And then the first problem starts, the Jewish shops get smashed, and when you go on to the street the next day, that was the Saturday, you had already people molesting you…You were completely outlawed, there was no protection from anywhere.

Anybody could come up to you and do what they want and that's it, and people came into flats which they wanted and took them.' The SS approved of all the humiliations local Austrian Nazis heaped on the Jews, especially when they made the Jews scour the streets clean: 'I remember I once had to scrub the streets as well,' says Walter Kammerling. 'I can't remember anything except that I saw in the crowd a well-dressed woman, you can't say the uneducated proletariat, and she was holding up a little girl, a blonde lovely girl with these curls, so that the girl could see better how a twenty- or twenty-two-year-old man (a Nazi Storm Trooper) kicked an old Jew who fell down because he wasn't allowed to kneel. He had to scrub and just bend down sort of, and he fell and he kicked him. And they all laughed and she laughed as well – it was a wonderful entertainment – and that shook me.'

Susi Seitz accepts that anti-Semitism was widespread in Austria: 'I must say the Jews were not very much liked in Austria...We never had the feeling that they were the same as us, they were different, completely different...We only knew our families made jokes about them and didn't like them. That we knew. But we didn't think much about it because we had other things to think about, and we liked to play games and do sports and liked to hike around in our country. And we knew that the Jews hadn't that feeling for our home country.' With prejudice like this to exploit, Austria became a happy home for the SS. Austrian Jews were forcefully encouraged to emigrate. Within six months of the Anschluss eager SS officers, organized by Adolf Eichmann, had expelled around a third of Vienna's Jews. The emigrants had to leave their wealth behind. The Nazis simply stole it.

Heinrich Himmler realized that territorial expansion meant the potential for a huge increase in power for the SS. In November 1938 he told his SS generals: 'Germany's future is either a greater Germanic empire or a nothing. I believe that if we in the SS are doing our duty, then the Führer will create this greater Germanic empire, this greater Germanic Reich, the biggest empire ever created by mankind on the face of the earth.'[22] The brutal way the SS acted in Austria in 1938 was a foretaste of how the Nazis would rule their empire. Outside the borders of Germany the SS intended to operate with little or no restraint.

The German Foreign Office basked in the glory of the Anschluss. 'The unification of Austria was really a national dream,' Manfred von Schröder told me. 'It was the summit of Hitler's popularity and that influenced everyone in Germany at that time.' The euphoria also affected Hitler, according to von Schröder: 'It must have been an enormous feeling of success and probably it made his megalomania grow.'

Spurred on by the bloodless success of the Anschluss, Hitler now turned to Czechoslovakia. Its strategic geographical position in Europe convinced Hitler that he could not expand further without neutralizing its army. The most obvious way of destabilizing Czechoslovakia was to incite the more than 3 million Germans who lived in the Sudetenland; they had already been calling for greater rights within Czechoslovakia as an ethnic group. Less than three weeks after his triumphant entrance into Austria, Hitler held a meeting in Berlin with the leaders of the Sudeten German Party and told them that he intended to 'settle' the Sudeten problem in the 'not-too-distant-future'. Hitler knew that world opinion would not permit him to attack Czechoslovakia without a pretext, so after approving the Sudeten German Party's tactic of agitation against the Czech government, he left events to escalate without his direct involvement.

The Czechoslovakian government suffered because their country was a creation of the post-World War I settlement. Not only did this mean that the Nazis despised it, but that the country's genesis had created a number of ethnic minorities within it, many of whom were suspicious of each other. To outside observers, such as the British, it seemed that there was some justice in the Nazi dislike of Czechoslovakia and their support for the Sudeten Germans. An editorial in *The Times* on 7 September 1938 even called for the Sudetenland to be given to the Germans.

As problems with the Sudeten Germans escalated, the British Prime Minister, Neville Chamberlain, intervened to try to solve the crisis. He began by making two visits to Germany to meet Hitler on 15 and 22 September. The dispute was finally resolved at the Munich conference on 29 September at which representatives from Italy, Britain and France agreed that the Sudetenland should be ceded to Germany in stages between 1 and 10 October.

The Czechoslovakian crisis allowed the British to see what sort of statesman Hitler actually was. Chamberlain called him 'the commonest little dog' he had ever seen.[23] The British and the French witnessed the rows, the vacillations, the bullying and the changes of mind that characterized Hitler's diplomacy. Nor was Hitler satisfied with the Munich Agreement. He had doubted all along whether the British and French would really have risked everything over Czechoslovakia and now believed he had been badly advised. He suspected that it had not been necessary for Göring and Mussolini to devise any form of compromise at the conference. Manfred von Schröder, who had been present at the signing of the agreement, heard only the day after the Munich conference that Hitler was saying, 'They have robbed me of my war.'

Hitler still had not finished with Czechoslovakia. Even though the Nazis now possessed the Sudetenland, and had thus deprived Czechoslovakia of her man-made fortifications and the mountains that were her natural defences, Hitler still saw the rest of Czechoslovakia as a threat. He now used the same tactic to destabilize the remainder of Czechoslovakia that he had used to gain the Sudetenland – he encouraged a minority to revolt. Now he pressed the Slovak leaders to declare full independence from the rest of Czechoslovakia. Their natural inclination to do so was reinforced by threats from Hitler that if they did not do as he wished, he would encourage Hungary to claim Slovakia as *her* territory. This was diplomacy the Darwinian way: we are stronger than you and if you don't do what we want, then you will be crushed. Treaties, international law, mutual policing of nations through organizations like the League of Nations – all were devices the weak employed to hide from the strong. Hitler practised not the diplomacy of Bismarck but that of the bully. Up to now he had cloaked his brutal bullying in such a way that it was capable of another interpretation – the Anschluss was Austria's wish, the Sudeten Germans were mistreated – but now he was to demonstrate openly the true essence of Nazi philosophy, in which the strong simply 'take over' the weak.

On 14 March 1939 the Slovaks declared independence (reading from a text prepared by Ribbentrop). That night the ageing Czech President, Emil Hácha, arrived in Berlin for talks. Hitler humiliated him, first by keeping him and his entourage waiting for hours, then by making them tramp through hall after hall of the new Chancellery to reach his office, and finally by meeting them at one o'clock in the morning and announcing that at six o'clock, in five hours' time, German troops were going to invade their country. Hitler was enjoying himself; Hácha was not. As the Czech President tried to telephone Prague, Göring joined in the fun and began describing to him how German planes would bomb the Czech capital. Manfred von Schröder witnessed what happened next: 'Hácha broke down and had a heart failure.' Von Schröder called Hitler's personal physician, Dr Theodor Morrell, who gave Hácha an injection. The Czech

President revived sufficiently so that at four o'clock in the morning he signed away the Czech people into Hitler's 'care'.

Manfred von Schröder witnessed the celebrations in Hitler's huge office following the submission of Czechoslovakia: 'It was a sort of victory party with champagne – Hitler had his mineral water. And then I got a very close impression of that man. It was amazing to see how he behaved when he was among friends, alone, and hadn't to behave like a statesman for the public. He was sitting first of all like this...' Here von Schröder demonstrates by tousling his hair, undoing the top buttons of his shirt and sitting across his armchair, his legs dangling over one side. 'He was talking the whole time, dictating to two secretaries; one proclamation to the Czechoslovak people, and a letter to Benito Mussolini. I thought he was behaving like a genius but that was wrong, of course. When I look back today and I have the clear picture of him standing up and then sitting down again I think he was absolutely behaving like a maniac.'

Hitler may have won the immediate prize of the Czech republic, but he had demonstrated, even to his own loyal diplomats, that he had extremely poor judgement. 'That was the most stupid act and he ruined practically everything,' says Reinhard Spitzy. 'There was no necessity to invade Czechoslovakia because all electric lines, the railways, the roads, the water pipes could be cut at the ethnic frontier. After the Munich conference the Czechs were absolutely in our hands and with nice treatment we would have won them all.' To Manfred von Schröder Hitler's actions were diplomatic suicide: 'That changed the whole of history because from that moment on it was clear that Hitler was an imperialist and he wanted to conquer – it had nothing to do with the self-determination of the German people.'

Hitler, of course, did not see his actions in this negative way. Removal of any potential threat from a country as strategically placed as Czechoslovakia was essential if the German Army was to move further east in search of conquest. But still nothing could be accomplished without a common border with Russia. Standing in the way was a country re-created at Versailles – Poland.

Paradoxically, since it was to be the invasion of Poland that would spark the war, Hitler's claims on it were not as unreasonable as his claims on Prague and the remainder of Czechoslovakia had been. Danzig, previously a German city, had been designated a Free City under the Versailles Treaty and sat in a Polish 'corridor' of land between German East Prussia and the rest of Germany. It was easy to argue that in this case Germany had experienced injustice.

Initially, Ribbentrop asked the Poles for the return of Danzig and a strip of German territory across the Polish corridor on which a German-run road and rail link between East Prussia and the rest of Germany could be built. This time Hitler met real resistance. On 31 March 1939 the British and French guaranteed the borders of Poland. Encouraged by the guarantee, the Poles were not about to compromise. Then, as 1939 progressed, the position of the Soviet Union became critical. If Stalin allied himself with Britain, Germany would run the risk of a two-front war if she pushed the world to conflict. British attempts at negotiation with the Soviet Union were, however, lacklustre, for both ideological and practical reasons (Stalin had purged thousands of officers from the Red Army and the Soviets were perceived to be a third-rate military force). Stalin was also unwilling to be pushed into a war that offered him little in terms of his own narrow self-interest. Then the Nazis pulled what Manfred von Schröder calls a stroke of 'courage' and 'genius' – they signed their own treaty with the Soviet Union, their greatest ideological enemy.

The German Foreign Office had noticed the significance of Stalin's speech in March 1939 when he had said, in a clear rebuff to Britain, that he would 'not let our country be drawn into conflict by warmongers, whose custom it is to let others pull their chestnuts out of the fire'.

'That was the turning-point,' says Hans von Herwarth, then a diplomat at the German embassy in Moscow. After Stalin's speech, Germany and the Soviet Union began negotiations on greater economic ties. As the summer progressed, Ribbentrop, with Hitler's blessing, pushed forward with negotiations for a political treaty, a 'non-aggression' pact, which was eventually signed on 23 August. At first sight, the treaty seemed incredible – totally at variance both with Hitler's expressed ideological view of the Soviet Union and the Soviets' own suspicions about the Nazi regime. But there was a secret part of the treaty, not revealed at the time, that shows why both countries, greedy for spoils, would have seen the agreement in their own national self-interest. Hans von Herwarth saw the secret protocol signed, and confirms that within it Hitler 'promised to give back to the Soviet Union all that they had lost through the results of World War I. And naturally that was a prize which France and Great Britain couldn't pay because that meant to sacrifice the freedom of the Baltic states, Poland and even, perhaps, Finland.'

Hans von Herwarth was clear what the consequences of the Non-Aggression Pact would be. 'Now we have lost the war,' he told his colleagues that summer. 'My opinion was that the Americans would come in and we would lose World War II.' But Hans von Herwarth was very much in a minority. The general view was that the Non-Aggression Pact with the Soviet Union was a major foreign policy coup. Britain and France realized that it made a Nazi invasion of Poland more likely. Hitler himself, according to notes of a meeting taken by Admiral Wilhelm Canaris (head of the Abwehr – the military intelligence of the German High Command), admitted to his military commanders: 'Now Poland is in the position in which I wanted her...Today's announcement of the Non-Aggression Pact with Russia came as a bombshell. The consequences cannot be foreseen. Stalin also said that this course will benefit both countries. The effect on Poland will be tremendous.'[24]

This meeting at Berchtesgaden on 22 August 1939 showed Hitler at his most frightening. All the threads of Nazi thought were pulled together: an overwhelming sense of the great Darwinian struggle ahead ('A life and death struggle...On the opposite side they are weaker men'), the importance of individual courage ('It is not machines that fight each other, but men'), and a complete rejection of 'weak' values such as restraint and compassion ('Close your hearts to pity. Act brutally.').

Yet as he gave this chilling speech to his military leaders, Hitler had put himself in the position of being allied to the one country in the world he wanted as an enemy – Russia – and was close to war with the one country in Europe he had originally wanted as a friend – Britain. When faced with this reality today, a number of interviewees answered us reproachfully: 'Please don't forget,' says Graf von Kielmansegg, then a Wehrmacht officer, 'England and France declared war, not Germany.'

'I always hoped,' says Karl Boehm-Tettelbach, 'that England – here I'm talking to you as an Englishman – that England would see what Germany was planning to do and would agree and share in Europe, whatever the politics.'

Even at this late stage – August 1939 – officers such as Karl Boehm-Tettelbach did not feel they were about to embark on a world war. 'Hitler's story was that he wanted to help Germans. He didn't want to invade Czechoslovakia. He didn't want to have Czechoslovakia, he wanted to help the Germans there. And it was the same with Poland. He wanted to erase the Versailles diktat that Danzig and Königsberg were separated from Germany. So therefore he had something good in mind: he wanted to help the Germans and to unite Germany...Politically, I approved of it.'

The Nazi leadership knew that Hitler was not limiting himself to 'uniting Germany' again. The tone of his 22 August meeting had shown that his desire for conquest was much more ambitious than that. On 29 August Hermann Göring beseeched Hitler not to 'go for broke'. Hitler replied that 'throughout my life I have always gone for broke'.

On 1 September German troops invaded Poland. Two days later Britain and France declared war. This war had not been planned, but with Hitler and the Nazis pursuing these particular policies, war of some kind was inevitable.

The chaos and rivalries that had characterized so much of the Nazi government were now exposed to the stresses of a world conflict. As Dr Goebbels heard the news that war had been declared, he turned to his hated rival Ribbentrop and said, 'Herr von Ribbentrop, this is your war. To begin a war is easy. To end it is more difficult.'[25]

4

THE WILD EAST

ON 20 JUNE 1946 THERE WAS A CELEBRATION IN POZNAN, Western Poland. Crowds gathered wherever they could, climbing fences and trees, all striving to find the best place to witness the much-anticipated hanging of Arthur Greiser, former Nazi ruler of the Polish Warthegau. Anna Jeziorkowska had taken a friend along: 'I can only say that at the moment when Greiser was hanged from the gallows, people were so overjoyed, so overcome by enthusiasm that they were kissing one another, jumping up and down, shouting, bursting into songs.' Anna walked home rejuvenated. 'After one has had to endure such suffering,' she says, 'then one is looking for some form of satisfaction, isn't one?'

No country occupied by Germany in the entire war endured as much as Poland. This was the epicentre of Nazi brutality, the place where Nazism achieved its purest and most bestial form. Six million Poles died in the war – around 18 per cent of the population; by comparison, the British lost fewer than 400,000.

Arthur Greiser was one of the men most responsible for the appalling suffering of the Poles. Along with Hans Frank, who ran the district the Nazis named the General Government, and Albert Forster, the overlord of Danzig/West Prussia, Greiser was one of the absolute masters of Poland.

But at his war crimes trial you would never have guessed the individual power he had once possessed. He pleaded with the court that he had really been a friend of the Poles and that Hitler was the man to blame for what had happened. Greiser said that he, too, had been a 'victim of Hitler's policies' and a 'scapegoat for the crimes of his masters'. In essence, he claimed he was simply acting under orders. But this was a lie. There were, in fact, hardly any orders (in the sense of binding instructions) given to men like Greiser.

Hitler referred to such men as a 'race of rulers, a breed of viceroys.'[1] These rulers of the east were allowed tremendous latitude in decision-making. The order they received from Hitler was simply: 'they had ten years to tell him that Germanization of their provinces was complete and he would ask no questions about their methods.'[2] The logical conclusion of a regime where party leaders were told to 'take over power themselves' (see page 35), or where in the absence of orders from the top, party functionaries worked 'towards the Führer' (see pages 53–4) was the terror and chaos of the Nazi occupation of Poland. A letter Greiser had written to Himmler was quoted at the trial. In it Greiser stated his belief that he could effectively treat the Jews of Poland as he liked: 'I, for my part, do not believe that the Führer needs to be consulted yet again about this matter, particularly in view of the fact that it was only recently during our last discussion concerning the Jews that he told me I could proceed with them according to my own discretion.'[3]

Hitler had promised a 'new order' for the east. What happened may have been new, but there was precious little order in it.

As the German troops crossed into Poland on 1 September, their political masters had still not made the most basic decisions about what political shape the newly acquired territory should have. How much of it should be incorporated into the Reich? Indeed, should any piece be left that could still be called 'Poland'? What was clear was what the Nazis wanted to do with the Poles themselves – turn them into slaves, educated only to the most basic level. Poland was thus about to become the scene of the biggest racial experiment the world has seen. In the process the belief that twentieth-century Europe was home only to civilized people would be shattered.

Sporadic signs showed from the first that this was no ordinary invasion. German SS units displayed terrible and casual brutality as they accompanied the regular army into Poland. Wilhelm Moses served in a regular army transport regiment during the invasion of Poland and what he saw led him to the conclusion that 'an animal isn't as dangerous as the Nazis were in Poland'. As he drove through one Polish village, he witnessed the brass band of the SS Germania Regiment playing as seven or eight people were hanged from the gallows. He could see that the SS had first tied the victims' feet together and then attached stones to them. This technique led them to die a deliberately slow death. Their tongues were hanging out, their faces blue and green. 'I no longer knew where I was,' says Wilhelm Moses. 'You can't really describe the way I saw it. The music was only playing because people were screaming so much.'

Later in the invasion, Wilhelm Moses and his truck were commandeered by the SS, and he was ordered to transport Polish Jews between towns, delivering them from one SS unit to the next. He is still haunted by their cries as they were loaded: 'Let me get down, don't take me, they will kill us,' he says the families would cry.

'Well, who said that they are going to kill you?' he asked.

'But of course they will kill us, they killed the others too, my mother, my father, my children have all been killed. They will kill us too!'

'Well, are you Jews?' asked Herr Moses.

'Yes, we are Jews,' they replied.

'What could I do?' says Herr Moses. 'I am a tortured person. As a German, I can only tell you that I was ashamed about everything that had happened. And I no longer felt German...I had already got to the point where I said, "If a bullet were to hit me, I would no longer have to be ashamed to say that I'm German, later, once the war is over."'

Wilhelm Moses has no clear idea why those he saw executed were murdered, or how the particular families he transported were selected. Even today, studying the documents, it is hard to make sense of why the terror occurred where it did. Unlike the systematic killing the Einsatzgruppen (Reinhard Heydrich's infamous 'special units') were to embark on in the invasion of the Soviet Union in 1941, the killings following the invasion of Poland were sporadic. The SS probably killed anyone they didn't like the look of – especially any Polish Jews who had in some way 'offended' them. There was no law to prevent their random cruelty.

Aside from individual acts of terror against Jews, or 'partisans' who had been resisting the invasion, the Nazis also victimized another particularly hated section of Polish society, the intelligentsia. Implementing a policy that was to be copied by the Cambodian Communist Pol Pot more than thirty years later, the Nazis proposed genetically engineering a country by killing. They believed that if intelligent people were removed, there would be less resistance to their plans for creating a state consisting of ignorant slaves. And if intelligent people could be prevented from breeding, the next generation would consist of only stupid people. A practical step to the fulfilment of this warped idea occurred in November 1939 at the Jagellonian University in Krakow.

The occupying Germans called the professors of the ancient university to a meeting in one of the lecture rooms.

One of those who attended was Mieczyslaw Brozek, an assistant professor of philology. He expected the representatives of the new German authorities simply to instruct the academics present how they were to carry on teaching. Instead, after he and his colleagues had been sitting in the lecture room for a few minutes, they turned round to see that a row of soldiers had appeared behind them. The Nazis ordered the academics to go downstairs, beating them with rifle butts as they went. Brozek was in shock as he saw elderly professors hit by young German soldiers. 'I had a very Catholic upbringing,' he says, 'and it did not enter my head that something evil could happen...For anyone to imagine anything like this. It was beyond our life experience.'

Professor Stanislaw Urbanczyk was another academic caught up in this diabolical German plan whose intention was, he says, for 'the Poles to remain only at the lowest levels...to be slaves'. In the concentration camps where the professors were imprisoned, 'What was really difficult to survive was the hunger and the cold. It was a particularly cold winter and in the space of one month over a dozen professors died.' Those who transgressed even the most minor camp rule were tortured. 'One of my colleagues had a letter from his mother in his pocket,' says Professor Urbanczyk, 'and when they found it during a search he was strung up on a post and had to hang there with his arms tied tight behind him for an hour or more. Another punishment was to be beaten with a stick.'

For these extremely intelligent men used to making sense of what was going on around them, the sheer injustice of their suffering was almost unbearable. Mieczyslaw Brozek remembers seeing a German guard cuddling his child in his arms and then thinking, 'Crowds of corpses lie in the cellar, and at the same time this man has a heart for his child, his wife and so on. The duality of this is unbelievable.' Brozek suffered the effects of this psychological torture for many years afterwards. His time in the camp persuaded him of 'the complete annihilation of values. After the experiences I had in the camp there are no values. I had a vision of the worthlessness of everything. The senselessness of everything. This tormented me desperately, to the brink of suicide.'

Fourteen months after the meeting at which they had been snatched, almost all the surviving professors were released. News of their abduction had reached the outside world and pressure had been growing, particularly from Italy and the Pope, for them to be freed. That the Nazis were susceptible to outside pressure of this sort may seem surprising given what was to happen during Operation Barbarossa (see page 156) and its aftermath; but the professors had the 'good fortune' to be victims of the regime in the very first year of the war when, particularly before the fall of France, the Nazis still took some notice of outside pressure.

In those early months of the war some of the German Army leadership also disliked the excesses they learnt had been committed, primarily by the SS. Colonel-General Johannes Blaskowitz, commander of the Ober-Ost region, wrote two memorandums of complaint; this extract is from his second, dated 6 February 1940: 'It is misguided to slaughter tens of thousands of Jews and Poles as is happening at present...The acts of violence against the Jews which occur in full view of the public inspire among the religious Poles not only deep disgust but also great pity...The attitude of the troops to the SS and police alternates between abhorrence and hatred. Every soldier feels repelled and revolted by these crimes which are being perpetrated in Poland by nationals of the Reich and representatives of State authority.'[4]

Hitler was not moved by such arguments. The diary entry of his army adjutant, Major Engel, for 18 November 1939 records Hitler's reaction to Blaskowitz's first memo: '[Hitler] starts making serious criticisms of the "childish attitudes" among the army leadership; one can't fight a war with Salvation Army methods. This also confirms his long-held aversion to General Bl. whom he had never trusted.'[5]

There was never any question about which side of the argument Hitler supported. But the very fact that generals such as Blaskowitz still felt able to protest at atrocities witnessed by the army may go some way to explaining why the killings and oppression in Poland were seemingly arbitrary. Less than two years later, following the invasion of the Soviet Union, the army leadership would be much more compliant in the face of Nazi atrocities.

Six weeks after the invasion and its initial chaos, the Nazi administrative plans for Poland had taken shape. The country had been split between Germany and the Soviet Union under the secret part of the Nazi–Soviet Pact signed in August 1939 by Molotov and Ribbentrop. The German part (188,000 square kilometres of Polish territory with a population of 20.2 million Poles) was either parcelled off to be part of existing Reich territory like East Prussia, or formed into one of three new districts, each run by a committed Nazi. Albert Forster ran the area called West Prussia, Arthur Greiser ran the Warthegau (an area with Posen – or Poznan, as the Germans called the city – at its heart), and Hans Frank ran the remaining occupied territory, now called the General Government. West Prussia and the Warthegau were integrated into the Reich, and the General Government was to be, initially at least, a dumping ground for unwanted Jews and Poles.

Hitler may have had a 'vision' for Poland – to reorder it racially so that West Prussia and the Warthegau became 'German' while the General Government became the dustbin into which the people not wanted elsewhere were thrown. But the enormity of accomplishing this vision at a time of war, plus the chaos endemic within the Nazi hierarchy, meant that those charged with carrying it out had great latitude in decision-making – even, as we shall see, to the extent of contradicting the spirit of the vision altogether.

Central to the task of racially reordering Poland was movement. The Nazis intended to treat the Polish people like so many parcels, throwing them from one place to the next until the pattern pleased them. Heinrich Himmler was charged with organizing this massive task. Space first had to be found in the incorporated territories for the hundreds of thousands of incoming ethnic Germans who, under the secret protocol with the Soviet Union, had been allowed to leave the Baltic states and other territories in the wake of Stalin's occupation. Meanwhile, 'unsuitable' Poles (such as the intelligentsia, or those who might present a 'threat' to the Germans) were to be deported south to the General Government. Simultaneously, the indigenous Polish population was to be assessed and graded according to racial value. Some might be classed suitable as 'additional population', others classed as 'unsuitable'. The Jews (who were certainly 'unsuitable' in the eyes of the Nazis) were to be gathered in ghettos until a decision could be made as to their eventual fate. In a regime within which there was already a predisposition to institutional chaos, this gigantic reordering of a population was a recipe for anarchy.

To try to understand the human impact of the Nazis' wild plan for Poland we traced individuals from every level of the Nazis' racial order, from the indigenous Germans of the Warthegau to the Jews of Łódź, from the dispossessed Poles of Posen to the incoming Volksdeutsche (ethnic Germans) of the Baltic states. Together they bear testimony to the consequences of an inhuman scheme.

Parts of Poland had, of course, been German before the Versailles Treaty, and large numbers of ethnic Germans were already living there. They presented no problems to the Nazi administrators in classification terms – they were simply

German and, therefore, at the top of the racial pile. Charles Bleeker-Kohlsaat belonged to one of the grand German families who lived in the province of Posen. His grandparents owned an estate of more than 600 hectares with a magnificent house. They kept fifty-four horses and employed twenty-eight Polish families, nearly 300 people altogether. The Bleeker family were proud of their German tradition and had refused to relinquish it after the Versailles Treaty made Posen part of Poland. Long before the German Army arrived, Charles Bleeker's grandmother, who had deliberately never learnt more than a few words of Polish, held the view that the Germans were superior to the Poles. 'She would say, "After all, we are the Germans, we are more highly evolved. Those are just Poles and there is no need to learn their language,"' says Charles Bleeker. 'We were rich and somehow the Poles were made to feel that.'

The Bleeker family were overjoyed at the news that the German Army was approaching: 'The adults were glad to be German again,' says Charles Bleeker. He remembers, when he was eleven, a German soldier arrived on a motorcycle, the first of an army they all felt would bring their liberation. 'I looked at him,' says Bleeker, 'and said "Good afternoon!" and he looked at me and said, "Good afternoon, lad. What good German you speak!" I said, "But I am German!" Then it was the soldier's turn to be astonished because he had thought that now that he was in Poland, there would only be Polish people living there. I was fascinated by his uniform, by the fact that he spoke German, that he was friendly to me, by his beautiful motorcycle. I was beside myself.' But within days, this feeling of euphoria became mixed with fear. As ethnic Germans the Bleekers were able to keep their grand estate – indeed, the Nazis renamed the whole area Bleekersdorf – but their Polish landowning neighbours suffered a very different fate. 'They were evacuated very early on,' says Charles Bleeker, 'and they came to us and begged us on their knees to intercede on their behalf so that they could stay on their own property. We did no such thing because we simply lacked the courage. Then we suddenly heard things like this person had been dispossessed and that person has been dispossessed, another one has been shot as a hostage, and we told ourselves, good heavens these people must have done something, otherwise the German government would not have dispossessed them or shot them as hostages. They must have done something.'

Still trying to rationalize the suffering they saw around them, the Bleekers went to welcome the trains bringing in ethnic Germans from the Baltic states, Bessarabia and the other regions now occupied by Stalin. At the station they experienced another disappointment: some of the incoming Germans were not the superior race they had expected. 'We were not at all keen on them, at least my family wasn't. These people spoke mostly very poor German. They had a terrible accent which nobody could understand and we almost took them for Poles.'

The Eigis were one incoming family of German ethnic origin. They had chosen to be deported by the Nazis from Estonia once they heard that Stalin was approaching. Irma Eigi was seventeen years old when she found herself with the rest of her family on a ship heading towards Poland. 'We were not happy at all,' she says. 'It was like standing next to yourself. It happened, you didn't quite grasp it. It was a bit like being in a state of shock.' Irma Eigi had loved living in Estonia; she and her family had found it a tolerant and beautiful country, but they felt they had little choice but to leave on the German ships when they came. Their only alternative had been to face Stalin and, they were warned, risk being sent to Siberia. Instead, they thought, the German ships would take them to Germany. But, like the Bleekers, they too were

disappointed by the harsh realities of the Nazi racial reorgan-
ization. When the Eigis learnt that their true destination was
not Germany but Poland, they were outraged. 'We hadn't
reckoned on that at all. When we were told we were going to
the Warthegau, well, it was quite a shock, I can tell you.' The
shock increased when, after the boat docked, the Eigis found
that their first home was a transit camp, a school strewn with
straw. But this was nothing to the surprise they experienced
on discovering how the Nazis went about finding somewhere
for the incoming ethnic Germans to live. 'Poles had to move
out of their houses for us so that we had flats to live in,' says
Irma Eigi. 'We had no inkling of that before it happened.'

Frau Eigi still remembers with horror the day, just before
Christmas 1939, when she went with her family to the Nazi
housing office in Posen to ask if there was a flat available for
them. The housing officials said there was. The Eigis were
given the keys, the address and a map of the city, and told to
go off on their own and find it. 'When we went to visit the
flat we had terrible feelings,' she says. 'It was a tall apartment
building, unrenovated and with strange windows.' They
climbed the stairs and opened the front door of the apartment. Inside there was chaos. 'You noticed there had been
people here who had had to leave very quickly,' she says.
'Some of the cupboards stood open. The drawers were open.
On the table were the remains of food. And then the unmade
beds, messed up.' Frau Eigi's father refused to stay in the flat
and the whole family went back to the Nazi housing alloca-
tion office. There they were told that since it was near
Christmas there was no other flat on offer, so the Eigis had to
move in. They chose to settle in only one room, huddled
together against their fears of what had happened. 'Strangely,
I can still see this flat today,' says Frau Eigi. 'And every time
I think about it I am still overcome by some fear. It is as if I
had goose pimples on my back. Always, when I'm frightened,

I see this flat in front of me, even in other situations of fear.'

Now that the Eigi family had a flat, the next stage in the Nazi resettlement programme was to find the head of the family a job. In Estonia Herr Eigi had run a hotel. There were no hotels available in Posen, but there were still some restaurants that had not yet been taken over by the Nazis. Herr Eigi was told to walk around town and see if he liked the look of any restaurant still owned and run by Poles. Off he went, accompanied by his wife and his daughter. 'Most restaurants were in German hands,' says Irma Eigi, 'we were relatively late. And the Baltic Germans had already taken possession of the better restaurants.' Eventually they managed to find a small restaurant still run by Poles, so her father went back to the Nazis and asked for permission to run this restaurant. After signing formal papers of ownership, he simply took over the restaurant. ('Taking over' is a recurrent theme in Nazi ideology. Herr Eigi was behaving as the Nazis believed all Germans, as a superior race, should. He wanted this restaurant, so why not just take it?)

Irma Eigi cannot remember what happened to the Polish owner, or even if she or her father ever met him. 'It could be that the Polish owner had already left,' she says. 'You live in a trance. If you were always thinking about it, you'd have to kill yourself. You can't live with this guilt. You can't even shrug off the guilt on to the government. But on the other hand, every person has an instinct for self-preservation. What else could we have done? Where else were we supposed to go?'

Frau Eigi still tries to imagine the suffering endured by the family evicted from the flat she and her family first inhabited in Posen. Anna Jeziorkowska doesn't have to imagine the suffering because she experienced it. She and her family, all Poles, were quietly at home in their flat in Posen on the evening of 8 November 1939 when Anna's mother looked out of the window and exclaimed 'Germans!' Buses and cars pulled up outside the block of flats and moments later German soldiers banged on the door. 'They burst into the room,' says Anna Jeziorkowska, 'into the kitchen, they were everywhere. Of course, there was great chaos, crying, wailing. The Germans pushed us, they hit father on the face, and we got so frightened that we started crying. My younger brother, he was very delicate, started vomiting.' The German soldiers demanded money and jewellery from her parents before they threw them out of the flat. Her mother gave them all the jewels she had, including her wedding ring. 'I was scared,' says Anna, who was then just 10 years old, 'as much as only a child can be'. The family, along with their neighbours from the same block, was taken to a transit camp where they slept on straw. 'The conditions were unbearable for children,' says Anna. 'The food was cold. There was a turnip soup. For us children it was uneatable.'

After a few days word reached them that Germans had moved into their flat. 'I cried,' says Anna. 'We cried together, my sister and I, cuddled to each other, remembering our toys, the good old days, what we had lost. And it was terrible, it is impossible to describe, even now it hurts to think about it.' After five months in the transit camp, they were herded out and shoved into train wagons that were normally used for transporting animals. They had eight or ten days in the dark and cold of the wagons before they reached their destination, the town of Golice in the General Government. There, an old man saw them huddled in shock in the town square and took pity on them. He took them to his own run-down house and offered them a room. 'The conditions there were also difficult,' remembers Anna. 'There were no beds, we slept on the floor, no comforts, no running water, and everything else was difficult. But at least we had a room, a very small room.'

Evictions and deportations, such as that suffered by the Jeziorkowska family, happened in town and countryside alike. In rural areas whole villages could be uprooted in one action. Franz Jagemann was a German of Polish ancestry who, as an interpreter, helped the Nazis in their dreadful work. He vividly remembers one action that took him to a remote village in the Gnesen district of Poland. Twenty or twenty-five police officers in vans drove to the village and were stopped by local Nazi Storm Troopers just outside the village boundary. The Storm Troopers had been keeping watch but the villagers suspected nothing. Then trucks arrived bearing the SS, members of the Totenkopf (death's head) division. At a little after three o'clock in the morning the police and SS swarmed down the central street of the village, breaking into the homes, while the local Storm Troopers surrounded the village from the outside. 'People were beaten,' says Franz Jagemann, 'people were kicked, there was blood. The worst thing about it for me was to see an elderly couple, they were over seventy and clearly didn't understand what was going on, they were beaten up and thrown on to a truck. One SS man, who was born in Upper Silesia, carried on as if he was berserk, screaming at the villagers and driving them together with violence. People were kicked, punched, pistols waved in their faces. It was like a proper hold-up.'

Stefan Kasprzyk, the son of a Polish peasant, remembers that night when the SS came to call: 'They surrounded the farms so that no one would run away. People took what they could carry. Only a few ever returned. My grandfather was tortured by them and after he was deported, he died. Our neighbour lost two children.'

The Nazis who terrorized this tiny Polish village needed space for the Germans who were arriving that very afternoon, so they solved their problem by simply removing the entire population of a village. Franz Jagemann also witnessed the arrival of the incoming Germans. 'You might say that the beds were still warm when they arrived,' he says. Some of the ethnic Germans expressed surprise that they were expected just to take over someone else's house in someone else's village. They said, "And we're supposed to take it over? It doesn't even belong to us!" I really did hear such comments,' says Franz Jagemann, 'but I would say that the majority were convinced that it was their new property now because the war had been won against Poland and that it was all in order.'

After witnessing the brutality of the SS, Franz Jagemann subsequently tried to get warnings to villagers who were to be deported, but he does not believe he was a hero: 'I was there to assist in what we today euphemistically call ethnic cleansing. I was conscious of that...I didn't immediately go into hiding or run away or join the underground. I displayed a lack of courage.'

There was no chance for any of the villagers caught up in these violent deportations to alter their fate by claiming, 'I am really of German origin – you must reclassify me.' Yet, for many thousands of other Poles, reclassification was a possibility. In pursuit of their aim to 'Germanize' the areas of Poland outside the General Government, the Nazi administrators had huge powers of discretion in deciding who was Polish and who was now German. These powers of discretion led to conflict between the two Gauleiters (district leaders) of the newly incorporated territories of Poland – Arthur Greiser of the Warthegau and Albert Forster of West Prussia – a conflict that shows how in wartime the notion of 'working towards the Führer' could assume arbitrary and contradictory dimensions on a massive scale.

Arthur Greiser was the hardest of the hardline Nazis, a man who had Himmler as a mentor. His aim was to turn the Warthegau into a model Gau (district). He expressed contempt for the indigenous Poles and took care to implement seriously the detailed criteria the Nazis used to determine which of the Poles could be Germanized and which could not.

His policy was one of ruthless, uncompromising racial segregation. Albert Forster, ruler of the adjacent Nazi district, Danzig/West Prussia, though also a committed Nazi (and a man later sentenced to death for war crimes), had a very different attitude to racial classification. Forster had been overheard to joke that if he 'looked like Himmler' he wouldn't talk about race so much.

The dispute between Forster and Greiser is personified by the experience of Romuald Pilaczynski of Bydgoszcz, a town in what was then Albert Forster's kingdom. Forster did not enforce tedious individual classification on the population. He decided to reclassify some Poles as Germans *en masse*, without detailed examination. After all, hadn't Hitler said that in the pursuit of Germanizing Poland he would 'ask no questions about their methods'? 'According to materials known to me,' says Mr Pilaczynski, 'about 80 per cent of Bydgoszcz's population responded to Forster's announcement: "If you want to be in Germany, sign the 'Germanization list'." ' The Pilaczynski family signed and became German 'in the third category'. This gave them important advantages denied to ordinary Poles: the right to increased rations, the right to an education and the right to remain in the incorporated territories. But signing the paper didn't make Romuald Pilaczynski feel German: 'We lived the Polish way, we spoke Polish...The 80 per cent who obtained the identity cards of the third group did not consider themselves in any way German.' But Mr Pilaczynski had an uncle who lived in the Posen region, Arthur Greiser's realm: 'The uncle from Posen was not offered the Volksliste (the chance to be Germanized) but was deported.' Of course, as the Pilaczynskis realized at the time, there was no sense to this. They were from the same family and had the same ethnic background. One was no more German than the other. Yet the Pilaczynskis of Bydgoszcz escaped the suffering of deportation while their relatives in Posen had to endure it.

Unlike Forster, Greiser was pursuing a policy of debasing the Poles and Polish culture out of pure ideological zeal. In September 1940 a directive was issued in Greiser's name. It said: 'It will require a long period of education to achieve a state of affairs in which every German citizen adopts an attitude to Poles which corresponds to our national dignity and the aims of German policy.'⁶ In other words, Germans were still being too friendly to Poles. Now, if they did not treat them as slaves out of conviction, they would be made to treat them as slaves out of fear. The directive went on: 'Any individuals belonging to the German community who maintain relations with Poles which go beyond those deriving from the performance of services or economic considerations will be placed in protective custody...In all cases the maintenance of repeated friendly contacts with Poles must be regarded as failure to observe the prescribed distance.'

At his country house outside Posen, Greiser himself certainly strove to live up to his own ideals. Danuta Pawelczak-Grocholska was a servant in the Greiser household. She remembers him as 'a powerfully built figure. He was a tall man, you could see his arrogance, his conceit. He was so vain, so full of himself – as if there was nothing above him, a god, almost. Everybody tried to get out of his way, people had to bow to him, salute him. And the Poles, he treated them with great contempt. For him the Poles were slaves, good for nothing but work.' Danuta Pawelczak-Grocholska was terrified when first told that she had to work in Greiser's house. 'The very sound of Greiser's name made people shake with fear because they knew who he was.' Greiser had grown up in Poland of German descent, spoke Polish, gone to a Polish school and yet now he was nicknamed the 'Pole hater'. Danuta had already witnessed what he was capable of. In a reprisal action ordered by him, she had seen the Germans shoot twenty Poles in the local village square. 'They shot them solely because they were Polish,' she says. 'It was incredible. That image has stayed with me for so long that whenever I walk through the square, past that place, I see those people. And it was all Greiser's doing.' When he heard the name of his daughter's new employer, Danuta's father said to her, 'You are walking into the lion's den; who knows if you will leave it alive.' Danuta had walked the 6 kilometres from her own home to the Greisers' house in tears. Once there she was put to work cleaning the house – to the 'German' standard: 'You were not supposed to see a speck of dust. Carpet fringes had to be combed in straight lines. God help us if there was one out of place! It was all done to perfection, with exaggerated opulence. On the coldest day of the winter, her ladyship would order the cleaning of the windows for New Year's Eve. Our hands would freeze to the window panes. We blew on our fingers but we had to carry on with the cleaning.' Everything in the seventy-room palace and estate was kept immaculate, all for the use of just Greiser and his wife. 'The orangery, the fishponds, the gamekeeper…. The whole economic base of the place was geared exclusively for the use of these two people. It was luxury, in every respect pure luxury.'

Greiser was not just another conqueror who was exploiting the vanquished in order to live in comfort. He lived this way because, as a German, he believed it was his right. He was at the top of the racial ladder and, as a member of a superior race, he had to be true to the laws of nature and live better than his racial inferiors. Greiser was later to explain his philosophy thus: 'If, in past times, other peoples enjoyed their century-long history by living well and doing so by getting foreign peoples to work for them without compensating them accordingly and without meting out justice to them, then we, too, as Germans, want to learn from this history. No longer must we stand in the wings; on the contrary, we must altogether become a master-race!'[7]

Equally, Greiser felt it essential for the future of the Reich that the racial classification of the incorporated territories was completed diligently and systematically. He was therefore deeply irritated when he saw the casual way in which his neighbour, Albert Forster, was treating the whole question of racial assessment. In a letter dated 16 March 1943, Greiser complained to Himmler about Forster's attitude: '...right from the start I avoided trying to win cheap successes by Germanizing people who could not provide clear proof of their German origin...As I have frequently pointed out in my discussions with you, my ethnic policy is threatened by that pursued in the Reich Gau Danzig/West Prussia in so far as the policy followed there initially appears to many superficial observers to be more successful.'[8]

Himmler replied to Greiser that he was 'particularly pleased' by his work on Germanization. In contrast, Himmler had written a letter of complaint to Forster sixteen months previously, on 26 November 1941 in which he had expressed Hitler's view that: '"I do not wish the Gauleiters of the eastern Gaus to enter into a competition to see who will be the first to report after two or three years, 'My Führer, the Gau has been Germanized.'[9] Instead, I wish to have a population which is racially impeccable and am content if a Gauleiter can report it in ten years' time..." You yourself are such an old National Socialist,' added Himmler, 'that you know that one drop of false blood which comes into an individual's veins can never be removed.'

The fact that Himmler wrote such a letter to Forster in 1941 but was still hearing Greiser's complaints about Forster in 1943 demonstrates that even Himmler was fallible. As far as Forster was concerned, the only order he was following was the vague instruction from the Führer to Germanize his *Gau*. How he did it was his business. Forster, in his own eyes, was simply pursuing Hitler's vision in the way he thought best. It scarcely mattered to him that Himmler thought he was Germanizing in a way contrary to racial theory; he knew that Himmler could do little about it. Thus, the lack of firm orders and the absence of specific job descriptions defining the scope of any individual's responsibility, all attributes of Nazi administration which had been present in the party from the 1920s, had their bloody impact on the gigantic canvas of Poland.

Nothing better illustrates the conflict between the Nazi lords of Poland, or the inherent lack of a detailed plan for the Nazi administration of Poland, than a row that flared up early in the occupation between Hans Frank, who ran the General Government, and Arthur Greiser. Himmler and Greiser were keen to rid the Warthegau of 'undesirables' as soon as possible and, as we have seen with the tragic story of Anna Jeziorkowska and her family, herded unwanted Poles on to trains that took them to the General Government. Frank protested. The trains arrived and disgorged their human cargo but he had nowhere to put them. 'Night after night trains of evacuees came to the General Government,' says Dr Fritz Arlt, who was a former Nazi Storm Trooper and, in 1940, head of the Department for Population Affairs and Welfare in the General Government (someone who has never, incidentally, been convicted of war crimes). 'The people were thrown out of the trains, whether in the market-place or on the train station, or wherever it was, and nobody cared about it…We received a phone call from the district officer and he said, "I don't know what to do any more. So and so many hundreds have arrived again. I have neither shelter nor food nor anything…" Without doubt, the most awful things were also happening.' The situation was not helped by the antipathy that existed between Frank and SS-Obergruppenführer Friedrich-Wilhelm Krüger, who was the senior SS man in the General Government. Frank believed that since he was in charge of the General Government, then Krüger was subordinate to him. Himmler countered with the view that Krüger was simply 'assigned' to Frank, not 'subordinate'. Hitler never decided who was right.

The disagreement between Frank on the one hand and Himmler and Greiser on the other wasn't just about the administrative difficulties of trains turning up unannounced and leaving thousands of deportees out in the cold. There was a fundamental conflict of ideology between them. Frank wanted the General Government to be the 'granary' of the Reich. He wanted to keep the farmers in their place and to maximize the economic exploitation of the area with as little inconvenience as possible caused by what he believed were unnecessary transportations. Greiser and Himmler had a bigger vision; the priority for them was not tawdry economic need, but the racial and ideological goal of incorporated territories that were 'pure' and of German blood. If that meant that the General Government would become a dustbin into which all the undesirables of the Reich would be thrown, then so be it.

On 12 February 1940 there was a meeting at Göring's Karinhall estate near Berlin in an attempt to thrash out the difficulties. All the key participants in the dispute were present: Himmler, Frank, Greiser and Göring. Frank allied himself with Göring, who supported him in the meeting. The General Government should become the 'granary' of the Reich, said Göring; the priority must be to strengthen the war potential of the Reich. Himmler protested that he needed space in which to put the incoming ethnic Germans. A compromise appeared to be reached when Himmler stated that he and Frank would 'agree upon the procedures of future evacuations'.[10] Frank was delighted. He thought that Himmler's racial vision of a reordered Poland had received a body blow. Göring's argument that the demands of an ongoing war in France must take priority seemed decisive.

Himmler, however, was not to have his vision dashed so easily. Just as Frank had appealed to Göring, so Himmler decided to appeal to Hitler. A study of the way he did so is particularly instructive because there was no greater manipulator of the Nazi system than Himmler. First, he timed his approach to Hitler perfectly, presenting him with a memo innocuously entitled 'Some Thoughts on the Treatment of the Alien Population in the East' on 15 May 1940, once it was obvious that the German Army was progressing well in France. In the memo he again called for the General Government to be a dumping ground for undesirable Poles, and since it was clear that the Nazis would now have possession of France and her colonies, he proposed a new solution to the problem of the Polish Jews. Instead of transporting *them* to the General Government, he suggested that they be sent to a colony in Africa. The memo also outlined the methods that would be used to turn the remaining 'unGermanized' Poles into a 'leaderless labouring class'.

Himmler later noted that Hitler read the memorandum and found it 'good and correct'. Furthermore, Himmler felt authorized to tell others that Hitler approved of the memo. Professor Christopher Browning, who has made a particular study of Nazi resettlement policy in Poland, told me: 'This is the way decisions are made: Hitler does not draw up an elaborate plan, sign it and pass it down the line. What you get is an encouragement to Himmler to fight it out with the others and the ability now to invoke Hitler's approval if they don't give way. And Hitler can still back out later, of course. You see, he's reserving his options, but he's encouraging Himmler, who has anticipated that this is really the sort of long-range thing that Hitler would like.'

Hans Frank now learnt that there had been a change in policy since his meeting with Göring and decided to put the best face he could on it. On 30 May 1940, at a meeting of police chiefs in Krakow, Frank announced the change of policy caused by Himmler's victory. Referring to a recent conversation he himself had had with Hitler, he talked openly of the difficulties of resettling the incoming Poles and of trying to turn them into a leaderless class that could never rise against the Germans again. His speech was extraordinary in its casual brutality even by the standards of the Third Reich: '...we, as National Socialists, are faced with such an incredibly difficult and responsible task that we can only talk about these things in the most intimate circles...The Führer told me that the implementation of German policy in Poland is a matter for the men who are in charge of the General Government to deal with themselves. He put it this way: we must liquidate those people whom we have discovered form the leadership in Poland; all those who follow in their footsteps must be arrested and then got rid of after an appropriate period. We do not need to burden the Reich organization of the German policy with that. We don't need to bother to cart these people off to concentration camps in the Reich because then we would only have trouble and an unnecessary correspondence with their relatives. Instead, we will finish the thing off here. We will do it in the simplest way.'[11] As a result, during the summer of 1940, thousands of Poles, many from the intelligentsia, were simply murdered.

What sort of man makes a speech like that? Hans Frank had been Hitler's lawyer, more used to talking to judges than Nazi executioners. At his enormous and elaborate country retreat outside Krakow we talked to some of Frank's servants and asked them what it was like to work in the household of such a man: 'Wonderful,' says Anna Mirek, a Polish cook, 'even though we worked very hard, sometimes sixteen hours a day, depending on the need, if there were guests. But the atmosphere was jolly, pleasant: people were polite, and even if one was tired it gave one strength...To me Frank seemed a

nice man, polite.' Bemused by this response we asked how
Anna Mirek reconciled this memory with the knowledge that
Frank had been involved in the mass killing of Poles. 'As for
those higher political affairs that's something different,' she
answered, 'I know nothing about it. I'm not good at it. I'm
good at cooking, observing the stars, telling the weather. That
I'm good at.'

Zbigniew Bazarnik worked at Frank's country house as a
furnace-stoker. 'We all felt quite relaxed here,' he says, 'not,
as one used to hear, like in a camp, where one was shaking at
the sight of a German.' He did, though, remember one incident that showed a darker side to life in the Frank household.
Polish Jews were working at the house doing renovation
work in the early years of the German occupation. One day it
was discovered that one of the Jews had decided to have a
bath in Hans Frank's own bathroom when he thought no one
was looking. Mr Bazarnik later learnt what happened to him:
'Here in the courtyard he was pushed into the boot of a small
car – an Opel – and they could not fit him in so they broke his
arms and legs, took him somewhere outside Krzeszowice and
shot him…A sad story but then why he took such a fancy into
his head, it is difficult to understand.'

Dr Fritz Arlt knew Hans Frank not as a servant knows a
master but as a valued subordinate knows a boss. Dr Arlt
worked for Frank in the early years of the war in Krakow. 'If
I think about Frank, then I have to say that he was a tragi-
comic figure,' says Dr Arlt. 'Frank was a highly intelligent
chap. He was a good musician, a pianist.'

Our interview with Dr Arlt was one of the most extraordinary we conducted because, even though he was a senior
Nazi figure involved in population affairs in the General
Government, he said he never knew of the atrocities ordered
by Frank and carried out by the SS. Dr Arlt talked of a 'conspiracy of silence' and said that he himself had done his best

to implement Nazi policies humanely and that Poles had spoken up in his defence after he had tried to help them. Only once, because we confronted him with a specific document, did I see what I took to be the granite heart of a true Nazi administrator. In Götz Aly's book *Endlösung* a frightening letter is quoted that called for the removal to a concentration camp of ethnic German farmers who were complaining because they were 'homesick'. These ethnic Germans simply refused to accept naturalization. An official letter ordered 'arrangements to be made for the transportation into a concentration camp' of the recalcitrant 'gang leaders' of the homesick farmers.[12] The letter, signed by a *Gauleiter*, bears the dictation mark Dr A – Dr Arlt's initials. 'Yes, it is without doubt the Dr Fritz Arlt who is sitting in front of you now who is named there,' says Dr Arlt when we asked him about the letter. 'What am I supposed to do now?' We asked him what he knew about the concentration camps to which the letter called for the ethnic Germans to be sent. His reply was illuminating. 'This was a regulation passed by Herr Himmler. And I knew about regulations which were in this connection, that people who were not willing to be resettled were to be sent to a concentration camp.' Dr Arlt, of course, had not answered the question. He had simply stated, in effect, that he was 'acting under orders'. When we pressed him and asked what he thought a concentration camp was, he replied: 'What I thought a concentration camp was? Exactly what it says: a camp in which people who somehow or other represented a danger against law and order were concentrated.' We pressed him again, asking if he did not think that this was a severe punishment. 'I'm sorry, but the people knew that they probably would have to expect that. I don't know. I was never a camp administrator.' Here was a man who had been a key part of a process in which homesick ethnic Germans who refused resettlement were consigned to a concentration camp, who had not the slightest remorse about his actions. Indeed, he expected those who questioned him to be satisfied with a response which was that in 1943 all he knew about concentration camps was that they were places where people were 'concentrated'. In our interview with Dr Arlt it was a moment of revelation. Who can tell where coldness and indifference end and criminality begins?

As a group, of course, it was the Jews of Poland who were to suffer most. But in the initial months of the war a racially obsessed Nazi like Greiser perceived himself as having less a Jewish problem than a Polish one. The difficulties of resettling incoming ethnic Germans from the east plus the need to Germanize the Warthegau were his immediate priorities. The Jews were perceived at first as a problem whose solution was imminent, then, as difficulties arose, as one whose ultimate solution could be postponed. As a first interim measure, the Nazis ordered the concentration of Jews in ghettos, the biggest of which in the Warthegau was Łódź. This was always intended to be a temporary solution until the Jews could be deported, so Greiser and his minions presumed, down to the 'dustbin' of the General Government.

Estera Frenkiel, who came from a Łódź Jewish family, read in her local newspaper in early 1940 that a ghetto for Jews was to be established in the northern part of the city. The streets of Łódź were listed according to the dates by which their Jewish inhabitants had to leave their flats. 'It was just as though a bomb had gone off over our heads,' she says. 'We were used to anti-Semitism. Anti-Semitism was also rife among the Poles...Polish Anti-Semitism was perhaps more financial. But German anti-Semitism was: Why do you exist? You shouldn't be! You ought to disappear!'

The Jews of Łódź rushed to find somewhere to live within the designated area of the ghetto. Housing conditions there were appalling from the very beginning. Out of a total of 31,721 flats, the majority of which consisted of just one room, only 725 had running water.[13] Estera Frenkiel's mother found that the apartment they thought they had reserved, a shop with a small flat attached, was already occupied. 'And then my mother went out on to the street and walked up and down talking to herself: "What shall I do now? Where shall I go with my children? There remains nothing else other than to commit suicide." The people who had taken the flat heard this, called her over and said, "Please, listen. The room and kitchen are enough for us. You can move into the shop."' So the Frenkiel family, with immense gratitude, moved into a shop measuring 12 metres square.

There were rich pickings for those of German descent left in Łódź. Eugen Zielke was an ethnic German who watched an employee of his father's 'take over' a big grocery store in Łódź that had previously been owned by Jews who had now been forced into the poverty of the nearby ghetto. Zielke accompanied his father's employee as he went on to choose an apartment for himself from the accommodation abandoned by the Jewish residents of Łódź. 'The flat was locked up and sealed,' he says, 'but we opened it. It was indescribable. Things were strewn all over the floor, all the clothes. The table in the dining-room was laid for supper, there was bread, there was tea, there was even sausage. But when he saw all that and how it was, he said, "It's not possible! It's unbelievable! What on earth was going on here?"' They both left the apartment, shocked, though not sufficiently so for Zielke's acquaintance to give up the Jewish grocery store he had already accepted from the Nazis.

Greiser asserted that the Jews had 'hoarded colossally'. Therefore, once in the ghetto, they were made to give up their money for food. It was an act of pure gangsterism, a means of plucking all the valuables from the Jews before they were transported to whatever 'dustbin' or reservation was to be their future home. And not only the incoming Nazis benefited from selling food at inflated prices to the Jews trapped in the ghetto. One of Eugen Zielke's relatives participated in the crime, and he himself benefited from it. 'I saw it from the point of view of a businessman,' says Zielke. 'They couldn't nibble on a ring, but if they could get a piece of bread for it, then they could survive for a day or two.' Jewellery would be smuggled out of the ghetto and bought for a fraction of its worth. 'If I got something in my hand for 100 marks and it was worth 5000 marks, then I'd be stupid not to buy it,' says Zielke. 'You don't have to be a businessman – that's what life's about.'

We put the following statement to Eugen Zielke: 'You could say that you became rich on the backs of people in the ghetto, the misery, the poverty of the ghetto dwellers.'

'You can say "Yes" in reply to that question,' answered Herr Zielke. 'The Poles got rich. The Germans got rich. Everyone got rich…some of them with gold and silver and others with food, simply to survive. I already told you. I saw it from another point of view. I saw it as a businessman.'

By August 1940 the Jews trapped in Łódź ghetto had no money left to pay for food, so a decision was forced upon the Nazis. Should they let the Jews starve or should they feed them? The decision-making process, which took place in Łódź that autumn, once again involved minor Nazi functionaries having to thrash out policy for themselves in the face of silence from Berlin. Hans Biebow, a former coffee importer from Bremen, was the Nazi chief of ghetto administration. He came up with a solution to the problem – the Jews in the Łódź ghetto could be made to work and would thus be able to produce goods that could be sold in order to buy food. Biebow's deputy, Alexander Palfinger, disagreed. He believed that the Jews must still be concealing money. Only by the threat of total starvation would the Jews finally reveal their last hoarded gold. If he was mistaken, and the Jews did die, then so be it. 'A rapid dying out of the Jews is for us a matter of total indifference,' he wrote, 'if not to say desirable, as long as the concomitant effects leave the public interest of the German people untouched.'[14]

Palfinger lost the argument. Hans Biebow's immediate superior, Dr Karl Marder, sided with what has been termed Biebow's 'productionist' argument. The Łódź ghetto was now to become a business enterprise. Palfinger left Łódź in disgust. As Professor Browning discovered, Palfinger's 'parting gesture, an obvious ploy to attract attention to what he considered the intolerable coddling of the Łódź Jews, was to order from Berlin 144,000 eggs per week for the ghetto, leaving the embarrassed Biebow to explain that the request had been made without his knowledge'[15].

Greiser was happy with the proposal that the ghetto become a generator of wealth because he had arranged to pocket the profit from the scheme himself. 'The Jews are going to be providing labour at a set rate,' says Professor Browning, '35 per cent of that is going to go to the Jews themselves so that they can buy food, 65 per cent is going to go into a special account of Greiser's, one that he controls, his slush fund.'

Estera Frenkiel worked for the Jewish administration inside the ghetto and got to know Hans Biebow well. Her first meeting with him demonstrated at once the schizophrenic attitude of the well-mannered Nazi who had to deal with Polish Jews. Estera Frenkiel remembers how she was introduced to Biebow by another secretary Dora Fuchs: '"This is a new secretary," said Dora. Biebow got up from his chair, came over to me and introduced himself. He shook hands with me. He immediately thought, "What have I done!" and said, "I shake hands only when first introduced."'

Hans Biebow was a man who 'worked towards the Führer' not just for the good of Nazi Germany but for the good of himself. He exploited his position of absolute power over the Jews of Łódź ghetto at every opportunity – sometimes in direct contravention of the strict Nazi rule that Germans should never be physically intimate with Jews. 'One day a 16-year-old girl was engaged in the office,' says Estera Frenkiel. 'She was told to take Biebow some coffee in his office. She gave him the coffee. He saw the pretty girl and touched her up. In all her life the girl had not seen a German man. She had seen Germans from afar, but not close up. She didn't want this. She was still an innocent girl and she fought back. Thereupon he tore off her dress. It is highly likely that nothing happened because she ran away. But he shot at her and hit her in her ear. She bled profusely. She went back to her room and lay down. It was terrible.'

Estera Frenkiel told us this dreadful story – as she told us all her experiences in the Łódź ghetto – dry-eyed while sitting in the Jewish cemetery of Łódź, only yards away from the graves of thousands who had died of the maltreatment they had suffered in the ghetto. I remarked to her after we had filmed the interview that she was one of the toughest and most decisive people I had ever met. She looked at me for a moment and half smiled. 'If I wasn't tough and decisive,' she replied, 'I wouldn't be standing here today.'

As 1940 drew to an end, the Jews in the Łódź ghetto, despite suffering hunger and abuse, had at least not been left to starve to death. From being a temporary measure the ghetto had become a mini-manufacturing camp that had effectively become self-sufficient. It is worth remembering just how the Nazis ended up in this position. For the decision-making process by which the Nazis created a ghetto that could last indefinitely demonstrates the ability individuals had not only to act opportunistically within the Nazi administrative system but in the process to create new crises that needed to be solved. Since the Nazis were operating expediently in circumstances of crisis, only short-term decisions were made. The Jews were first concentrated in ghettos, something that was intended to be only a brief incarceration, preparatory to shipping them off to the General Government. But Frank objected to large numbers of Poles being simply dumped in his area. Then came the ambitious suggestion that the Jews might be shipped not to the outer reaches of the Nazi empire but to far-flung parts of the world, such as Africa, a solution made possible by the defeat of France and by the expected imminent defeat or capitulation of Britain. This modified proposal allowed Frank to argue that it was a waste of time sending the Jews a few hundred miles down to the General Government first, so they remained even longer in ghettos that had been intended only as temporary holding pens. This allowed the local Nazi administrators to come up with another short-term idea – selling them food as a means of extorting their money. Only when the Jews' money was exhausted did the local Nazis face a real policy decision – whether to let them all starve or not. Once that was answered in the negative, and the plan to allow the ghetto to become a manufacturing base was accepted, the relationship with the Jews changed; they had now become slave-workers employed in semi-permanent camps.

This end result was never 'planned' if by a 'plan' we mean that someone sat down at the beginning and chose to arrive at this destination. Instead of working to a 'plan' the Nazis were taking short-term decisions when each mini-crisis occurred. Crucially, none of these decisions was an 'order' from Hitler. The Führer had communicated broad objectives but local Nazis on the ground made these life and death decisions on their own.

The atmosphere in which the Nazis made each decision was one of contempt for the Poles and hatred for the Jews. In

Poland during the early years of the war the Nazis initiated a racial policy the like of which had never been seen before. Hundreds of thousands of people were uprooted and cruelly cast to the wind. But suffering on an even greater scale was about to follow.

5

HIGH HOPES

ON 22 JUNE 1941 THE GERMAN ARMY INVADED THE SOVIET UNION.
What followed was a racist war of annihilation that spawned
the Holocaust and led eventually, more than any other single
event, to the destruction of Germany. With hindsight, Hitler's
actions in ordering the invasion seem woefully misguided –
almost crazy. Yet, at the time there were many people – and
not just Germans – who thought that the decision to invade
the Soviet Union was a rational act in pursuit of German self-
interest and, moreover, that this was a war the Germans
would win.

In the summer of 1940 Adolf Hitler, despite his swift and
dramatic victory over France, faced a major military and
political problem. The British would not do what seemed logical and what the Führer expected – they would not make
peace. Yet Hitler was frustrated by geography – in the shape
of the English Channel – from following his immediate
instincts and swiftly crushing the British just as he had the
French. Hitler did order preparations to be made for an invasion of England, but he was always half-hearted in his desire
to mount a large seaborne landing. Germany, unlike Britain,
was not a sea power and the Channel was a formidable
obstacle. Even if air superiority could be gained, there
remained the powerful British Navy. And there was another,

ideological, reason why Hitler was not fully committed to invading Britain. For him, it would have been a distraction. Britain contained neither the space, nor the raw materials, that he believed the new German Empire needed. And he admired the British – Hitler often remarked how much he envied their achievement in subjugating India (see page 79). Worse, if the Germans let themselves be drawn into a risky amphibious operation against a country Hitler had never wanted as an enemy, every day the potential threat from his greatest ideological opponent – the Soviet Union – would be growing stronger.

All this meant that, from Hitler's point of view, there was an alternative to invading Britain: he could invade the Soviet Union. Both Hitler and his military planners knew that Germany's best chance of victory was for the war in Europe to be finished swiftly. Hubert Menzel was a major in the General Operations Department of the OKH (the Oberkommando des Heers, the German Army headquarters), and for him the idea of invading the Soviet Union in 1941 had the smack of cold, clear logic to it: 'We knew that in two years' time, that is by the end of 1942, beginning of 1943, the English would be ready, the Americans would be ready, the Russians would be ready too, and then we would have to deal with all three of them at the same time…We had to try to remove the greatest threat from the East…At the time it seemed possible.'

Germany's need for new 'living space' (*Lebensraum*) had been a recurring theme in Hitler's early political testimony. And he had always been clear about where Germany should find its new empire – Russia and the border states subject to her (collectively the Soviet Union).

Hitler was deeply prejudiced about the Soviet Union – this one country became the particular focus for his anti-Semitic, anti-Communist, anti-Slav beliefs. He would describe Moscow as the headquarters of the 'Judaeo-Bolshevist world conspiracy'.[1]

Associated with this overwhelming ideological hatred of the Soviet Union was a more concrete fear: Hitler was concerned about the higher birth-rate of the Slavs. He remarked that they were 'an inferior race that breed like vermin'.[2] Hitler foresaw grave danger if eventually the Soviet Union became a 'modern' nation with a vastly larger population than Germany's. To eliminate the need for future conflict – on less advantageous terms – Germany had to act swiftly.

None of that, however, meant that Hitler was driven to war with the Soviet Union by a kind of myopic fanaticism. He had already shown that he was perfectly prepared to put aside his deeply held beliefs when it was politically expedient. That was the reason Ribbentrop, the Nazi Foreign Minister, had flown to Moscow in August 1939 to conclude the Non-Aggression Pact with the Soviet Union.

On 31 July 1940 it was once again pragmatic – not ideological – considerations that were voiced by Hitler at the Berghof, his mountain retreat in southern Bavaria, when he met with his military commanders. Yes, he believed that an invasion of Britain should be considered – air attacks would begin as soon as possible – but the whole enterprise remained fraught with risk. Now, logically, he was driven to another possible way of finishing the war. Hitler asserted that, since Britain's hopes were kept alive by the thought that the Soviet Union was still out of the war and might one day come to its aid, the destruction of the Soviet Union would shatter Britain's last reason to continue the war.

It's hard to accept now, given today's relative balance of armed forces between Britain and Russia, but at the time the Germans gave every impression of being more frightened of the British – with their mighty fleet and empire – than the

Soviet Union. So when, at that meeting on 31 July, Hitler voiced his intention to crush the Soviet Union, there was no evidence that his military commanders were appalled by the news. Just like Hitler, they seem to have thought at the time that a land war against the Soviet Union was preferable to a seaborne invasion of Britain.

The context of that meeting is important. As Hitler gathered with his military leaders, they were flushed with a remarkable victory over France. In numbers there had not been much to choose between the two sides, and yet under Hitler the German Army had crushed the French in six weeks. This would have been a major achievement on its own, but set against the background of the disastrous way in which the German advance had bogged down far short of Paris in the trenches of World War I, the spring 1940 victory must have seemed phenomenal. Any war against the Red Army would be conducted using the same apparently unstoppable Blitzkrieg tactics of swift motorized attack that had just proved so successful in France; as Hitler put it, this was a new type of war that would be 'unbelievably bloody and grim', but it would always be 'kindest because it will be the shortest'.[3]

As the Soviet Marshal Georgy Zhukov later put it: 'The German forces invaded the Soviet Union intoxicated by their easy victories over the armies of Western Europe…and firmly convinced both of the possibility of an easy victory over the Red Army and of their own superiority over all other nations.'[4]

Hindsight allows us to condemn the military judgement of these men who so fatally underestimated the warlike capacity and will to fight of the Soviet Union. The war on the Eastern Front has come to seem uniquely insane; the act of a single power-crazed individual who held his generals in thrall. What act could be more guaranteed to fuel the unquenchable fire of the dictator's ambition and more certain to destroy his nation in the end? That is certainly the easy explanation that

Franz Halder, one of the military commanders closest to Hitler, gave after the war. Halder, who was Chief of the Army General Staff between 1938 and 1942, spoke during his de-Nazification (and in an interview in the 1960s) of a meeting he had had with the Commander-in-Chief of the German Army, Walter von Brauchitsch, at the end of July 1940. Halder described how Brauchitsch asked him, 'Have you ever thought about [attacking] the East?' Halder said he replied, 'That fool [Hitler]. I honestly believe he will even get Russia on to us. I won't even think of preparing anything for it.' What could be more understandable than this response? By telling this story, Halder positions himself as just another of the mad Führer's victims.[5]

But there's a problem with Halder's convenient version of history – it doesn't stand up to scrutiny. On 3 July, weeks before the meeting with Brauchitsch, Halder revealed in his private war diary that he had already floated with his planners the idea of a campaign against the Soviet Union, a 'military intervention' that would 'compel Russia to recognize Germany's dominant position in Europe'.[6] Halder had decided on this action himself, without any direct order from Hitler. Like all of those who wished to survive and prosper in the high reaches of the Nazi state, Halder had learnt that it wasn't sufficient simply to follow orders – they had to be anticipated.

Nor are Halder's actions in the early days of the German campaign in the East those of a sceptic. On 3 July 1941, just 12 days into the war, Halder wrote in his diary: 'It is thus probably no overstatement to say that the Russian campaign has been won in the space of two weeks.'[7] That same day he wrote to one of his colleagues, Luise von Benda (who later married General Alfred von Jodl, see page 156), also voicing the view that the Soviet Union had all but lost the war; he added that Hitler had come round to his quarters to chat and congratulate him on his birthday, and had stayed for an hour at teatime. 'I will keep this day as precious in my memory,' writes the clearly euphoric Halder.[8]

The temptation to alter the past must have been over-whelming for Halder – after all, no general wishes to go down in history as playing a significant part in the greatest defeat his country has ever suffered. It is this all too human desire to rewrite history that has fuelled over the years the popular myth that the only proponent of the German inva-sion of the Soviet Union in 1941 was one power-crazed lunatic. It was simply not so.

Part of the reason for the Germans' over-confidence was contemptible then and is still so now. The Nazis believed that the inhabitants of the Soviet Union were racially inferior – from its planning stage this was to be no ordinary war, but a racial war of annihilation against a 'sub-human' people. They also thought that the whole Jewish/Bolshevik system they saw in place in the Soviet Union was rotten and would crumble in the face of the expected early military losses of the Red Army. But there were other, more rational, reasons why they (and many of the western Allies) thought that the Soviet Union was scarcely capable of putting up a fight.

Along with the rest of the world, Hitler and his military commanders had watched the effect of Communist rule on the Soviet Union's military capacity. And the Germans were encouraged by what they saw, for they believed that the Soviet leader Josef Stalin had, during the 1930s, substantially weakened the Red Army. Stalin's character, which would help shape and define the course of the forthcoming war in the East, was, in the eyes of the Nazis, devastatingly flawed.

Unlike Hitler, who had essentially created the Nazi Party, Stalin had not been the vital driving force behind Soviet Communism – that role had fallen to Lenin. Hitler's charis-matic authority was irreplaceable in the Nazi Party – he never had a serious rival. Stalin was a black hole of charisma, a fixer, a *praktik*, a 'man who got things done', the silent figure at the back of the room who waited, listened and was underestimated until the moment came.[9] Amongst the leading Communists he had seemed least likely to succeed Lenin in 1924; Zinoviev and Trotsky were more gifted speakers, Bukharin more engaging. Even after he became leader of the Soviet Union, Stalin remained a man of the shadows. He made but a small fraction of the number of personal appearances that Hitler did during the 1930s. Paradoxically, this worked in Stalin's favour – the image was created that he was always working for the Soviet Union, hidden but watchful. Yet at the annual parade in Red Square Stalin looked out not just on his own portrait but on Lenin's as well. Stalin was constantly reminded that he was the follower – and followers can be replaced. As Bukharin once said: Stalin 'is unhappy because he cannot convince everyone, even himself, that he is greater than everyone, and this is his unhappiness…'[10]

Stepan Mikoyan grew up in the Kremlin compound in the 1930s. His father Anastas was a leading member of the Politburo and he himself met Stalin on many occasions. 'Stalin was by nature very attentive,' says Mikoyan, 'and he watched people's eyes when he was speaking – and if you didn't look him straight in the eye, he might well suspect that you were deceiving him. And then he'd be capable of taking the most unpleasant steps…He was very suspicious. That was his main character trait…He was a very unprincipled man… He could betray and deceive if he thought it was necessary. And that's why he expected the same behaviour from others…anyone could turn out to be a traitor.'

The later Communist leader Nikita Khrushchev put it this way: 'All of us around Stalin were temporary people. As long as he trusted us to a certain degree, we were allowed to go on living and working. But the moment he stopped trusting you, the cup of his distrust overflowed.'[11] Trotsky, who always felt himself Stalin's superior, gave this judgement on the new Soviet leader: 'Being enormously envious and ambitious, he could not help but feel his intellectual and moral inferiority every step of the way...Only much later did I realize that he had been trying to establish some sort of familiar relations. But I was repelled by the very qualities that would strengthen him...the narrowness of his interests, his pragmatism, his psychological coarseness and the special cynicism of the provincial who has been liberated from his prejudices by Marxism but who has not replaced them with a philosophical outlook that has been thoroughly thought out and mentally absorbed.'[12]

This, of course, was an underestimation of Stalin. He might not have possessed Trotsky's charisma, but Stalin was the more politically astute; his combination of natural intelligence, pragmatism, suspicious nature and ruthlessness enabled him to develop an extremely effective way of retaining power: terror. The Nazis took careful note of how, during the 1930s, Stalin eliminated anyone whom he, or his secret police, the NKVD, thought presented the remotest threat.

As a consequence, Stalin specialized in using fear as a factor of motivation. One historian describes it as 'negative inspiration' – the idea that his followers had constantly to prove themselves to him.[13] It was foolhardy in the extreme to criticize the system in front of him. One young Air Force general boldly stated, at a meeting at which Stalin was present, that the number of accidents in military planes was so high because 'we are forced to fly in coffins'.[14] Stalin replied: 'You should not have said that, General,' and had him killed the following day.

From 1937 Stalin presided over the purging of the Red Army. Thousands of its most senior officers were tried and executed in an atmosphere of paranoia. Mark Gallay was a Soviet test pilot who lived through this horror. 'In 1937 the conditions in our country were oppressive,' he says. 'There was the heavy atmosphere of the Stalinist repressions. It concerned everyone: scientists, the military, and amongst the military the Air Force. Suffice to say that, within the space of a few years, the head of the Air Force was changed many times. One after the other, they were repressed and eliminated.' Gallay explained how he led a 'dual existence' during this time. On the one hand he was starting his career, courting his future wife, 'in the prime of my youth', someone who would set off for work each day with 'pleasure'. On the other, as a candidate-member of the Communist party, two or three times a week he would attend sinister meetings. 'And we tried to pick someone at random from our own milieu and to get him to talk about his links with "enemies of the people"... But the vast majority of people were innocent. And at these meetings someone would make a speech. Well, you know, there is a breed of person who likes to give a condemned man that final push. Someone would get up to make a speech because they were forced to do so. The majority maintained a gloomy silence. And they knew that if they voted to exclude someone from the party, he would be arrested that night.'

This charge of 'enemy of the people' was an extremely effective device for the security forces; few allegations could appear at first sight more serious, and yet the actual details of the offence remained vague.[15] Lavrenti Beria, the head of the NKVD, is said to have quoted the theory, which he assigned to Stalin, that 'an enemy of the people is not only one who makes sabotage, but one who doubts the rightness of the party line. And there are a lot of them among us, and we must liquidate them.'

This policy of terror did not even spare those who were valuable to the military machine. On a 'dank and cold' October day in 1937, Mark Gallay arrived at the aerodrome to witness a chilling sight. The tailplanes on the aircraft in front of his hangar were being painted over. Each experimental plane carried the initials of its designer, and now the painters were obliterating 'A.N.T.' – the mark of one of the most gifted aero-engineers of the time, Andrei Nikolaevich Tupolev. Gallay realized that Tupolev must have been arrested; that the very man who had designed the new warplanes had just become 'an enemy of the people'.

An insight into the way Stalin wished the secret police to deal with these 'enemies of the people' is contained in this instruction sent to local NKVD authorities: 'The Central Committee…authorizes the use of physical coercion by the NKVD beginning in 1937. It is well known that all bourgeois intelligence services use physical coercion of the most disgusting kind against representatives of the socialist proletariat. The question therefore arises why socialist organs should be more humane towards the rabid agents of the bourgeoisie and sworn enemies of the working class and collective farms?'

It is not hard to guess the effect such arbitrary arrests, torture and murder had on the morale of the Soviet military – particularly in areas such as experimental plane design, an environment in which progress can be made only through trial and error. 'Naturally,' says Mark Gallay, 'when the general atmosphere is oppressive, it does not facilitate the flourishing of initiative…Under the conditions of the Stalinist terror, everyone was afraid of making mistakes.'

Goebbels recorded Hitler's view of Stalin's purges in 1937: 'Stalin is probably sick in the brain,' said Hitler. 'Otherwise you can't explain his bloody regime.'[16] For Hitler himself had practised nothing like this. On the contrary, (as discussed in Chapter Three) when he came to power he had initially worked with the generals who were already in place. Even when, in the late 1930s, he had been presented with an opportunity to remove those military figures who were still not enthusiastic about Nazism, he had merely forced the wavering generals into retirement – they had been given not a bullet in the head but a pension.[17]

Stalin did more than purge the Red Army to confirm to the Nazis that he was 'sick in the brain'. Even his own family fell victim to his obsessive paranoia. Two of his brothers-in-law were arrested and shot, two of his sisters-in-law were arrested and imprisoned. A third brother-in-law, Pavel Alliluyev, died of suspected poisoning after going to work in the Kremlin one day in November 1938. 'That was his character,' says Kira, Pavel Alliluyev's daughter and Stalin's niece. '"Stalin" – it means "steel".' (Born Iosif Dzhugashvili, he had adopted a pseudonym, like many Communist agitators, in his case Stalin – 'of steel'.) As Kira explains, 'He had a heart of steel...It would seem that Stalin had hinted to someone that Papa had to be got rid of because he was continually compromising him [Stalin] by getting him to set people free. And obviously Stalin got fed up with it...Of course, he knew that he couldn't arrest my father. He wouldn't be able to prove to my mother that he was an enemy of the people. So he got rid of him.'

Kira and her family spent time at Stalin's dacha in the country, where she marvelled at the other side of his character. 'He was very fond of my younger brother – he called him "mushroom", he would sit him on his knee and chat to him affectionately...And I could say that I didn't want to eat something or that I didn't like something. He'd say: "Leave her alone! If she doesn't want to, then she doesn't have to!"'

But after her father's death, Kira and her mother's relationship with Stalin changed. 'He became very strange. He kept us at a distance. We no longer saw him after 1939...The way we lived after Papa had been poisoned, it was like something out of a Shakespearean tragedy.' Kira and her mother were both imprisoned, though neither of them could see the reason why. 'A normal person would think, how is it possible to destroy your own family? But his power was greater than

anyone else's. He was clearly above everyone else. He didn't
see anything around him, he just wanted everyone to say
"Yes" to everything he did. Anyone who said "No" or who
doubted anything would be made an "enemy of the people".
His enemy...My whole life was destroyed. My husband left
me because his parents said to him: "They'll put you in prison
too!" I married again but it was too late the second time...it
was too late to have children. My life was really destroyed.
But what should I do about it? I decided to be an optimist. So
I go on living. You can't go back and change things.'

Of course, terrible as these stories of personal suffering
are, they would have given the Nazis no concrete reason to be
certain that Stalin had so damaged the Soviet Union that the
country would collapse under the German attack. Even today
there is argument about the extent to which the purges alone
harmed the Red Army. For the Soviet military machine was
also weakened by its chaotic expansion in the years preceding
the war when inexperienced officers were thrust upwards in
the hierarchy into positions for which they had little training
(a situation, of course, exacerbated by the purges). While
during 1937–8 more than 30 per cent of officers were
expelled from military service, only in recent years have the
original Western estimates of officers *arrested* during the
same period dropped from between a quarter and a half of
the total number to well below 10 per cent. But what the
argument about numbers fails to do is recognize the harm
done to the morale and initiative of the Soviet armed forces
by the knowledge that the merest error could result in arrest
or even execution.

Indeed, as Hitler and his generals began in the summer of
1940 to assess how the Red Army might fight in the forthcoming war, they had more compelling evidence than knowledge of
the purges to make them feel optimistic about the conflict
ahead. Nine months before, in November 1939, the Red

Army had attacked Finland. Stalin had planned to take the country forcibly into the Soviet Union as the Karelo-Finnish Soviet Republic. On paper the Finns appeared to have little hope. They faced a numerically stronger Soviet force – one estimate says the Red Army had nearly a three-to-one advantage. But it didn't work out the way Stalin desired. 'It was a terrifying scene,' says Mikhail Timoshenko, who fought on the Soviet side with the 44th Ukrainian Division in the Finnish War. 'It gave you the impression that someone had intentionally sent our people to freeze to death. There was no enemy visible anywhere. It was as if the forest was doing the shooting all by itself.'

The Red Army received a lesson in how a small, motivated and lightly armed force could conduct effective guerrilla war. 'In small groups, of say 10 or 15 men, the Finns were sneaking up to our bonfires, firing short bursts from their machine guns and then immediately running away again…when we sent our men to follow the tracks that we'd observed in the snow, they didn't return. The Finns lay in wait for them and killed them all in ambush. We realized that it simply wasn't possible to wage war against the Finns.' As a result of failures in tactics, leadership, equipment and communications, Timoshenko's division began to fall apart. By February 1940 they were down to 10,000 men – less than half strength. 'Personally, I thought that there had been some kind of misunderstanding – the decision made no sense to me. Why had they sent our division there when there was no enemy, when it was so dreadfully cold, when people were freezing to death?' Out of his regiment of 4000 only about 500 escaped from Finland unharmed. The Soviet system dealt with this failure in a familiar way. The 'guilty' commanders were shot. In Timoshenko's case, both his regimental commander and commissar (see page 159) were executed. A peace treaty was finally signed with Finland in March 1940. By sheer superiority of numbers the Red Army had gained some territory – but at the terrible cost of 130,000 Soviet dead.

Even a committed Communist like Mikhail Timoshenko realized the message being sent to the Soviet Union's fellow signatory of the Non-Aggression Pact: 'The Germans, naturally enough, came to the conclusion that the Red Army was weak. And in many respects they were right.' The German General Staff examined the Red Army's tactics in the Finnish War and reached a simple but damning conclusion: 'The Soviet "mass" is no match for an army with superior leadership.'[18]

All this goes some way to explain why, on 21 July 1940, nearly two weeks before the major military conference at the Berghof, Hitler went so far as to ask General Alfred von Jodl, Chief of the Operations Staff of the High Command of the Armed Forces (OKW), if the German Army could move into action against the Soviet Union that autumn. Jodl rejected the idea of attacking so soon; there wasn't enough time to complete the necessary planning. Instead, preparations were begun that summer for an attack the following year.

The formal directive for the invasion of the Soviet Union was issued on 18 December 1940. Up to then the codenames Otto and Fritz had been used for the operation, but Hitler now renamed it Barbarossa after the nickname of Emperor Frederick I, who, according to ancient belief, would rise again to aid Germany when the country needed him most.

As 1940 came to an end, all the various strands of Hitler's thinking must have confirmed him in his view that this giant undertaking was the right way forward. On a practical level, the failure of the Luftwaffe in the Battle of Britain had destroyed any chance of a successful German invasion of England – so how else could Britain and the USA be neutralized except through the elimination of their potential ally on the European continent, the Soviet Union? On a political level, the visit of Soviet Foreign Minister Vyacheslav Molotov to Berlin in November 1940 had demonstrated to Hitler the dangerous way in which the Soviet Union wished to exploit the Non-Aggression Pact. Had not Molotov announced that the Soviet Union wanted to annex part of Romania? On an economic level, Germany was hugely dependent on the Soviet Union for raw materials with which to fight the war – suppose at a crucial moment the Soviet Union simply turned off the tap? On an ideological level the Communists were, of course, loathsome to Hitler and the Nazis. Wouldn't the Führer feel 'spiritually free' (as he later wrote to Mussolini) by breaking the Non-Aggression Pact, this marriage of political convenience? On a military level, what more evidence did the German Army need of their own innate superiority than to compare their own swift subjugation of the French with the inability of the Red Army to crush the puny Finns?

Not until the beginning of 1941, after the timing and objectives of Barbarossa had been laid down, were any practical doubts voiced. The head of the Wehrmacht's Office for Armament Economy, General Thomas, now raised with the High Command some of the difficulties that the German Army would face during the invasion – how would they be supplied with sufficient fuel and provisions inside Soviet territory? At a meeting with Hitler on 3 February, Halder mentioned these problems and suggested ways of overcoming them (the idea that the German Army might 'live off the land' and loot the resources of the Soviet Union to augment any deficiencies in supply was optimistically put forward by the Wehrmacht's central economic agency; see page 182). A later, more devastating, assessment, again from General Thomas, of the logistical challenge that the German Army would face was probably never even shown to Hitler.

That February another flaw in the invasion plan was discussed, albeit briefly. Barbarossa was not intended to be an invasion of the whole Soviet Union. The Germans would stop at the Ural Mountains, leaving the Soviets to retreat beyond – to the forests and swamps of Siberia. Not even Hitler thought he had the military power at his disposal to march east to the Pacific Ocean. (As Hubert Menzel, a Panzer division officer, put it: 'This was Blitzkrieg – but without borders.') Field Marshal von Bock, who was to command Army Group Centre (the military thrust charged with advancing along the central Minsk–Smolensk–Moscow axis), asked how, after the defeat of the Red Army, the Soviets would be 'forced to make peace'.[19] Hitler replied vaguely that 'after the conquest of the Ukraine, Moscow and Leningrad...the Soviets will certainly consent to a compromise'.

Despite all this, the confidence of some in the German High Command remained overweening: 'The Russian colossus will be proved to be a pig's bladder,' said General Jodl. 'Prick it and it will burst.' Perhaps Jodl was thinking of the humiliation the generals had suffered when their pessimistic assessment of the German Army's chances against the French had proved so wrong. This time, the generals would not be accused of being 'negative'.

During that spring Hitler made changes to the OKH's three-pronged invasion plan. He thought their emphasis on the need to push on to Moscow was misplaced. Central to Hitler's conception of the forthcoming hostilities was his belief that this was a new kind of war, a war of destruction, and it was more important that the enemy's forces be eliminated in vast encirclement battles than that their capital be taken. Hitler's change of emphasis was accepted without protest. His expectation was clear – the Red Army would be surrounded and eliminated far west of Moscow and then the country would collapse because of the loss of its industrial capacity.

That spring key decisions were also taken about the manner in which the invasion should be conducted. To Hitler and the Nazis, the Soviet Union was not like France or

Belgium or any other 'civilized' country in the West. From the beginning, this was viewed as a war against savages who carried within them the dangerous, corrupting belief of Communism infested with Judaism. Halder, reflecting Hitler's desires, noted on 17 March 1941 that 'The intelligentsia put in by Stalin must be exterminated' and that 'In Great Russia force must be used in its most brutal form.' Hitler did not hide from his generals his view that this was to be a war of 'annihilation' – he said as much to them in a speech on 31 March. They, in turn, did not resign or protest, as these views were codified in a series of orders that set the letter and spirit in which the war was to be fought. These orders, which were labelled 'criminal' at the Nuremberg trials after the war, were prepared not by the SS but by the legal arm of the Army's own High Command.

The first 'criminal' order was the Barbarossa-Decree, under whose terms partisan fighters were to be shot out of hand and collective reprisals against whole communities were authorized. This was followed by the infamous Commissar Order, which called on soldiers to shoot Soviet political officers – the commissars. (For much of its life the Red Army operated under 'dual command', with the professional military officers having to consult political commissars before issuing substantive orders. One of the great fears of the early revolutionaries had been that the Army might one day move against the Communist Party – they hoped the presence of the commissars ensured this could not happen.)

It is hard today to understand how the modern army of a cultured people like the Germans could have accepted that they were about to fight a war outside international convention – a war in which they were expected to be not just soldiers but murderers. But to meet Bernhard Bechler is to comprehend the mentality of the time that made it possible. He wasn't just a soldier who accepted the contents of the

Commissar Order – he was one of the people who put his name to it. Acting as ADC to General Müller, a 'General for Special Tasks' in the Army High Command, he signed to witness the signature of Field Marshal von Brauchitsch. 'I was proud of the fact that my name was on the order,' says Bechler. 'But back then one shouldn't think of it as a special event. There were 20, 30 events happening at the same time and this is just one of them…Insights never come until after the fact. Afterwards, when I realized its significance, what a dirty business it actually was, yes. But at the time one didn't really notice much of it.'

In so far as he did stop to think about it, Bechler felt that 'at the time we were still convinced that there would be a victory. And if we had won, everything would have been right. You must not forget that. If we had won the war against the Soviet Union, none of this, not even the crimes or whatever, would have mattered.'

When pressed harder on the ethical question – the sort of moral standards he was working to in issuing such orders – Bechler replied: 'If I believe that there is a danger for the Western world, that the Soviet Union is a threat to civilization, if this is what I believe and embrace, I take a moral stance. I am morally obliged to prevent this, and my morals prompt me to avail myself of means which I wouldn't have used otherwise – in order to prevent Bolshevism prevailing in Europe…One didn't see it as a crime against the Russian people because Hitler had said: "There is no such thing as a crime on the part of the Germans." This was simply our moral stance: they had to be destroyed. The potential had to be destroyed, everything that kept the system going.'

Bernhard Bechler's response, with its convoluted logic, is significant. It represents the same reasoning process that Heinrich Himmler, Reichsführer SS, used in order to justify the killing of Jewish children. In essence it amounts to: 'The threat to our society from these people in the future is so great that in this case the end justifies the means.' By such reasoning do intelligent people justify their most bestial acts. It shows that sophistication and culture are no bar to atrocity – indeed, they can be an aid, for once the intelligent mind devises a justification, there is no limit to the consequent brutality.

The German Army had already seen how the Einsatzgruppen – the special 'task forces' charged with liquidating the Nazis' ideological enemies under Reinhard Heydrich, Head of the Main Reich Security Office – had operated in Poland against Jews and the Polish intelligentsia. Nearly two years on, the German Wehrmacht – and especially its more ambitious members – knew that brutality was to be expected. But this wasn't a case of just 'putting up' with a war of annihilation. The Army and its High Command knew they had to compete with Himmler's SS for a role in the future Great German Empire. If they were perceived as 'weak', they would later be brushed aside. After the conquest of the Soviet Union, only those military leaders who showed 'ideological purity' could hope to receive the Führer's blessing.

Not everyone in the German Army went along with the 'criminal' orders. But the majority of German Divisions did enforce them.[20] The forthcoming war was presented to them not only as a 'crusade' against a brutal, savage enemy, an attempt to bring civilization in the form of a German empire to the East, but also as a struggle that seemed to be a military and economic necessity – if it was lost, then Germany was lost. Such circumstances made it easier for them to understand why this had to be a war without rules. As Goebbels recorded in his diary of 16 June 1941: 'The Führer says that we must gain the victory no matter whether we do right or wrong. We have so much to answer for anyhow that we must gain the victory because otherwise our whole people…will be wiped out.'[21]

The Germans set about assembling the force of 3 million men that would invade the East, and inevitably Stalin learnt of the new troop concentrations. But what should he make of this intelligence? Was this just a provocation – a means of ensuring that the Soviet Union did not interrupt the flow of raw materials to the German war machine? Or was it more serious – did it mean war? One of those Soviet agents who did learn the true reason behind the German military build-up was Anatoly Gurevich, head of Soviet military counter-intelligence in France and Belgium. Established with a cover as a South American company director, he managed to infiltrate himself into a circle of German commanders in Belgium. In October 1940 Gurevich learnt that the Germans planned to attack the Soviet Union the following year. 'I started to find out how the troops were moved,' he says, 'and that they were being transferred to the Eastern Front.' By the beginning of 1941, Gurevich recalls, he was sending messages to Moscow via the Soviet embassy in Brussels that 'the war had to start in May 1941'. Richard Sorge, the Soviet agent in Japan, sent messages to Moscow to much the same effect.

Stalin's attitude can be gleaned from a secret document released only since the fall of Communism. Dated 16 June 1941, it was sent by the People's Commissariat for State Defence of the USSR, V.N. Merkulov, and reads: 'A source working in the German Aviation Headquarters reports: 1. Germany has concluded all necessary measures for war in preparation for an armed assault against the USSR and an attack can be expected at any moment...In the Ministry for the Economy they are saying that at a meeting of all the economic planners destined for the "occupied" territories of the USSR, Rosenberg [who was shortly to be appointed Minister for the Occupied Territories by Hitler] also made a speech, stating that "the very notion of the Soviet Union must be wiped off the map".' Across the front of this report Stalin has scrawled: 'Comrade Merkulov, you can send your "source" from his position on the staff of the German Air Force to his fucking mother. He is not a "source" but a disinformant.'

Stalin has often been berated for not taking warnings such as these more seriously. But, once more, it's easy to mount such criticisms with hindsight. At the time, it can't have seemed so clear-cut. As Stalin would have seen it, Hitler's prime concern was Britain, and invading the Soviet Union would have committed Germany to a war on two fronts. Furthermore, the Soviet Union was keeping to its various agreements with Germany to provide raw materials for the Nazi war effort. In October 1939 the Soviet Union had even let the German Navy use an ice-free port east of Murmansk to repair its U-boats for the war in the North Atlantic. Why would Hitler want to jeopardize this fruitful relationship?

On 10 May 1941 Rudolf Hess, Hitler's Deputy, had parachuted into Scotland. What prospects did this conjure up in Stalin's mind? Were the British and the Nazis colluding with each other? If they were, this was good reason to ignore the British intelligence information he was now receiving, which claimed there would be a German invasion. Perhaps the British were trying to force the Soviet Union into a foolish strike against Germany so as to let themselves off the hook. The British, remember, had been less than enthusiastic about an alliance between themselves and the Soviet Union in 1939.

Stalin considered all these possibilities against the background of his overwhelming desire to do nothing to provoke the Germans. A war against the Nazis in 1941 would not have been in his interests. It is likely that he thought the Soviet Union could not escape an eventual conflict against the Germans, but he felt that this war would not come until 1942–3 at the earliest. In the meantime he could prepare his army and benefit from the secret protocol of the Non-

Aggression Pact with Germany which gave the Soviet Union increased territory in Europe – including a large portion of Poland. So a part of Stalin's determination to believe that there was no definite plan to invade the Soviet Union must have been wishful thinking – what seemed a good idea to the Germans would have seemed a very bad idea indeed to Stalin.

Stalin was not alone in believing that appeasing Hitler would enable the Soviet Union to escape invasion. Marshal Zhukov, appointed Chief of the Soviet General Staff in February 1941, later said, 'Most of the people around Stalin supported him in the political judgements he made before the war, especially the notion that, as long as we did not rise to any provocation, or make any false step, then Hitler would not break the Pact and attack us.'[22]

It is against this background that one should judge the claims, which have emerged since the fall of Communism, that the Soviet Union itself was planning a strike against the Germans in 1941. (This was also the claim that Hitler and the Nazi propagandists made immediately after the invasion to justify their attack – although there is no evidence that they actually believed it when they were planning the invasion.) Such hard evidence as has emerged essentially revolves around one Soviet document, dated 15 May 1941, entitled 'Considerations for planning the strategic deployment of the Soviet Union's Armed Forces in the event of war with Germany and its allies'.

A study of the complete document reveals that it is far from being the 'smoking gun' that justifies the conspiracy theorists in claiming that Stalin was planning an imminent attack on Germany. The context of the document makes it clear that it is written in response to the information reaching the Soviet military that the German Army is massing on the borders of the Soviet Union: 'The situation, in the current political climate, suggests that Germany, if it were to attack the USSR, would be able to raise against us as many as 137 infantry divisions, 19 tank divisions, 15 motorized divisions, 4 cavalry divisions and 5 landing aircraft divisions – a total of 180 divisions…' The report goes on to talk of the probable direction of the main thrust of the German attack 'south of Demblin' and that 'This attack will, in all likelihood, be accompanied by an attack in the north from East Prussia against Vilna and Riga, as well as a short, concentrated attack from around Suvalki and Brest against Volkovysk, Baranovichi.'

After listing the possible route of the German attack, the report suggests that 'we should attack the German Army when it is still at the deployment stage and has not yet had time to organize the front and co-ordinate the different arms of the service'. Two counter-offensives are then suggested into German territory.

A careful reading of the report shows that it represents not a plan for an unprovoked attack on Germany but a response to German mobilization and an attempt to frustrate a possible invasion. It is also evident that far from being a secret plan kept hidden until that moment, the document is the last in a series of deployment plans – a contingency in the event of invasion from the West.

Despite the popular myth that the Soviets did nothing to prepare for a possible German attack, the truth is that the leaders of the Red Army did consider in detail how their forces should be deployed – the only problem was that they deployed them in the wrong way. The basic military assumption that the 15 May document, and those that preceded it, rested upon was that in the event of war the Red Army should practise 'active defence'. Instead of using the vast depth of the Soviet Union to soak up the enemy, Stalin believed that large portions of the Red Army should be positioned right against the frontier, ready for a massive counter-attack into enemy territory.

Stalin's behaviour in the spring of 1941 is that of a man desperately trying to do nothing to antagonize the Germans, rather than that of a warlord waiting to strike. (The Russian historian Professor Viktor Anfilov states that Marshal Zhukov told him that Stalin did see the 15 May document and reacted angrily: 'Are you mad? Do you want to provoke the Germans?') And newly declassified documents confirm that the Soviet Union was still honouring its deliveries of raw materials to Germany up to the moment of the invasion.

Just because Stalin had no desire to invade Germany at this time, it doesn't mean, of course, that had the war gone on he would have felt his Pact with the Nazis was sacrosanct. But Stalin's natural caution made him wary of over-committing himself. He did not break his neutrality treaty with Japan until after the Americans dropped their first atomic bomb. Only then did Stalin order the Red Army to invade Japanese-held territory in China and rush towards Japan itself. In parallel, then, one can posit a scenario in which Stalin would first have waited to see how the war in the West progressed and then, if he could have moved in the endgame to the benefit of the Soviet Union, no treaty would have prevented him.

This is, it is worth remembering, exactly the reason why the Germans felt they needed to eliminate the threat from the Soviet Union so quickly. Both Hitler and Stalin knew that time favoured the Soviet Union. To this limited extent, then, not just the Nazi leadership but many former German soldiers still consider this a preventive war: 'I don't want to claim that Hitler waged a preventive war in the sense of forestalling a looming attack,' says Rüdiger von Reichert, then an artillery officer with Army Group Centre. 'You can use the term "preventive war" only in so far as saying that he [Hitler] knew that the conflict was necessary, and that he was in a more favourable position if he launched an attack first, and that he had to take into account that Stalin might launch an attack too. So in this way there was sympathy for the decision to attack Russia.'

The original plan for Operation Barbarossa had called for an attack in May 1941, but this start date could not be met because in March a military coup in Belgrade had overthrown the Nazi ally Prince Paul. As a result, on 6 April German troops invaded Yugoslavia. For strategic reasons Hitler ordered them to carry on into Greece. The Italians had botched their own invasion of the country some months earlier, and Hitler could not risk the German Army's southern flank being exposed during Barbarossa. Both Yugoslavia and Greece swiftly fell to the German Blitzkrieg and the war was over by the end of April. But because of these unforeseen military actions Barbarossa could not be launched until June.

Hitler himself, as the Eastern campaign fell around him in 1945, was to blame the eventual German failure in the Soviet Union on the delay in implementing Barbarossa. Whilst there was some confusion caused by the swift redeployment of German units back into their start positions for Barbarossa, it was a particularly wet spring and the likelihood is that the invasion date would have been in June regardless. In any event, it was not the matter of a few weeks' delay that spelt doom for Operation Barbarossa, but a fundamental miscalculation about the true nature and difficulty of the task ahead.

Certainly none of the German veterans we spoke to felt at the time that Barbarossa was going to fail because it was launched in June rather than May. On the contrary, many were filled with optimism about the ease of the task ahead. On the morning of the attack Bernhard Bechler went to his sister's to say goodbye – he was about to travel to Hitler's new advance headquarters in East Prussia: 'I said, "Listen, we will part now. In a few weeks I'll ring you from Moscow."... I was utterly convinced that this would happen, and I was in fact proud of our plans.'

Just before dawn on Sunday 22 June 1941 Rüdiger von Reichert, as an artillery officer with the 268th infantry division, waited to cross the border into Soviet-held Poland. 'The situation was made so grotesque because approximately an hour before a brightly lit, peaceful train had driven by, destined to go to our then ally who was about to be attacked.' At half past three they attacked 'with a huge burst of fire, and on the demarcation line opposite the guards were shot down'. For Wolfgang Horn, a soldier in the 10th Panzer Division, the massive artillery barrage that signalled the opening of the war gave him 'a great feeling about the power being unleashed against the dubious and despisable [sic] enemy'.

The Germans moved forward in three great thrusts along an invasion front of 1800 kilometres, the longest in history: Field Marshal von Leeb with Army Group North aiming for the Baltic states and Leningrad, von Bock with Army Group Centre attacking towards Minsk, Smolensk and eventually Moscow, and von Rundstedt with Army Group South heading into the Ukraine.

Though the Soviet defenders were roughly equal in numbers of fighting men to the German invaders (just over 3 million on each side), they were little match for them. A combination of their weak deployment close to the border (based on the military doctrine of 'defence through attack' which did not allow effective defensive operations), lack of training, inexperience of their commanders, and inadequate military hardware (much of which was outdated or in need of repair) meant that the Soviet forces were easy prey for the encirclement tactics of the Germans.

The invaders had elevated their Blitzkrieg attack to a new level of tactical deftness. Conventional military theory had asserted that armoured attack should be in waves – first bombers, then artillery, then tanks, then motorized infantry and so on. But under General Heinz Guderian, Commander-in-Chief of Panzer troops and the man whose original think-ing about armoured warfare had made successful Blitzkrieg possible, the Germans had revolutionized that approach. Instead their tanks, dive bombers and artillery all focused simultaneously on one narrow point in the enemy line – sometimes no wider than a single road. This level of coordination was possible only because of both sophisticated communications – spotters inside the forward tanks would radio back the exact position that the artillery batteries should shell – and extensive previous battle experience. 'We were well trained in it,' says Wolfgang Horn. 'We had done it in France – when breaking through to the port of Calais, for example. So we knew how to attack as a spearhead, regard-less of what was on the sides...it was a very coordinated attack, always.'

Once the Panzers had burst through the enemy line, they forced their way on, leaving the following infantry to plunge through the gap and encircle the bewildered opposition. In the early days of Barbarossa it was Army Group Centre that had most success with this tactic, swiftly advancing to Smolensk deep inside the Soviet Union. But Blitzkrieg tactics had not been designed for such an enormous country and in the vast distances involved the conventional infantry could not keep up with the Panzer advance, so the spearheads had to stop and wait for them.

But these were problems of success, and from the indi-vidual German soldier's point of view the early weeks of Barbarossa were essentially days of glorious victories. 'You thought it was a doddle,' says Albert Schneider, a soldier in the 201st Assault Gun Battalion. 'The Russians will all defect in droves or will be taken prisoner and detained in a camp somewhere.' The ease of the initial advance made him think 'we will have a splendid life and the war will be over in six months – a year at most – we will have reached the Ural

Mountains and that will be that...At the time we also thought, goodness, what can happen to us? Nothing can happen to us. We were, after all, the victorious troops. And it went well and there were soldiers who advanced singing! It is hard to believe but it's a fact.'

On the morning of 22 June Stalin was awoken at his dacha at Kuntsevo just outside Moscow when Marshal Zhukov, then Chief of the General Staff, telephoned him with the news of the invasion. Initially Stalin thought there must have been a mistake – perhaps there had been a coup and Hitler's generals had taken over, or perhaps this was just another provocation. Stalin ordered the Foreign Ministry to ask the Japanese to help – maybe they could mediate with the Germans. Stepan Mikoyan's father was summoned to a crisis meeting that morning at Stalin's office in the Kremlin. Then, and for the first few days of the war, 'nobody understood what was going on...communications had been disrupted. It wasn't clear where our army was or where the Germans were.'

'I fought on the border for three days and three nights,' says Georgy Semenyak, then a twenty-year-old soldier in the Soviet 204th Division. 'The bombing, shooting...explosions of artillery gunfire continued non-stop.' On the fourth day his unit began to retreat – into chaos. 'It was a dismal picture. During the day, aeroplanes continuously dropped bombs on the retreating soldiers...When the order was given for the retreat, there were huge numbers of people heading in every direction – although the majority were heading east.' As he trudged east through Belorussia, Georgy Semenyak watched in despair as his officers deserted. 'The lieutenants, captains, second-lieutenants took rides on passing vehicles...mostly trucks travelling eastwards.' By the time his unit approached Minsk, capital of Belorussia, his section was left with 'virtually no commanders. And without commanders, our ability to defend ourselves was so severely weakened that there was really nothing we could do...The fact that they used their rank to save their own lives, we felt this to be wrong. But every man has his weaknesses.'

Blame should not be unqualified for those officers who deserted their men. For by the time of the German invasion in 1941, one estimate is that, as a result of the purges and the hasty expansion of the Red Army, about 75 per cent of officers and 70 per cent of political officers had been in their jobs for less than a year.[23]

Stalin's actions, in those early days of the war, bore little relation to the reality on the battlefield. He berated his generals and called for advances into enemy territory, action in pursuit of the original Soviet plan of counter-attack – a plan now utterly unrealistic in the face of German advances of up to 60 kilometres on the first day of Operation Barbarossa.

As Hitler saw the early German successes, he must have felt confirmed in his belief that the Red Army would be destroyed within weeks. And he was not the only one, as the invasion began, to have little faith in the Soviet capacity to resist. The US Secretary of the Navy wrote to President Roosevelt on 23 June: 'The best opinion I can get is that it will take anywhere from six weeks to two months for Hitler to clean up on Russia.' Hugh Dalton, the British Labour politician, recorded in his diary on 22 June: 'I am mentally preparing myself for the headlong collapse of the Red Army and Air Force.'[24] Just before Barbarossa had been launched, the British Joint Intelligence Committee had stated that in their judgement the Soviet leadership lacked initiative and the Red Army had 'much obsolete equipment'.[25] The British War Office told the BBC that they should not give out the impression that Russian armed resistance would last more than six weeks.[26]

A crisis occurred in Moscow on 27 June when Stalin and other members of the Politburo attended a meeting at the Commissariat of Defence on Frunze Street. Stepan Mikoyan's father was there: 'They began asking Zhukov questions and they realized that the military were almost totally in the dark. They couldn't tell them anything: where the army was…where our army was…where the Germans were…how far they'd advanced…Nothing was clear. Zhukov was so shaken up that, as my father described it, he was on the verge of tears.' Stalin was now aware that the Germans were about to take Minsk – and the Red Army could do nothing to prevent it. He stormed out of Frunze Street, saying: 'Lenin founded our state and now we've fucked it up.' Shortly after the meeting he left for his dacha – and stayed there.

In Germany, Goebbels had been concerned about how the public would react to news of the invasion. He had been the one who had read out Hitler's proclamation at 5.30 a.m. on 22 June, stating that the war was necessary to 'counter this conspiracy of the Jewish-Anglo-Saxon warmongers and the equally Jewish rulers of the Bolshevik headquarters in Moscow'. Maria Mauth, then a seventeen-year-old schoolgirl, recalls hearing her father react to the news of the invasion in the way Goebbels must have feared: 'I will never forget my father saying: "Right, now we have lost the war!"' But then, as the accounts of the first easy successes arrived, the attitude changed. 'In the weekly newsreels we would see glorious pictures of the German Army with all the soldiers singing and waving and cheering. And that was infectious of course. We thought about it in those terms and believed it for a long time, too. We simply thought it would be similar to what it was like in France or in Poland – everybody was convinced of that, considering the fabulous army we had.'

The fact that Germany was attacking a country with which it had signed a Non-Aggression Pact made little difference. It was the Pact itself that had been the aberration. Now Germans could voice once more their comfortable prejudices about the nature of the hordes who lived on their Eastern borders. 'Russian history had always been barbaric,' says Maria Mauth, 'and we now thought, well, there must be something to it – just look at them! And everybody said: "Gosh, just look at them! Right, well, that's not a life worth living!" Those were the actual words. That was the image of the Russians, and on top of that they were cowardly too, because they had retreated so quickly.'

Germans like Maria Mauth didn't form their views about the Russians out of fear of denunciation if they failed to spout these prejudices – she is a sincere woman who at the time believed that 'We were not like them. We were much better.' The propaganda newsreels confirmed her view that the 'Russians' were 'ugly, underdeveloped. Sometimes they were shown with faces like apes, with huge noses, no hair, in rags, filthy – well, that was the image, so you said to yourself, well, God, OK, why not?'

Such sentiments as these were widespread not just amongst German civilians but throughout the army as well, and helped ensure that this war did not just begin as a brutal racist war but escalated from there. On the battlefield, in those early days of the war, Walter Schaefer-Kehnert, an artillery officer in a Panzer division, found his belief confirmed that these 'Russians' – as the Soviet people were most often referred to by the Germans – were 'more stubborn, more primitive, less civilized'. 'When they counter-attacked and we had to leave the wounded behind and then we came back again, we found all the wounded had had their heads split open with short infantry blades. Now you can imagine our soldiers, when you see your wounded friend has been brutally killed, then they were furious.'

Another reason why the war in the East was so 'different' from the one in the West was the murder away from the battlefield. According to plan, the Einsatzgruppen began their terrible work in the very first days of the war. They immediately killed, amongst others, 'Communist party officials and Jews in the service of the party or state' – a definition that was interpreted in the widest sense. (See Chapter Eight for a fuller description of the work of the Einsatzgruppen.)

'Jewish-Bolshevism, you see, that was the big enemy,' confirms Carlheinz Behnke, then a soldier in the SS-Panzer Division Wiking. 'And these were the people to fight against because they meant a threat to Europe, according to the view at the time...And the Jews were simply regarded as the leadership class or as those who were firmly in control over there in the Soviet Union.' (In fact, contrary to the Nazi stereotype, Jews were no longer very prominent, with a few exceptions, in the Soviet leadership.)

This comforting prejudice also made the killing of the Soviet political officers, the commissars, easier. 'Our task was absolutely clear to us,' says Walter Traphöner, a soldier in an SS cavalry regiment that fought in the East. 'We knew that Bolshevism was the World-Enemy Number One...And we were told that their aim was to overrun Germany and France and the whole of Europe down to and including Spain. That's why we had to fight.' In the context of this fight against 'World-Enemy Number One' the commissars were 'particularly dangerous' and 'when we caught any of them, they just had to be killed'. When pressed on how it could be right to execute somebody just because of their political opinions, Traphöner replied: 'We never really asked about the reasons for anything much. I mean they were just blokes who were supporting their system, just like it was with us...The commissars just had to be killed...We wanted to prevent the Bolsheviks from conquering the world.'

Back in Moscow, Stalin was coaxed out of his dacha at the end of June after two days, when a delegation from the Politburo 'convinced' him to lead the Soviet Union to victory. (At least one historian believes that Stalin, in retreating to his dacha, was following a ruse of Ivan the Terrible's – feigning collapse to see who supported him and who didn't.) In any event, there was no alternative leader of the Soviet Union. Stalin had helped get them into this disastrous situation – now he would have to help them get out of it.

On 3 July Stalin finally made a radio broadcast to the Soviet people and spoke about the German invasion. 'Comrades, citizens, brothers and sisters, men of our Army and Navy,' he began (the reference to 'brothers and sisters' was significant – it appealed to a nationalist rather than Communist sentiment), 'my words are addressed to you, dear friends! The perfidious military attack begun on 22 June is continuing. In spite of the heroic resistance of the Red Army, and although the enemy's finest divisions and finest Air Force units have already been smashed and have met their doom, Hitler's troops have succeeded in capturing Lithuania, a considerable part of Latvia, the western part of Belorussia and part of western Ukraine. The Fascist aircraft are extending the range of their operation, bombing Murmansk, Orsha, Mogilev, Smolensk, Kiev, Odessa, Sevastopol. Grave danger overhangs our country. How could it happen that our glorious Red Army surrendered a number of our cities and districts to the Fascist armies? Is it really true that the German-Fascist troops are invincible, as the braggart Fascist propagandists are ceaselessly blaring forth? Of course not!'

Stalin went on to defend the Soviet Union's participation in the Non-Aggression Pact ('we secured our country's peace for a year and a half') and to promise military success ('this short-lived military gain for Germany is only an episode'). But there is no disguising the defensiveness of his comments nor the self-justifying thread that runs through them.

One way out for Stalin, of course, would have been to try to make peace with the Germans. There was a precedent for this. In order to extricate the Soviet Union from World War I and to consolidate the Revolution, Lenin had concluded the Treaty of Brest-Litovsk. Under this agreement, which Lenin never intended to be permanent, he had ceded large tracts of territory (nearly 1.4 million square kilometres, including Latvia, Lithuania, Estonia, the Ukraine, Georgia and Armenia) to Germany. Was something like this contemplated – even as an option – in the first weeks of this war? In the rigid Communist version of the history of their 'Great Patriotic War' any peace treaty with the Germans would have been unthinkable treachery. (And any peace negotiations would also, incidentally, have broken the treaty of alliance signed by Britain and the Soviet Union on 12 July, which stated that neither country would 'negotiate nor conclude an armistice or treaty of peace [with Germany] except by mutual agreement'.)[27]

The truth is rather different. Anecdotal rumours that approaches were made through one of Beria's agents to get Ivan Stamenov, the Bulgarian Ambassador in Moscow, to intercede with the Germans have been known in the West for many years. But no document from the Communist period confirmed it – until now. A research team led by Professor Vladimir Naumov, one of the academic consultants for the television series on which this book is based, recently discovered in the Presidential Archive in Moscow a report from Pavel Sudoplatov, one of Beria's most trusted officers. This report was written in 1953 at the time of Beria's arrest, and describes how an approach to the Bulgarian Ambassador took place between 25 and 27 July 1941. Sudoplatov writes: 'Beria instructed me to pose four questions in my discussion with Stamenov. Beria listed these questions looking at his notebook and they amounted to the following:

'1. Why did Germany break its pact of non-invasion and start a war with the USSR?

'2. If Germany were to arrange it, under what conditions would Germany agree to stop the war?

Above Austrians in
Linz greet Hitler's
arrival on 12 March
1938, boosting his
already sky-high
self-confidence.
Left Austrian Nazis
make Viennese Jews
scrub the streets in
the aftermath of
the Anschluss. The
crowds were so big
that they had to be
held back.

Above A child gives
the Führer flowers
in 1938, the year
of his greatest
popularity so far.
Right The Union
Flag and the
Tricolour hang
above an SS guard
of honour outside
the 'Führerhaus'
in Munich during
the conference of
September 1938.

Above A passer-by surveys the damage to a Jewish shop in Berlin after Kristallnacht, November 1938.
Left Philipp Bouhler, the ambitious Nazi who organized the child 'euthanasia' policy.

Above Proof that history can be stranger than fiction. Ribbentrop shakes hands with Stalin, the man who represented the ideology the Nazis despised – Communism. The Hitler–Stalin Pact, signed in Moscow on 23 August 1939, was an act of pure pragmatism by both sides.

Above right Albert Forster (right) and Arthur Greiser in August 1939 when Greiser still worked for Forster in Danzig/West Prussia. Once Greiser was given his own area to control he complained constantly about his former boss.

Right A Polish family run from their home during the Nazi occupation. A scene of panic and suffering that was seen in Poland a hundred thousand times.

Left Himmler examines a child, eyeing up his racial potential. Himmler treated such children as a farmer treats his animals, deciding which should be allowed to grow and breed, and which should be slaughtered young.

Below German officials in Albert Forster's area determine the suitability for Germanization of the Poles sitting opposite; with Forster's attitude to Germanization, the discussion should not have taken long.

Top left and right Scenes of life in the 25d4 ghetto. The old man might well be asking, 'What more can I sell to survive?' Notice how the Jewish workers do not even stop working whilst their photo is taken.

Above Hans Biebow (right), ghetto manager of 25d4, counts the money extorted from the Jews in 1940. Biebow was careful to share the loot around – especially with Arthur Greiser.

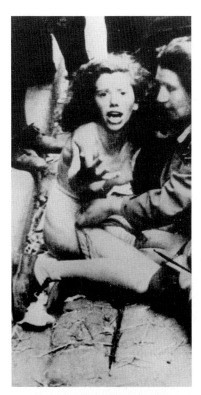

Left A Jewish woman who has been abused by the citizens of Lemberg (Lvov) in the Ukraine, after the Germans arrived in 1941.
Below The 'Death-dealer of Kaunas' holds the iron bar he used to dispatch many of his victims.
Bottom A photograph of the so-called 'garage' killings in Kaunas. The Germans stood and watched as the Lithuanians did their work for them, killing the Jews.

Above Jewish women in Latvia are forced to pose for the camera just before they are shot, December 1941. Within months the Nazis would have developed a more efficient way of committing mass murder – the gas chambers of the extermination camps.

Right The face of a killer: Petras Zelionka in the uniform of a Lithuanian soldier.

'3. Would the Germans be happy with the handing over of such Soviet lands as the Baltic States, the Ukraine, Bessarabia, Bukovina and the Karelian peninsula?

'4. If not, which territories would Germany want in addition?'

In 1991, shortly before his death, Sudoplatov was interviewed by the KGB about his life as an officer of its predecessor, the NKVD. He briefly mentioned the Stamenov affair, recalling that Beria had been supposed to meet Stamenov personally but Molotov had objected since 'it would be too official' if he went. Sudoplatov also revealed that Stamenov was selected as the go-between not just because as Bulgarian Ambassador he now represented German interests in the Soviet Union, but also because Beria believed that he was sympathetic to the Soviet cause. Beria had done Stamenov favours in the past, including organizing a job in Moscow for his wife, and Sudoplatov goes so far as to describe Stamenov as a Soviet agent.

On Beria's orders the meeting was to take place at the Georgian Aragvi restaurant in Moscow. Sudoplatov records that his boss added one more condition: 'Beria gave me the strictest warning that I should never tell anyone, anywhere, at any time about this commission of the Soviet government; otherwise myself and my family would be destroyed.'

Sudoplatov dutifully posed the four questions to Stamenov in Beria's private room at the Aragvi restaurant. The Bulgarian Ambassador reacted nonchalantly. 'Stamenov tried to behave as a man convinced of Germany's defeat in the war. He attached little significance to Germany's rapid gains during the first few days of the war. The thrust of what he said boiled down to the USSR's forces, without question, surpassing those of the Germans, and that even if during the initial period the Germans took substantial territory from the USSR and maybe even reached the Volga, in the long run

Germany would none the less suffer defeat and would be smashed.' Immediately after the meeting, according to Sudoplatov, he briefed Beria on his conversation with the ambassador; his own involvement in these peace feelers stopped at this point.

What are we to make of this report? It was written in the context of the attack on Beria after Stalin's death. That explains one strange contradiction: at the beginning of the report Sudoplatov writes that he believed Beria was acting with the full consent of the Soviet government, whilst at the end he says he is now convinced (because of what Beria's 'investigators' have just told him) that his former boss acted on his own in 'these actions of betrayal and sabotage'. Obviously, the report has no merit as an attack unless it is asserted that Beria was acting alone, but this is implausible and illogical – what possible reason could Beria have to think that it was worth pursuing an individual attempt to gain peace? Equally, since Beria's career was built upon his closeness and subservience to Stalin, why would he take such a gigantic risk and act in this way without his master's consent, especially since Stalin *was* the Soviet leadership, as head of the government, Defence Commissar, Supreme Commander-in-Chief and Party General Secretary?

Sudoplatov also writes that Beria told him the motive for this approach to Stamenov was to give 'the Soviet government room to manoeuvre and gain time to muster strength'.[28] After the fall of Communism he reiterated that 'the aim of this disinformation was to play for time'. This justification too should be treated with scepticism. For even if this peace approach had been deadly serious, Beria would still have briefed Sudoplatov in this way – it would be the only possible means of denial if news of any negotiations leaked out. 'Of course,' Beria would say, 'this was all part of a massive disinformation campaign...' This also meant that, should the negotiations subsequently be discovered (as they indeed were, and used against Beria at his trial in 1953), there was a chance they might be explained away.

The Russian historian Dimitri Volkogonov, drawing on previously secret sources for his biography of Stalin, unearthed evidence that also contradicts the idea that the Soviet leadership was, by these actions, merely trying to 'gain time to muster strength'. He writes that 'Molotov described the offer of territory in exchange for an end to the fighting as "a possible second Brest-Litovsk Treaty", and said that if Lenin could have the courage to make such a step, we had the same intention now'.[29]

The final significant feature of Sudoplatov's hitherto secret report is the date of the contact with the Bulgarian Ambassador – late July 1941. This means that the following anecdotal story told by a Russian historian who knew Marshal Zhukov becomes of particular importance. In the 1960s Zhukov was out of favour and Professor Viktor Anfilov befriended him. Zhukov told him how he was called to Stalin's dacha in early October 1941, at the lowest point of Soviet fortunes: 'When I was asked in I said, "Good afternoon, Comrade Stalin." Stalin obviously failed to hear me – he was sitting with his back to me. He continued talking to Beria, who was in his room. And I overheard the following: "...get in touch through your agents with the German intelligence service, find out what Germany is going to want from us if we offer to sign a separate peace treaty".'

Until recently there was dispute about when this approach to the Bulgarian Ambassador had taken place – July or October. Sudoplatov is clear – it was in late July. Yet Zhukov overheard the conversation between Stalin and Beria in October. Therefore what the confirmation of the date of the original approach to the Bulgarian Ambassador in July now leads to is the new and intriguing possibility that, with Stalin's authorization, Beria was ordered to pursue peace feelers in both July and October (and maybe in between as well). And if Zhukov honestly and accurately reported what he heard Stalin saying to Beria, this doesn't sound like 'disinformation' but desperation. It's not surprising, therefore, that after the war the Soviet leadership wanted to pretend that these thoughts were never in their minds – or at least to shove the blame solely on to the shoulders of Beria and Sudoplatov. Just as German generals wanted to rewrite the past once the result of the war was known, so did Stalin and the rest of the Soviet leadership.

During the first months of the invasion, the Germans, of course, weren't about to let Stalin make even a humiliating peace – not least because, as a result of their victories, they were accumulating Soviet prisoners by the million. 'I witnessed the huge, incredibly enormous numbers of prisoners of war,' says Rüdiger von Reichert, 'which naturally left a deep impression, and helped to get rid of any scepticism one had had when the war started.' The sight of these Soviet prisoners also confirmed to Reichert the accuracy of the Nazi stereotype of the 'sub-human' Slav: 'You saw people who you felt were inferior to you in terms of their level of civilization, their spiritual and mental capabilities – I'm ashamed to say this now, for today we see things entirely differently.'

The fate of these Soviet prisoners of war is one that has not received, in the West, the attention it deserves. Knowledge of the 6 million who died in the Holocaust is, rightly, widespread. But how many in the West know the terrifying statistic that out of a total of 5.7 million Soviet soldiers taken prisoner between June 1941 and February 1945 a staggering 3.3 million died – the majority as a result of disease and starvation?[30] The treatment these POWs received was very different from that experienced by captured British or US servicemen. For the

Soviet prisoners there was often no food, no shelter, no camp to speak of at all – just an open field enclosed with barbed wire. The experience of Georgy Semenyak, captured by the Germans near Minsk in July 1941, was typical. Once taken prisoner, he and 80,000 of his comrades were herded into a vast open space, guarded by German soldiers with machine guns. For the first week they were given neither food nor water – they could drink only from a muddy stream at the edge of the camp. At the start of the second week the Germans threw a few boxes of food – mostly salted herring – into the crowd of prisoners and then watched as the Soviet prisoners fought for the contents.

That autumn Semenyak was transferred to an even worse camp in Poland. About 100,000 Soviet prisoners were held in an open space without shelter from the elements. To amuse themselves the German guards would often fire directly into the camp. Lice were everywhere, and as a result there was an epidemic of typhus. A combination of disease, hunger and desperation led to cannibalism amongst the prisoners. During the night bodies were cut open. The buttocks, the liver, the lungs – all were removed, to be fried and then eaten. After beating the odds and surviving all this horror (and without, he says, resorting to cannibalism himself), Semenyak sums up his treatment at the hands of the Germans simply: 'They just never considered us humans.'

After the war some German officers claimed that such huge numbers of prisoners had never been anticipated, so the German Army had lacked the necessary means to deal with them. But at the very least, this is disingenuous. Whilst no direct evidence has surfaced that in the planning stages of the war the death of so many prisoners was specifically ordered, there is more than sufficient circumstantial evidence to conclude that such suffering was an obvious consequence of the way the war was conceived.

During the planning stage of Barbarossa it became clear that the vast distances to the front line and the inadequate Soviet transport system would prevent German troops being adequately supplied from the Reich. By 1941–2 the 'entire German Army' would therefore, as a document of 2 May 1941 from the Wehrmacht's central economic agency states, have to 'be fed at the expense of Russia'.[31] The consequence of this was obvious, as the document records: 'Thereby tens of millions of men will undoubtedly starve to death if we take away all we need from the country.'

Another document from the same agency, dated 23 May that year, goes even further in its prediction of the consequences of the German invasion on the Soviet people's food supply. Entitled 'Political-Economic Guidelines for the Economic Organization East', it states that the goal was to use Russian resources not just for feeding the German Army but also for supplying Nazi-controlled Europe.[32] As a consequence, 30 million Soviet people in the northern part of the region to be occupied were expected to die of starvation.

The Wehrmacht leadership must have foreseen that large numbers of Soviet prisoners would be taken – even if they did not anticipate as many as 3 million in the first seven months. But adequate preparations were not taken even for a lower number of captives – hardly surprising given the tone of documents like those quoted above. If, in planning the war, it was possible to assert that perhaps 30 million people would die of starvation as a result of German policy, then why, in parallel, would anyone have been trying actively to save the defeated enemy's soldiers?

That summer, whilst the Soviet prisoners of war died in the German camps, Hitler became concerned about the state of his army's advance. Despite the initial power of the German attack, the Soviet system showed no signs of imminent collapse. And although enormous numbers of prisoners had been taken, the Soviets had been able to call up military reserves – something the Germans had underestimated. In places the Red Army was putting up fierce resistance. Above all there were problems caused by the sheer scale of the German operation. By the middle of July some Panzer units were over 600 kilometres inside Soviet territory and the view voiced before the campaign that such units could, if necessary, 'live off the land' was proving to be a ridiculous fiction. The Soviets had burnt or otherwise destroyed anything that could be of value to the Germans, and supplies from the rear were hampered not only by the distances involved but also by the poor Russian infrastructure (almost all the roads were unmetalled, and what railway track existed was a broader gauge than the German system). In addition, the forward Panzer spearheads had suffered terrible losses. This was only to be expected in Blitzkrieg, where these units bore the brunt of any enemy resistance – Walter Schaefer-Kehnert's spearhead Panzer unit, for example, lost 50 per cent of its personnel within the first eight weeks of the war. But Blitzkrieg operations were not designed to last for month after month.

In July and August 1941 there was conflict at the Wolf's Lair, Hitler's Field Headquarters in East Prussia, between the Führer and his generals. The argument was over how to deal with a new strategic problem. The German front was effectively cut in half by the Pripet Marshes, a remote area all but impenetrable to armoured forces. Whilst Army Group Centre, operating north of the marshes, had made spectacular gains, Army Group South, fighting south of this region, had run into tougher resistance. Hitler's generals still favoured Army Group Centre pushing forward at once to Moscow. Hitler disagreed; not only had he asserted since December 1940 that it was more important to destroy the industrial base of the Soviet Union than to capture its capital, but he was concerned about possible flank attacks on Army Group Centre.

The atmosphere was not helped when Hitler, suffering from dysentery in the early days of August, vacillated about what the German Army should do next. One day Moscow was going to be the priority, then a few days later he insisted that there were other tasks to fulfil first. On 19 August it appeared to Josef Goebbels, the Propaganda Minister, that Hitler might even be doubting the ability of the German Army to crush the Red Army as planned: 'The Führer is very annoyed at himself for letting himself be fooled about the potential of the Bolsheviks by reports from the Soviet Union. His underestimation of the enemy's armoured divisions and Air Force, in particular, has meant an extraordinary amount of trouble for our military operations. He has suffered greatly as a result. It is a serious crisis.'[33] On 21 August Hitler made his decision clear: more important than the capture of Moscow was the encirclement of Leningrad in the north and the destruction of Soviet forces in the south, which would eliminate the threat of a flank attack on Army Group Centre.

Subsequently, this decision has been seen by some as another example of the ignorant corporal crippling the chance of victory created by his generals. But compelling military studies demonstrate that it was Hitler who had the more sound military sense.[34] An advance on Moscow in August by Army Group Centre would have been fraught with risk – not least from flanking attack, since considerable Soviet forces were still concentrated south of the Pripet Marshes in the Ukraine. The Germans might have reached Moscow but then been cut off inside the city, as they were later at Stalingrad.

Hitler's decision to order Guderian's Panzer Group south to Kiev in the Ukraine brought about an astonishing victory – one that restored the Führer's optimism. The Germans took more than 600,000 prisoners at Kiev in the greatest encirclement battle fought in modern times. Whole Soviet armies were caught, some trapped on the eastern bank of the River Dnieper as Kiev fell on 18 September.

Stalin was responsible for this disaster. Dominating the Stavka, the command body that controlled all Soviet forces, and believing in his own genius despite his almost total ignorance of military strategy, he ordered the Red Army to attempt the impossible and hold Kiev. One of the very few who dared stand up to him was Zhukov. He suggested to Stalin that the Red Army should withdraw in the face of the German advance on Kiev, only to be told by Stalin that he was talking 'rubbish'. Zhukov asked to be relieved at once of his post as Chief of the General Staff – a proposal that Stalin instantly accepted.

Nikolay Ponomariev, Stalin's personal telegraphist, witnessed the Soviet leader's response to the frantic calls from the Red Army commanders in Kiev. 'They were saying that they were not strong enough to maintain control over Kiev,' he says. 'They asked to be allowed to move the troops away, but Stalin insisted on the opposite – "Hold out as long as you can."' Stalin's intransigence cost the Soviet Army dear – the paucity of his strategic thinking is no better illustrated than by this catastrophe. Stalin's idea of defence at this time was as simple as Hitler's was later to become – hold your ground and fight to the last.

German soldiers were elated. 'We succeeded, didn't we!' says Hubert Menzel, who fought as a German tank officer at Kiev. 'We did wage encirclement battles across distances which we'd been simply incapable of imagining before.' Hitler too was euphoric. This was, he believed, the turning point of the war. With the threat from the flanks now clear, Hitler accepted that the German Army should push on towards Moscow, with the Soviet capital the target of the German Operation Typhoon.

On the Soviet side, in the wake of the dramatic loss of Kiev, there was bewilderment and fear. 'We simply kept wondering why our Army was surrendering one town after another,' says Viktor Strazdovski, who was eighteen years old in 1941. 'It was a real tragedy. It's difficult to express by words how we lived through that.' That autumn Strazdovski joined the Red Army and was shocked to see the equipment he was expected to use to defend his country. 'The 60-millimetre guns that we were given were trophies left from World War I – they didn't have modern sighting devices. And we only had one rifle between five soldiers.'

Strazdovski, badly equipped and poorly trained, was about to take part in the Battle of Vyazma – around the town that was the last great obstacle in the way of the German advance on Moscow. At the beginning of October 1941 the 3rd and 4th Panzer Groups linked to form the Vyazma pocket. Five Soviet armies were trapped. 'We were face to face with the Germans,' says Strazdovski, 'and we had to use these primitive weapons in real combat. We didn't feel confident enough...When I was sent to the place where the Germans broke our defence line, you can imagine how we felt – we felt we were doomed. There were four of us, with two rifles between us, and we didn't know in which direction we would run into the Germans. The woods around us were ablaze. On the one hand we couldn't disobey our order, but on the other hand we felt doomed.'

Soviet soldiers tried frantically to break through and escape the German encirclement. 'I saw one of these attacks coming early in the morning,' says Walter Schaefer-Kehnert, an officer in the 11th Panzer Division. 'We were sitting on top of the hills, there was a fog going down to the river valley, and when the fog came up it was like a herd of vehicles and men coming up by the thousand and it made your blood freeze...and then the Russians came into the ground where there was a swampy area, and then all the vehicles at once sunk in the mud, and then the people came on to us like a herd of sheep.' Schaefer-Kehnert shouted to his men, 'Let them come, let them get nearer, let them come on!' until they were close enough for the German 2-centimetre anti-aircraft flak cannon and machine guns to mow them down.

The next day Schaefer-Kehnert looked out over the battlefield at the thousands of Soviet dead and dying lying in front of him: 'And there were some Russian girls – I will never forget them – in trousers and dressed like soldiers, and they got in a cart, with a horse, and had a barrel of water and then went around giving water to the dying Russian soldiers lying on that field…They were lying there by the thousand like the battlefield of old history.'

Wolfgang Horn was in another Panzer division at Vyazma facing a different section of the encircled Soviet armies. As he looked across at the Red Army through special field glasses, he saw an 'incredible' sight. Only the front row of Soviet soldiers rushing towards the Germans had rifles – the row behind was unarmed. 'As the first row was mowed down,' says Horn, 'they [the second row] bent down and took the guns of those who were dead – they were destined to attack without weapons…something that was totally unfamiliar to us.'

That night, as more Soviet troops tried to find a way past the Germans, Horn's unit spotted several trucks full of Red Army soldiers coming towards them. The Soviet soldiers opened fire. But standing close together in the trucks they made a 'beautiful target' for Horn and his comrades, who lobbed hand grenades at them. Horn himself sustained a minor wound, which so angered him that he fought back even more fiercely at the enemy soldiers trapped around their trucks. 'Then the Russians were so cowardly,' says Horn, 'that some of the crew of these trucks cowered behind the vehicle.' As the Soviet soldiers lay huddled together, their hands and arms covering their heads, Horn shouted, 'Hands up!' in Russian at them, and then, when they didn't immediately respond, he and his comrades opened fire and killed them all. 'When they don't surrender,' he says, 'we shoot them. It was natural for us to do...They are cowards – they didn't deserve any better, anyhow.'

Even if Horn had accepted the surrender of these Soviet soldiers that night, they still might not have been saved because the lieutenant commanding his unit decided to order the murder of many of the Soviet prisoners taken. Horn felt this behaviour not just 'unchivalrous' but 'stupid' because 'Russians hiding in the forest might have seen the prisoners being shot and so they might fight better the next time'.

Viktor Strazdovski sums up the battle succinctly: 'What happened there is like a mincing machine, when people are sent to a sure death, unarmed to fight a well-trained army.' Walter Schaefer-Kehnert came to another conclusion: 'A life wasn't worth much for the Russians. Their deaths were not taken as seriously as with us...we were of the belief that there shouldn't be much left of the Red Army now.'

October 1941 marked the high point of Operation Barbarossa. Army Group Centre's defeat of the Red Army at Vyazma and the nearby Battle of Bryansk had eliminated the last serious obstacle on the road to Moscow. In the Ukraine, after the capture of Kiev, Army Group South had consolidated its position and the bounty of the Soviet Union's 'breadbasket' lay open to be plundered for the Reich. Outside Leningrad Army Group North had succeeded in cutting off the city and was attempting to starve out the inhabitants. It was the beginning of a 900-day siege of appalling suffering – in the winter of 1941–2 half a million people would die of starvation. All of this German military success led Hitler to declare at the Berlin Sportpalast that the Red Army 'would never rise again'.[35] Jodl remarked: 'We have finally and without any exaggeration won the war!' And Otto Dietrich, the Führer's own Press Chief, stated: 'For all military purposes Soviet Russia is done with.'[36]

At Vyazma (combined with the Battle of Bryansk) the Germans took another 660,000 prisoners. The news from the front line filled Muscovites with despair – just 90,000 Soviet troops now defended the capital. In this despondent atmosphere Nikolay Ponomariev, Stalin's telegraphist, was ordered to make contact with Zhukov, now back in favour as Commander of the Western Front, so that the Soviet leader could seek his advice. 'I knew that the situation was really bad,' says Ponomariev. 'Life in Moscow had stopped, the Metro had stopped running. Stalin came up to me, said, "Hello", as if nothing was happening, and asked, "What are we going to do? The Germans are pushing through to Moscow." I didn't expect such a question. I said, "We can't let the Germans into Moscow, they have to be beaten." "I think so too," he said. "Now let's ask Comrade Zhukov what is his opinion on the subject."'

Stalin listened for more than an hour and a half as Zhukov outlined what he needed for the defence of Moscow – tanks, artillery and, most importantly of all, rockets. 'It was a really difficult conversation,' says Ponomariev. 'I learnt from that how short of supplies and undermanned our army was.' Stalin told Zhukov that at least some of the supplies he needed were already on their way. Then, witnessed by Ponomariev, he asked Zhukov a question. '"Tell me, Georgy Konstantinovich, as a Communist to a Communist, are we going to hold Moscow or not?" Zhukov paused and then replied, "Comrade Stalin, if I get even part of the help that I asked for, we will hold Moscow."'

That was not the end of dramatic events on 16 October 1941, as ten minutes after the phone call to Zhukov one of Stalin's senior aides told Ponomariev to pack all his equipment and get ready to leave. 'Half an hour later,' says Ponomariev, 'I was visited by one of Stalin's security guards, and he asked me if I was ready to go. "Where are we going?" I asked. And he said, "You'll see when you go. Get ready and come with me." There was a car waiting outside. We were driven away. Moscow was completely dark. The weather was wet. I saw we were heading for the railway station. I saw the armoured train and Stalin's guards walking to and fro on the platform. It became clear to me that I would have to wait for Stalin and go into evacuation with him.'

As Ponomariev sat on Stalin's train, other Muscovites came to the conclusion that they too should prepare to leave. Maya Berzina, a thirty-one-year-old mother, was one of those who decided to flee. 'We wondered what would happen if the government left,' she says. 'It must mean that Moscow would be surrendered. My husband was Jewish, I was half-Jewish and it meant we were doomed. My husband ran to the railway station and he was told that there would be no trains...he was advised to leave on foot. We had a three-year-old son and what could we do with him? He was too heavy to carry and too weak to walk. We realized there was also Moscow port, the southern port, and my husband went there and learnt there would be some ships. On that day of panic I saw how people began to show initiative – which was a long-forgotten thing. We're used to directives. It turned out that the chief of the port began to sell tickets for a ship that was already mothballed for the winter and somehow we managed to get on it.'

Maya Berzina was certain, on that day in mid-October, that the Germans would take Moscow: 'We heard there were people who put up posters that said "Welcome". There was panic. We were told by the conductor on the tram that she had seen Germans on another tram – I don't know if it was true...Directors of shops opened their shops and were saying to people, "Take what you want. We don't want the Germans to get these things.'"

In this atmosphere of panic even Stalin himself considered deserting the capital. A secret document only just declassified, number 34 of the State Defence Committee, dated 15 October 1941, reveals just how serious Stalin believed the situation had become. It states that the State Defence Committee had resolved 'To evacuate the Presidium of the Supreme Soviet and the top levels of Government... (Comrade Stalin will leave tomorrow or later, depending on the situation)...In the event of enemy forces arriving at the gates of Moscow, the NKVD – Comrade Beria and Comrade Shcherbakov – are ordered to blow up business premises, warehouses and institutions which cannot be evacuated, and all Underground railway electrical equipment.'

This was perhaps the key moment of the whole war. For if Stalin had climbed on board his train and fled, Soviet resistance might have weakened decisively. Many believe that, even without Stalin, a combination of the oncoming winter weather and the problems of fighting inside Moscow, street to street, would have broken the Germans. But what that scenario underestimates is the psychological effect of Stalin's presence on the population of Moscow. Many of those Russians we talked to emphasized the importance they placed on their leader's continued presence in Moscow. In propaganda terms Stalin *was* the Soviet Union. If he was a coward, why couldn't everyone be a coward? If he ran, why couldn't they?

Perhaps, even if Stalin had deserted the capital, the Germans would have been surrounded and trapped inside Moscow – that's almost certainly what would have happened if Army Group Centre had moved on the Soviet capital in August whilst the threat from the flanks remained. But by October, with that danger eliminated, why couldn't Moscow have become another Kiev or Minsk – cities that the Germans now held securely? Stalin's apparent cowardice and his inability to prevent the growing panic in the capital would have severely damaged his authority. And once the Soviet leadership lost Moscow, the centre of the Soviet communications and transport network, what terms of peace might they have been prepared to negotiate?

In the event, Stalin decided to stay in Moscow – but only after vacillating about what he should do. On 15 October, according to Politburo member Anastas Mikoyan, Stalin announced to them that he intended to leave Moscow 'tomorrow morning'. But by the night of the 19th Stalin had resolved to stay. V.S. Pronin, President of the Moscow Soviet, was present at that decisive meeting. This is his account of what happened – a notable first-hand description of how Stalin conducted business: 'When we assembled in the room leading to Stalin's office, Beria set about persuading everyone that we should abandon Moscow. He argued that we should give up Moscow and set up a defensive line on the Volga. Malenkov supported him, Molotov mumbled his disagreement. In fact, I particularly remember Beria's words: "But how are we going to defend Moscow? We have absolutely nothing at all. We have been overwhelmed and we are being shot down like partridges." Then all of us went into Stalin's office. Stalin came in as usual with his pipe. When we had settled down, Stalin asked: "Are we going to defend Moscow?" Everyone was silent. He waited a moment and then repeated his question. Again no reply. "Very well [said Stalin], we will ask individually." Molotov replied first: "We will defend [Moscow]." All, including Beria, answered the same: "We will defend [Moscow]."'[37]

So Stalin decided to stay in Moscow, which he insisted must be held by the harshest measures necessary. In order to counter the panic, he instituted a 'state of siege' in the capital from 20 October. A curfew was imposed from midnight to 5 a.m. and the task of enforcing law and order was entrusted to the NKVD.

Vladimir Ogryzko commanded one of the NKVD units which tried to restore order in Moscow that October. 'Panic was spread by diversionary groups and spies who had broken through Moscow's defences,' he says. 'There were robberies – everything you can imagine happened – because as usual the people lost their heads...the ill-educated ones. The scum of the earth did show its face. It seeped through.'

Men like Ogryzko interpreted Stalin's order as giving them total power. 'It isn't peacetime,' he says. 'You're not going to say, "Stop or I'll shoot!" a thousand times before you shoot, nor are you going to shoot in the air. Of course not. You shoot them on the spot. It was a tough command. Anybody who resisted and didn't obey orders on demand – especially if they moved away or opened their mouths – was eliminated on the spot without further ado. And that was considered a truly heroic act – you were killing the enemy.'

The streets were jammed with fleeing Muscovites, towards whom Ogryzko had a similarly uncompromising attitude. 'They were running away,' he says, 'they were marauders, bastards who thought they'd stay alive at the end of the day.' He overturned their cars into the roadside ditches and 'If the driver was crushed, well, even better...that wasn't my responsibility.'

A combination of Stalin's decision to stay in Moscow and the imposition of this brutal 'state of siege' did indeed restore order. 'These severe measures, these beautiful measures,' says Vladimir Ogryzko, 'are the essence and content of war. You cannot say that they go against human rights – they are neither cruel nor mad. It was right to execute the people who didn't understand their position at a time which had become more cruel for their country...Had there not been such a tough order, there would have been total panic. Anything could have happened. Literally. It was a very wise, resolute and correct decision taken by the Defence Council and Stalin.'

Outside the city the Germans, as the winter weather began, contemplated the final attack. They had travelled further and faster, and taken more enemy prisoners, than any invading army in history. The only problem was that, according to their original plan, by now they should already have won the war.

6

A DIFFERENT KIND OF WAR

MORE CIVILIANS DIED IN THIS WAR THAN ANY OTHER IN HISTORY.
Around 13 million Soviet civilians alone lost their lives under
German occupation (more than twice the entire population of
Scotland).[1] Set against the background of the Battle of
Moscow and then the Nazi occupation of Soviet territory in
1942 and 1943, this chapter therefore confronts one of the
most important questions of the conflict: why did this, of all
wars, result in such a human catastrophe?

A key reason, of course, was the character of the respec-
tive leaders. Both Hitler and Stalin shared a disregard for the
lives of those they ruled. Humanity had no place in their attitude to war. When one acted brutally, the other would
respond – with more brutality. Nowhere was that uncompromising attitude to human life made more clear than during
the struggle for the Soviet capital.

In mid-October 1941 it looked as if Moscow was about
to fall into German hands. But then Stalin decided to stay in
the city; NKVD troops quelled the panic and the winter rains
began, causing a three-week delay to the German advance as
the roads became impassable. Whilst the Germans waited,
Zhukov set about enforcing discipline at the front and nine
Soviet reserve armies were gathered east of the Volga, bol-
stered by the arrival of fresh troops from Siberia.

Operation Typhoon, the German advance on Moscow, began again on 15 November, and on the solid, frozen ground made good progress. By the beginning of December a few forward units were about 20 kilometres from the centre of the city – it was as near as the Germans were ever to get. Walter Schaefer-Kehnert's Panzer unit was one of those that came closest, on 4 December. As he studied his maps and examined the position of his artillery batteries, he realized an extraordinary truth: 'I measured this distance to the Kremlin and said, "Well, if we had a long-range cannon, we could shoot at the Kremlin."' Through the regimental commander they obtained a 10.5-centimetre gun and opened fire. 'With a 10-centimetre gun you won't do much harm,' he says. 'We thought only of the morale consequences on the citizens of Moscow – shooting to the town and the Kremlin!'

The ineffectual shelling of the Kremlin symbolized the German position – they had come so far and yet still had not accomplished the goal they had set themselves. The next day, 5 December, Schaefer-Kehnert's unit felt the weight of the Soviet counter-attack. As the Germans tried to defend themselves, they were hampered by the sudden, intense cold. 'When the temperature dropped to below minus 30 degrees Celsius our machine guns were not firing any more,' says Schaefer-Kehnert. 'Our machine guns were precision instruments but when the oil got thick they didn't shoot properly any more – this really makes you afraid.' All around him, he saw the devastating effect of the Germans' lack of winter clothing. According to the original Barbarossa plan, two-thirds of the German Army should have been withdrawn by now since the war would already have been won, so proper preparations had never been made for winter warfare. 'We had huge losses from frozen toes and fingers during the night,' says Schaefer-Kehnert. 'And when the infantry had to sleep in the open, you tried to make a hole in the snow. Then there was an order that a guard had to go round every two hours and look because you would freeze to death and you would not realize it was happening. Particularly if we had been fighting during the day and sweating and then we cooled off at night – that was when the greatest danger was of freezing to death. It's a very nice death but you don't want to have it!'

Rüdiger von Reichert's unit suffered when they could no longer move their heavy artillery. The guns were pulled by brewery horses, 'pampered creatures used to an abundance of food and warm stables, and these poor animals now suddenly found themselves drawing heavy pieces of artillery which they had to draw first through quicksand, then mud and then snow. And almost all of them died of heart disease.'

'The German Army near Moscow was a very miserable sight,' says Fyodor Sverdlov, a company commander in the Soviet 19th Rifle Brigade. 'I remember very well the Germans in July 1941. They were confident, strong, tall guys. They marched ahead with their sleeves rolled up and carrying their machine guns. But later on they became miserable, crooked, snotty guys wrapped in woollen kerchiefs stolen from old women in villages...Of course, they were still firing and defending themselves, but they weren't the Germans we knew earlier in 1941.'

Whilst the Soviet counter-attack continued, on 7 December Hitler received what he took to be good news – the Japanese had bombed Pearl Harbor. He believed this meant that the United States, with its hands tied by a wide-ranging Pacific War, would no longer be able to devote resources to helping Britain and consequently the Soviet Union. Only days earlier Hitler had been briefed by Fritz Todt, Reich Minister for Armaments and Munitions, that if the USA entered the conflict, the war would be lost for Germany. But Hitler still chose to see American involvement via Japan as a positive sign. On 11 December Germany formally declared war on the

United States. To Hitler this was doing little more than recognizing the inevitable; ever since the Americans had begun their package of war aid to the British, he had foreseen an eventual confrontation with the USA unless Britain could be removed from the conflict first. That, after all, had been one of the key reasons behind Operation Barbarossa – Hitler had wanted to eliminate the threat from the East before an American-backed front opened in Europe. Unfortunately for Hitler, not only had the Red Army not been destroyed in 1941 as planned, but the opening of hostilities between Japan and the USA and the subsequent Japanese advance south to Singapore meant that Stalin could now release more Soviet troops from his Western border, confident that he would not fall victim to an attack from the Japanese, Germany's Axis ally. With its military machine fully occupied on land fighting the British, and in the Pacific confronting the mighty American fleet, it was not in Japan's interests to provoke any conflict with the Soviet Union.

By the middle of December the situation of the German troops outside Moscow had become desperate. Halder called their predicament 'the greatest crisis in two world wars' and summed up a report from the Quartermaster General as saying 'we have reached the end of our human and material forces'.[2]

On 16 December Hitler ordered the German forces to stand firm, believing that any retreat might turn into a rout. He issued a directive to Army Group Centre calling for the 'fanatical will to defend the ground on which the troops are standing' to be 'injected' into the troops. If a staged withdrawal was ever necessary, then 'every place of inhabitation must be burnt down and destroyed without consideration for the population'.

The Panzer commander, Heinz Guderian, objected fiercely to Hitler's order. He argued that to insist the Army stood where it was would result in the senseless death of German soldiers.

They must retreat. Hitler seemed bemused by these objections. 'Do you think Frederick the Great's Grenadiers enjoyed dying for their country either?' he asked. Revealingly, he then criticized Guderian. 'You stand too close to events,' Hitler remarked. 'You ought to disengage yourself more.'[3]

Hitler's obvious contempt for those, like Guderian, who expressed any pity for human suffering was another key reason why the war became so brutal. In a crisis he believed the stronger 'will' would prevail – and 'will' became a synonym for cruelty. He always felt his generals had a dangerous tendency towards pity. On 22 December Guderian was relieved of his command. A few days earlier, on the 19th, Field Marshal von Brauchitsch had retired because of ill health. He received none of the traditional decorations or honours due on retirement. Instead he was vilified. Here – to committed Nazis – was another example of a German general who just hadn't demonstrated the strength of 'will' the Führer had a right to demand. Goebbels recorded in his diary the following March that Hitler called Brauchitsch 'a vain, cowardly wretch who could not even appraise the situation, much less master it'. Goebbels also recorded his own view that 'The senior officers who have risen from the General Staff are incapable of withstanding severe strain and major tests of character.' The pure Nazi view is here clearly expressed – deficient equipment and inadequate supplies were not symptomatic of disastrous planning but were, in fact, 'major tests of character'.[4]

As Wolfgang Horn and the rest of his unit discovered that winter, even getting frostbite would be to fail this 'major test of character': 'We had to warn each other if a nose was getting white. "Rub your nose otherwise you will be punished!" You see, those who had something frozen were punished for abandoning the Fatherland to some degree – sabotaging the war effort by letting something freeze.'

This same ruthless desire to enforce the harshest discipline on those who thought of retreat was evident on the Soviet side as well. As an NKVD officer, Vladimir Ogryzko fought alongside rearguard divisions behind the troops in the Battle of Moscow. Their job was simple. If Soviet troops ran past them in retreat, they killed them. 'The station I was protecting had the right to kill anyone who approached it,' says Ogryzko. 'They're given a chance, when you say, "Stop or I'll shoot!" And if they don't stop, then they're shot…There are a certain number of rules in life, especially in the army and even more so in war. There can't be demagogues. They are traitors, simply traitors. It should be considered as part of people's education – a traitor should get his come-uppance.' Ogryzko is still proud of his work: 'It was a very good decision to take and it shouldn't be judged. They used fear to crush fear. If it was right or wrong, so what? It was a time of war and there had to be certainty.'

Just as Hitler's personality helped shape the nature of the German defence outside Moscow, so Stalin's helped shape the Red Army's attack: 'I have to say that the cruelty and determination and will of Stalin were communicated to the commanders of the front and also reached us, the junior commanders,' says Fyodor Sverdlov, commander of an infantry company at the Battle of Moscow. 'Stalin was cruel, but even now I continue to think this cruelty was justified. There couldn't be any mercy, any pity.'

During a frank interview, Sverdlov admitted that in pursuit of Stalin's 'cruel' policy he personally shot one of his own men. 'It happened once during a successful attack. There was one soldier, I don't know what his name was, but because of his cowardice and because the combat was very severe he broke down, and he began to run, and I killed him without thinking twice. And that was a good lesson to all the rest.'

Sverdlov also revealed another element that contributed

to the brutality of the conflict – he, and the men he commanded, often fought under the influence of alcohol: 'There's a Russian saying that a drunken man can cross the sea. Whenever a man gets drowned in the Moskva River, he would always be a drunk. A drunk thinks that everything is easy, and this makes it clear why Russian soldiers were given vodka.' Every one of his soldiers was issued with 100 grams of vodka a day from the Ministry of Defence – this was known as the 'Minister's 100'. But this wasn't all they drank. 'You know that Russians are fond of drinking,' he says, 'but it was a must during the war. Of course, it was seldom that we drank 100 grams only because as we bore heavy losses every day that amount of vodka was meant to cover a bigger number of people than there actually were. I usually drank 200 grams of vodka at breakfast, 100 grams of vodka at lunch, and if there was no combat in the evening, I would drink another 200 gram glass sharing dinner with a company of friends.'

Fyodor Sverdlov doesn't feel that being drunk hampered the fighting ability of the Soviet soldier – quite the contrary: 'When a person gets drunk, he feels more determined, more courageous. He doesn't think about being killed in a minute. He marches on, trying to kill the enemy. Being quite frank, I have to say that in the course of the whole war both Germans and Russians were always drunk at decisive moments because a human mind cannot otherwise bear the horrors of the modern war. I don't know if the British and the Americans drank when they were landing in Normandy, but I bet they drank whisky.'

By the end of January 1942 the crisis was over for the Germans. The front had stabilized. Hitler believed this accomplishment had been his alone – after all, had he not been the one who had issued the stand-fast order? And, his conceit knowing no bounds, he had by now replaced

Brauchitsch as Commander-in-Chief of the German Army with the only man he felt certain had the strength of will to do the job properly – himself. But in reality Stalin and his generals were not yet in a position, in either their tactical thinking or the resources at their disposal, to impose a decisive defeat on the German Army. The eventual outcome of the war was far from certain and, in the meantime, the Nazis had a new empire to rule.

The way the Germans administered their conquered territories in the East (particularly the biggest of them all, the Ukraine) was to play another decisive part in the escalation of the brutality of this war. Ironically, given what was to happen, at the start of Operation Barbarossa many German soldiers thought the indigenous population of the East could be their allies, not their enemies. 'During the first few months of the war we were welcomed as liberators,' says Peter von der Groeben, who was a senior officer with the 86th Infantry Division. 'Sometimes they would bring you salt and bread [the traditional symbols of welcome and hospitality] because the peasants considered this their liberation from Bolshevism.' For Rüdiger von Reichert, an artillery officer with the 4th Army, the experience was the same: 'I experienced it again and again in these first months, that people would bring you something from their garden – we were very hungry for fresh vegetables. Not everybody was delighted, but many of them welcomed us warmly as their liberators.'

Many of the German soldiers, even those like Carlheinz Behnke who fought in an SS Panzer division, thought that this might turn into a 'conventional' occupation: 'We assumed that once the Ukraine had been occupied it would become an independent state and the soldiers would probably fight on our side against the rest of the Bolshevists. It might have been naive, but that was the general trend and mood amongst us young soldiers.'

The reason for the warm welcome the German soldiers received as they marched into the Ukraine is not hard to find. The Ukrainians had suffered hugely under rule from Moscow. The famine of the early 1930s – created by Communist policies – had resulted in an estimated 7 million deaths. And just before they retreated in the face of the German advance, the NKVD had murdered thousands of Ukrainian political prisoners. 'We dreamt about the new Ukrainian state,' says Aleksey Bris, who lived in the west of the Ukraine. 'Any war against the Soviet Union was perceived by us as a good war.'

As an eighteen-year-old student with a gift for languages, Bris started to work for the local German administration as an interpreter. As he sees it, this was not collaboration: 'I mean, every man is dreaming to have something better. Nobody would like to be a sweeper on the street.' For him, and for many other Ukrainians, the Germans appeared at first as just another in a long line of conquerors. And 'under all authorities, regardless of their character, their particular system was accepted as "normal". For example, if the Chinese had come, we would also have thought of them as "normal"...I would have to work for them somehow because I need to eat, I need to live, I need to work, and that's why we didn't have this kind of definition as "collaboration" as you have it in the West.' As Bris saw it, the Ukrainians had 'no other choice' but to work with the Germans.

Aleksey Bris's decision to assist the Germans was based on the judgement that the Nazis were 'like any other conqueror'. But they weren't. Hitler did not believe in a policy of cooperation with the indigenous population of the Eastern territories – in the way the British had ruled India or, indeed, the way the Romans had governed their empire. Whilst the conquered people in the West of the Nazi Empire, like the French or Dutch, could generally be treated less brutally because they were for the most part 'civilized', Hitler believed that since the people of the Soviet Union were 'inferior', they did not deserve the resources that nature had given them. 'It's inconceivable,' he said, 'that a higher people [i.e. the Germans] should painfully exist on a soil too narrow for it, whilst amorphous masses, which contribute nothing to civilization, occupy infinite tracts of a soil that is one of the richest in the world.'[5] Hitler preached that the Germans should be guided by only one natural law in this occupation – the stronger person must do whatever he liked.

Such a philosophy freed Hitler to dream of a form of conquest that would crush the inhabitants of the occupied Eastern territories for ever; he saw his mission to make them less civilized than even he thought they already were. Their level of education was to be, as he described it, 'just enough to understand our highway signs so that they won't get themselves run over by our vehicles'. For all his admiration for the British achievement in India, Hitler looked across the Atlantic to the violent colonization of the American West for a practical lesson in how to deal with the population of the German-occupied territories: 'There's only one duty: to Germanize this country by the immigration of Germans, and to look upon the natives as Redskins.'[6]

These extracts, from Hitler's private dinner-table monologues, carry the stamp of the authentic Führer. But he was not always so forthright, as Alfred Rosenberg, newly appointed Minister of the Eastern Territories, was to discover. Rosenberg met Hitler on 16 July 1941 at the Führer's headquarters in East Prussia, the Wolf's Lair, and voiced his view that the nationalist sentiments of the Ukrainians should be encouraged. Hitler did not object. At a later conference Hitler even hinted that the Ukraine might one day be considered independent within the German Empire. But these were simply words to keep the loyal but misguided Rosenberg happy. On 19 September Hitler revealed his true feelings to a more ideologically sympathetic Nazi. Notes survive of a meeting between Hitler and Erich Koch, the Nazi Gauleiter of East Prussia and recently appointed Reich Commissioner for the Ukraine. 'Both the Führer and the Reichskommissar [Koch] reject an independent Ukraine...Besides, hardly anything will be left standing in Kiev [the capital]. The Führer's inclination to destroy Russia's large cities as a prerequisite for the permanence of our power in Russia will be further consolidated by the Reichskommissar's smashing of Ukrainian industry, in order to drive the proletariat back to the land.'[7]

What pleasure it must have given Hitler, in a meeting with a Nazi hardliner like Koch, to state that it was his 'inclination to destroy Russia's large cities'. Here he could be honest. With Rosenberg, technically Koch's superior in the Nazi hierarchy, for long periods he was more opaque. Such behaviour seems curious at first, since it was Hitler himself who appointed Rosenberg. But Hitler's behaviour is explicable, consistent as it is with the methods he generally used to control and manipulate the Nazi state.

In the first place, Nazi hierarchies were not what they seemed. Koch had a very large degree of autonomy in how he decided to run the Ukraine and he was able to report directly to Hitler, should he wish it, through the automatic access guaranteed by his other position as Gauleiter of East Prussia, so Rosenberg could be bypassed whenever necessary. Second, Hitler was always loyal to those, like Rosenberg, who had stuck by him in the times of 'struggle' before the Nazis came to power – and here was a grand-sounding job as a reward for his loyalty. Third, the appointment of Rosenberg allowed Hitler to play off Koch against him if he wanted to. In-fighting amongst leading Nazis preserved the Führer's role as the final arbiter within the system. Finally, Hitler disliked issuing written orders to the likes of Rosenberg and Koch, so the presence of this conflict between them allowed him 'deniability' if anything went catastrophically wrong. As Hitler acknowledged when he spoke to the commanding generals of the German Army Groups in the summer of 1942, he was prepared to say whatever he felt any situation demanded: 'Were it not for the psychological effect, I would go as far as I could; I would say, "Let's set up a fully independent Ukraine." I would say it without blinking and then not do it anyway. That I could do as a politician, but (since I must say it publicly) I can't tell every [German] soldier just as publicly: "It isn't true; what I've just said is only tactics."'[8]

Inevitably, there was a series of disruptive rows between Rosenberg and Koch about how the Ukraine should be run. Whilst Rosenberg toyed with the idea of treating the Ukraine in a more conventional colonial way, Koch's attitude is best expressed in his statement to the Nazis on Kiev city administration that 'we are a master race that must remember, the lowliest German worker is racially and biologically a thousand times more valuable than the population here'.[9] Whilst Rosenberg dreamt one day of a university in Kiev, Koch closed the schools saying, 'Ukrainian children need no schools. What they have to learn will be taught them by their German masters.'[10]

'You would not believe the kind of confusion there was,' says Dr Wilhelm Ter-Nedden, who worked in Rosenberg's ministry in Berlin. 'The administration melted away.' Even though Rosenberg was technically his superior, Koch treated him with open contempt. Ter-Nedden attended meetings between the two men and was shocked at what he saw: 'On these occasions I witnessed Koch tearing Rosenberg off a strip, in such a manner that I would have thrown him out! And Rosenberg put up with it.' At one lunch Koch ignored Rosenberg completely, only talking to the person next to him, until finally he leaned across the table and said loudly, 'Is this as boring for you, Rosenberg, as it is for me?' To Ter-Nedden this was all symptomatic of the same warped political system that had previously allowed Hermann Göring to control the economic destiny of Germany via the Four-Year Plan: 'When Göring arrived we all had to line up to meet him – and Göring said, roughly, "Of course, I know nothing about economics, but I have an unbridled will!"'

Koch's own 'unbridled will' was creating a very different Ukraine from the one Aleksey Bris had anticipated: 'Little by little, between Germans and Ukrainians there was a feeling of separation – an edge.' To Bris this was summed up one day by a conversation he had with Ernst Erich Haerter, the German commissar of Horokhiv, his local town. Bris said that one day he would like to continue his studies and become a doctor. The German commissar replied, echoing Koch: 'We don't need you Ukrainians as doctors or engineers, we need you as people to tend the cows.' As Bris now saw it, the Germans regarded themselves as 'gods on the earth'.

However, Nazi policy towards these occupied territories was never straightforward, and not just because of the inherent tension between functionaries like Rosenberg and Koch. Sometimes it was impossible for Nazi administrators accurately to second-guess just what the Führer's policy would be on any particular issue, as the saga of the availability of contraceptives to the Ukrainians amply demonstrates.

In July 1942 Hitler moved from East Prussia to new field headquarters near the town of Vinnitsa in the Ukraine, and stayed there until October of that year. This location allowed his faithful lieutenant, Martin Bormann, to observe the local population in the surrounding villages. He was outraged at what he saw; the Ukrainian children did not look like sub-humans at all. On the contrary, many were blond and blue-eyed. Seeking an explanation of this phenomenon in Nazi evolutionary theory, he concluded that these impressive children were the product of their grim living conditions – as a consequence of the poor housing and sanitation only the strongest children had survived. It was not in the interests of the Reich, as Bormann saw it, to allow the Ukrainians to breed further. Hitler agreed. Only a few months before, in February 1942, Hitler had fumed about the mistakes that previous German colonizers had made: 'No sooner do we land in a colony than we install children's crèches, hospitals for the natives. All this fills me with rage...The Russians don't grow old. They scarcely get beyond 50 or 60. What a ridiculous idea to vaccinate them!...No vaccination for the Russians and no soap to get the dirt off them. But let them have all the vodka and tobacco they want.'[11]

Now, after discussions with Bormann, and notwithstanding his desire to deny the Ukrainians other modern medical care, Hitler accepted that the local population should be encouraged to use contraceptives provided for them by the Nazis. But only weeks before Bormann's eye-opening trip around the Ukrainian countryside a zealous Nazi official, acting no doubt on what he believed would be Hitler's wishes, had decided to ban contraceptives in the occupied territories, arguing that since they were evidence of sophisticated medical knowledge, the Führer would wish them to be denied to these 'natives'. Hitler fumed: 'If some idiot should actually try and carry out such a prohibition in the occupied East, he [Hitler] would personally shoot him to pieces. In the occupied Eastern territories a brisk trade in contraceptives shall not only be permitted but even encouraged, for one could have no interest in the excessive multiplication of the non-German population.'[12]

The day after Hitler had uttered these words, Bormann relayed the Führer's wish that there be a 'brisk trade in contraceptives' in the East to Rosenberg. (Bormann's memorandum also emphasized that 'German public health services shall under no circumstances be established in the occupied Eastern territories.')[13] The administrators in Rosenberg's ministry were outraged, some complaining that the phrase 'brisk trade in contraceptives' should not be associated with the Führer. But at least Rosenberg's ministry was not ordered to carry out these instructions. That fell to Koch, who was only too eager to add these racially inspired measures to his long and vindictive action plan against the Ukrainians.[14]

The story of the contraceptives is instructive not just because it shows how obsessive Hitler and Bormann could be about such a matter of detail, but also because it demonstrates the power of Hitler's underlying racist belief. From his perspective, part of the reason for Operation Barbarossa was, indeed, to stop the Slavs 'breeding like vermin'.

For Aleksey Bris the tension inside him caused by the way the Germans were treating the Ukrainians – beatings and hangings in his local town were commonplace – finally burst out in dramatic fashion on 12 September 1942. It was a bright autumn day, and Bris was standing idly in a street near the centre of Horokhiv, watching as townspeople queued to buy the belongings of Jews whom the Germans had killed – pots and pans and other kitchenware. But it wasn't this fact that prompted Bris to action. (When pressed on why he seemed so relaxed about both the Germans and the Ukrainian townspeople profiting from the murder of the local Jews, he replied: 'I don't think they thought much about *what* they were buying – they just thought about the chance of buying *anything*.') One of the locals tried to jump the queue and was beaten with a cane by one of the German soldiers supervising the sale. Something snapped inside Bris as he saw this fellow Ukrainian being whipped, and he grabbed the German policeman by the collar. 'How could you allow him to hit this person?' Bris shouted to members of the German administration who stood nearby.

The Germans stared in shock. Who was this 'inferior' who had dared lay his hand upon a member of the master race? Then a member of the German administration recovered himself and screamed '*Raus*!' ('Get out!') at Bris, who stayed still – he didn't know what to do. The German shouted again and then hit Bris with his own cane. And that was the moment Bris's life changed. He fought back. 'I had this kind of chivalrous knight idea…I felt on the edge of mental collapse…at that moment I wasn't afraid of the Germans. When you are hit like that, the emotions come first and you don't think about the consequences.' Bris darted forward, grabbed the cane from the German and pushed him over. Then he kicked him on the head. Another member of the German administration standing nearby made a grab for his pistol. As he fumbled to undo the straps on his holster, Bris started to run.

Meleti Semenyuk was among the townspeople who witnessed Bris's actions that day: 'I felt that he was a hero, especially because I knew that he used to work for the Germans.' As he watched the German policeman beat the queue-jumper, Semenyuk too was ready to react against them. 'I hated all of them. But Bris was the first man to act.'

The Germans mounted a massive search for Bris. They went straight to the house where he lived with his relatives and beat them severely before taking them to a concentration camp. They posted leaflets around the town offering a reward of 10,000 Reichsmarks for his capture. But Bris had escaped to the forest. Having once worked for the Germans, he was now determined to fight against them.

Bris's own personal history mirrors the experience of thousands of other disillusioned Ukrainians, though few began their resistance to the Germans in such a dramatic way. And since this link between the cruelty of the German civilian administration and the creation of a resistance movement seems clear, the result has been that men like Koch – as the physical embodiment of Hitler's sentiments – have become convenient scapegoats. Artillery officer Rüdiger von Reichert noticed that the 'friendly attitude' of the local population changed only 'when the effects of the civilian administration, which followed after the military administration, were felt. Naturally word got round very rapidly that in general they would behave as members of a master race and treat everyone like slaves and exploit them.' Former Panzer officer Walter Schaefer-Kehnert agrees: 'We came for them as a kind of liberator,' he says, 'liberating them from the Bolshevistic community system. My personal opinion is that the Nazis were too stupid to exploit that. You see, we could really have come as liberators but their [the Nazis'] idea that they were second-class human beings was ridiculous…The Russians and the Ukrainians, they were people like we were ourselves, with a great feeling for human dignity.'

Many other German soldiers expressed a similar view, claiming that the maltreatment of the civilian population in the occupied territories was the responsibility of Nazi administrators such as Koch. As a result, they exonerated the German Army from blame. But that's not what actually happened – for not all of the Ukraine was in the hands of Koch. Whilst the majority of it was in his Reichskomissariat, Galicia and Volhynia in the west were incorporated into the General Government under his fellow Nazi administrator Hans Frank, and the territory nearest the front line, including the eastern Ukrainian city of Kharkov, came under the jurisdiction of the German military authorities. And that city's population suffered more under the German military administration than Bris's home town of Horokhiv did under Koch's rule.

The military rulers of Kharkov were responsible, in the winter of 1942–3, for a famine in which thousands died (the precise number who died in the German occupation of Kharkov will probably never be known – one estimate is about 100,000). Whilst the Army requisitioned huge quantities of food for themselves, the vast majority of the population received nothing to eat at all from the Germans. The soldiers watched as the weakest members of the population – most often women, children and the elderly – simply starved to death.

'They didn't pay much attention to people dying,' says Inna Gavrilchenko, talking of the attitude of the German military administrators. 'They took it easy. I don't think they were shocked.' Inna, a teenaged girl during the occupation, witnessed how the townspeople tried to survive: 'First they killed dogs and ate them. But the dogs didn't last long. So they ate rats, pigeons, crows.' When the animals ran out, the most desperate started to eat human flesh. 'There were some people who excavated fresh graves to get the bodies. And they boiled them and cooked them in all possible ways. They made meat jelly out of bones and ate some cakes with human flesh.'

The German military administration didn't just give the non-working inhabitants nothing to eat, they also sealed Kharkov as a security measure, preventing the townspeople from being able to barter for food with the local farmers. As a result, Inna's beloved father died of starvation in front of her. Almost delirious with hunger herself, she sat talking to his body for eight days in their flat before a neighbour came and helped prepare the body for burial: 'For a very long time I had a fear that they buried him alive. Sometimes [sitting with her father when he was dead] I heard sighs. Maybe it was just gases in his body as a result of decay...I don't know.'

Inna believed she too was going to die of starvation. But she was lucky. A neighbour who worked in a German canteen used to take the water in which she had washed the Germans' dirty dishes, boil it up and make her drink it – there were occasional remnants of food floating in it. Inna also worked for a short time as an errand-girl in a German meat factory in the town. Sometimes the Germans who worked there would give her a scrap of bone or a bottle of blood: 'With blood,' she says, 'you can make an omelette...just like you make scrambled eggs, but without the eggs.'

When a blood omelette wasn't possible, she ate what she could find in the nearby woods within the city limits: 'Have you ever tried the bark of a birch tree?...It is sweetish. And you can try the leaves and young twigs of jasmine. There are a lot of edible things that you hate to think of today.'

Heartbreaking as Inna Gavrilchenko's story is, there are even worse examples of the suffering the German Army brought to Kharkov – and many of them relate to the maltreatment of children. Anatoly Reva was only six years old when the Germans arrived. His torment began when some prisoners of war were temporarily held behind his family house. Anatoly's father, seeing their suffering, threw food over the fence to them. The Germans shouted at him to stop, but he didn't hear, so they shot him dead. As a result of the shock, the little boy's mother lost her sight and was taken for treatment to a hospital that Anatoly could not find. So in March 1942, without any relations to care for him, he found himself alone.

He began to beg in the streets. But since as a child he was what the Germans called an *unnützer Esser* (useless eater), his prospects were bleak. Then his fortune seemed to change. One day he was befriended by a woman who took him to an orphanage in Kharkov. He slept that night on a bed of hay and the next morning awoke and waited for some breakfast – but the orphanage had no food that day or the next. The children were fed on scraps just twice a week. So, to survive, they had to run into the forest and scavenge. 'I was so hungry that I was eating nuts,' says Reva, 'and these nuts were poisonous, but I had to eat them because my stomach required some kind of food. Other children ate grass or leaves.'

Children in the orphanage regularly died of hunger, most often at night. But starvation was not the only cause of death in that institution. From time to time German soldiers came, looking for anyone who was circumcised, anyone who was Jewish. Once, Anatoly watched as a Jewish boy was discovered and taken away to be shot.

The selection of these Jewish children would almost certainly have been done by the SS or other security forces. But for the most part the town was home to 'ordinary' soldiers of the German Army. Once, Anatoly approached a group of these men and, his desperation overcoming his fear, begged for some food. One of them said, 'Hold on a minute' and reappeared moments later with a 'bag full of excrement'. 'They didn't have any kind of human feelings,' says Anatoly. 'They didn't feel sorry for children.'

It was administrators from the German Army, not Nazis like Koch, who presided over this nightmare world and orchestrated the famine. But the guilt and responsibility of the German Army for the savage way in which civilians were treated during the war in the East does not stop there. Academic researchers, studying the detailed records of individual Wehrmacht units in the East, have shown in recent years that, especially in the rear areas, the committing of atrocities against the civilian population was widespread. And the evidence against the Wehrmacht is not contained just in documents – it comes from the testimony of surviving German soldiers themselves.

Walter Schaefer-Kehnert's Panzer group participated in the burning down of Soviet villages as part of the German scorched earth policy in the wake of their repositioning after the Battle of Moscow: 'You see, the soldiers disliked it utterly. They said better to have a real battle than to burn the houses of the civilian population, so we were very reluctant to do so.' When asked what happened to the people whose houses he burnt, he said: 'Well, they had to look somewhere else, going to the next village or wherever they could.' But surely the next village might have been burnt as well? 'Sure,' he replied, 'but you were busy enough looking after yourself....'

Wolfgang Horn of the 10th Panzer Division personally ordered the burning down of a Russian village in a reprisal action. Crucial to his ability to deny women and children shelter was his overall belief about the sort of people he was fighting. 'One divided Europe into three areas,' he says, 'Europe A, B and C. So Russia was Europe C – the lowest standard of all. England or Germany or France were Europe A and Poland maybe Europe B.' He didn't think the Russians were 'as civilized as we are...They were not accustomed to normal behaviour, like coming in on time and doing one's work efficiently, as we were in Germany.' All this meant that to burn down a Russian village was of no great consequence to him. 'Burning down a civilized house' would have been very different. As he saw it, a Russian house was primitive and not of much value.

Adolf Buchner served in an SS unit on the Eastern Front, near Leningrad, and he too witnessed the consequences of Hitler's desire to fight a war of annihilation. Under the guise of suspecting particular villages of sheltering 'partisans', Buchner's unit would set fire to wooden houses with flame-throwers and then shoot anyone who emerged. 'These were defenceless people and perhaps they could have been gathered together and brought to a camp and given a chance to survive, but this was sheer brutality, totally stubborn. Anything that moved – bang! There were children among them too. There were no scruples, everybody was a target.' Adolf Buchner denies shooting women and children himself, but he does admit shooting at the men who emerged from the burning houses. 'What can you do?...It feels like being hypnotized, you cannot really describe it.' The brutality of the German soldiers even extended to shooting stray children. 'The child has to be fed, so they'd sooner simply get rid of it.

Put it in a ditch and the matter was over and done with.' Once, when a school was being stormed, Buchner said to his comrades, 'Don't you feel sorry for the children?' 'Why?' came the reply. 'A child might also be holding a weapon.'

Still troubling Adolf Buchner today is the knowledge that some of his German comrades enjoyed the killing: 'Was there any need, for example, to shoot the children in front of the women and then shoot the women after that? That happened too. That is sadism. There were officers like that, they liked sadistic things, they liked it when the mothers were screaming or children were screaming – they were really hot for that. In my view these people are not human...to see a child crying "Mummy" or "Daddy"...a human being capable of thought who is capable of doing such things, I cannot get it into my head that such things exist, but they do.'

Adolf Buchner is clear about the extent of German participation in the atrocities in the east. 'Virtually all units were involved...It did not matter whether it was Wehrmacht or SS, both of them.'

The last of these witnesses who bear testimony to atrocities committed by the German Army is Albert Schneider, who was a mechanic in the 201st Assault Gun Battalion. He told us how, as his unit passed through a Russian village, a comrade of his stole a pig from one of the peasants. The owner of the pig objected and started to wail in protest. So his comrade drew his pistol and shot him. 'I was unable to say anything about it,' says Schneider. 'Perhaps I was too much of a coward. I'm not all that brave.'

Not only did Schneider witness the aftermath of atrocities committed by individual Wehrmacht soldiers (on top of a heap of corpses in one village he saw the body of a woman with a German bayonet thrust into her vagina), but his unit, under instructions from its commander, systematically perpetrated a war crime. Staying overnight in a remote Russian village, his unit garaged some of their vehicles in a barn. During the night one of the engines blew up. Next morning, the officer commanding his unit ordered all the men from the village – some as young as 12 – to be gathered together. Then they were told to run away from the German soldiers, and as they scattered they were shot in the back. This all took place 'without any investigation at all as to what had actually happened', says Schneider. 'Why, it might have been that the engines overheated because they were Maybach engines which tend to overheat very quickly.' The officer who ordered this terrible reprisal should not be thought of today as unique. At the time he would have felt his actions were justified by the special powers, for use only in the East, given to him by the German Army (see page 159). (General Halder had asked for a provision to be inserted in the infamous Barbarossa Directive of May 1941 that allowed a commanding officer to order the burning of villages and the killing of some of the inhabitants if he believed they were supporting Soviet partisans.)[15]

Having witnessed theft and mass murder, Albert Schneider also admits that rape was commonplace. Many Wehrmacht soldiers still say today that sexual molestation of the local women was out of the question – not least because these women were, the German soldiers were repeatedly told, members of an 'inferior' race and such an action would have been judged a 'race crime' and severely punished. But that was not Schneider's experience. He saw one of his comrades take a Russian woman into a barn and heard the woman scream as she was raped. After it was over his comrade boasted, 'Well, I showed that one!'

'But that was not an isolated incident,' says Schneider. 'There were several cases in this village in particular when women were actually raped...it was well known throughout the ranks that things like this were going on. And nobody said a word about it....I once asked a sergeant why nothing was being done about it. And he said: "Because half the army would have to face trial!" In my opinion that says it all.'

The mass of the civilian population of the occupied areas could therefore be violated and oppressed by any combination of German agencies – the Army, the SS, the Einsatzgruppen (see Chapter Eight) and the civilian administration under fanatical racists like Koch. All of them are responsible both for the escalation of the suffering of the civilian population and for helping to create greater resistance to the German occupation.

On the Soviet side, Stalin had called for a partisan movement to rise and fight against the Germans as early in the war as 3 July 1941. In a speech made that day he announced: 'Conditions must be made unbearable for the enemy and his collaborators – they must be pursued and annihilated wherever they are.'

Hitler's response to Stalin's call is instructive. 'This partisan war in turn has its advantages,' Hitler said. 'It gives us a chance to eliminate anyone who turns against us.'[16] This meant, of course, that the suffering of the occupied population could only increase. Since neither Hitler nor Stalin was held in check by moral considerations, neither were the forces they controlled – such as the Soviet partisans or the German forces who tried to track them down. In most guerrilla wars, such as that in Vietnam, one side (in that case the Americans) is trying to preserve the status quo. In this partisan war neither side wanted to keep the status quo – the Germans wanted to reorder the occupied areas to create their new, racially inspired empire, and the Soviet partisans wanted not just to disrupt the Germans but to impose their will on the local population as well. Part of the role of these partisans was to root out 'collaborators' and remind the indigenous population that Stalinist terror could still operate even in German-occupied territory.

The partisan movement didn't develop systematically.[17] The first phase, from the outbreak of the war until the spring of 1942, was characterized by failure. Despite Stalin's rhetoric, the Soviet Union was not prepared to fight a guerrilla war. The concept of 'defence through attack' – the idea that any future war should be carried out on the enemy's soil – had, in theory, rendered partisan warfare unnecessary. And Stalin's natural suspiciousness meant that he was innately ill-disposed to the idea of armed bands operating behind enemy lines far from the control of Moscow. That, plus the belief in many quarters in the early months of the war that the Germans would win, combined with the hopes of those, like Aleksey Bris, that the Germans would prove sympathetic conquerors, meant initially that Soviet partisans were isolated. The massive German anti-partisan actions of early 1942, such as Operation Hanover, marked the partisans' lowest ebb. But with Stalin's growing support, and motivated by the belief that Germany might conceivably be defeated, the movement began to grow in effectiveness. The actual number of Soviet partisans engaged in the fight against the Germans is notoriously difficult to estimate.[18] One of the latest calculations is that at the end of 1941 there were 2000 partisan detachments giving a total of 72,000 partisans, and that by the summer of 1944 around 500,000 partisans were fighting the Germans. (Communication with Moscow was spasmodic – for much of the war 90 per cent of the partisans had no radio contact with their own side.)

Mikhail Timoshenko was one of Stalin's Soviet partisans – a member of an NKVD special unit. He conducted the fight against the Germans and the 'traitors' in the occupied civilian population with a ruthlessness that the Soviet leader would have approved of. As a general rule he ordered any German prisoners whom his unit captured to be shot. 'What could we do with them?' says Timoshenko. 'Release them so they could kill us again?' He would ask for volunteers from amongst his men to do the actual shooting, and there was never a shortage of willing killers. 'You know they considered them as enemies they had to destroy,' says Timoshenko. 'Understand that these people had had their houses burnt down – with their parents still inside them. These men were vengeful.'[19]

Living behind the lines, mundane considerations, such as where to get enough food, became a major problem. The partisans occasionally had parachute drops of supplies, but for the most part they lived off the land – or off the Germans. Timoshenko always snatched the packs of the Germans he had shot 'because in them, especially those belonging to the divisions that had come from Europe, there was rum and chocolate. There were salami tins! They were stuffed with food and we needed to be fed.'

When there were no Germans to ambush, the partisans took food from the local villagers. And that could be a major cause of conflict. Ivan Treskovski was a teenager living with his family in a ramshackle farmhouse on the edge of the village of Usyazha deep in the Belorussian countryside. He remembers how he cowered upstairs and listened when the Soviet partisans came to pay a call on his father: 'They'd be drunk, drunk!' he says. 'They'd take our fat, our chickens and our clothing. They'd take it to another village and sell it or change it for vodka – that's what they did.' On one occasion in the winter of 1942 he heard the partisans shout at his father, 'Give us some bacon fat or we'll kill you!' For the locals in this region life became a daily round of terror. In the daytime there was always the fear that the Germans would come, and during the night they were at risk from the partisans.

Whilst German lines of communication did risk disruption at their hands, the greatest impact the partisans had was on the lives of the occupied population. Stalin himself authorized his partisans to kill any locals who were helping the

Germans. Mikhail Timoshenko admits that he and his band of partisans killed those who they thought had collaborated.[20] Indeed, so strong was his reputation for shooting 'traitors' that one of the German propaganda newspapers printed a caricature of him. Underneath there was the caption: 'This is the leader of the partisan movement who destroys everything he gets his hands on: he steals cows and robs collective farms.' Timoshenko remembers that his hands were shown 'covered in blood'. He felt this attack was 'unfair': 'They'd written that I killed local traitors. Well, there were instances when we did kill traitors. We killed any of the population who helped the Germans. But they said that I shot people who wouldn't give me their cattle. That's nonsense, of course.'

These partisan groups made their own laws, and Timoshenko admits that part of his job was, as Stalin would have wished, to deal with those 'who had lost the conviction that Soviet power would be victorious'. If he suspected a particular villager was a 'traitor', he would send two men to his house at night to snatch him. They would interrogate him and then, as was most likely, believing him to be an informer, they would shoot him. 'There were no courts,' says Timoshenko. 'There was no power other than my own…. It was essentially a terror, but a terror against dishonourable people.'

The potential for abuse in such a system is, of course, enormous. Ivan Treskovski recalls that there were villagers who might, out of spite, tell the partisans that someone had links with the Germans – and then the one who was denounced was murdered. As he puts it: 'Whoever had the gun was the master and did whatever he wanted.'

Eastern Belorussia, with its thick forest close to isolated villages, was ideal country for partisan activities, and teenager Nadezhda Nefyodova and her family discovered personally how they could bring their murderous vengeance down on anyone they chose. One night in November 1942 the local partisans came to the tiny village of Prilepy, just out-side Minsk, and murdered her sister and her husband. There was no explanation – the partisans didn't need to justify their murder. The deaths led to speculation that perhaps one of them had been seen talking to the Germans. Then, since other people were also killed that night, a theory grew that the whole village had in some way offended the partisan leader. In a civilized society someone is accused, convicted and pun-ished. In this shadowy world of suspicion and revenge, vil-lagers were first murdered and then speculation grew about what crime they might conceivably have committed.

Nadezhda Nefyodova's family took in and hid the mur-dered couple's two small children, who were little more than babies and had been cowering underneath the bed while their parents were murdered. But the local partisans seemed to want to kill the children as well, because now they pur-sued the whole of Nadezhda's family. During the day it was safe for them to stay at their house, but at night, when the partisans might come, the family scattered. Her father slept concealed in hay at the other side of the village, whilst Nadezhda, her mother and the two little children all went to other relatives in nearby villages. The next day they would reassemble and begin work in the fields around their home, trying to grow enough food to survive.

The local partisans were led by Petr Sankovich, a commit-ted Communist who had been the chief vet for the area before the war. His most faithful lieutenant was Efim Goncharov, the local headmaster and a member of the district party committee. The lawless atmosphere of the time is captured in this official report from another Belorussian partisan, Vladimir Lashuk, dated May 1942: 'I served with Goncharov, and we completed a whole series of attacks on the Fascist occupiers, turncoats, traitors and other German supporters.'[21] And, of course, they themselves decided who was a 'turncoat' or a 'traitor'.

But Nadezhda Nefyodova and her family didn't suffer only at the hands of the Soviet partisans. In March 1943, a drunken Soviet partisan shot at a German plane from just outside Usyazha, Nadezhda's village. Reprisals followed. The next day Stukhas dive-bombed the village, and then the German-controlled police arrived. Most of the villagers hid in the nearby woods as soon as the bombing started, but Nadezhda's brother Siyonas stayed behind. Bravely, he climbed on to the wooden roof of their house and tried to put out the fire caused by the incendiaries. He managed to save the house but it cost him his life because he was still in the village when the German police arrived. They set fire to the barn in which he took refuge and then, as he emerged, shot him. Twenty-seven out of twenty-eight houses in the village were destroyed in the German reprisal attack and twenty-nine villagers died.

'Do you know how hard it was to live in the middle of all those garrisons?' Nadezhda asks. 'Germans during the day, and at night those bandits would arrive. You had to be afraid of all of them because none of them came with good intentions. And if you protested, what did it mean to them to kill you? You were a mere fly! You were living all the time – from morning till evening and evening till morning – in such tension... You didn't know what tomorrow would bring, so you just lived for that day...just for that hour.' Surprisingly, given the Western perception of Hitler's war in the East, she concluded by voicing her view that as far as she was concerned it had been the Soviet partisans – not the Germans – who had been the more 'terrifying' enemy: 'Of course the partisans were crueller – they came at night and to their own kind.'

Petr Sankovich, the local partisan leader, was killed in an ambush with German forces in February 1944, but Efim Goncharov survived the war, was awarded a medal and became chairman of the district committee. Whilst there are still calls for the prosecution of remaining German war criminals, it is worth remembering the criminals on the Soviet side who prospered long after the war and were never punished. 'If my sister and her husband had lived, then all our lives would have been different,' says Nadezhda today. 'There remains an aftertaste of spite in my heart.'

Nadezhda Nefyodova and her family in Belorussia lived between the Germans and the partisans and suffered cruelty at the hands of each. But in nearby German-occupied Ukraine there were those who were caught in an even tighter trap. For here there was a third force, the Ukrainian Nationalist partisans, committed to fighting both the Germans *and* the Soviet partisans.

Meleti Semenyuk fought with the Ukrainian Nationalists (the Ukrainska Povstanska Armiia or UPA). The disillusionment caused by the harsh German rule offered an opportunity to fight for an independent Ukraine. To the Soviet partisans, and to Stalin, they were as much an enemy as the Germans. 'The aim of the Red partisans was to eliminate our movement so that they could come back to a clean area,' says Semenyuk. 'And those partisans – like animals – I cannot describe them.' Stories of atrocities committed by the Soviet partisans (often long after the war with the Germans was over, as Stalin ordered the Ukraine to be 'cleansed') are commonplace in the Ukraine. A secret Soviet Interior Ministry report acknowledges that the Soviet forces committed 'anarchic and oppressive actions against local citizens'. In one example of such an action, the report describes how an undercover Soviet group that had infiltrated the UPA 'brutally tortured a sixty-two-year-old man and his two daughters'.[22]

After escaping from his village, Aleksey Bris joined the UPA. He remembers the cruelty of the conflict with the Soviet partisans: 'The Germans just killed us, but with the Red partisans the bestialities were different. Some of them were cutting the ears off our members. In rare cases they have this Asian way of torturing people – cutting your ears and tongue off. I don't know if they did this to people who were still alive, but these events happened quite often. It's sadism which exists in every system. The Germans just hanged people, but I never saw anything like tortured bodies. But, of course, we were quite cruel...we didn't take any prisoners of war and they didn't take any prisoners either, so we killed each other. That was natural.'

The secretive and arbitrary way in which the partisans most often conducted their fight, together with the fact that the majority of atrocities against the local population were never reported for fear of further reprisal, means that it will never be possible to quantify accurately the precise numbers of crimes the partisans committed. Nor is it easy to assess the damage these partisan movements actually inflicted on their German occupiers, for their impact was as much psychological as physical. Mere figures for the number of Germans killed by partisans during the war (one estimate is about 50,000) underestimate the effect of their presence on the German infrastructure. This plaintive letter from a Herr Schenk, who ran a mining and steel company in eastern Ukraine, gives some sense of how the Germans could be affected in practical terms by the virtual civil war that erupted during their occupation. He writes, in April 1943, that around him are '1. Partisans, who are nothing but Bolsheviks...' and '2. There is a large number of national Ukrainian partisans who are also located in these forests...' He sums up the situation between these two groups succinctly, for as well as attacking him, 'Groups 1 and 2 are also fighting against each other.' In addition, 'There are so-called bandits...who are disrupting the main-line traffic.' In this morass 'travelling by car is today extremely dangerous'. One local police officer remarked to Schenk as he began a journey,

'If you're lucky, you'll make it through.' Schenk concludes his letter by writing: 'The economic situation is suffering greatly under these conditions to the point that there is no German administration left at all in many regions.'[23]

Hitler's solution to these problems was simple: more brutality, more killings, more oppression. This view was shared by the Wehrmacht Commander-in-Chief in the Ukraine, who reported as early as December 1941 that 'The fight against the partisans succeeds only if the population realizes that the partisans and their sympathizers sooner or later are killed… Death by strangulation inspires fear more particularly…only measures that can frighten the population more than the terror of partisans can lead to success. The Army Group recommends resort to such measures as needed.'[24]

But, as with most Nazi policies that involved individual discretion, the anti-partisan policy was anything but consistent. Local commanders were free to a large extent to determine their own actions – some even did deals with the partisans in their area. Führer Directive No. 46 of August 1942 attempted to clarify the way the German forces should deal with the partisan problem. But it served only to muddy the waters still further. On the one hand it recognized that the cooperation of the local population was important in the fight against the partisans, but it also warned against confidence in the local population being 'misplaced'. This one directive shows in microcosm the inability of Hitler and the Nazi hardliners to accept the idea that the population they were dealing with were proper human beings. They knew they needed the locals to help against the partisans, but they also knew that a necessary precondition of gaining their help was to treat them decently – something that went against their basic ideological beliefs.

Yet it was clear by the end of the summer of 1942 that this policy of harsh repression was not getting the desired results. An alternative was suggested by Colonel Reinhard Gehlen, head of the German Army's Intelligence Agency for the East, who concluded in a report in November 1942: 'If the population rejects the partisans and lends its full support to the struggle against them, no partisan problem will exist.'[25] The resulting debate mirrored that between Koch and Rosenberg on the Ukrainian political question. This time it was a few army commanders, such as Gehlen, who argued for partnership with the local population against the partisans. Gehlen called for captured Soviet partisans to be treated as 'normal' prisoners of war – and in some cases this was done in Army Group Centre (who faced the Red Army east of Smolensk) in 1943. He also mounted propaganda leaflet campaigns against some partisan groups with varying results.

Unsurprisingly, Hitler did not share Gehlen's views. The Führer had concluded that 'only where the struggle against the partisan nuisance was begun and carried out with ruthless brutality have successes been achieved'. Just like the whole war on the Eastern Front, the struggle against the partisans was viewed by Hitler as 'a struggle of total annihilation of one side or the other'.[26] The natural consequence of this attitude was that, despite the best efforts of a few soldiers like Gehlen, the brutality escalated. If each side believes that the only way to fight fear is 'with more fear', as Vladimir Ogryzko put it in the context of the battle for Moscow, then the only limit on cruelty is the human imagination.

Some of the harshest German anti-partisan actions of all were launched in eastern Belorussia in the summer of 1943 – a few months after the 'invincible' German Sixth Army had been destroyed at Stalingrad and whilst the Red Army fought back the German summer advance at the Battle of Kursk. During this 'cleansing' in the countryside around Minsk, on 22 July, German units came to the tiny village of Maksimoky. They burst into the house of teenager Aleksandr

Mikhailovski and awoke both him and his deaf and dumb brother. On the dusty road outside, as dawn broke, the Germans assembled eight villagers, including Aleksandr and his brother. They tied their hands behind their backs and ordered them to walk down the road, with the Germans following about 50 metres behind.

Aleksandr knew what this meant, for the Germans had used this same technique in nearby villages. Partisans had planted mines on many of the roads in the area, and the Germans used the locals as human mine detectors. (This kind of sadism was not uncommon. Curt von Gottberg, the SS-Obergruppenführer who, during 1943, conducted another huge anti-partisan action called Operation Kottbus on the eastern border of Belorussia, reported that 'approximately two to three thousand local people were blown up in the clearing of the minefields'.)[27]

'Your heart turned to stone and you went to a living death,' says Mikhailovski of his treatment at German hands. 'The people went along just like they were already dead. They knew that only despair and tears awaited us.' Their dilemma as they walked along the road was a stark one. 'Whenever we felt there was something suspicious, we'd try to avoid it. But we knew that if we avoided a mine and it blew up a German behind us, then we'd die all the same because they'd shoot you.'

The Germans forced them along the dusty road for eight hours as they walked nearly 30 kilometres to the next village. The terror was constant: 'Our mouths were dry and because of our tears we couldn't see the road.' But they were lucky. On this stretch of road there were no mines. At the end of this ordeal they owed their lives to another piece of good fortune. The Germans were about to kill them, but the locals protested vehemently to the army commander that these were not 'bandits' but innocent villagers and their lives were spared.

An insight into the mentality of those German soldiers who had to grapple with the partisan problem is given by Peter von der Groeben, the Operations Officer of Army Group Centre and its most senior staff officer after the Commander-in-Chief. He acknowledges that the partisans 'were conducting a highly successful war against our reinforcement troops. On the railways, the roads, everywhere, blowing up the railway lines, destroying roads, attacking columns.' In addition he 'assumes' that, since his soldiers were angry when they saw German columns attacked and mutilated, then 'if they captured a partisan village, I am quite convinced that their behaviour wasn't very gentle. I assume they more or less killed everybody they came across there.'

Confirmation of this behaviour comes from Carlheinz Behnke, a soldier with the 4th SS-Police Panzergrenadier Division. His section came upon some 20 or so German soldiers from his own unit who had been left behind wounded, and who had since been murdered and mutilated by Soviet forces 'in the most bestial manner – their ears had been cut off, their eyes had been gouged out and their genitals had been cut off'. The commander of his detachment gave the order that any civilians still present in the area were to be shot as a reprisal, 'without any consideration being given to the women or even the children'. Behnke thought this order 'logical and correct', and he himself participated in the subsequent killing of civilians. A sleigh was crossing the ice about 400 metres away from him and he, along with his fellow soldiers, fired at it and saw the three occupants topple over. 'I don't know whether they were children, women...obviously you look at these things differently nowadays...but it was a moment which is impossible to describe and nobody who didn't witness it can understand it, I think.'

Behnke admits that his unit became incensed and vented their anger in indiscriminate murder. Only after 24 hours, their blood lust sated, did they regain some control. Their wild emotional state, which Behnke, in common with Peter von der Groeben, sees as some kind of justification for the subsequent committing of atrocities, is in fact the reverse – an example of how units of the German Army lost their discipline and permitted themselves to behave like crazed bandits.

We traced a revealing report read and initialled by Peter von der Groeben in his capacity as Operations Officer (Ia) of Army Group Centre about the German anti-partisan Operation Otto. It lists around 2000 'partisans' and their 'helpers' killed, but it details only 30 rifles and a handful of other weapons recovered from them. This extraordinary disparity, even today, does not surprise him. 'Look, the partisans must have had the necessary weapons – otherwise they could not have done anything to us,' he argues. And in response to the argument that this might be evidence that German troops were killing indiscriminately, he replies: 'I can't remember. As I said, the troops' fury was immense. Well, I would imagine that they also killed some innocent people. But who could tell who was innocent?' When pressed, he would only accept: 'Well, if the counter-actions themselves did go over the top, I think they were regarded as unpleasant but necessary counter-measures which were, of course, also meant to be a deterrent.'[29]

Similar discrepancies between the number of 'partisans' killed and the number of weapons recovered occurred in the SS statistics for their own anti-partisan operations. When Himmler was asked why this was happening he replied: 'You appear not to know that these bandits destroy their weapons to play the innocent and so avoid death.' Not surprisingly, these harsh measures did not eradicate the partisan problem. The German Army High Command conceded in 1943 that they had not been able to rid the occupied territories of these 'bandits'.

It is simplistic to state that the Nazis' racism was the only cause of the cruelty of the partisan war. Other factors clearly contributed to the escalation of the brutality, not least the vast area that the Germans had to control, the despair felt by many German soldiers that the war as a whole was not going in a way that favoured them, and the ruthless way in which Stalin's partisans could terrorize the locals and murder and mutilate captured German soldiers. But it is true to say that to stand a chance of eliminating the partisan threat, the Germans needed the cooperation of the indigenous population, and it was Nazi racist beliefs that made such assistance impossible.

It's easy to argue that this failure was simply another of Hitler's tactical mistakes. 'If only he had been more flexible,' the argument goes, 'and treated the inhabitants of the occupied territories with the basic respect due to all human beings, then the partisan war would not have escalated as it did.' But even to suggest this possibility is to misunderstand the nature of the whole war in the East. Hitler could never have moderated his policy towards the occupied territories. These racist beliefs were at the core of his being. They were almost how he defined himself. There were no circumstances in which Hitler would give up his vision of the new German Empire. Indeed, as the war progressed, far from doubting these central convictions, he became reconfirmed in his view that he was right. If the policy of treating the people of the East as 'sub-humans' was failing, then it was always the fault of other people around him – these 'vain, cowardly wretches' – who were not pursuing the policy of persecution with sufficient zeal.

Against the background of the growing partisan threat, Hitler set about trying, once more, to win the war on the battlefield. Now the Germans would advance south-east in a campaign that would be decided at a place then little known outside the Soviet Union – a city called Stalingrad.

7

THE TIDE TURNS

1942 WAS A YEAR OF TRANSFORMATION ON THE EASTERN FRONT.
At the start of it the Red Army was grappling with the
Germans at the gates of Moscow. By the end of it the mighty
German 6th Army was on its knees at Stalingrad.

It is easy, then, to characterize this as the year when the
Soviets made the Germans pay for the arrogance of the original Barbarossa plan; to see this 12-month period as the time
when a combination of the vast reserves of population from
that the Red Army could draw, military aid from Britain and
the USA, and the tanks and artillery from Soviet factories that
had been dismantled in the face of the German advance and
reconstructed far behind the front line, resulted in an
inevitable change of fortune for Stalin and the Soviet Union.
In short, it is easy to regard 1942 as the year when, day by
inexorable day, the inevitability of a Soviet victory became
obvious to the world.

But to judge that year in such a way would be a mistake.
Instead, what the history of 1942 demonstrates is that,
despite all the foreign help, all the manpower at their disposal, all the output of their factories, the Soviet Union could
still have lost the war against the Germans. Both Stalin and
the Red Army had to change the way they conducted the fight
– and in the process, they had to learn from the enemy.

The Red Army performed badly in the first months of 1942 after the Battle of Moscow, and Stalin was the man most responsible. On 5 January he announced to the Stavka (the Soviet High Command) a plan almost as overambitious and contemptuous of the enemy as Hitler's original Barbarossa plan had been. Instead of concentrating the resources of the Red Army on one point of attack, Stalin proposed that they should advance on *all* fronts. In the north they would push to relieve Leningrad, in front of Moscow they would attack Army Group Centre, and in the south they would confront the Germans in the Ukraine and the Crimea. In 1941 Stalin had demonstrated his military incompetence when it came to defence; now, at the start of 1942, he was showing his weakness as a commander in attack. Zhukov spotted the plan's flaws and said so. Nikolai Voznesensky, the economist, pointed out the grave logistical problems that would result from such an overarching campaign, but was ridiculed as a man who 'only ever mentioned problems'. Against such protests the Soviet offensive began.

Not surprisingly, the Red Army made little progress as it attempted simultaneously to take on the Germans on all fronts, but at least there were no disastrous defeats. However, all that was to change when Stalin ordered a new offensive in the south, around the Ukrainian city of Kharkov, to begin in May 1942. The General Staff view was that the Red Army should be much less ambitious and consolidate its position around Moscow. But Stalin wanted action. 'Don't let us sit down in defence,' he stated baldly as he endorsed Marshal Timoshenko's plan for a major campaign. (Timoshenko, the offensive's main proponent and a comrade of Stalin's from the civil war, had previously seen his army encircled in 1941 by the Germans at Smolensk.)

Boris Vitman was an officer in the Soviet 6th Army and took part in the ill-fated Kharkov offensive of May 1942. At headquarters he saw that 'those who were planning the operation were certain that it would be completed successfully and the mood was very cheerful...the idea was that by 1943 the war would be finished.' Vitman noticed that the offensive was ambitiously called 'The campaign for the complete and final liberation of the Ukraine against the Nazi invaders'.

Stalin believed that the Germans' major campaign that year would be mounted in front of Moscow, and the Kharkov plan was based on that assumption. By attacking in the south, the Red Army hoped to disrupt the German preparations further north and strike the enemy at their weakest point. Unfortunately for the Soviets, their assessment of the German intention was wrong. The Germans were indeed planning a major offensive – but not on the Moscow axis. Instead they intended to attack through the Ukraine towards the southeast of the Soviet Union. Thus the Red Army unwittingly attacked the Germans at the very place where they were preparing their own build-up. But even so, the Red Army still had superiority in numbers against the Germans for the forthcoming offensive – at least three Red Army soldiers to every two German ones, with the ratio even more favourable to the Soviets at the concentrated points of attack.

'On 12 May 1942, early in the morning, large numbers of artillery were lined up – so long that you couldn't see an end to them,' says Boris Vitman, who took part in the initial advance. 'The morning was misty, the sky was overcast, and this was good because it prevented German planes from seeing our divisions. All of a sudden you could hear a terrible noise. The earth was shaking. All the cannons opened fire simultaneously and this cannonade went on for more than an hour. Then when the cannonade stopped, the order came, "Go ahead!" and we advanced. Seeing such big power, such superiority, we were so inspired, we were going ahead thinking that victory was in our hands.'

Such optimism was misplaced. Anticipating an attack, the Germans had withdrawn and the mighty Soviet artillery barrage had been worthless. 'When we reached the German line, we saw that the defences were empty,' says Boris Vitman. 'There was not a single German dead body. There were only destroyed mock cannons. It was all a simulation of the German defence line, which in fact had been abandoned long ago. And we went on and on without meeting any resistance. We kept marching and marching. We did not give much thought to the fact that there were no Germans around. We thought we were marching towards Berlin.'

But, as Vitman and his men were about to discover, they had been lured into a German trap. 'On the outskirts of Kharkov all of a sudden our attack faced very strong resistance as the Germans had prepared a powerful defensive line. Our attack was choked.' And then their predicament grew worse. 'There was the rumour that, as we were advancing, the Germans struck on the flanks and crushed the two armies that were covering our advance, and that the Germans were almost about to encircle us.'

Nine days into the offensive, with the attack stalled, Vitman was ordered to report to the headquarters of the 6th Army about 6 kilometres from the front line, still within the threatened German encirclement: 'I saw there a lot of panic. They were packing headquarters documents in a great hurry.'

Almost immediately he arrived at headquarters Vitman was told to return to his regiment. On the road back to the front line he passed a convoy of Soviet soldiers going in the other direction. The officer in command told Vitman that his regiment had been cut off by the Germans and that he should join this unit, which was trying to break out. But as they retreated, they were caught in the open and shelled and bombed by the Germans. 'You could only hide in the old shell holes,' says Vitman. 'Actually I always preferred to lie not with my face down, but with my face up so I could see where the bombs were falling.... The earth was shaking. There was smoke going up, bits of bodies and uniforms flying into the air, and next to you there were bullets and splinters falling around. You don't think about anything. What can you think about? When I saw several bombs flying directly on me, I said to the soldier who was lying near me, "Let's run!" I managed to stand up and run away, but I was hit by the blast. Later, when I came back to see what had happened, all that was left of this other soldier was his bag and his gas mask.'

The Soviet troops became surrounded as the German flanks closed in on them. The panic intensified with each passing hour. Vitman watched as a commissar ripped the red star – the insignia that marked him as a political officer – from his sleeve and then, noticing there was a mark on his uniform showing where the star had been, began desperately rubbing mud over the fabric. When that failed he gave his tunic jacket away to a passing soldier and ran. Vitman saw another soldier throw down his rifle and say, 'For many years I was like a prisoner in a collective farm, and now it doesn't matter to me whether I live or not,' and then run to surrender.

Joachim Stempel fought on the German side at Kharkov. He remembers 'the astonished eyes of the Russians, who just couldn't believe what was going on here. They couldn't believe how much ground we had made up in the rearguard of their advance troops.' He describes the nights of the battle as 'unforgettable': 'The sight of thousands of Russians, who were trying to escape – a heaving mass of them – trying to reach freedom, shooting at us and being shot back at. Then, with a lot of shouting, trying to find gaps through which they could escape, and then being repulsed by the hail of bullets from our artillery and our guns...The most horrifying pictures and impressions were the ones immediately after the attempted break-outs; awful, horrible wounds and many, many dead. I saw people with entire lower jaws just torn away, people with head wounds who were barely conscious but still driven on…I had the impression that, at that point, it was every man for himself trying to find a way to get out of the cauldron.'

All around him Boris Vitman heard the moaning of the Soviet wounded, but no one was paying any attention to them. Nearby, in a dugout, the Red Army doctors and nurses lay completely drunk. 'I pointed my gun at them,' says Vitman, 'and said, "Come out and do something!" But they had got drunk because they could see that they wouldn't be able to help so many wounded.'

Vitman watched with horror as the Germans continued fighting. 'I thought they were real butchers because they were still firing when there were so many dead. And I realized that they couldn't take so many people prisoner, so they were trying to destroy as many of us as possible. German tanks began to approach, as well as armoured vehicles. At that moment our captain turned up. His head was bandaged and had blood on it. He shouted: "Attack!" About 20 people rose up, and I was one of them, even though my machine gun had no ammunition. We followed him, simply to die. Our group came under fire. People were falling down next to me and I kept thinking, well, when will my turn come? Then I saw an explosion, the earth went up, I lost consciousness for a moment, but quickly recovered and knew I was wounded in the leg.' Vitman looked up and saw a German armoured car about 20 metres away from him. Two soldiers with machine guns got down from the vehicle and walked towards him. 'Russ, komm, komm,' they shouted. 'I found it difficult to stand because of my wound,' says Vitman. 'One ran towards me, whilst the other aimed his machine gun at my head. When they saw I really couldn't stand up they pulled me to my feet and threw me into the back of an open truck.'

Vitman was driven to a collection point for the wounded. The able-bodied were imprisoned nearby behind barbed wire and guarded by SS soldiers. He heard an announcement over a loudspeaker: 'Jews and commissars come forward!' The commissars were taken away, leaving about ten Jews behind. 'The Jews were given spades and told to dig a trench. It began to rain. After a while I could only see the tops of their heads. An SS man was hitting them to make them dig faster. When the trench was deep enough, he picked up a Russian machine gun and fired, shooting several salvos into the trench. We could hear them moaning. Then some more SS men turned up and finished them off. They were killed only because they were Jews. This had a shocking effect on me because then I saw what Nazism was. We were told that the Jews and commissars cannot have control over us any more, that the Germans had come to liberate us and soon we're going home. But I only knew I had to fight the Germans to the very end.'

Even though Boris Vitman had escaped immediate murder, since he was neither a commissar nor a Jew, he was still in great danger. A German doctor arrived and began a selection of the wounded – those still 'useful' to the Germans would be allowed to live for the moment, the rest left to die. Next to Vitman was a Soviet soldier who had been shot in the stomach. Knowing the importance of looking as though he had only a minor wound, he was trying to shove his intestines back inside his body. 'He looked so much at a loss,' says Vitman, 'and his eyes were asking: what shall I do with all this?'

Vitman himself was saved because he had learnt German at school and was able to act as a translator for the doctor. 'I noticed later that if a Russian could speak German then their attitude was quite different. When the man couldn't speak a foreign language the Germans thought it indicated that he was from an inferior race. But when they heard me speak German, they brought us water and didn't shoot us down.' Vitman was able to understand the conversations the Germans had amongst themselves, most notably when two senior SS men arrived in a headquarters car and stood nearby, looking at the mass of prisoners. 'I could hear one of them saying, "It's a shame Marshal Timoshenko is not present to see all this. The Führer has reserved a medal for him – the iron cross with oak leaves – to thank him for making such a big contribution to the German victory."'

Timoshenko had indeed made a large contribution to the German victory. Despite superiority in numbers, his attack had been crushed. By 28 May 1942 he had lost over a quarter of a million troops. The two Soviet armies caught around Barvenkovo (in what became known as the Barvenkovo 'mousetrap') were almost completely destroyed. 'It was a real disaster, a big disaster,' says Makhmud Gareev, a Red Army officer during the war who went on to the highest reaches of Soviet command in the post-war era. 'The failures of 1941 could be put down to the unexpected nature of the invasion and our unpreparedness, but in 1942, after we had carried out some defensive operations and after the front line had sta-bilized, all of a sudden such a major defeat.' And it was clear to soldiers like Gareev what one of the key reasons for this failure had been: 'It is linked to what happened in 1941 – to Stalin's incompetence, his lack of understanding of a strategic situation and his unwillingness to listen to others.'

'We [the German soldiers] were proud that we had managed to succeed so quickly,' says Joachim Stempel. 'I have to say that we all shared in the belief and the feeling that what we're doing will work. There's nothing we can't do, even if it's difficult and we're ill-equipped. We still believed and had faith that the leadership would provide, and then we'd make up the rest. And again, after the Kharkov cauldron [encirclement] where, once again, we were able to leave the battlefield victoriously, we were in high spirits and looked forward to what lay ahead.'

The German victory that soldiers like Stempel hoped for was not an impossibility in 1942. The Germans already held the agricultural heartland of the Soviet Union – the Ukraine – as well as the Donbas (Don River Basin) region, which had been the Soviets' main centre for coal and steel. With Stalin demonstrating at Kharkov that he appeared to have learnt nothing from the military disasters of the previous year, eventual Soviet defeat looked conceivable.

Hitler capitalized on the Soviet defeat at Kharkov with his own ambitious Operation Blue – the plan to advance in the south towards Stalingrad, the mountains of the Caucasus and down to the Caspian Sea. This would deprive the Soviet war machine of access to its supply of oil and, Hitler believed, deal it a crushing economic blow from which it would not recover. The campaign's aim, he stated, was 'finally to annihilate what vital defensive strength the Soviets have left and to remove from their grasp as far as possible the principal sources of energy for their war economy'. A glance at the map shows how grandiose Operation Blue actually was – yet if Stalin had carried on leading the Red Army in such a foolhardy way, the German campaign could well have succeeded.

On 28 June 1942 the Germans attacked along virtually the whole southern front, with the 4th Panzer Army pushing on to Voronezh and the 1st Panzer Army advancing out from south of Kharkov. The Blitzkrieg moved swiftly, attempting as before to encircle whole Soviet armies, and initially as the Red Army fell back, the signs were that this might be a repeat of 1941. 'The main reason [for the German success] was that after we suffered defeat near Kharkov, a big gap appeared,' says Makhmud Gareev. 'The stability of the front had broken down. We didn't have any ready reserves. They had been used up for the offensives in different directions. Reserves had to be transferred from the Moscow direction, from the Leningrad direction, but the trouble was that these reserves were sent into combat immediately. Sending every new division into combat without proper preparation led to a worse and worse situation.'

At the end of July, after his troops had pushed on towards the River Don, Hitler decided to split his forces in two. Whilst Army Group A turned south to the oilfields of the Caucasus, the other spearhead, Army Group B, continued towards Stalingrad on the Volga. By this action Hitler demonstrated not just his impatience to accomplish several military objectives simultaneously but his own contempt once again for the Red Army.

Stalin watched the progress of Operation Blue and reacted with fury. He had preferred to believe that the German attack in the south was a mere diversionary thrust preparatory to the main attack on Moscow; now he searched for scapegoats amongst his intelligence officers. Then, as the Soviet forces fell further back, he issued his infamous order 227 – 'Not a step back' – which, amongst other harsh measures, confirmed the power of the 'backmarker' divisions to shoot any Soviet troops who tried to retreat without authorization, and formally introduced penal battalions to punish cowardice. Once again, at a moment of crisis, he believed the Red Army was best motivated by fear of terrible retribution if it failed.

The brutality of Soviet discipline – particularly the personal experience of those who survived the penal battalions (*shtrafbaty*) – is an aspect of the war that the Communist Party historians preferred not to publicize. Only since the fall of Communism have men such as Vladimir Kantovski, who was sent to a penal battalion in 1942, felt free to tell their extraordinary true story.

Kantovski's troubles began in the spring of 1941 when, as an eighteen-year-old student in Moscow, he learnt that one of his teachers had been arrested. (Only recently has he been allowed access to the secret NKVD file that shows, ironically, that his teacher was imprisoned because he had been overheard voicing the view, just before the German invasion, that 'the Hitler/Stalin pact was dangerous for the safety of the Soviet Union'.) So angry were Vladimir and his school-friends at their teacher's arrest that they typed out a leaflet of protest and circulated it around the neighbourhood. They were all committed Communists and felt that the purity of their ideals had been sullied by this arbitrary oppression. 'We had our own understanding of Communism,' says Kantovski, 'and this honesty demanded that we act...We didn't take Stalin and his henchmen seriously. But at the same time we remained patriots and in essence Communists. Although not Communists in the way Stalin understood it.'

Shortly after the war had begun, the NKVD came to Kantovski's flat and arrested him. By July he had been transferred to Omsk prison, east of Moscow, where he stayed for several months. 'You can write novels or poems about Omsk prison,' he says. 'Imagine a cell which has nine bunks. And there were between 50 and 60 of us in that room with nine beds and people were sleeping in the beds, under the beds, between the beds and in the gangway. We could leave the cell twice a day to go to the toilet and once a fortnight we were taken to the bath-house. But we were never allowed to walk in the courtyard and go out into the open air.'

For writing the pamphlet protesting at his teacher's arrest Kantovski was sentenced to ten years in a labour camp. But as soon as he was transferred from Omsk, he asked to be sent to the front line, since 'while the country was at war we felt guilty about sitting in prison'. To those in the West who want to believe that the undoubted brutality of the Soviet system was the sole reason the Red Army was capable of sacrificing so many of its soldiers in battle, Vladimir Kantovski's action will be inexplicable. For here is a man who *volunteered* to serve in one of Stalin's notorious penal battalions. What his story demonstrates is that the terror prevalent in the Soviet system is only part of the reason the Red Army fought as it did. In 1942 even prisoners unjustly held in the gulag could feel motivated to fight the Germans by their own patriotism and belief in the Communist ideal.

After Stalin issued order 227 in the summer of 1942, Kantovski learnt that his request had been granted; he would be sent to the front line, his sentence commuted from ten years to five. He became one of the 440,000 Soviet soldiers who served in penal battalions; how many survived the war is not known for sure, but it is likely to be the merest handful.[1]

Once at the front line he met the other members of his battalion: 'I was the only one who was convicted on political charges – usually the penal battalions were made up of people who had committed various minor crimes like being late for work, which was a crime at that time. If you were more than 21 minutes late, it meant a year in prison, but instead of that you could go to a penal battalion. Or a small theft or if you were rude to someone in the street – that could all be considered a crime and you could be sent to a penal battalion.'

Kantovski knew that in a penal battalion 'my old sins could only be pardoned through my blood' – and that the only realistic chance he had of survival was to be wounded in combat. Yet he 'never regretted for a single minute' that he chose to join. 'It's my nature. I don't like to muse over decisions I've taken – I never do it on principle. And in spite of everything, some opportunities were opening up for me. There was a small chance of survival – even if 10 people survived out of 250 it meant that you had a chance.'

After receiving 'no training whatsoever', Kantovski's unit was marched to the front line and told they would have the opportunity of serving the Motherland by 'reconnaissance through combat'. They were required to advance towards the German lines and 'make the enemy's weapons fire so that our reconnaissance people could spot the sources of the enemy's fire and later destroy them'. They were ordered forward at dawn towards a wood occupied by Germans about 400 metres from the Soviet positions. 'As soon as we showed ourselves, the enemy opened fire. And our officers shouted, "Onwards, onwards!" I don't think you can feel any patriotism when you are participating in such an attack. I think the over-riding feeling is one of bluntness – your feelings are blunted. You feel fatalistic. You know what's happening is unavoidable, fatal, and it's like a game of Russian roulette. Well, what is your lot going to be?'

As the penal battalion advanced, the German machine gun fire intensified. The four or five Soviet tanks that accompanied them were swiftly destroyed. Then Kantovski felt bullets hit his arm and shoulder: 'I was wounded and I began to bleed. You had to be heavily wounded to be pardoned, but how can you know whether you are badly wounded or not badly wounded? Until I became convinced that I was heavily enough wounded I didn't dare set off towards the first aid centre. It was very hard to move – my arm was not working, so I had to crawl lying on my back.'

Out of his unit of 240, only nine escaped being severely wounded or killed. Luckily for Kantovski, his wound was considered serious enough for him to be medically treated and released from the penal battalion. He then returned to Moscow where he was able to continue as a student. But his story does not end there. In 1944 he was arrested again and charged with the same offence he had committed in 1941. His NKVD investigator just told him, 'In 1941 you were sentenced to ten years. All right, go back and do your time and you'll finish in 1951.' Kantovski never knew why he had been sent back to the gulag. 'We lived under Stalin's personal dictatorship,' he says. 'I didn't query whether Stalin was just or unjust – he was simply a tyrant. All of it rested on fear, on cruelty, on informing – on sticks without any carrots.'

In the course of making the television series on which this book is based some truly exceptional people emerged. But Vladimir Kantovski was one of the most impressive. Sitting in his small Moscow flat, he unravelled a personal story that was rife with injustice at every turn. Yet all his personal misfortune – even the wounds whose scars he still bears today from his experience of 'reconnaissance through combat' – stemmed from writing that pamphlet of protest in 1941 about the arrest of his teacher. It was hard to see what that pamphlet had achieved apart from his own suffering. Looking back, didn't he regret ever having written it? 'I don't regret having done it,' he replied. 'Because not everyone could say at the time that he had the liberty to express himself. My personality grew stronger.' He paused for a moment, trying to find the exact words that would convey his feeling. Then he finally said, 'I don't regret it because it gives me self-respect.' In a war that is rich in stories of suffering which have no redemption, it is worth remembering the personal experience of Vladimir Kantovski – a man who was prepared to die not just for his country, but for his own sense of self-worth.

Yet no amount of personal sacrifice seemed able to stem the advance of the Germans in the summer of 1942. On 23 July Panzer divisions advanced into Rostov as far as the bridge across the River Don. 'The Germans were so confident,' says Anatoly Mereshko, a Soviet officer who fought against them that summer, 'which was natural because they moved from Kharkov to the Don... It would make anyone confident. They walked, having rolled up their sleeves, wearing shorts and singing their songs. As for our retreating units, they were really completely demoralized people. They didn't know where they were going and they didn't know where to look for their units. For example, they were told to reassemble in Marinovka, but where was Marinovka? About five or six soldiers would turn up and ask: "Where is Marinovka?" So they just walked and walked, carrying their weapons with them – because without weapons they would be interrogated.'

Tamara Kalmykova, then an eighteen-year-old student, witnessed the Soviet retreat: 'There was terrible panic – each was frightened for his life. And I used to say that if I had a machine gun I would have killed all those who were retreating. Because every step of the retreat doubled the amount of blood that needed to be shed – afterwards you will need two or three times the casualties to win it back.'

Stalin must have felt similar sentiments – that was why he issued his order: 'Not one step back.' But that summer he also accepted that on occasion it would be necessary to conduct staged withdrawals to prevent his forces being encircled. It was a breakthrough – the first significant sign that he was prepared to learn from his earlier mistakes and listen to the generals around him. Only by a fighting retreat could similar disasters to Kharkov that spring and to Kiev and Vyazma the previous year be avoided.

That summer Anatoly Mereshko commanded an élite unit of officer cadets in the fight against Operation Blue. For him and his unit, each day had the same essential pattern. 'Usually the Germans attacked twice and then waited for the main forces to pull up for a larger attack the next morning. When the evening came, all warfare stopped. But they sent their motorcyclists to the flanks where they fired light rockets – they just did it to give the impression of encirclement. The Germans did everything according to schedule. At dawn their reconnaissance plane usually arrived. Then the bombers came. They bombed the front line, and then the shelling began, and then infantry and tanks attacked. If you could withstand the bombing and the shelling, it was fine because you could always fight back against the tanks and the infantry. If they had no success, they stopped their attacks.' During the night, whilst the Germans called up more rein-forcements, the Red Army melted away. 'We had no strength to hold the defence,' says Mereshko. 'If we had been given the order to hold out and stay, we would have stayed, but the command preferred to save us.' Ironically, these new prag-matic tactics did not please either him or his men: 'We felt desperation and anger because of our helplessness, and we also wondered: "Why do they not let us properly fight the enemy? Why do we have to keep on withdrawing?" And we kept withdrawing, as far as the River Don.'

'Our initial impression was that the Russians were flee-ing,' says Joachim Stempel who, as a German tank officer, fought his way across the steppes in Operation Blue. 'But that turned out to be a mistake.' The Red Army was, of course, making a strategic retreat – though to many of the soldiers on the ground the impression must have been that this was a repeat of 1941. But this time there were no great German encirclements, and the hit-and-run Soviet defensive tactics sapped the strength of the German advance. 'If we caught up with the Russians during the day,' says Gerhard Münch, who fought in Army Group B, 'then during the night they'd go fur-ther away from us. This is the time when I first heard the term "The Russians fighting by space", which means he lets us enter and our difficulties with supply get bigger and the ways of supply get more complicated.' Münch's regimental com-mander expressed similar doubts to him during the advance to Stalingrad. 'He was very sceptical after Kharkov because he said, "This huge space – what on earth are we supposed to do here?" And when we were not able to get at the enemy, he made the point that our opponent was using space against us.'

That summer the Red Army was careful about choosing the moment to mount a defence against the Germans and the moment to withdraw. Bridgeheads and other important strategic positions would be held and fiercely defended until the threat of encirclement became too great. Joachim Stempel and his men saw at first-hand this new sophistication in Red Army tactics once they crossed the River Don and encountered a Soviet defensive obstacle the like of which they had not seen before. 'Here we experienced incredibly heavy losses,' he says. 'Behind every little hill, every little rise, there were built-in T.34 tanks. Only the gun barrels were visible, and we were really surprised when they opened fire – we hadn't really recognized them. And particularly terrible were the Russian flame-thrower divisions, who, at temperatures of 40 degrees, just lit up everything that was at all flammable and we had the most terrible injuries and burns...And the closer we got to Stalingrad, the harder was the resistance of the Soviet troops.'

Hitler was determined that Stalingrad should be taken. The city was an important industrial centre and dominated the Volga, the river along which the Soviets moved vital supplies up from the Caucasus. If Moscow and the other northern cities could be cut off from this southern oil, the Soviets would be struck a devastating economic blow. (Hitler's intense interest may also have been fuelled by the city's very name – Stalingrad had been renamed in honour of the Soviet leader after his alleged exploits there during the civil war.)

The 4th Panzer Army, together with the 6th Army, converged on the city, which lay spread out in front of them like a ribbon for 50 kilometres or so along the Volga. A more difficult city to defend could scarcely be imagined. The river formed a natural barrier, and once the Germans surrounded the city on the remaining three sides, all reinforcements would have to make the dangerous journey across the water.

On Sunday, 23 August the Germans launched a 600-bomber raid on Stalingrad – the most intense aerial bombardment so far seen on the Eastern Front. That morning Valentina Krutova, an eleven-year-old schoolgirl, and her fourteen-year-old brother Yuri were picking berries on the city outskirts when they heard the sound of a massive armada of planes. As they looked up, the bombs began to fall. 'Everything was ablaze,' she says. 'There was screaming... While an adult could have been able to understand that there was a war going on, what could we understand, being children? We were only scared that we would be killed.'

'When the bombing began, it was really horrible,' says Albert Burkovski, who was fourteen in 1942. 'I can still remember the planes, the noise they were making, and it became real hell. I don't know how people managed to bear it. It was all one big fire. We climbed to the roof and we could hear the moaning, groaning from down below.' Once the bombing had stopped, Albert ran back home towards the house he lived in with his grandmother. When he turned on to their street, he saw that his house had become a pile of rubble. 'Once we came back there was only moaning and more moaning coming from under the ruins. My grandmother had been hiding in the basement of the house, but it was all closed in by the ruins – everyone in there was crushed. I thought for some time that I had better be killed because such was my grief, my misery, because I was all alone.'

Stalin resolved to hold the city. The Red Army had retreated hundreds of kilometres from Kharkov in the Ukraine, and a stand had to be made on the Volga. Initially he refused to allow even the civilian population to escape across the river. There would be no more running away. Here the Red Army would stay and fight.

At his new headquarters at Vinnitsa in the Ukraine, Hitler sweated in the fierce summer heat. Despite the progress that had been made by both Army Groups, no Soviet armies had been encircled. Fanning Hitler's annoyance, General

Halder, the Chief of the Army General Staff, suggested that there might not be enough resources available to support both Army Groups and enable them to meet their objectives simultaneously. Hitler was furious. Halder recorded in his war diary on 30 August: 'Today's conference with the Führer was again an occasion for abusive reproaches against the military leadership abilities of the highest commanders. He charges them with intellectual conceit, mental inadaptability, and utter failure to grasp the essentials.'[2]

At the beginning of September there was another row as Field Marshal List's Army Group A, fighting in the Caucasus, appeared to slow in its advance. Jodl, Chief of the Operations Staff of the High Command of the Armed Forces, supported List's actions, saying that he was following previous instructions from the Führer. Hitler was beside himself with anger. List was removed and on 9 September Hitler personally took command of Army Group A, which was advancing across the steppes about 1600 kilometres away. This led to a bizarre command structure in which, as commander of an army group, Hitler was answerable to himself as Commander-in-Chief of the Army, then to himself again as Supreme Commander-in-Chief of the Wehrmacht (all the German Armed forces), and finally to himself again as Head of State. Then, as if the atmosphere of change was not fetid enough, on 22 September Hitler replaced Halder as Chief of Staff with Kurt Zeitzler, a general famed for his obsequiousness. So, at the same time as Stalin was learning to listen to the advice of those around him, Hitler was creating an impractical military structure that crushed individual initiative and in which his military commanders knew what fate to expect if they dared criticize their all-knowing Führer.

Meanwhile, after the bombing of Stalingrad, in the last week of August the Germans finally reached the Volga. By 3 September the city was surrounded. 'We came to a rise which offered a very good view of Stalingrad,' says Joachim Stempel. 'The city was in flames and suddenly, like a silver ribbon, I saw the Volga. It came as quite a surprise. We all knew we had to get there – that's our goal, maybe the goal of the whole war…It was a very impressive thing to be standing on the border with Asia and being able to say – we're at the Volga! In spite of all the casualties, all the hardships, we had managed to attain this goal, this victory. The Volga! It was within our grasp! The Volga was a very impressive sight in the autumn sun. A river of a width which we don't know in Germany. And this incredible view into the depths of Asia – nothing but forests, more forests, plains and the endless horizon. It was an inspirational feeling for anyone who had been involved in breaking through the Russian defences, the taking of ground, the loss of good comrades who couldn't experience this with us. And now before us, this picture, the Volga, close enough to touch. We thought, it can't take much longer now – we're here.'

As the Germans moved forward into the city, thousands of civilians became trapped behind their lines. Valentina Krutova, together with her brother Yuri and five-year-old sister, were amongst those cut off from the narrowing Soviet-held section of the city. They lived with their grandmother, who was badly wounded as the result of an explosion. 'Germans often came into our house,' says Valentina. 'They would open the door and look in. But as our granny was really rotting alive and the Germans were very much afraid of various diseases, they didn't come very close. The Germans saw there were blisters on her body and little worms had appeared in her wounds. It smelt terrible.'

There was no medical care available, and shortly after the Germans arrived her grandmother died. 'When she died we carried her, we actually pulled her body on some piece of cloth into a trench and put the piece of cloth on her to protect her face from the earth, and then we buried her. We couldn't find the place afterwards. It was very hard for us because we used to feel some support from her when she was alive. Although she was bedridden, she was with us, she was a living human being. We could talk to her. She would hug us and express her sympathy and this warmed our hearts. We didn't feel too burdened by fear, although we were living on the territory occupied by the Germans. But when we lost her, it began to be emotionally very difficult for us. We had no one else to support us.'

Three children on their own amongst the thousands trapped in Stalingrad had little chance of survival, but four-teen-year-old Yuri did what he could to scavenge food. 'My brother used to go to a grain elevator where a small amount of grain remained, and he gave us a little bit every day and it helped us. He kept the bag between the window panes. One day a German officer and two soldiers – they were either Germans or Romanians – came in and began demanding food. They wanted eggs and chicken and bread. And we had nothing. They began to search for food, and were clever enough to look between the window panes and they found that little bag with wheat. They wanted to shoot us down. My brother and I went down on our knees and pleaded with them not to kill us. The German officer was young. He began to say something to his soldiers. They took away the grain but they left us alone.'

Albert Burkovski was another child left on his own in the city, but he was lucky – he was on the Soviet side of the divide. In the first days of the bombardment he and a school friend helped transport wounded Red Army soldiers down to the landing stage on the Volga by pushing them in a cart. 'We brought the wounded to the river crossing and could see cut-ters and boats and rafts approaching. The Germans were firing, and the firing was heavy.' Many of the Soviet boats were destroyed before they reached the bank. 'The crossing was terrible. There was so much shelling and bombing that, even if you could swim – well, you could get killed.'

Hitler had ordered that Stalingrad be taken, but Stalin had commanded that it be held. This city, which at the start of Operation Blue had been seen as merely one target amongst many, had unexpectedly become the operation's main objective – almost the focal point of the whole war. Stalin ordered the Red Army to retain the Stalingrad bank of the Volga, using whatever means were necessary.

In such brutal circumstances the character of the two commanders in the battle was to prove crucial. Leading the German 6th Army was the sophisticated Friedrich Paulus, an experienced staff officer who had previously served as deputy Chief of Staff under General Halder. 'Paulus was very tall and he was very calm and poised,' says Günther von Below, who served under him in the 6th Army. 'He was a very wise man with a very humane attitude. He was always somewhat hesitant in his decisions – one had to help him decide…On one occasion I said to him, "General, if you don't sign here and now, I will sign on your behalf this very instant." And then he signed the paper. And he laughed and said: "So much for that."'

In command of the Soviet 62nd Army at Stalingrad, from September 1942 onwards, was a very different man – Vasily Chuikov. If Paulus was a strategist, aware of the grand sweep of war, then Chuikov was a tactician, focused on the struggle to take an individual street or building. If Paulus was courteous, almost deferential, then Chuikov was a bully whose brutal treatment of those he believed had failed him was legendary.

'Chuikov could sense the nature of a battle,' says Anatoly Mereshko, who served with him at Stalingrad. 'And he could take timely decisions in spite of all obstacles to carry out that decision. He had persistence and perseverance…Chuikov combined the Russian features, which are, as one song puts it,

"If you shoot, you shoot; if you make merry, you make merry," and for Chuikov shooting came first. He had colossal energy that was very catching, and it passed on to more junior commanders and then on to soldiers. If Chuikov's character had been different, then we wouldn't have held Stalingrad.'

A crucial part of Chuikov's character was his brutality. If a commander acted in a way he disliked, Chuikov would physically assault him: 'He went as far as beating people with his fists or with a stick,' says Mereshko, 'for which Stalin told him off. He used to lean on a stick, and if he didn't like the behaviour of a particular commander, he could hit this commander with his stick on his back.' Later in the war Mereshko had personal experience of this side of Chuikov: 'I went into the house where the operational department was, and I could see my boss leaning against the wall with the table overturned. He was holding a handkerchief to his nose and there was blood on it. He said to me that Chuikov had hit him.' Mereshko's superior officer explained the simple reason he had been assaulted by Chuikov: 'The General Colonel had hit the Lieutenant Colonel because he was dissatisfied with the report he had received.' Then his boss added, 'Well, it's good that you've just come, not one minute before, because otherwise he would have hit you too.'

Chuikov was one of a new breed of Soviet commander, not one of Stalin's creatures picked primarily for his subservience but a ruthless and competent leader. He knew that he was required to hold Stalingrad or die in the attempt. He also knew that he had to impose the harshest discipline imaginable on the troops he commanded in order to achieve his aim; more than 13,000 of them were arrested – and many of that number executed – during the Battle of Stalingrad. Yet again, the Soviet system sought to fight 'fear with fear', as the Red Army was told retreat was impossible and that 'there is no land beyond the Volga'.

The shrewd tactician in Chuikov also realized that the ruined city allowed the Red Army, for the first time in the conflict, to fight a different kind of war – one in which individual bravery and resilience would count as much as high-flown strategy. The Soviet troops would inhabit the city like 'living concrete' and take on the Germans in hand-to-hand fighting. Chuikov decreed that the Soviet troops must station themselves as close as possible to the German front line. That way the German bombers and artillery risked hitting their own men in any attack. The motto of the Soviet defenders became, 'Don't get far from the enemy.' 'Our principle was, we'll put claws in the throat of the enemy and hold them very close,' says Anatoly Mereshko. 'That way you can stay alive. These were Chuikov's tactics. The gap between you and the enemy should not be bigger than 50 or 100 metres, or not more than a grenade's throw. If we threw a grenade, we had only four seconds before the explosion happened. When the Germans threw their grenades, they fell into our trenches and our soldiers could lift the grenade up and throw it back because the German grenades exploded after nine or ten seconds. So we took advantage of the weakness of the German grenades. That was also due to Chuikov.'

Chuikov also perfected the use of assault groups to clear German-held houses. 'Such a group could vary between five and 50 people, without their rucksacks, only with grenades, and their job was to rush into the house,' says Mereshko. 'And then this assault group would be followed by a consolidation group. The assault group had to send the Germans into panic, but the consolidation group that followed had to repel the Germans' counter-attack.'

These house clearances were the stuff of nightmares. Suren Mirzoyan is one of the few survivors of these operations from the Soviet side, and described a typical assault group encounter with the Germans: 'Only the outer wall of the house survived, but inside there was rubble and the Germans had hidden amongst it. Suddenly one German jumped on my friend and he reacted and hit the German with his knee. And then a second German jumped on him and I lashed out against him – we had knives. Do you know when you press a ripe tomato, juice comes out? I stabbed him with a knife and everything around was in blood. I felt only one thing – kill, kill. A beast. And another German jumped on me and he was shouting and then he fell. If you were not strong enough physically, the German would have swallowed you. Each metre of Stalingrad meant possible death. Death was in our pockets. Death was always on our steps.'

During these primitive encounters Mirzoyan preferred not to use modern weaponry: 'I tried not to use [these] weapons against people. I had a knife or a spade – a very sharp spade. It's better than a machine gun sometimes. I also used the spade in the front lines. You dig with your spade and then you can use it in man-to-man fighting. A machine gun takes a long time – you have to load it. But with a spade you simply lift it and you strike. It makes sense. These spades were very crucial in fighting.'

In the middle of September the Germans mounted a determined attack and managed to reach Stalingrad's central railway station. Supported by the 13th Guards Division, Chuikov and his men fought back. Chuikov's own determination to cling to the river bank or die in the attempt became an inspiration to his men. Every factory, every street, every house became a battlefield.

The savagery of the fighting amongst the rubble of Stalingrad was the antithesis of Blitzkrieg. This was not sophisticated combat but primitive struggle, as Helmut Walz, a private in the German 305th Infantry Division, discovered to his cost on the morning of 17 October when he and his unit were in the ruins of a factory: 'We had the order to advance, in the open space, to the factory buildings. It was a desert of rubble. Everything was mixed up together.' About 15 metres in front of him he saw Soviet soldiers in a dugout: 'I advanced about 10 metres, so that I was roughly 5 or 6 metres away from them, and hid behind a heap of concrete. I called out to them in Russian to surrender, but they didn't. Everywhere it was burning – bullets were flying through the air – so I threw a hand grenade right into the middle of them. And then one of them came out with blood running from his nose, his ears and his mouth. I don't know anything about medicine but when I saw him I knew that he wouldn't be able to survive – something inside his body was torn. And he aimed his machine gun at me – the Russian machine gun with the little drum at the front – and I said to myself, "Boy, you ain't going to get me!" And I aimed my gun at him. And then I saw little stars shooting out of the air. For a moment I was numb. What's going on? I ran my left hand over my face and a jet of blood came out and my teeth flew out of my mouth.'

One of Walz's comrades, seeing what had happened, leapt up on to a mass of concrete and then crashed down hard on top of the Soviet soldier. 'He jumped straight into the face of that Russian with his boots,' says Walz. 'I can still hear the face cracking – he kicked him to death, probably.' Walz's lieutenant gestured to him to move into the protection of a bomb crater where the officer bandaged Walz as best he could, but then another Red Army soldier appeared above them. 'The Russian aimed his machine gun at him [the lieutenant] and then his steel helmet flew off – it was a bull's-eye shot, right into his head,' says Walz. 'His head was open and I could see his brain, on the right, left and in the middle – there was water but no blood. He looked at me and then he fell into the rim of the crater.' Another German killed the Red Army soldier who had shot the lieutenant, and Walz crawled away to search for a medic.

By the end of that one day in October, out of a total of 77 soldiers in his company 'nobody was left – they were all either dead or wounded. The whole company had gone.'

The very proximity of the enemy in Stalingrad also led to bizarre, almost friendly, encounters. 'Imagine us in house-to-house fighting,' says Anatoly Mereshko. 'We took the third floor and the Germans took the first and second floors. By midday both sides get tired and the Germans shout, "Hi, Russians!" "What do you want, Germans?" we'd say. "Can you send us some water?" they'd answer. And we'd shout, "Let's swap pots filled with water for a pot filled with cigarettes." And then one hour later we'd carry on, we'd open fire again. Or the Germans cry, "Well, we have no cigarettes. We can send you a couple of clocks or watches." Well, then we swapped water for cigarettes or water for vodka or for schnapps, and we honestly stopped fighting during that hour of swapping. Eventually either they kicked us out of the house or we kicked them out – it was proper fighting, the strongest side winning.'

This was a form of warfare for which the Germans had not been prepared. 'Hand-to-hand combat, positional warfare,' says Joachim Stempel, 'I don't want to say it was entirely foreign, but they were elements of our training which were very much on the fringe. We were an offensive army, trained for attack, and we were able to defend ourselves, of course, but we didn't have the experience of the Russian soldiers, whose training, whose nature and whose psyche of being tied to his native soil were all thrown into the mix. We didn't have that, and I think that we had more casualties because we weren't as close to nature as the Russians...The Russians had the advantage in trench warfare and hand-to-hand combat – there's no doubt. As a tank unit, we were used to driving tanks and trying to bring the enemy down with tanks and then stopping, clearing the area and moving forward. But that was all forgotten in the past, a long time ago.'

The frustration for the Germans was intense, for the Volga was so close. 'Again and again, we heard, "Another hundred metres and you're there!" But how can you do it if you just don't have the strength left? It wasn't attacking as we were used to attacking. Here we remained in position for weeks and tried hard to win some land, even if it's only 10 or 15 metres which we managed to take from the Russians – that was considered a success. But the main thing was that the Russians were defending a narrow strip of land, maybe 300 metres deep, on the steep slopes down to the Volga where the command headquarters of the Russian armies and divisions were located. And the soldiers who were on duty there were completely fanatical about it, and obsessed with their mission. "You have to hold this because your generals are behind you!" And that made it impossible for us to take those last hundred metres, which was our constant aim.'

Gerhard Münch, by now a battalion commander, quickly realized that with the available resources house-to-house combat could not be won by either side: 'If the enemy has the stairwell or is on the first floor, then you don't even need to try [to take the house] because you just won't succeed. Once you get a demonstration of how unsuccessful any attempt to get into another building is, and if you're lucky enough to get back the injured people, then you just stop trying it. And so, in this section, the whole battle came to a standstill…it was not possible to change anything – unless you got five new divisions that came in, but I think they probably would not have been able to do anything either.'

Throughout the city, the German advance bogged down. The Soviet snipers who hid in the rubble of the city made any movement from cover during daylight potentially fatal. These snipers were feared and detested. They became symbolic of the dishonourable, degrading and primitive way in which many Germans believed the Battle of Stalingrad was being fought. 'The Russian sniper who worked in our sector is again and again celebrated as a major hero,' says Gerhard Münch. 'I found it inwardly revolting. I always compared it with sitting in a raised hide and shooting deer – that's got nothing to do with soldiership in my personal opinion.'

'It became increasingly more difficult,' says Joachim Stempel, 'because every attack cost us so many casualties that it was possible to work out that, soon, there won't be anyone left. And we knew that the Russians at night were taking people across the Volga, but we had nothing left and so we had to keep going, nailed to the spot.' The German side received reinforcements too – but inexperience could prove swiftly fatal in the ruins of Stalingrad: 'I can remember something that was unforgettable, a cry of joy from the battalion, when we heard: "Tonight you'll get 60 or 70 men from the reserves." And, of course, that was such a message of hope that it just made you forget about everything else. And then, when they arrived, these boys, all about 18 or 19 years old, had had about four weeks' training. But that night, all hell broke loose. First, there was Russian artillery fire, then a Russian night offensive into our trenches. And with great difficulty – in fact, the commander of the battalion personally came down to the front to help me – we managed to push the Russians back out of the trenches. We lost more than half of these boys, dead or wounded, and they'd only just arrived. And the reason for that was because they lacked that sense, that instinct for danger, crisis, that you need in such situations – they just couldn't react like the old hands were able to react.'

Some of the fiercest fighting was for the Mamaev Kurgan, the ancient burial mound on the edge of the city. Whoever held this hill commanded a clear view of the centre of Stalingrad and the Volga just beyond. This key strategic point changed hands many times during the battle, sometimes several times in one day. Albert Burkovski took part in the fight. He had been 'adopted' by the Soviet 13th Guards Rifle Division, and at fourteen became one of the youngest soldiers to fight in the defence of Stalingrad. 'I remember walking on the dead, decomposing bodies on the Mamaev Kurgan,' he says. 'Imagine, I put my foot on the ground and when I lift it I see that it's all dirty with somebody's intestines. It will never get erased from my memory... But the most horrible experience was when I killed the first German. The Germans made about fifteen or twenty attacks [on the Mamaev Kurgan] during the day. First came the bombing, then the artillery fire, then tanks went ahead and then the infantry. And all of a sudden I saw this German standing and looking away from me. He didn't see me because I was all covered with dust and earth. When I saw that huge German, I immediately fired at him without standing up. When you shoot at short range, then bits of the body immediately go up. I could see bits of him and I could smell the smell of his clothes because it was very close. And my comrades began to calm me down...I was vomiting. Other men were saying to me, "Come on, this is just a German," but none the less I was shivering all over. And it stayed in my memory forever.'

To escape German bombardment the Soviet defenders dug a series of underground hideouts in the bank of the Volga. Chuikov's headquarters were built deep in the earth only a few metres from the river. 'If you wanted to live, you had to dig trenches and shelters,' says Burkovski. 'There were a lot of lice because there was no time to take a wash. But no one fell ill because our nerves were so much on edge that they didn't let us become sick.' A short distance along the river another Soviet commander lived in a sewer and held command meetings on planks just above the running water. The Germans had not witnessed this level of determination from the Red Army before. 'I think only Russians can get used to such hardships,' says Anatoly Mereshko phlegmatically.

And it wasn't just Soviet men who were fighting to defend Stalingrad. Relatively little attention has been given in the West to the vital contribution that female soldiers made to the fighting strength of the Red Army – at least 800,000 women served in Soviet forces during the war. Tamara Kalmykova, who became a communications officer that summer with the 64th Army, was one of the thousands of female soldiers who helped defend Stalingrad. 'When we reached the Stalingrad front,' she says, 'we learnt we had to rely on ourselves and set right all the mistakes that were made in the first years of the war...Women were more enduring, although they are the weaker sex. As Chuikov put it, "You can trust something to a woman. You feel confident that your order will be fulfilled at any cost." Because a woman is a mother who gives birth. Any mother is going to stand firm to protect her children the same way animals defend their cubs...And women were merciless. They were avenging their husbands or brothers – in the families of practically all the women who were fighting, somebody had died. And nothing remained of their homes but ashes. Anyone, from any country, would want to take revenge. And this is what called them to action and gave them the strength and patience and courage to fulfil such a difficult job.'

Even though she was classed as a communications officer, Kalmykova also took part in the savage fighting just outside the city: 'During the battle, when we were walking along the communications channel, there was a cry that a gunner had been killed. I ran and my friend, a nurse, ran after me. She began to bandage him but he was dead. So she lay down next to the machine gun and started firing and I helped her, giving her the cartridges, and we managed to repel the German attack. But she was killed. I felt such anger against the enemy for killing my friend...and I was so sorry for her. She was only eighteen. She hadn't seen anything in life.'

Shortly afterwards Tamara Kalmykova was able to take her revenge on the Germans – but at great personal risk. The communications cable laid to the neighbouring battalion had been cut and her commander had sent two soldiers – a man and a woman – ahead to follow the wire and repair the damage. But neither of them had returned. So he ordered Kalmykova to find out what had happened to them. 'I followed the cable for 3 kilometres,' she says. 'And then I saw our young man – killed. He was lying dead, shot in the head. I went on following the cable and saw the girl. She was also dead, shot in the back of her head and in her spine. I picked up the documents of each of them and went on to look for the break in the cable so that I could repair it.'

'Suddenly I noticed a German in the bushes. I thought it was my end. I began to crawl back, but the heavy rifle that I had made it difficult. But the German had a sub-machine gun. It was easy for him to fire his sub-machine gun and to kill me, but he wanted to take me alive as a prisoner for interrogation because he saw I was a communications officer and knew a lot. But I managed to shoot at him. He fell down. At first I didn't believe he was really dead because I thought he was playing a trick and that he wanted me to go towards him. When I was sure he was really dead, I approached him. I didn't look at his face. I just put my hands into his pockets to get his documents. I felt a real repulsion when I was picking things from his pockets. But if I hadn't brought his documents back, they wouldn't have believed that I had killed him. When I returned, my commander was surprised to see me with a German backpack and a machine gun. I fell on my bunk bed and felt very weak. It was very frightening. But nevertheless I had to do what I had done – because if I hadn't I would have been killed. If you stayed idle, then you would surely die. Either you act against him or he acts against you. The logic is clear.'

Determined Soviet resistance had meant that the initial German thrust into the heart of the city had been held in September. By October, despite more fierce German attacks, the Red Army still held a strip of land in front of the Volga. Hitler was impatient. The 6th Army contained more than 300,000 men – why couldn't they take one ruined town? But the problem, as the German veterans of Stalingrad still emphasize today, was that even Paulus did not have enough men at his disposal to be sure of eliminating the Red Army soldiers who hid in the buildings and the sewers. The Volga, which the Germans had initially believed acted to their advantage in that it prevented the Soviets' retreat and made reinforcement hazardous, now became a hindrance since it prevented the 6th Army completely encircling their enemy.

Whilst the Germans wrestled with the unexpected difficulties that this new situation presented, Stalin and his generals debated how they should respond. Gradually, since the débâcle at Kharkov in May, Stalin had become less dogmatic in his military thinking. Now junior commanders were taught the German tactics of Blitzkrieg. 'I have to admit that we learnt to fight from the Germans,' says Tamara Kalmykova. 'Specifically, in coordination of troops, reconnaissance, communications and cartography.'

A key part of the learning process was to build on the practice of sending snatch squads across the German lines to capture prisoners for interrogation. These missions were dangerous in the extreme. Suren Mirzoyan was selected with one of his comrades for just such a task in the summer of 1942. They crept across no-man's-land until they encountered the enemy: 'We found out in what buildings the Germans were and then we crawled through the potato fields, we crawled and crawled and crawled until we got near one German guard. He was pacing to and fro with his machine gun. I was very nervous – I was sweating with nerves because I wondered what would happen if other Germans detected us. As soon as this guard turned round, I hit him on the head. I was very strong. He immediately collapsed, screaming, but I shut his mouth and began to pull him along. After we'd dragged him for several metres the Germans opened fire, but we successfully got him back to headquarters about 8 kilometres away.'

The psychological impact of these snatch squads on the German soldiers was enormous. Helmut Walz, fighting in the rubble of Stalingrad, remembers once looking round to see that their medical orderly had disappeared from view: 'We called out, "Medical, where are you?" But he didn't answer.' During their search for him the Germans found a drain cover leading to the underground tunnels of the sewage system. Shocked, Helmut Walz shouted to his comrades: 'They pulled him down there!'

The pressure on the Soviet intelligence officers to get every scrap of useful information from these captured German soldiers was intense. An insight into just how such interrogations could be conducted during the war comes from Zinaida Pytkina. At first glance today she resembles one of the many grandmothers who trudge the streets of Russian provincial towns, wrapped like parcels against the biting wind. But her penetrating stare and directness of manner mark her out. For Zinaida Pytkina was selected during the war to serve in the most secret security service of all in Stalin's state – SMERSH. Until the fall of Communism she dared not tell even her own close friends just what she had done during the war.

So beloved of thriller writers, SMERSH (the Russian acronym stands for 'Death to Spies') actually did exist. Officially known as the Main Directorate for Counter-Intelligence, it was formed on 14 April 1943, three months after the Red Army retook Stalingrad, and replaced the so-called Special Departments of the People's Commissariat of Internal Affairs' Third Directorate. Their job, as Pytkina puts it discreetly, was 'to look after order' but 'silently'. As well as searching for enemy agents – and interrogating prisoners captured by the snatch squads – SMERSH also policed the loyalty of Soviet soldiers under the guise of investigating 'subversion'.

When Pytkina was told that she had been selected for SMERSH (she had not applied to join – they had chosen her) she was frightened. Perhaps, she thought, she had done something wrong: 'They look for offenders against the law, and I thought in the beginning that maybe I was a law offender too.'

When Pytkina was asked to 'describe her mission' within SMERSH she replied: 'My mission was to fulfil all the orders of my commanders.' But what did she actually do? 'Whatever we were told,' she answered. Only later did she become more forthcoming and admit that part of her job was to recruit informers inside the Red Army to spy on possible deserters. Another of her tasks was to participate in the interrogations of German soldiers captured by the Soviet snatch squads – work she describes as 'hard, tricky and interesting'.

How, when interrogating captured German soldiers, could SMERSH officers tell if their captive was telling the truth? 'We knew in advance about the kind of information the officer had,' she replied. 'Both SMERSH and military intelligence already had part of the information that was expected from this German, and the rest was up to the specialist.'

'How did the "specialist" extract this information?'

'If he [the prisoner] doesn't answer, then we had to make him talk.'

'How did they make them talk? Did the Russians give the prisoners vodka?'

'I've never seen anyone being given vodka: just hit him or beat him,' she answered. 'Well, there's an enemy in front of me and this enemy is reluctant to give me what I want. If he gets a "wash" once or twice, then he will sing. This is why he was taken prisoner, to give information.' ('Wash', it transpires, was a euphemism for torture beatings. Later in the interview, when she was again asked, 'How did you make the Germans talk?' she answered even more equivocally and with deliberate irony: 'I don't know how to put it. Those who kept silent – they were treated "gently". No one wants to die.')

Zinaida Pytkina didn't just, on occasion, interrogate snatched prisoners but also took part in what could be the final stage of their journey through SMERSH – their execution. On one occasion she was told by her commanding officer to go and 'sort out' a young German major whose interrogation had been completed. Outside the interrogation building a pit had been dug and the German officer was ordered to kneel beside it. Pytkina drew her pistol ('My hand didn't tremble'), pointed it at his neck and pulled the trigger. His body fell into the pit. 'It was joy for me,' she says, describing her emotions at that moment. 'The Germans didn't ask us to spare them and I was angry…I was also pleased. I fulfilled my task. And I went back into the office and had a drink.'

When asked to explain in more detail why she felt this way after killing this German officer in cold blood, she replied: 'I am sorry for my people. When we were retreating we lost so many seventeen-, eighteen-year-olds. Do I have to be sorry for the German after that? This was my mood…As a member of the Communist Party, I saw in front of me a man who could have killed my relatives…. I would have cut off his head if I had been asked to. One person less, I thought. Ask him how many people he killed – did he not think about this?…

'I understand the interest in how a woman can kill a man. I wouldn't do it now. I would do it only if there was a war and I saw again what I had seen during the war…They had been captured, and people like him had killed many

Russian soldiers. Should I have kissed him for that?...I even used to ask to be sent on reconnaissance missions to capture a prisoner, but it wasn't allowed. Women were not sent on such missions – but I wanted to go. I wanted to crawl to the enemy's side and to capture a prisoner, perhaps kill him.'

Stalin would have admired Zinaida Pytkina's ruthless attitude, and back in the autumn of 1942 he called for similar cold-blooded determination from the defenders of Stalingrad. But determination alone would not win the battle. During the Germans' Operation Blue, the Red Army had demonstrated how they had mastered the art of retreating. Now they had to prove they could mount an effective attack. For the first time in the war the Red Army had to show that it understood how to prevail in a modern, mechanized war, and that they possessed tactical understanding as well as courage.

The first real sign of that change occurred in early autumn 1942 in Moscow. Stalin was on the telephone, and Zhukov and Vasilevskii (who was made Deputy Commissar for Defence in 1942) were discussing the strategic alternatives facing the Red Army in the south. 'Zhukov and Vasilevskii were talking to each other,' says Makhmud Gareev, who was a close colleague of Zhukov's, 'and Zhukov said, "We have to look for a new solution," and Stalin immediately overheard them, stopped speaking on the phone and asked: "Well, what solution do you mean?" Zhukov and Vasilevskii explained. Stalin said, "You've got a week to study the situation, but don't involve any other Stavka members."'

That conversation led to the first major Soviet victory of the war – Operation Uranus. The plan was ambitious: to attack the Germans from the flanks and encircle the entire 6th Army. Both the conception and implementation of Operation Uranus demonstrated that the Red Army had changed its approach from the desperate days of Kharkov five months earlier. 'They learnt from the Germans,' says

Makhmud Gareev. 'They not only learnt from the Germans, but they learnt from their own mistakes.' The Uranus plan was inspired not just by the huge, pincer-like encirclements the Germans had mounted in 1941, but harked back to the theory of mechanized 'deep operations' that innovative Red Army commanders had proposed in the early 1930s and which had subsequently been denounced. In accepting Zhukov and Vasilevskii's thinking, Stalin demonstrated both his flexibility and his cynicism – who cared if Soviet officers had been persecuted for suggesting similar ideas in the past? Perhaps the plan would work now.

The main thrust of the proposed Soviet attack would be not on the powerful German units of the 6th Army but on the Hungarian, Romanian and Italian soldiers who were stationed on the flanks. The Germans had been forced to use these armies from their Axis allies to fill in the gaps in their line – a situation that had arisen because Hitler had split his attacking force in two back in the summer.

Many of Stalin's previous operations had been distinguished by the ease with which the Germans had learnt of Soviet intentions, but Operation Uranus was different. This offensive was to become famous as the first example of the Soviet talent for military deception – *maskirovka*. Ivan Golokolenko was an officer in the 5th Tank Army who took part in Operation Uranus, and to start with even he and his comrades were deliberately misled about the true nature of the operation ahead. 'On 20 October 1942 we received an order to prepare wood for the frosty winter to help Moscow with supplies,' he says. His unit took the wood to a nearby train station only to discover that it wasn't destined for Moscow at all, but was needed to camouflage their tanks which were being loaded on to railway trucks. 'In the course of two or three days all three echelons travelled away – but no one knew in what direction we were finally going. We didn't know our destination; even the commander of the brigade did not know, and the station masters along the route did not know either.

'About 24 October we unloaded during the night at Kamulka station, north of Stalingrad. After that we travelled 55 kilometres without headlights. We travelled in complete darkness, very slowly, one car after another...I remember at one of the crossroads there was a group of generals standing nearby, and one of the truck drivers felt at a loss and by mistake turned his front headlights on. He heard some swear-words and then the strike of a stick against the headlights and the sound of cracking glass. Then you could hear voices saying, "Zhukov! Zhukov!", and I could recognize Zhukov with the group of generals.' It was Zhukov himself who had smashed the headlights on the truck. 'He was there personally watching the progress of our convoys,' says Golokolenko. 'He was strict about camouflage and attached great importance to it. He would stop at nothing to achieve results...He was cruel and merciless with people who disobeyed orders. I think it was necessary during that war.'

The concealment and deception of Operation Uranus went beyond merely denying the enemy knowledge of troop movements. Golokolenko's unit was one of many ordered to build trenches and other defensive fortifications in the open, so as to give the German reconnaissance planes the impression that an offensive was not contemplated. Bridges that the Germans could actually see from the air were deliberately built many kilometres from the proposed area of offensive operation: 'There were fake bridges as well as fake areas of troop concentration far from the direction of the attack. These bridges were built in order to distract the attention of the enemy from the direction of the main thrust.' When it was necessary to construct genuine river bridges for the forthcoming advance they were camouflaged: 'Some of the bridges were built as underwater bridges. They were built at a depth of 50 or 70 centimetres down in the water. From the air it was more difficult for the reconnaissance planes to spot the presence of such bridges.'

While they waited for the order to attack, Golokolenko's unit practised the coordination of infantry and tanks in offensive operations – incredibly, a task they had not undertaken before. They also trained to overcome one of their greatest fears – 'tank phobia': 'We had to sit in trenches and tanks travelled over us, and we soldiers were supposed to stay in the trenches without fearing the oncoming tanks.' The problem was a serious one: 'As soon as tanks appeared, our infantry would run away. This was a real scare. I remember also this fear of encirclement. As soon as somebody said, "They're about to encircle us!" this caused immediate panic.'

The Red Army also prepared a form of Blitzkrieg offensive that mirrored the one used against them in 1941 by the Germans. 'Previously tank units were used mainly as a support for infantry,' says Golokolenko. 'But this new idea was very different. At some narrow stretch of the front the defence would be broken and then through this narrow gap two tank corps would be introduced. The objective of the tank corps was to bypass the enemy's fortified areas and points of resistance and go deeper and deeper to capture the really important points like bridges or city towers. Infantry was supposed to follow the progress of the tanks and clear up whatever was left – this was the new thing.'

The Red Army also benefited from one of the most extraordinary and surprising achievements of the Soviet people during the war – their ability to out-produce the Germans in military hardware. The industrial facilities available to the Germans ought to have produced much more war material than a Soviet manufacturing base that had been disrupted by the invasion and the consequent need to relocate further east.

Yet working in factories, often under appalling conditions, the Soviet workforce – half of whom were women by 1942 – utterly outperformed the Germans. In 1942, for example, they manufactured 25,000 aircraft – 10,000 more than the Germans managed to produce. And much of this military hardware (the later versions of the T34 tank in particular) was as good as or better than anything the Germans possessed.

In readiness for Operation Uranus the Soviets managed to assemble, undetected, a force of more than a million men. A measure of their success at deceiving the Germans is given by the comment of Zeitzler, Hitler's newly appointed Chief of the Army General Staff, on 23 October, less than four weeks before the launch of Uranus, that the Red Army were 'in no position to mount a major offensive with any far-reaching objective'.[3]

At six o'clock in the morning on 19 November, the day on which Operation Uranus was to be launched, Ivan Golokolenko's unit knelt down before the banner of the brigade whilst an address from Stalin was read to them: 'There was something fatherly, something parental about it. It said, "Dear generals and soldiers, I address you my brothers. Today you start an offensive and your actions decide the fate of the country – whether it remains an independent country or perishes." And those words really reached my heart…. I was close to tears when the meeting was over. I felt a real upsurge, a spiritual upsurge.'

No one can know just how many Red Army soldiers reacted to Stalin's message as Ivan Golokolenko did. One of the great unanswered questions of the war is whether Soviet citizens resisted the Germans out of fear of punishment if they didn't, out of patriotism, out of love of Stalin or out of faith in Communism. The answer, almost certainly, is a mixture of all these reasons, with different motivations surfacing not just in different people but in the same person at different times. But those of us looking back today are almost certain to underestimate Stalin's importance to the majority of the population of the Soviet Union. Given what we now know about Stalin's terror, it is easy to overlook the extent to which he was a powerful – almost a vital – focal point during the war. Typical of the views of many Soviet veterans today is Anatoly Mereshko's comment: 'What people say now about Stalin killing millions of people – we didn't know anything about it. And when we went into battle we shouted, "For Motherland! For Stalin!" Now we have no ideology. There are no slogans that would bring the people together, like "Everything for the Front! Everything for the Victory!" A lot of women and children worked at the factories with this motto. It wasn't just hot air – it was based on people's beliefs.'

The artillery barrage that marked the start of Operation Uranus began at 7.30 a.m. on 19 November 1942. Just like the detailed training and deception that had preceded the operation, it too was conducted in a new way, and again in a Germanic style: 'Previously artillery was used for 10 or 15 minutes' shelling before the attack,' says Golokolenko. 'But now the big mass of the artillery – up to 500 artillery pieces – was relatively concentrated at a narrow stretch of the front, and all this mass was aiming at that narrow stretch of land with all its firepower.'

Golokolenko rode in a truck with his men to the front line: 'When I heard the artillery fire, it began to snow and the visibility got worse. Later that morning we heard the order to move forward. As soon as we reached the enemy's front line of defence, we came under very powerful fire. One of our tanks exploded, then another, and yet another caught fire. The truck in which I was riding was hit in the radiator. My men dismounted and ran after the tanks. They advanced about 300 metres and the tanks stopped and the infantrymen lay down on the ground…I really felt horrible because in all my previous battles, like those near Leningrad, often when we started the offensive things began to go bad very quickly, and I was frightened that we would never learn to fight well, and so again when things went bad, when we began to fail, I also felt quite desperate and depressed.'

But his unit was just unlucky – it faced a part of the enemy line that had been undamaged by the artillery fire. Elsewhere other units had made good progress, and soon Golokolenko's brigade too was pushing on through the snow, advancing most often at night, further into German-held territory. The Romanians had been given the task of holding the flanks by the Germans, and their poor performance has been the subject of debate ever since. 'I don't want to hurt the feelings of the Romanians,' says Golokolenko, 'but they were less battle-ready than the Germans. The German Army was well trained and they were braver. Romanians didn't have a real goal – what were they fighting for? You can't say that we went on without facing the enemy's resistance, but it was easier than it used to be. They didn't seem to have prepared any defensive areas.'

The main thrust of Operation Uranus was west of the River Don, more than 150 kilometres away from Paulus and Stalingrad to the north. Even if the Germans had responded quickly to the threat, it would have been hard for them to move their armour out to deal with the Soviet attack. But the Germans didn't act swiftly. Paulus's ability to react to the constantly increasing threat of encirclement was compromised by the necessity of consulting Hitler, who was taking time off from his headquarters in East Prussia and was staying at the Berghof in southern Bavaria. Those inadequate units that were sent by the Germans to counter the Soviet advance also had to deal with the snow and the consequent poor visibility. The previous German advantages of surprise and lightning attack were lost.

In one of the legendary Soviet feats of the war, Lieutenant-Colonel Filippov and his men drove brazenly straight into the German-held town of Kalach with their lights turned off, and then, when they reached the bridge across the Don near the centre of the town, suddenly opened fire. This one dramatic action came to epitomize for the Red Army how far they had come, not just courageously but tactically as well. They had beaten the Germans and their Axis allies not because of superior numbers, but because of superior thinking. On 23 November units of the Red Army met up near Kalach and completed the encirclement of the German 6th Army. 'We felt inspiration,' says Ivan Golokolenko. 'We felt confidence that we were capable of beating the enemy successfully, and this operation remained the most memorable – the brightest – event. I remember I felt as if I had wings, I felt as if I was flying. Before that I used to feel depressed, but now it was as if I opened my wings and I was capable of flying in the sky.'

Even though they knew they were encircled, many soldiers of the 6th Army refused to accept that they were in danger. The Red Army, they believed, was composed of inferior people, badly armed and worse trained. Moreover the Führer would not, could not, let them down. The last vestiges of the overweening confidence that had created the Barbarossa plan in the first place had still not disappeared. 'Stalingrad was surrounded,' says Bernhard Bechler, a German officer caught within the encirclement. 'But even then I believed that the Führer would not give us up; that he wouldn't sacrifice the 6th Army, that he would get the 6th Army out of there.' This faith in Hitler during the early stages of the encirclement was voiced by many surviving Stalingrad veterans. 'Everybody thought, well, this can't really last long,' says Gerhard Münch. 'It'll only last a few days – we thought this was a temporary situation.'

Hitler, no doubt influenced by his belief that his own 'will' had prevented a collapse in front of Moscow a year earlier, ordered Paulus to stay where he was and make no attempt to break out of the pocket. Göring, anxious as ever to curry favour with the Führer, boastfully promised that his Luftwaffe would supply the 6th Army by an 'air bridge'. There was a precedent; earlier in 1942, at Demyansk, German planes had successfully air-dropped supplies to troops surrounded by the Red Army – although the Demyansk operation was on nothing like the scale of the one proposed to keep the 6th Army functioning as an effective fighting force. Simultaneously, Field Marshal von Manstein was ordered to attack from the south-west of the front to cut a relief corridor through the Soviet encirclement and relieve Paulus. His Operation Winter Tempest began on 12 December 1942 and pushed on through the snow and sleet into the Soviet ring around Stalingrad.

When the men of the 6th Army learnt of the rescue attempt, they thought it concrete proof of the Führer's commitment to them. 'Allegedly Manstein was approaching,' says Bernhard Bechler. 'They kept telling us this story and sometimes people even imagined: "We've heard the roar of the guns of Manstein's army today – he must be near!" Suddenly these ideas were cropping up, although it wasn't true, but it was fear of the future that made people imagine these things.'

The Soviets had placed 60 divisions inside their ring around Stalingrad and Manstein's task was hopeless. On 19 December, the 57th Panzer Division reached the River Mishov 50 kilometres from Stalingrad – it was as near as the German relief force was ever to get. On Christmas Eve Manstein's own force was threatened with encirclement by the Soviet troops and withdrew.

As 1942 drew to a close it was also clear that the ambitious air bridge promised by Göring could provide but a fraction of the supplies needed within Stalingrad. Those German planes that did manage to get through often dropped their load on the Soviet positions because of wind conditions or a change in the position of the front line. Day by day, as conditions worsened for the 6th Army, their faith in the Führer's power to rescue them began to disintegrate.

'If you haven't experienced it yourself,' says Bernhard Bechler, 'you won't know how cruel it was. When I lay down and stuck my hand under the collar, my hand would be full of lice. And the lice carried typhus…We had nothing to eat. There were some frozen horses and we took an axe and chopped some meat and heated it up in a pot just to have something to eat. We were just lying there, without any food, almost frozen to death, it was dreadful…Just imagine the scene: steppe, everything frozen, sub-zero temperatures of minus 20 or 30 degrees, masses of snow. We were lying in dugouts in the snow…German soldiers were lying on the ground and German tanks ran over these soldiers because they were no longer able to get up and make themselves known. I was thinking to myself, subconsciously: if people at home could see us here, if they could only see our soldiers dying so wretchedly! And as I was thinking, I was beginning to have my first doubts, asking myself; what are you doing here at Stalingrad? What are you doing here, a German officer, thousands of miles away from home? Are you defending Germany in this place? And why?'

After Manstein's relief effort failed, and in the emotional atmosphere of Christmas and New Year in Stalingrad, some officers in the 6th Army were so desperate that they considered suicide. 'After our Christmas "party",' says Gerhard Münch, 'I went to the regimental staff to wish them Merry Christmas. Then I learned that officers of our artillery regiment had shot themselves…And at New Year's Eve my own company commanders came to me and said that, since all of this did not make sense any more, and that everything was finishing anyway, shouldn't we all shoot ourselves together?

We discussed for a whole night with each other what we should do. And at the end of this discussion it was clear that, as long as soldiers had to be led under our command, we did not have any moral right to commit suicide.'

That January Joachim Stempel visited his father, the general commanding the 371st Infantry Division (and a professional soldier before the war), who was fighting in a different section of the Stalingrad encirclement. The encounter would turn out to be one of the defining moments of Joachim Stempel's life: 'I drove to his command centre in a jeep and talked to him about the situation, about which as a divisional commander he knew more than I did as a small platoon leader. And so I realized how bad the situation really was. And my father said, very realistically, "We are being sacrificed in order to save others." And then the door opened and Paulus entered the bunker. My father reported to him and immediately said, "Should my son be sent out?" Paulus said no, that he might as well stay and listen to this. And then they discussed the situation. And Paulus finished by saying this: "My proud 6th Army is meeting a fate it does not deserve. For us, Stempel [he meant my father], the last road we have to take calls for strength, which we also have to ask of our men. As a German general, you know what is required of you at the end. My men and I will defend our position in the bunker until the Russians storm us, and then the bunker will be blown sky-high with us inside. I wish you all the best for your last stand." And he shook hands with both of us and disappeared.'

After Paulus left, Joachim Stempel and his father sat discussing what they had just heard. Its meaning seemed clear: 'My father too said that none of the generals would be taken prisoner – it's impossible, as the commander had said. "You try," he said. "You're still young. You try to get out of this cauldron, somehow to get through…But I will shoot myself. I don't want to be a burden to my staff officers in their attempt to break through. I'm fifty years old, I can't be a burden to them. So I'll take care of it here. I will do it when the Russians are outside my bunker, here in this room in which you're standing…I will act like a captain of a sinking ship. A captain doesn't get into the lifeboat, a captain goes down with his ship. And my men die here for their country, and will never see their homes again, and I won't see my home again either. I will stay here with my men."'

Joachim Stempel had one last conversation with his father: 'I thanked him for the way I had been raised and trained. For my schooling, the good home I'd had, the care I'd been given, and the opportunity to follow a career of my choice that I'd had. And I wished him all the best. And he said, as I saluted him with military honours, he said, "We'll see each other again soon, up there, where all brave soldiers meet again. Take care, my son." I saluted…and walked out to my friends.'

On 10 January 1943 the Red Army mounted Operation Ring to squeeze the noose tighter on the 6th Army, and by 26 January forward Soviet units had linked up with Chuikov's 62nd Army on the Volga. As January came to an end, so did the German resistance. 'One day three Red Army soldiers approached our little foxhole,' says Bernhard Bechler. 'We were living in there, my adjutant – a young lieutenant – and me. The regiment's command post was only a few metres away. Suddenly these Red Army soldiers were coming towards us. And we both thought in a flash, we don't have any ammunition, this is the end. They're either going to shoot us or they'll take us prisoner. What shall we do? At that point I saw my adjutant pull a photo from the pocket of his uniform jacket. I looked at it, and it was a photo of his young wife with two very young children. He glanced at the photo, tore it to pieces, pulled his hand-gun, shot himself in the head and was dead. I experienced it there and then, but one can't imagine what it's like when a person is suddenly lying there dying. The following moment the

Red Army soldier was upon me. He held his pistol to my chest, but he didn't pull the trigger, and at that point, when I realized he wasn't going to shoot me, my second life began.'

As the German defence crumbled, Gerhard Münch, who only a few weeks before had counselled his junior officers not to commit suicide but to stay with their men as long as they were needed, received unexpected orders from a colonel at 51st Corps Headquarters. 'You are flying out, today,' he was told. Münch had been selected as one of the last 'special envoys' to carry documents out of Stalingrad. At the makeshift airfield desperate German soldiers milled around as Münch clambered aboard the plane. 'Then Russian artillery started to shoot at us and, as the pilot took off, soldiers who had not been able to get into the plane clung to the bottom of it. He tried to shake them off and they actually fell down. You can hardly describe it: you had to have seen it – all the hopes that these people had to get out of there.'

Münch had left his men behind in the encirclement – he had not even been allowed to telephone his own regiment to say that he was leaving them: 'It took me a long time, internally, to cope with it, the fact that I had not personally kept to the principle by which I had been brought up and educated – to stand by your men. It was very, very tough to cope with. It took me years…the soldiers believed in me and there was a relationship of trust, which is key for any soldiers' relationship. And then, in the last consequence, I am flown out.'

As the fate of the 6th Army became inevitable even to Hitler, he promoted Paulus to the rank of field marshal. No German field marshal had ever been taken prisoner. The message was clear – Paulus was expected to kill himself.

On 30 January, as Soviet troops closed in on Paulus's headquarters at the Univermag store on Heroes of the Revolution Square, Gerhard Hindenlang, one of his battalion commanders, received a radio message containing news of this promotion. Hindenlang was told to take the news to Paulus – along with the intelligence assessment that the Red Army was about to overwhelm the last German resistance: 'I went over and reported to the general and told him that on the radio we had heard about his promotion to field marshal. But I also had to say that at the same time I would have to ask him to capitulate because the Russians had positioned themselves around this store [his command post] and further defence was pointless. And he said to me, approximately, "Hindenlang, I am the youngest field marshal of the German Army and I have to become a prisoner of war." And I was a bit surprised – stunned even – to hear that, and he saw the surprise on my face and he said, "What do you think of suicide?" And I said, "Field Marshal, I lead troops and I will do so right until the last moment. I will go and become a prisoner of war if needs be, but you – you haven't got any forces any more." And he said, "Hindenlang, I'm a Christian. I refuse to commit suicide."'

The next day Paulus was captured alive by the Red Army. The minutes of Hitler's midday situation conference of 1 February 1943 survive, and demonstrate the combination of rage and bewilderment with which the Führer greeted the news: 'What hurts me so much,' he said, 'is that the heroism of so many soldiers is cancelled out by one single character-less weakling...What is "life"?...the individual must die anyway. It is the nation which lives on after the individual. But how can anyone be afraid of this moment which sets him free from this vale of misery, unless the call of duty keeps him in this vale of tears!' Still later in the conference Hitler repeated his main theme. 'What hurts me the most personally is that I went on and promoted him to field marshal... That's the last field marshal I promote in this war. One must not count one's chickens before they are hatched...I just don't understand it...He could have got out of this vale of tears and into eternity and been immortalized by the nation, and he'd rather go to Moscow. How can he even think of that as an alternative? It's crazy.' The transcript reveals a man almost in shock – less at the failure to hold Stalingrad than at the actions of Paulus.[4]

For Günther von Below, who was Paulus's chief of operations and who went into captivity along with him, the field marshal's decision not to commit suicide is easy to explain. 'He [Paulus] said, "As a human being, and above all as a Christian, I do not have the right to take my own life." And my attitude was the same... It wasn't cowardice. It was quite simply our duty to go into captivity with our soldiers. And if I had taken my own life there, that would have been cowardice. That is my conviction.'

But the idea that Paulus, by not taking his own life, was able to 'go into captivity' with his men is dismissed by Joachim Stempel: 'It's just a joke, because minutes later the general was no longer with his troops – he was in a heated fast train, with white linen on the bed and table, on his way to the generals' camp in Moscow.' Paulus was indeed separated from his men – and photographs in an album still kept in the secret archive of the Russian Security Service show the relative comfort of the field marshal's captivity. The conditions of his imprisonment were, if not luxurious, certainly far superior to the degradation that awaited his men in the Soviet camps. (Just over 90,000 German soldiers were taken prisoner at Stalingrad; of these, 95 per cent of the non-commissioned officers and ordinary soldiers died, along with 55 per cent of the junior officers but only 5 per cent of senior officers.)[5]

'I was disappointed,' says Joachim Stempel of his reaction to the news that Paulus had decided to allow himself to be captured. 'And I mistrusted everything. Because I thought, well, what is the word of a superior officer worth?' As far as Stempel was concerned, the conversation he had witnessed between Paulus and his father had been unequivocal – Paulus was calling on his senior officers to commit suicide. 'If my father had been uncertain in any way, he might have thought, well, OK, if Paulus, as commander-in-chief, survives and is taken prisoner, why should I, a divisional commander, not be taken captive as well?'

As Paulus was captured by the Red Army, elsewhere in Stalingrad Valentina Krutova and her brother and sister lay huddled in bed – by now too weak to scavenge for food: 'My brother was lying on one side of the bed, I was lying on the other side and my young sister was between us. The only thought we had was where to find something to eat. We were so hungry. I can't imagine now myself what I lived through... We simply stayed in bed and were lying all day silently; clinging to each other, hugging each other. Trying to keep our sister warm. We would turn our faces to her and press ourselves to her body.' Then, one day, they heard knocking at their door: 'And we could hear somebody shouting [in Russian], "Why are you knocking on the door? Don't knock. Maybe there are Germans inside, they'll shoot us. Throw the grenade." But one soldier did open the door, and to start with they couldn't make out who was inside. But we began to scream, "Don't kill us! We're Russians!" The soldier who was first to come in shouted, "There are children here." When they came in and saw us, they burst out crying.'

For the Red Army, the victory in Stalingrad was more than just a military triumph: it marked a spiritual watershed. 'I drank a toast,' says Suren Mirzoyan, 'and said after Stalingrad I am no longer afraid.' For Anatoly Mereshko, the victory gave him 'a supernatural, extraordinary feeling – that I won't be killed in the war. When I saw the surrendering Germans, and when I realized they hadn't killed me in Stalingrad, I felt I would live to see the victory. I felt confident. It was a real certainty that I would not die.'

But Stalingrad was not the single decisive moment of the war on the Eastern Front that is sometimes claimed. The Germans did not give up after this defeat, and the continued resistance of the 6th Army enabled the Germans to extricate Army Group A safely from the Kalmyk steppes and the Caucasus to the south, and thus avoid another encirclement. But the defeat at Stalingrad was none the less hugely significant. Never again would the German Army cast their eyes on the Volga.

While these dramatic actions were taking place on the front line, hundreds of miles away a crime was being committed by which the Nazis would, for all time, be defined – the mechanised extermination of the Jewish people.

THE ROAD TO TREBLINKA

IMAGES OF AUSCHWITZ ARE AMONG THE MOST FAMILIAR ON the planet: the row upon row of huts, the emaciated corpses staring out at us from old newsreels. Film exists of Auschwitz because it was a work camp as well as an extermination centre, and this also partly accounts for why there are many more survivors of this camp than the others. But Auschwitz, though a place of nightmares, is not *the* quintessential example of Nazi horror. The Nazis created other hell-like places that were killing factories – pure and simple – designed to produce nothing but corpses. These places, far from German soil, achieved their devilish purpose and were destroyed by the Nazis before the end of the war to hide the enormity of their crime. Such a place was Treblinka. If you visit the site of Treblinka camp today, deep in the isolated Polish countryside, you will stand in a forest and hear only birds. Yet you still stand on a spot that marks one of the lowest points to which human beings have ever descended. The memorial stone at what was the camp boundary is inscribed with the words 'Never Again'. It should also bear another word, written in letters of fire – 'Remember'.

Samuel Willenberg, whom the Germans had caught in a round-up of Jews in Opatów, southern Poland, was in a train rattling towards Treblinka in 1942. Now, crammed into a cattle truck, he heard Polish children shout as they passed different stations, 'Jews! You'll be turned into soap!' As the train snaked through the countryside, Samuel heard other Jews in the cattle truck whisper, 'It's bad. We are going to Treblinka.' Yet still nobody in the truck wanted to accept that a place could exist simply for the elimination of innocent human beings. 'It was hard to believe,' says Samuel Willenberg. 'I was here and still I could not believe it at first.'

The train arrived at Treblinka station, the cattle truck doors crashed open and suddenly there was shouting, '*Schnell, schnell*!' Ukrainians in black SS uniforms herded the Jews off the platform and through a gate into the lower part of the camp. Men were pushed to the right, women to the left. A young Jewish man carrying pieces of string and wearing a red armband approached the men and told them to take off their shoes and tie them together. The young man looked familiar to Samuel. 'I asked him, "Listen, where are you from?" He told me and asked me where I was from. I said, "Czestochowa, Opatów, Warsaw." "From Czestochowa?" "Yes." "What's your name?" "Samuel Willenberg." "Say you are a bricklayer," and he left.' That chance meeting and those five words of advice saved Samuel's life. He told the guards he was a bricklayer and so became one of the tiny handful of Jews selected to help in the camp, not for immediate death.

Some 800,000 people (other estimates say more than one million) were exterminated in Treblinka camp over a period of thirteen months between July 1942 and August 1943. It took just 50 Germans, 150 Ukrainians and just over 1000 Jews forced to work with them to accomplish it all. Standing in the clearing where the camp used to be, what strikes one first is its size – a mere 600 by 400 metres. It is a profoundly upsetting moment when one realizes that if people are to be murdered there is no need of space.

The layout of the camp could scarcely have been simpler. The victims arrived on train trucks and were then herded from the station to a central courtyard in the camp where the men were ordered to undress. On one side of the yard was a barracks where the women undressed and where their hair was shaved. 'At that point,' says Samuel, 'the women gained hope, for if they are going to have their hair cut, it means there is going to be some life after, for hygiene is necessary in a camp.' The women did not know, of course, that the Germans wanted to stuff mattresses with their hair. The nakedness of the victims also worked in the Germans' favour. 'A man who takes his shoes off and then is ordered "Strip!" and is naked – that man is no longer a human being, no longer a master of himself,' says Samuel. 'He covers certain parts of his body, he is embarrassed. Suddenly, he has a thousand problems of which he has not been aware in his normal life, which he did not have as he was never forced to walk about naked – except perhaps as a child – among people, among friends. Suddenly everyone is naked! And the Germans, you see, took advantage of that. And on top of that, the lashing, "Quick! *Schnell, schnell*!" At that point one wanted to run somewhere as fast as one could, run somewhere, no matter where.' The men, women and children were harried down a path (the Germans called it 'The Path to Heaven') less than a hundred metres to the gas chambers where they were murdered. Once dead, their bodies were thrown into pits next to the gas chambers.

The whole process, from the arrival of the train to the remains being hurled into the pit, took less than two hours. Most of the victims were never certain where they were or what was happening to them until the last moment. Every effort was made to try and deceive them about their fate. Treblinka station was decorated like a real station with a clock and timetables. The victims were told they had arrived at a transit camp where they would have to take a shower. High barbed-wire fences, in which branches were entwined, wound through the camp so that no one could see what was about to happen to them next.

After the murder of the victims, Treblinka became a vast sorting area. In a huge yard on the east side of the camp Jewish workers, such as Samuel Willenberg, had to sort out belongings which, until moments previously, had been someone's treasured possessions. 'It looked like a Persian bazaar,' says Samuel, 'open suitcases, spread-out sheets, and on each sheet lay different things. Trousers separately from shirts, from woollen things, it all had to be sorted. The gold lay separate in the bags...Each of us had a sheet spread out next to him where we put photos, documents, diplomas.' Samuel worked under the eyes of a sadist, an SS guard they called 'Doll'. He had a St Bernard dog called Barry, which he had trained to tear out human flesh, to bite at a man's genitals, on the command 'Man bite dog'. (As the verdict at 'Doll's' later trial stated: 'By the word "man" he meant Barry: the word "dog" referred to the prisoner.')[1] Every moment of the time that Samuel worked in Treblinka until his escape into the surrounding forest seven months later, he risked being killed in an instant, on a whim.

More than fifty years on Samuel Willenberg can still only scarcely comprehend what he saw. 'They alighted on to the platform in the usual manner, as if they had arrived in a health resort. And here, on this small plot of land, was taking place the greatest murder that ever took place in Europe, in the entire world. Before he died, Professor Mering [Samuel's history teacher, who worked alongside him at Treblinka] said, and I will never forget it: "You know, I look at it from the point of view of history." "Excuse me?" I looked at him as if he had gone mad.'

At night Samuel and the other Jews made to work in the camp would try to make sense of what was happening to them: 'There were discussions, quietly, people asked each other, "Why?" That question, all the time – why? Why? And, "For what crime? Why small children? What have they done? What have I done? What has each of us done?" There was no answer.' These same questions still resonate today. How was it possible that Germans ordered and organized this mechanized extermination? Not just in Treblinka, but in Auschwitz, Belzec, Sobibór and the other death camps. In all history there is no crime to equal it. No one before has ever sought to kill men, women and children on this scale and to justify such killing by the simple expedient 'They were Jews' or 'They were Gypsies' or 'They were homosexuals' – to kill people just because they did not fit, were not wanted. How could it happen? How could a place like Treblinka come to exist on the face of the Earth?

No single cause is itself sufficient to explain it. Rather, there were a number of preconditions without which the final decision to order this mass extermination could not have been made. Chapter One described how anti-Semitism grew in Germany after World War I and how some extreme right-wing parties used rhetoric calling for the Jews to be killed. But before he became Chancellor of Germany, Hitler himself, at least in his public speeches and writing, never openly called for the Jews to be murdered. His public stance in the 1930s was consistent with calls for the Jews to be excluded from German citizenship and to be forced out of Germany altogether. Many Jews were subsequently pressed into leaving Germany, and this method of dealing with the Nazi-created problem of the Jews was to exist almost until the moment when the killings were ordered.

Yet behind the idea of 'purifying' Germany by ridding it of Jews there had always lain a far more sinister philosophy. As early as 21 March 1933 a Leipzig newspaper had announced: 'If a bullet strikes our beloved leader, all the Jews in Germany will immediately be put up against the wall and the result will be a greater blood bath than anything the world has ever seen.' As Arnon Tamir told us, Nazi anti-Semitism can be summed up in the simple words, 'The Jew is guilty, for everything, always.'[2]

The idea of *blame* is a crucial one. Even the mentally ill, whom the Nazis despised, were never held personally to blame for their own illness. The Jews, however, were always blameworthy: they were held responsible for the loss of World War I and were behind the hideous creed of Bolshevism. It did not matter that this analysis was simply wrong; it was still possible for the Nazis to believe it – after all, Germany had clearly lost the war and suffered as a result. Furthermore, the Nazis said *every* Jew was to blame because, as Nazi propaganda made clear, the Jews were all part of one homogeneous mass, loyal to each other rather than to their Fatherland. If one Jew had committed a crime, then all Jews had committed it.

None of this meant that the extermination of the Jews was inevitable from the moment the Nazis came to power. For most of the 1930s many Jews managed to live relatively peacefully in Hitler's Reich. After the chaotic violence of the early months of the regime and the abortive boycott of 1 April 1933 there was less violent oppression. Segregation and discrimination remained widespread, but many Jews managed to tolerate these everyday abuses. Then, on 9 November 1938, came Kristallnacht. The horror of that night is encapsulated in the experience of 18-year-old Rudi Bamber, who rang the police to report that Storm Troopers were smashing up his family's house, only to realize that they would not help; the police approved of the crime.

Kristallnacht is important in the development of Nazi anti-Semitism because it illustrates once again how the Jews were held collectively to blame for any crime. The Jew who shot the German diplomat in Paris was not treated as an individual criminal, but as one cell in an organism that consisted of all Jews. Rudi Bamber tried to work out why the Storm Troopers had picked on his family. What had they done wrong? But the Nazis did not think that way. *All* Jews were held responsible for any crime committed by any other Jew. It did not matter that they had never met or that they might condemn his crime; one Jew was all Jews.

This all meant that the Jews were in a uniquely vulnerable position in Nazi Germany. On 30 January 1939 Hitler gave a speech that included these words: '...if the international Jewish financiers in and outside Europe should succeed in plunging the nations once more into a world war, then the result will not be the Bolshevizing of the Earth, and thus the victory of Jewry, but the annihilation of the Jewish race in Europe.' At first reading these words seem unequivocal. Hitler talks of the 'annihilation of the Jewish race in Europe' – what could be a clearer promise of the Holocaust than that? But it is not necessarily that obvious. We have already seen how the ghetto managers of Łódź in 1940 knew nothing of any planned extermination; instead, they had initiated a scheme whereby the ghetto was functioning as a slave factory. And another significant clue about Nazi thinking in 1940 exists in Himmler's memo, 'Some thoughts on the treatment of the alien population in the east'. When writing about his plans to educate Polish children only at the lowest level and to kidnap any Polish children who seem to be 'racially first class', Himmler adds the paragraph: 'However cruel and tragic each individual case may be, if one rejects the Bolshevik method of physically exterminating a people as fundamentally un-German and impossible, then this method is the mildest and best one.' Thus to Himmler, writing in the spring of 1940, 'physically exterminating a people' is 'un-German'. Of course, he could have been lying. He could already have known of a secret plan Hitler had hatched to exterminate another group – the Jews. But why would he bother to dissemble in a memo destined for Hitler? Himmler had no difficulty in making inhuman statements once the Holocaust had been decided upon. (In a speech at Posen in October 1943, talking of the 'extermination of the Jewish people', he said, 'We had the moral right, we had the duty to our people, to destroy this people which wanted to destroy us,' and, 'We have exterminated a bacterium because we did not want in the end to be infected by the bacterium and die of it.')[3]

It therefore seems highly unlikely that, despite Hitler's speech in 1939, there was any systematic plan to exterminate the Jews until 1941. But we can never know for sure because we cannot know the content of Hitler's mind – his secret intention. Maybe he longed to implement extermination but was restrained enough to wait until he thought he could do so with impunity. Alternatively, and perhaps more probably, Hitler always loathed and despised the Jews and simply wanted to get rid of them. What form that 'getting rid of' would take was something the Nazis were capable of revising given the circumstances. Initially, the overt policy was clearly one of expulsion. Before the war Adolf Eichmann ran the SS 'Office for Jewish emigration' in Vienna after the Anschluss, which served effectively to steal the Austrian Jews' money before they were allowed to leave. In one sense this was working towards 'annihilating' the Jewish race in Austria.

A grander plan to expel the Jews from Europe took shape in 1940 at the time of the fall of France. At first sight it is an incredible, almost unbelievable plan – to send the Jews to Madagascar. Franz Rademacher, who worked in the German Foreign Ministry, wrote the following memo dated 3 July 1940: 'The imminent victory gives the Germans the possibility, and in my opinion also the duty, of solving the Jewish question in Europe. The desirable solution is: All Jews out of Europe...In the peace treaty France must make the island Madagascar available for the solution of the Jewish question, and must resettle the approximately 25,000 French people living there and compensate them. The island will be transferred to Germany as a mandate...The Jews will be jointly liable for the value of the island. Their former European assets will be transferred for liquidation to a European bank to be set up for the purpose. In so far as these assets are insufficient to pay for the land which they get and for the necessary purchase of commodities in Europe needed for developing the island, bank credits will be made available to the Jews by the same bank.'[4] Outlandish as it appears, this plan was the logical conclusion of the expulsion policy which the Nazis had been following up to this point. The Madagascar version was simply more ambitious: to send the Jews to an island off the coast of Africa and to steal all their money by making them pay for the privilege of going there. And Madagascar was not going to be a tropical paradise for the Jews, it was proposed that the Chancellery of the Führer organize transportation to the island under its head, Philipp Bouhler, the man behind the murderous Nazi euthanasia policy.

In the event, the Madagascar plan came to nothing. A precondition of its success was that the sea route to Africa needed to be safe for German shipping. With Britain still in the war, this could not be guaranteed. Of course, when Rademacher wrote his memo in July 1940, the Nazis thought it likely that Britain would shortly be out of the war. Hitler had never wanted to fight the British and was prepared to discuss peace terms – a peace that would have probably turned Britain into a satellite of the Nazi empire, like Vichy France.

As 1941 dawned, no practical progress had been made on the ambitious Madagascar plan. Deportations of Poles and Jews to the General Government had begun again, but not in sufficient numbers to solve Greiser's problems. Hans

Frank still complained that the General Government did not have the resources to take the deportees and the transports temporarily stopped again in March 1941. The squabbling between the competing Nazi barons of Poland over the destination of Polish 'undesirables' seemed never-ending.

By now preparations were in hand for the invasion of the Soviet Union, an event that was to be the catalyst for a radical change in Nazi policy towards the Jews. This time a much more extensive role for the Einsatzgruppen was openly acknowledged.

Instructions dated 2 July 1941 tell of the proposed scope of the work of the Einsatzgruppen: '4. Executions. The following will be executed: all officials of the Comintern (most of these will certainly be career politicians); officials of senior and middle rank and 'extremists' in the party, the central committee, and the provincial and district committees; the people's commissars; Jews in the service of the Party or the State...No steps will be taken to interfere with any purges that may be initiated by anti-Communist or anti-Jewish elements in the newly occupied territories. On the contrary, these are to be secretly encouraged.'[5] Reinhard Heydrich, Head of the Reich Main Security Office and close colleague of Himmler, who issued these instructions, is thus openly calling for the execution only of 'Jews in the service of the Party or State', but the fact that purges are to be 'secretly encouraged' and that implicitly such purges may include the killing of women and children shows that there is an inherent contradiction in the instructions, unless the reference to 'Jews in the service of the Party or State' constitutes the bare minimum of Jews to be murdered.

Let us look at how one of the Einsatzgruppen went about its hideous tasks. Einsatzgruppe A was under the command of Police General and SS Brigadeführer Dr Walther Stahlecker. They moved into Lithuania behind the German

Army on 23 June 1941 and swiftly reached the town of Kaunas, Lithuania's second city. Given that Lithuania had been incorporated into the Soviet Union against her will in 1940 (as a result of the Molotov/Ribbentrop secret protocol), Stahlecker hoped that the Lithuanians themselves could be persuaded to turn on their former enemies. The Nazi lie that Communism and Judaism were virtually synonymous had also spread in Lithuania during the brief period of Communist rule. According to a report by Stahlecker, 'The task of the security police was to set these purges in motion and put them on the right track so as to ensure that the liquidation goals that had been set might be achieved in the shortest possible time.'[6]

Just after the Germans arrived in Kaunas, a sixteen-year-old Lithuanian girl called Viera Silkinaite walked past a row of garages just outside the city centre. She saw a group of people gathered around what looked like some drunks having a fight. As she drew closer, she saw that one man was lying on the ground, hardly breathing. Another man was standing above him holding a wooden club. This was not a drunken brawl, but the brutal clubbing to death of unarmed Jews by Lithuanians who had just been released from prison by the Germans. 'I was very frightened,' she says. 'I was lost, worried. I cannot describe my state of mind. Even now I can see that picture in my eyes.' Some of the crowd watching the killing shouted encouragement to the murderers, screaming, 'Beat those Jews!' and one man even held his small child up so that he could see. Viera Silkinaite could scarcely believe that a child was watching: 'What kind of person would he be when he grew up? If, of course, he could understand what he had seen. And what could you expect of such a person who was shouting? It was as if he was going to step into that garage and join the beating.'

Reports survive from some Germans who happened to witness these killings. One, written by an army officer, reads: 'There was a large number of women in the crowd and they had lifted up their children or stood them on chairs or boxes so that they could see better. At first I thought this must be a victory celebration or some type of sporting event because of the cheering, clapping and laughter that kept breaking out. However, when I enquired what was happening, I was told that the "Death-dealer of Kovno [Kaunas]" was at work...In response to a cursory wave, the next man stepped forward silently and was then beaten to death with the wooden club in the most bestial manner...'[7] A German photographer witnessed that, 'After the entire group had been beaten to death, the young man put the crowbar to one side, fetched an accordion and went and stood on the mountain of corpses and played the Lithuanian national anthem.'[8]

After witnessing just a few minutes of the killing, Viera Silkinaite ran off to seek sanctuary in a nearby cemetery. 'I was ashamed,' she says. 'When I went to the cemetery, I sat down and I thought: "God Almighty, I heard before that there were windows broken or something like that done, that was still conceivable, but such an atrocity, to beat a helpless man...it was too much."'

From the first, Einsatzgruppe A was more murderous than the other three groups. We know this because of extensive documentation generated by the groups themselves. Different Einsatzgruppen appear to have interpreted their initial orders in different ways, but even Einsatzgruppe A stopped short of murdering women and children in the initial weeks of the occupation.

Riva Losanskaya, who lived in the village of Butrimonys, roughly halfway between Kaunas and the Lithuanian capital of Vilnius, was twenty-one years old when the Germans invaded. Until the war she had spent a happy life in Butrimonys with her father, mother and two sisters. They were Jewish, but that was of little consequence before the war as everyone rubbed along together without a problem. 'When the war began,' says Riva, 'although we knew that the Jews were suffering in Poland, we still could not believe that the same thing could happen to us. How could innocent people be detained and killed? My father used to say that without a trial no harm could be done to anyone.' But as the German troops advanced, Riva saw people rushing around shouting 'We must flee!' There were rumours of Jews being killed in reprisals by Germans in the local town and that 'the streets were scattered with corpses'. Riva and her family gathered a few possessions together and travelled 10 kilometres to a nearby village where they tried to hide. They still thought that the Russians had been pushed back only temporarily and that the Germans would be swiftly thrown out of Lithuania. Soon, however it became clear that the Russians were not returning and that there was little point, as a family, in trying to hide in another village. 'The people in the village wouldn't give you a crust of bread,' says Riva. 'We had nowhere to go.' So the family returned to Butrimonys, where they lived uneasily in their own house.

Within days of the German occupation, all the Jewish young men of the village were rounded up and taken away. The remaining Jewish villagers were told that the young men had been taken to the nearby town of Alytus, where they had been put to work for the Germans. Riva's father was among those taken after the initial arrests. Days later some locals called on her and her mother and said they had good news. 'These "nice" people with whom we had been on such friendly terms all our life came to us,' says Riva, 'and told us, "We've seen your father, don't cry!" It was Vaitkevicius [a local who has since died], who came to tell us, "Here is a letter we got from him. We'll read it to you and then I'll take a parcel back for him." He had been very friendly with my father. I went to see my neighbours to tell them that everyone was still alive. "Why the tears? My father is still alive and I'm sending him clothes and food via Vaitkevicius." My neighbours said, "Riva, you have such nice friends. Can we pay him to take parcels to our husbands and fathers too?" So we got our parcels ready and gave them to Vaitkevicius who took them all. Other people were collecting up parcels in all the other streets too.' But it was a trick, breathtaking in its callousness. Just before they were killed by the Lithuanian police acting on German orders, the Jewish men had been made to write letters to their families asking for money, clothes and food to be sent to them. Then locals had been given these letters by the police so that they could steal from the victims' families. By the time Riva was told by her neighbours, 'We've seen your father,' he was already dead.

After her father was taken, Riva and her family never spent a night at home. Instead they slept out in the potato fields or in the homes of their neighbours, being careful never to spend more than one night in any one place. Nonetheless, they never went far from their house and still visited it during the day. Then, in September 1941, rumours of a change in policy towards the Jews began to spread around the village. It was said that the Germans had ordered the killing of every Jew in Lithuania, including women and children. 'A woman had even said, "I know that they've already dug the pits,"' says Riva, 'but we thought that maybe the pit was for potatoes...for the war. She was running round the ghetto saying, "They're going to shoot us tomorrow, you must flee!" But the people were thinking, "Perhaps they aren't going to shoot us, perhaps they dug those pits for no particular reason." That's how stupid we were. We didn't imagine that they would come to kill us so fast. The clever Jewish people said that since some kind of holiday was coming, we could relax for a few days.'

As 9 September was a church holiday, many Jews in Butrimonys thought it would be the one day on which their safety was guaranteed. They were wrong. That morning Lithuanian policemen, helped by enthusiastic locals, began rounding up the women, children and old people who constituted the remaining Jewish population of Butrimonys. Riva and her mother were part of a column herded along a road out of the village. Their destination was about 2 kilometres away – a pit that had been dug about 200 metres from the road among grassland and trees. The Jews shuffling to their deaths were weak with hunger, many shaken by living rough in the fields. 'I was thinking they'd kill everyone and the survivors would be cursed,' says Riva. 'But right up until the very last moment, I still had a faint vestige of hope.' When they were a little over 500 metres from the place of execution, Riva saw a path leading off into the forest on the other side of the road. She dragged her mother towards it and together they hid behind some shrubs. The guards had grown lazy because the rest of the Jews were so compliant and Riva and her mother were not missed. Minutes later they heard gunshots. 'Dogs were barking, perhaps they were frightened by the sound of the shooting,' says Riva. 'My mother said, "They're already shooting!" I said, "No, no, they're dogs." I only said that because I was scared that my mother would go mad.'

That same day Alfonsas Navasinskas was crossing a nearby meadow with a friend, Kosima. 'We saw people being driven along from Butrimonys,' he says. 'Someone on horseback came first and then some policemen and then some ordinary people – a shopkeeper and some clerks who worked in the offices distributing food coupons. They had all gathered together to take the Jews along. They were given sticks and the odd rifle.' Navasinskas and his friend followed the group and watched as the Jews were ordered to lie down on the grass. 'Then along came the men who did the shooting.

"Everybody get up," the Jews were told.' Navasinskas noticed that torn banknotes lay scattered on the ground. The Jews had ripped up their money to prevent the killers profiting from them. 'I waited a little and then went closer,' says Navasinskas. 'I could hear them as they shouted, "Choose your space, you so and so!"' He watched as a new group of Jews were ordered to strip at the side of the pit. As they did, some threw their clothes to people they knew in the crowd to prevent their killers from stealing their possessions. Navasinskas later heard remarks by a villager, who had been given an overcoat by one of the condemned Jews just before he was shot: 'Had the Jews survived, I wouldn't have got it. I'll wear it to a dance tonight!' He also heard a Jewish woman tell another local, 'Here's a cardigan, give it to your wife.' The buttons were covered with cloth but they were gold coins from the Tsar's time. The recipient of the cardigan, unaware of its hidden value chucked it in the farmyard with the chickens. In time, the chickens pecked holes in the cloth and revealed the glittering coins to the farmer. 'He has since died, but he told me that to have deserved finding the coins he must have been deemed "good in the eyes of God".'

After he had seen five groups of Jews shot at the pit, Alfonsas Navasinskas went home alone (his friend stayed on to collect the torn-up money). 'I kept turning round to look behind me, wondering whether anybody was coming after me. It was such a horrible feeling. Nobody spoke up for the Jews, nobody said a word. It was as if it were all quite normal.'

Another villager who came to witness the murders was Juozas Gramauskas, then twenty-one years old. 'The women, children and old men were shot inside the pit,' he says. 'The children were going from person to person, shouting, "Mummy, Daddy, Mummy, Daddy, Mummy!" I think someone was calling for his daughter. And along came a really fat chap with a pistol and...bang, bang! All the grief and weeping was just heartbreaking. Even now, I cannot bear the memory of all the lamenting and crying there. To this day I cannot imagine what was going on.'

The shooting was carried out by Lithuanian soldiers acting under German orders. There were German soldiers present but they simply observed the slaughter. The killing went on until evening, when fires were lit in order to see if there was any movement inside the pit. 'I constantly see it before my eyes, the beasts!' says Juozas Gramauskas.

All this horror is registered in the report of Einsatz-kommando 3 simply as follows: '9.9.41 Butrimonys – 67 Jews, 370 Jewesses, 303 Jewish children – (total) 740.' Some villagers remember the execution day as 8 rather than 9 September and recall seeing as many as 900 Jews killed. In the savage circumstances precise record-keeping was hardly practicable.

It is almost impossible to understand how human beings could do this. An easy route, and one that has been taken by some, is to say that those involved were all 'mad', but the evidence scarcely supports this easy conclusion. The diary of a German/Austrian member of an Einsatzkommando, Felix Landau, survives. He was a cabinet-maker by trade, who joined the Nazis in 1931 at the age of twenty-one and became a member of the Gestapo in Vienna in 1938. He reported to the Einsatzkommando in June 1941, initially for duty in Poland. His diary is an exceptional document because it mixes the horror of his days of killing with sentimental longing for his girlfriend. The entry for 3 July 1941 concludes: 'I have little inclination to shoot defenceless people – even if they are only Jews. I would far rather good honest open combat. Now good night, my dear Hasi [bunny].'[9] The entry for two days later records the shooting of members of the Resistance: 'One of them simply would not die. The first layer of sand had already been thrown on the first group when a hand emerged from out of the sand, waved and pointed to a place, presumably his heart. A couple more shots rang out, then someone shouted – in fact the Pole himself – "Shoot faster!" What is a human being?' The next paragraph begins: 'It looks like we'll be getting our first warm meal today. We've all been given 10 Reichmarks to buy ourselves a few necessities. I bought myself a whip costing 2 Reichmarks.'[10]

On 12 July 1941 he writes: 'Isn't it strange, you love battle and then you have to shoot defenceless people. Twenty-three had to be shot...The death candidates are organized into three shifts as there are not many shovels. Strange, I am completely unmoved. No pity, nothing. That's the way it is and then it's all over.'[11]

Felix Landau's diary shows a man to whom remorse is an unknown emotion. He is a selfish and base human being, but not a madman.

There are many advantages to studying such a diary, not least that it represents the moment with a lack of hindsight. But there is no substitute for the additional insight to be gained by meeting the participants, so we set out to find one of the killers who had operated in Lithuania. Eventually we traced a former Lithuanian soldier who had murdered Jews alongside the German Einsatzgruppe and who spent twenty years in Siberia as a result. Petras Zelionka was born in 1917 and came from a peasant background. His family was not badly off for the region, owning a small farm with two cows. Under the Russian occupation he heard rumours that 'in the security department people were mostly tortured by the Jews. They used to put screws on the head and tighten them, thus torturing the teachers and professors.' He joined the Lithuanian Army because, as he says, 'I respected Lithuania and I am a real Lithuanian...I was attracted to military things, I liked it very much.'

Petras Zelionka was first involved in the killing of Jews in the Seventh Fort at Kaunas in the early days of the German

The entrance to Bremen station. This photograph was taken in 1941 when the Nazis were at the height of their power.

Above Himmler pays a visit to a concentration camp in the east and examines the Russian prisoners. In the conflict in the east the POWs (on both sides) were treated appallingly. The Germans took 5 million Soviet prisoners – only 2 million survived the war.
Right German soldiers conduct an execution in a forest somewhere in the east, 1941. Shootings like this were widespread on the Eastern Front.

Above Jews are deported from Würzburg in Germany in 1942. Knowledge varied wildly amongst the German Jews about their possible fate – most could probably not conceive that they would be exterminated. Germany, after all, was a civilized country.

Left An unknown man and boy stare out from behind the wire of Auschwitz, January 1945. Suffering like this was the logical conclusion of the Nazis' pseudo-Darwinian theories.

Right Count von Stauffenberg. The man who tried to kill Hitler on 20 July 1944.
Below The aftermath of the bomb at the Wolf's Lair. No wonder, seeing this destruction, that Hitler felt divine providence had saved him.
Opposite Women run with their children from the advancing Red Army, Danzig, March 1945.

Above The aftermath of the fire-bombing of Dresden, February 1945. Destruction like this reinforced, for many Germans, the need to fight to the end.

Opposite top A German soldier gives a thumbs-up sign to a Frenchman who has volunteered to fight for the Germans against the Soviet Union. The Nazis dreamt of an alliance of the west against the east.

Opposite below German soldiers shoot 'deserters', April 1945. That spring the Nazis turned on their own countrymen in an unprecedented way.

Above Soviet soldiers shelter behind a sign which says, in Russian, 'Onwards Stalingraders, the victory is close!', in the Kreuzberg district of Berlin, April 1945.

Left The grave of a German soldier is marked by a cross and three helmets as holidaymakers sunbathe by one of the lakes in Berlin in the summer of 1945. The war was over, but it couldn't be forgotten.

occupation, during the period when the Einsatzgruppen killed predominantly men. As a guard, he patrolled the ramparts and watched as Jewish men were shot, fifteen at a time, at the edge of a pit which had been dug within the confines of the fort. Earth was thrown on each layer of bodies, then the whole process was repeated until there were no more Jewish men left to kill that day. He recalls that the men went to their deaths with little resistance, 'totally as lambs'.

From the late summer of 1941 the killing widened to include women and children in outlying villages, and Zelionka became one of the murderers himself. His answer to our question, 'When was the first time you had to shoot?' is revealing. 'Where? Where was I? Maybe I was in Babtai? Or maybe near Joniskis, around there…I had to take them somewhere. To take them first from the ghetto and to bring them somewhere.' As the statement he gave to the Russian authorities after the war confirms, Zelionka participated in many mass killings – so many that today he cannot remember where he first committed murder.

Describing a typical day's killing, he told us how soldiers from his battalion would leave their barracks after breakfast, not knowing their destination. There would be the simple command, 'Men, we have to go!' Then they would clamber aboard their lorries and leave. The mood in the lorry he describes as 'not very good. Sometimes I thought I would have to shoot an innocent man.' (His concept of 'innocence' is a diabolical one that excludes all Jews, even women and children.)

Once they reached their destination they would harry the Jews from the village out to the pre-prepared execution site. The Germans would strip the Jews of their 'golden things', such as jewellery and watches, and then order them to lie down. A certain number would then be counted off and taken to the pit, where they were shot. His battalion was assisted by a German detachment. 'You could not do it without the

Germans. They had machine-guns. We had just to shoot.'

The murderers were allowed to drink vodka during the killing. With vodka 'everyone becomes braver' says Zelionka. 'When you are drunk, it is different.' Sometimes, after the murders, the Germans would thank the Lithuanians for their help. In his statement to the Russians after the war, Zelionka revealed what he and his comrades did after murdering up to five hundred people in Vikija: 'When we had finished the shooting, we had lunch at a restaurant in Krakes. Spirits were consumed.' Murder did not diminish his appetite.

The murderers were all volunteers. There is no record of anyone being shot or imprisoned for refusing to murder. This is a reality that Zelionka finds hard to admit to today. 'You could refuse,' we told him.

'You could shoot and you could not shoot,' he replied. 'But you just pressed the trigger and shot. And that was it, it was not a big ceremony.'

'Did you ever think of refusing to shoot?'

'Now it is very difficult to explain all that, all those things: to shoot or not to shoot. I do not know. The others did it because of their indignation...The Jews are very selfish, how could I say...'

We asked him about shooting women and children. 'Let's say there is a Jew in front of you, not a man, but a woman or a child. A child has certainly never been a Communist. And you shoot that child. What had he done?'

'This is a tragedy, a big tragedy, because...how can I explain it better? Maybe it is because of a curiosity – you just pull the trigger, the shot is fired and that is it. There is a saying, "Youth is foolishness".' Talking later about the murder of children, he remarked, 'Some people are doomed and that is it.'

We tried in vain to get an emotional response from this mass murderer. 'Who was the man you shot first? Do you remember him?' we asked.

'No, I cannot tell you,' he replied. 'There were only the Jews, no one was our countryman. They were all Jews.'

'But were they men, women or children?'

'What can I say? It could be a man, a woman or...after so many years, how can you remember everything that happened?'

I asked our interpreter to press this convicted killer harder about his apparent lack of guilt. Did he not feel any shame? The result was both illuminating and the end of the interview.

'My colleague, an Englishman, asks me to translate this question to you: he says that English people, watching this film, will hardly understand how somebody, a soldier, used to shoot other people like this but he does not feel guilty.'

'They can accuse me, if they want. I was sentenced for twenty years for that. Short and clear. I was guilty and I carried out the sentence of twenty years...penal servitude.'

'But that was an official punishment. What does your *conscience* say?'

'I do not know. I am not going to answer such questions...I am not going to explain or tell you any more.'

So the interview ended.

It was an extraordinary experience to meet Petras Zelionka. It is rare for someone who has committed war crimes as horrendous as this to admit it openly, even if he has served a long sentence for the offence and does not risk prosecution again. Yet here before us was a man who killed alongside the Einsatzgruppen and who did not try either to hide the fact or to glory in it. He sat and talked about committing mass murder in a reserved and matter-of-fact way.

When reading documents relating to the Einsatzgruppen killings, one is always tempted to think that the men who committed them were not really human. Perhaps they were collectively insane. But Petras Zelionka gave every impression of being a sane man. If you met him in the street and were introduced to him, you would not notice anything out of the ordinary. Yet he murdered in cold blood, standing feet away from his victims. Today, when the mass killers we read about tend to be the crazed murderers featured in the tabloid press, it is important to meet a man like Petras Zelionka who killed more than any tabloid monster and yet sat before us as composed and normal as any grandfather.

Zelionka took part in many murders in Lithuania, but denies having visited Butrimonys. If not him precisely, then it would have been men like him from the Lithuanian Army who killed Riva Losanskaya's Jewish neighbours and from whose guns she herself had such a narrow escape.

In the weeks after the killings at Butrimonys, Riva became increasingly sickened by the behaviour of her fellow villagers, whom she saw profiting from the disappearance of the Jews. She recalls that as soon as she and the other Jews had been marched along to the pits, many of the remaining villagers rushed to the victims' houses to plunder them. 'Even the wives of two priests were fighting with each other,' she says, 'arguing over who was to have what.' Riva learnt that one local woman helped undress the Jews at the execution site and then kept their clothes for herself. 'She didn't even leave their knickers on, their clothes were so precious to her,' says Riva. 'When the Russians came, her children used to go to the cinema wearing those same clothes, sometimes even wearing the Rabbi's clothes.'

Throughout the German occupation Riva and her mother lived in constant fear of denunciation. 'Many people informed the authorities about the ones who had managed to escape,' she says. 'Even the kind-hearted ones did this. One Jew went to see a Russian family hoping that he could stay with them. First, he was given some food, then he was taken to the police and shot along with all the others. Everybody was doing it because they wanted the clothes and they believed that the Jews had lots of gold...But where would all that gold have come from? People didn't even have enough food, they didn't have enough potatoes.'

Riva Losanskaya's life has been spent searching for an answer to the same question posed by Samuel Willenberg in Treblinka – why? 'Fifty years have passed and I'm still wondering how people could do such things. I have always respected intelligence, I love and revere intelligent people. But then I saw them killing...Nobody can explain why the Germans did it. They are a cultured nation and have such a fine literature: Goethe, Schiller, Heinrich Heine...' Even though it was Lithuanian soldiers who shot the Jews of Butrimonys, she blames the Germans more. 'They were the cause of all our unhappiness. The Lithuanians hadn't killed any of us before the Germans arrived.'

The whirlwind of killings the Nazis organized in the first months of the occupation of Lithuania was documented by them in the so-called 'Jäger Report'. This shows a huge increase in the number of Jews killed, especially women and children, from about mid-August 1941. Until 15 August there is no mention of any children killed, but from then on they are killed in their thousands (1609 Jewish children murdered between 18 and 22 August in Kreis Rasainiai alone).[12]

This is a turning point in the killing process. Jewish women and children had, of course, already died in the ghettos of sickness or starvation, but this was different. Now they were being specifically targeted and murdered in cold blood.

Many factors came together to cause this change in policy. There was, for the Nazis, one straightforward 'practical' consideration – the need to feed these so-called 'useless eaters' once the male adults had been killed. From a Nazi perspective it was inconceivable that these people would be provided for at the expense of the German Army.

Ideological factors entered the decision-making process as well. In July Hitler had announced that he wanted a

German 'Garden of Eden' in the East and, by implication, there would be no place for the Jews in this new Nazi paradise. (And it can be no accident that Himmler ordered the extension of the killing to include women and children after attending several secret one-to-one meetings with Hitler in July; this move would not have occurred without the Führer wishing it so.)

However, the conclusion shouldn't be reached that this was somehow the moment that the entire Nazi 'Final Solution' – encompassing millions of European Jews – was decided upon. One document does perhaps suggest a connection between the two, but it is not quite as conclusive as it seems at first sight.

On 31 July Heydrich obtained Goering's signature on a paper that stated: 'To supplement the task that was assigned to you on 24 January 1939, which dealt with the solution of the Jewish problem by emigration and evacuation in the most suitable way, I hereby charge you to submit a comprehensive blueprint of the organizational, subject-related and material preparatory measures for the execution of the intended Final Solution of the Jewish question.' The timing of this document, on the face of it, is crucial: Goering signs Heydrich's general authorization for the 'Final Solution' of all the Jews under German control at exactly the moment the killing squads are to be used to shoot Jewish women and children in the East.

However, a recent discovery in the Moscow Special Archive casts doubt on the special significance of the 31 July authorization. This document contains a note from Heydrich dated 26 March 1941, which states: 'With respect to the Jewish question I reported briefly to the Reich Marshal [Goering] and submitted to him my new blueprint, which he authorized with one modification concerning Rosenberg's jurisdiction, and then ordered for resubmission.'[13] Heydrich's 'new blueprint' was most likely a response to the change in the Nazis' anti-Jewish policy caused by the forthcoming invasion of the Soviet Union. The idea of transporting the Jews to Africa had been abandoned, and early in 1941 Hitler had ordered Heydrich to prepare a scheme to deport the Jews somewhere within German control. Since the war with the Soviet Union was expected to last only a few weeks and be over before the onset of the Russian winter, it was reasonable, Heydrich and Hitler must have felt, to plan for the Jews to be pushed further east that autumn in an internal solution to their self-created Jewish problem. In the wasteland of eastern Russia the Jews would suffer grievously.

As the 31 July authorization makes clear, Heydrich was first assigned the task of planning the 'solution of the Jewish problem by emigration and evacuation' at the start of 1939, and so discussions about his jurisdiction and room for manoeuvre within the Nazi state on this issue must have been ongoing since then. Alfred Rosenberg (mentioned in the 26 March document), who was formally appointed Minister of the Occupied Eastern Territories by Hitler on 17 July 1941, was a potential threat to Heydrich's own power in the East, and the 31 July authorization may well have been issued to help Heydrich clarify his own position.

So on balance the new evidence does not support the once prevalent view that there was some conclusive decision taken by Hitler in the spring or summer of 1941 to order the destruction of all the Jews of Europe, of which the 31 July authorization is an important part. The more likely scenario is that as all the leading Nazis focused their attention on the war against the Soviet Union, the decision to kill the women and children in the East was seen as the practical way of solving an immediate and specific problem.

To begin with, the Jews of western Europe and the German Reich remained relatively untouched by this slaughter. The Nazi assumption was still that they would be 'transported

East' once the war was over, and in the optimistic minds of Hitler, Himmler and Heydrich that meant some time in the autumn of 1941. What was to happen to these Jews once they went East 'after the war' is unclear, since there were, as yet, no death camps waiting to receive them. Most likely they would have been sent to labour camps in the most inhospitable parts of Nazi-controlled Russia, where genocide would still have taken place, albeit a longer and more protracted one than the swift killing that was to follow in the gas chambers of Poland.

But that August some leading Nazis grew impatient with this plan. They knew that, in the East, Soviet Jews were already being 'dealt with' in the most brutal ways imaginable. Why, they began to suggest, should German Jews not be sent into the epicentre of this killing operation immediately? Joseph Goebbels, the Nazi Propaganda Minister and Gauleiter of Berlin, was one of those who took the lead that summer in pushing for the Jews of Berlin to be forcibly deported East. At a meeting on 15 August Goebbels' state secretary, Leopold Gutterer, pointed out that of the 70,000 Jews in Berlin only 19,000 were working (a situation, of course, that the Nazis had created themselves by enforcing a series of restrictive regulations against German Jews). The rest, argued Gutterer, ought to be 'carted off to Russia...best of all actually would be to kill them.'[14] And when Goebbels himself met Hitler on 19 August he made a similar case for the swift deportation of the Berlin Jews.

Dominant in Goebbels' mind was the Nazi fantasy of the role that German Jews had played during World War I. While German soldiers had suffered at the front line, the Jews had supposedly been profiting from the bloodshed back in the safety of the big cities (in reality, of course, German Jews had been dying at the front in proportionately the same numbers as their fellow countrymen). But now, in the summer of 1941, it was obvious that Jews remained in Berlin while the Wehrmacht were engaged in their brutal struggle in the East – what else could they do, since the Nazis had forbidden German Jews to join the armed forces? As they did so often, the Nazis had created for themselves the exact circumstances that best fitted their prejudice. But despite Goebbels' entreaties, Hitler was still not willing to allow the Berlin Jews to be deported. He maintained that the war was still the priority and the Jewish question would have to wait. However, Hitler did grant one of Goebbels' requests. In a significant escalation of Nazi anti-Semitic measures, he agreed that the Jews of Germany should be marked with the yellow star. In the ghettos of Poland the Jews had been marked in similar ways from the first months of the war, but their counterparts in Germany had up to now escaped such humiliation.

That summer and early autumn Goebbels was not the only senior Nazi figure to lobby Hitler to permit the deportation of the German Jews. In the immediate aftermath of the British bombing raid on Hamburg on 15 September the Gauleiter of Hamburg, Karl Kaufmann, decided to write to Hitler, asking him to authorize the deportation of the Jews of the city in order to release housing for non-Jewish citizens who had just lost their homes. Hitler was now in receipt of proposals to send the Jews East from a whole variety of sources, including a suggestion from Alfred Rosenberg that Jews from central Europe be deported in retaliation for Stalin's recent action in sending the Volga Germans to Siberia. Now, suddenly, just a few weeks after saying the Reich Jews could not be deported, Hitler changed his mind. That September he decided that the expulsions East could begin after all.

However, it is important not to see in this reversal of policy a picture of an indecisive Hitler somehow bending to the will of his subordinates. He was influenced at least as much by the latest developments in the external military situation as by the pleas of his underlings. Hitler had always said that the Jews could be deported at the end of the war, and in September 1941 it seemed to the Nazi leader that there might be only a matter of a few weeks' difference between deporting the German Jews 'after the war was over' and doing so now. Kiev was about to fall and Moscow seemed wide open to German assault, so Hitler still hoped that the Soviet Union would be defeated before the winter.

There remained, of course, the question of where to send the Jews. Himmler immediately had one answer – why should the Reich Jews not join the Polish Jews in ghettos? On 18 September Himmler wrote to Arthur Greiser, Nazi Gauleiter of the Warthegau in Poland, and asked him to prepare the Łódź ghetto for the arrival of 60,000 Jews from the 'Old Reich'.

Protests began as soon as the figure of 60,000 Jews to be deported from the 'Old Reich' to Łódź had been proposed by Himmler. As a result, the number was reduced to 20,000 Jews and 5000 gypsies. But even this influx still presented major difficulties for the Gauleiter, Arthur Greiser. Together with Wilhelm Koppe, the Higher SS and Police Leader for the region, he sought a solution to the problem of overcrowding in the ghetto. And it is hardly surprising, given that ever since the summer of 1941 murder had been the preferred answer in the East to this kind of crisis, that their minds turned to methods of killing. They called upon the services of SS Hauptsturmführer (Captain) Herbert Lange, who had been in command of a special unit charged with murdering the disabled in East Prussia and the surrounding area. For some of the killing he and his team had used a 'gas van' with a hermetically sealed rear compartment into which bottled carbon monoxide gas was pumped, and such vans were now seen by local Nazis as the most appropriate response to the sudden overcrowding in the Łódź ghetto.

According to his SS driver, Walter Burmeister, late that

autumn Lange hit upon a suitable site for his gas vans in the Warthegau. 'To make it plain from the start,' Lange told his driver, 'absolute secrecy is crucial. I have orders to form a special commando in Chełmno. Other staff from Posen and from the state police in Litzmannstadt [the German name for Łódź] are going to join us. We have a tough but important job to do.'[15] At the small village of Chełmno, some 50 miles northwest of Łódź, Lange and his team prepared a country house – 'the Schloss' – for the 'tough but important job' of mass murder. Chełmno, not Auschwitz, was about to become the first location for the killing of selected Jews from the Łódź ghetto.

But Chełmno was not the only extermination facility under construction towards the end of 1941. On 1 November work began on a camp at Bełżec in the Lublin district in eastern Poland. Most of the personnel for Bełżec, including the first commandant of the camp, SS Hauptsturmführer (Captain) Christian Wirth, were taken from the adult euthanasia programme. Deep in the General Government, Bełżec seems to have been established, like Chełmno , with the intention of creating a place to kill 'unproductive' Jews from the local area. But unlike Chełmno it was the first camp to be planned from the start to contain stationary gas chambers linked to engines producing carbon monoxide gas.

Meantime, the deportation of Jews from the Old Reich continued. Between October 1941 and February 1942 a total of 58,000 Jews were sent East to a variety of destinations, including the Łódź ghetto. Everywhere they were sent, the local Nazi authorities had to improvise a solution to deal with their arrival, acting sometimes on the authority of Berlin, sometimes on their own initiative. Around 7000 Jews from Hamburg were sent to Minsk, where they were found shelter in a part of the ghetto that had recently been cleared for them by shooting the nearly 12,000 Soviet Jews who lived there. Jews from Munich, Berlin, Frankfurt and other German cities were sent to Kaunas in Lithuania, where around 5000 of them were shot dead by members of Einsatzkommando 3. They were the first German Jews to be murdered on arrival as a result of being transported East. Another transport from Berlin reached Riga in Latvia on 30 November, and all aboard were also killed as soon as they arrived. But this action was against Himmler's wishes; he had previously rung Heydrich with the message: 'Jewish transport from Berlin. No liquidation.' Friedrich Jeckeln, the SS commander who had ordered the execution, was subsequently reprimanded by Himmler.

As these events demonstrate, during the autumn of 1941 there was little consistency of policy regarding the fate of the Reich Jews: Himmler protested at the shootings in Riga, but did not object to those in Kaunas. Nonetheless, despite these confused indicators, there is plenty of evidence that the decision to send the Reich Jews to the East was a watershed moment. In October, talking after dinner, Hitler remarked, 'No one can say to me we can't send them [the Jews] into the swamp! Who then cares about our people? It is good if the fear that we are exterminating the Jews goes before us.'[16] And it is clear that discussions were also taking place amongst the Nazi leadership that autumn to send to the East all the Jews under German control. In France, Reinhard Heydrich justified the burning of Paris synagogues by saying that he had given the action his approval 'only at the point where the Jews were identified on the highest authority and most vehemently as being those responsible for setting Europe alight, and who must ultimately disappear from Europe.'[17] That same month, November 1941, Hitler, in a discussion with the Grand Mufti of Jerusalem, who had fled to Berlin, said that he wanted all Jews, even those not under German control, 'to be destroyed'.[18]

By deciding to deport the Reich Jews, Hitler had begun a

chain of causation that would eventually lead to their extermination. In the Soviet Union Jewish men, women and children were already being shot by the killing squads. By sending many of the Reich Jews into this exact area, what else did Hitler think would happen to them? The line between killing local Jews to provide room for the arriving Reich Jews, and killing the arriving Reich Jews instead, was a thin one from the first – as Jeckeln's actions in Riga demonstrate. That distinction became even more blurred for the Nazi leadership of the General Government once Galicia, in the far east of Poland and bordering the killing fields of the Soviet Union, came under their control as the war progressed. The Einsatzgruppe had been killing Galician Jews for weeks, and it would be hard for the local authorities to hold to a position that Jews could be shot in one part of the General Government but not in another.

But this does not mean that Hitler and the other leading Nazis took a firm decision in the autumn of 1941 to murder all the Jews under German control. In the first place, there simply was not yet the capacity to commit such a crime. The only killing installations under construction in November 1941 were a gas van facility at Chełmno and a small fixed gas chamber installation at Bełżec. An order was also placed around this time with a German firm for a large 32-chamber furnace crematorium to be built at Mogilev in Belorussia, which some see as evidence of an intention, never fulfilled, to build another extermination centre far in the East. But all of these initiatives can also be explained by the desire of the local authorities to have the capacity either to kill the indigenous Jews in order to make space for the arriving Reich Jews, or to murder those Jews in their control incapable of work whom they believed were no longer 'useful' to them.

This confused state of affairs was to be clarified, with disastrous consequences for the fate of the Jews, by events that took place halfway round the world. On 7 December 1941 the Japanese bombed Pearl Harbor. On 11 December, as allies of the Japanese, the Germans declared war on the United States. For Hitler all this was 'proof' that international Jewry had orchestrated a world conflict, and in a radio broadcast to the German people immediately after the declaration of war he explicitly stated that 'the Jews' were manipulating President Roosevelt just as they were his other great enemy, Josef Stalin.

Hitler went still further in a speech he gave to the Nazi leadership, both Gauleiter and Reichleiter, the following day. He now linked the outbreak of this 'world war' with his prophecy uttered in the Reichstag on 30 January 1939 in which he had threatened that 'if the Jews succeed in causing world war' the result would be the 'extermination of the Jews of Europe'. On 13 December, Propaganda Minister Joseph Goebbels wrote in his diary: 'As far as the Jewish question is concerned, the Führer is determined to make a clean sweep. He prophesied to the Jews that if they once again brought about a world war they would experience their own extermination. This was not an empty phrase. The world war is here, the extermination of the Jews must be the necessary consequence. This question must be seen without sentimentality.'

Further evidence that the air was thick with talk of 'extermination' that week is provided by a speech that Hans Frank, ruler of the General Government, made to senior Nazi officials in Krakow on 16 December: 'As an old National Socialist, I must state that if the Jewish clan were to survive the war in Europe, while we sacrificed our best blood in the defence of Europe, then this war would only represent a partial success. With respect to the Jews, therefore, I will only operate on the assumption that they will disappear...We must exterminate the Jews wherever we find them.'[19] Frank, who had been one of those briefed by Hitler on 12 December, also added that 'in Berlin' he had been told that he, and people like him, should 'liquidate the Jews...themselves'.

The discovery of Himmler's complete desk diary in the 1990s also provides one tantalizing further link with Hitler during this most crucial period. On 18 December, after a one-to-one meeting with Hitler, Himmler notes: 'Jewish question – to be exterminated [auszurotten] as partisans.' The reference to 'partisans' is part of the camouflage language that allowed the murder of the Jews to be concealed as necessary security work in the East.[20]

Although no document written by Hitler linking him with a direct order to pursue the 'Final Solution' has ever been found, this body of evidence does demonstrate beyond reasonable doubt that he was encouraging and directing an intensification of anti-Jewish actions that December. It is likely that, even without the catalyst of US entry into the war, the deportations of the Reich Jews to the East, directly ordered by Hitler, would eventually have led to their deaths. The anger and frustration Hitler felt at the launch of the Red Army's counterattack at the gates of Moscow on 5 December had already probably predisposed him to vent his rage further upon the Jews. But what happened at Pearl Harbor brought a murderous clarity to Hitler's thinking. All pretence amongst leading Nazis that the Jews would simply be deported and kept in camps in the East was dropped. One way or another, they now faced 'extermination'.

On 20 January a meeting was held at an SS villa on the shores of the Wannsee, a lake outside Berlin. This gathering has become infamous as the single most important event in the history of the Nazis' 'Final Solution', an epithet it does not quite merit. The meeting was called by Reinhard Heydrich, who invited the relevant government state secretaries to take part in a discussion about the Jewish question. Included with each invitation was a copy of the authorization that Goering had given Heydrich on 31 July 1941 to pursue the 'Final Solution' (although, it is highly unlikely that the phrase 'Final Solution' had the same meaning in July 1941 that it had acquired by January 1942). Notoriously, because the meeting was due to begin at midday, the invitation also mentioned that 'refreshments' would be provided. The address at which the meeting was held was Am Grossen Wannsee 56–58, a villa once used by Interpol, the organization that coordinated international police activity. It is a useful reminder that the individuals who sat round the table at the Wannsee conference were salaried functionaries from one of Europe's great nations, not back-street terrorists, though their crimes were to be greater than any conventional 'criminal' act in the history of the world. Equally instructive, when today some still refer to an ill-educated 'criminal under-class', is that of the fifteen people around the table eight held academic doctorates.

Invitations had originally been sent in November 1941 and the meeting scheduled for 9 December, but the bombing of Pearl Harbor had resulted in its postponement. One of the unanswered questions of history is therefore what the content of the Wannsee meeting would have been had events in the Pacific not caused a delay. Certainly the intention would still have been to implement an ultimately genocidal 'solution' to the Nazis' 'Jewish problem', but perhaps the discussion would have focused more on an eventual post-war solution or a real attempt to set up work camps for Jews deported to the East. We can only speculate. What is certain is that, whether the USA had entered the war or not, Wannsee was always going to be an important meeting for Heinrich Himmler and Reinhard Heydrich. During the autumn of 1941 a variety of killing initiatives had emerged from a number of sources within the Nazi state. For Himmler and Heydrich, Wannsee was necessary above all else to coordinate them and to establish beyond doubt that the SS were the ones in control of the whole deportation process.

The issues discussed at the Wannsee conference are known primarily because a copy of the minutes, taken by SS Obersturmbannführer (Lieutenant Colonel) Adolf Eichmann, Heydrich's 'Jewish expert', survived the war. Eichmann's record of the meeting is of great historical importance, since it is one of the few documents that shine a light directly on the thinking process behind the 'Final Solution'.

At the start of the meeting Heydrich made reference to the administrative authority given him by Goering that allowed him to preside. Then he announced the formal change in Nazi policy that, no doubt, all the delegates would already have known. Instead of the 'emigration' of the Jews to countries outside Nazi control, there would now be 'evacuation...to the East' within the Nazi sphere of influence. In total 11 million Jews, a figure that included several million in countries such as Ireland and Britain that were not yet under Nazi domination, would eventually be subject to such 'evacuation'. On arrival in the East these Jews would be separated by sex, and those who were fit and healthy employed in building roads (Heydrich was almost certainly thinking of projects such as the Durchgangsstrasse IV, a road and rail link from the Reich to the Eastern Front already under construction). Those Jews who were not selected for this work would, the implication is clear, be murdered immediately, whilst the rest faced only a stay of execution since large numbers were expected to die as a result of harsh manual labour. Heydrich went on to express particular concern about any Jews who might survive the attempt to work them into the ground: these were the very Jews that natural selection would have determined were the most dangerous to the Nazis. They, said Heydrich, must also be 'treated accordingly'. There could have been no doubt in the minds of the other delegates just what Heydrich meant by this.

Significantly, there was no dissent at the meeting over the broad principle of killing the Jews. Instead, the greatest area of debate focused around the exact legal definition of 'Jew', and thus precisely who would be subject to deportation and who would not. The question of what to do with 'half Jews' stimulated a lively exchange of views. There was a suggestion that such people should be sterilized, or offered a choice between that operation and deportation. Alternatively they might be sent to a special ghetto – Theresienstadt, the Czech town of Terezin – where they would be housed alongside the elderly and those Jews with a high profile whose deportation directly to the East would have caused disquiet amongst the ordinary German population.

The discussion then passed to the more immediate 'problem' of the Jews of the General Government and the occupied Soviet Union. In the latter the Jews were being murdered by shooting, whilst in the former the death camp at Bełżec was already under construction. But millions of Jews were still alive in these areas, so Eichmann recorded in the minutes that 'various possible solutions' were mentioned in this context, an innocuous phrase that masked a discussion of specific methods of extermination.

The minutes of the Wannsee conference are deliberately opaque. Eichmann's draft of them was worked on several times by Heydrich and Heinrich Müller, the head of the Gestapo, to create that exact effect. Since they were intended for wider distribution, it was necessary for them to be written in camouflage language: those who understood the context would realize exactly what was intended, whilst the lack of crude terminology meant they would not shock the uninitiated should they catch sight of them. Nonetheless, they remain the clearest evidence of the planning process behind the Nazis' 'Final Solution' and the strongest evidence of widespread state complicity in the murders that were to follow.

But does that mean that the Wannsee conference deserves its place in popular culture as the most significant meeting in the history of the crime? The answer must be no. The misconception in the popular consciousness rests on the belief that this was the meeting at which the Nazis decided to embark upon their 'Final Solution'. This is simply not the case. Certainly Wannsee was important, but it was a second-tier implementation meeting, part of a process of widening out knowledge of an extermination process that had already been decided upon somewhere else. Much more important than the conversations at Wannsee were the discussions Hitler held in December 1941. If proper minutes were available of the Führer's meetings with Himmler during that period we would truly see the bleak landscape of the mind that made all this suffering enter the world.

The practical consequences of these decisions taken at the highest level were, of course, horrendous. During the autumn of 1942, for example, in one of their most heartless acts the Nazis decided to remove children under the age of 10 from the Łódź ghetto. Parents were told to take their children to a collection point, put them on trucks and walk away. 'The children were taken away from their parents,' says Estera Frenkiel. 'Their screams reached the sky…Every mother went with her child and put it on the cart, pressed it to them. The child screamed and cried. She pressed it to her breast and calmed it down and then went away.' Many mothers decided to leave their husbands in the ghetto and accompany their children to share their fate. One family who had hidden their child in their ghetto flat returned to their room later, to discover the child had suffocated in the confines of his hiding-place.

Working as she did in the office of the Jewish manager of the ghetto, Estera Frenkiel had privileged access to information, some of which she would rather not have learnt. One day a letter arrived, via Biebow's office, asking for information:

'I request that you ascertain immediately whether there is a bone-grinder in the ghetto. Either to be electrically or manually operated.' There was a postscript. 'The Sonderkommando of Chełmno is interested in such a grinder.'

'One's heart misses a beat,' says Estera Frenkiel talking of her reaction to reading the letter. 'The thoughts come flooding in. What for? Why? For whom? For what purpose?' Rather like the Jews in Samuel Willenberg's train *en route* for Treblinka, even in the face of evidence to the contrary, many of the Łódź Jews simply hoped for the best. But hope on its own was no protection.

Eventually, Estera Frenkiel and her mother were sent to Ravensbrück concentration camp. 'The ghetto was a story in its own right: that was a tale of hunger and starvation – a battle for food, avoiding deportation. But there in Ravensbrück it was hell: neither day, nor night.' She puts her survival down to one thing above all – 'luck'.

In 1942 extermination camps were established at Treblinka, Sobibór and Majdanek, as well as Bełżec. Auschwitz, which had existed as a concentration camp, had its massive new extension at nearby Birkenau also converted into an extermination camp.

At Auschwitz, unlike Treblinka, a systematic selection was periodically made of those inmates who were to be killed and those who were to be allowed to live, however temporarily. Nazi doctors were quick to grasp the infinite possibilities for human experimentation which this endless supply of human guinea pigs offered them. They devised a series of devilish experiments, the details of which haunt the mind of anyone who has studied the subject. The notorious Dr Josef Mengele systematically tortured young children, mostly twins. Another Nazi doctor, in pursuit of his own warped theory, quizzed a starving inmate about the effect of undernourishment on his metabolism before having him murdered so that he could dissect his internal organs and then judge the anatomical effects for himself.

The Nazis had now arrived at a destination no one had travelled to before – they had created killing factories where men, women and children could be disposed of in hours. The images of the gas chambers would forever shape and define Nazism. But one should not read history backwards. As we have seen, the journey to the gas chambers was not a simple one. Stages along the route included the anti-Semitism engendered in the wake of World War I defeat; the desire to exclude Jews from German life and the Nazis' belief that Jews were both a dangerous and inferior race; the invasion of Poland, which brought 3 million Polish Jews (considered the worst inferior racial combination) under Nazi control; and finally the decision to kill Communists and Jews in the wake of Operation Barbarossa. No blueprint for the Holocaust existed before 1941: the Nazi regime was too chaotic for that.

Above all, it was the invasion of the Soviet Union that caused a radical change in the Nazis' approach to the Jews. Hitler wrote that he felt 'spiritually free' at the time of the invasion, which for a character such as his, meant feeling free to be true to his own emotional view of the world – a world in which, as he said to his generals in August 1939, a human being should strive to 'close your heart to pity – act brutally'. Prior to Barbarossa, there are countless examples where the Nazis restrained their own brutality – the release of the Polish professors, for example – but once Barbarossa began, the Nazis were true to themselves and indifferent to the morals of the world.

They didn't know if it was possible to murder so many people, but twentieth-century technology made it easy.

9

REAPING THE WHIRLWIND

AFTER THE BATTLE OF STALINGRAD IN THE AUTUMN AND WINTER of 1942–3, Hitler and the Germans experienced nothing but disaster. So why, when the war must have seemed lost, did the Germans fight on to the end? Why did Germany have to suffer so, and in her suffering inflict destruction on countless others? The answers to these questions contain fundamental truths about Nazism, for this was an ideology that, under its Führer, would sooner destroy itself than surrender. As a result, in the last months of the war, the Nazis came to reap the suffering they had sown.

Until recently historians have concentrated their efforts on examining the major strategic turning points of the war. Only lately has there been much detailed research on the final period of the war when the regime descended into destruction. Between July 1944 and May 1945 more Germans perished than in the previous four years put together; roughly 290,000 German soldiers and civilians died per month. Yet one neighbouring Fascist country in the Axis successfully managed to remove its dictator before the end of the war and so escape further involvement in the conflict.

On 25 July 1943 the Italian Fascist dictator Benito Mussolini had an audience with the king of Italy. He was told that the Grand Fascist Council had voted by nineteen votes to seven to replace him as head of state. Mussolini was arrested as he left the room; thus was the first Fascist dictator bloodlessly removed from power. This prompts the question – if the Italians were capable of seeing the way the war was inevitably going and acting accordingly, why couldn't the Germans?

The first reason, of course, is that there was no German equivalent to the Grand Fascist Council which could collectively pass judgement upon Hitler. He had destroyed the normal apparatus of the state which would have served as a check on his absolute power. There were no cabinet meetings, no national assemblies, no party senate, no forums in which Germans could legitimately come together to question the conduct of the war. A system had evolved that protected Hitler not just from being constitutionally removed from office, but from coherent criticism of any sort.

Hitler himself would not seek surrender as the military situation grew ever more desperate. His whole character militated against such action. Consumed by hatred as he was, suicide was always his preferred escape, but only when Nazism had reached the very end of its long and bloody road. He would never capitulate. In order for Germany to be saved her suffering he would have to be removed.

If there was no prospect of removing Hitler from office constitutionally, as Mussolini had been, the only alternative was to remove him violently. Any conspirator seeking to do this would need a privilege rare and precious in those last years of the war – access to the Führer. The only people who were now admitted to Hitler's presence were either members of the Nazi leadership or the Armed Forces. Many obstacles prevented the former from acting against their Führer. Their commitment to Nazism was based on a belief in the supreme ability of Hitler, something which had been inculcated since the Nuremberg rallies of the 1920s. To challenge Hitler meant going against nearly twenty years of subservience and belief.

In addition, the Nazi leaders were hopelessly split among themselves by a series of personal enmities. (Goebbels disliked Göring, Göring hated Ribbentrop, Ribbentrop loathed Goebbels.) Finally, most, if not all, of the leadership were implicated in the crimes of the regime, as the Nuremberg trials later showed. They would have had little to gain by removing Hitler and making peace. Just as they had prospered with him, now they would suffer with him.

Only the leaders of the Armed Forces, who came into regular contact with Hitler, could hope to topple him. For many, however, the oath of allegiance they had sworn to the Führer proved too much to overcome. 'It was simply understood,' says Bernd Linn, an officer who served in the east, 'that the soldier has sworn an oath and stood by his oath.' Then there was Hitler's ability to change minds by the power of his own conviction, the effects of which Karl Boehm-Tettelbach, a Luftwaffe staff officer, regularly witnessed at the Wolf's Lair. On one occasion he drove to a local airfield to collect a field marshal who had just flown in from Paris to brief Hitler on the war on the Western Front. On the drive back to the Wolf's Lair, the field marshal asked Boehm-Tettelbach what mood Hitler was in because, he said, 'I'm going to give him hell. He should know what's going on in France.' On the return journey to the airfield the field marshal said, 'Boehm, excuse me, I was mad today but I made a mistake. Hitler convinced me that it was justified and I'm wrong. I didn't know what he knows. So therefore I feel very sorry.' As Boehm-Tettelbach says today, 'The flair Hitler had was unusual. He could take somebody who was almost ready for suicide, he could revive him and make him feel that he should carry the flag and die in battle. Very strange.'

It wasn't just Hitler's powers of persuasion, or the oath of allegiance, that kept many of the army in line: it was the often unspoken knowledge of what was happening in the east. And the horror intensified as the German Army retreated, step by bloody step.

Walter Mauth, a German infantryman with the 30th Division, took part in the scorched earth retreat from the Soviet Union in 1944: 'I never noticed anybody bothering to have a look inside the house to see whether there was a sick woman or anybody else in there. The houses were simply brutally shot at and burnt down. That's just the way it was. Nobody cared. There was no consideration – they were "sub-human creatures" after all, weren't they?' As part of the rearguard of his unit, Mauth watched as his comrades committed murder. 'I witnessed how they shot into the houses...But since they were Russian, it did not matter. On the contrary, you were even decorated – the more people you shot, the higher was the decoration you received. That's the truth.'

He confesses that 'personally, I consider the acts that have been committed a crime, then and now – in retrospect I consider it a damn scandal! I would like to pass on my experience, as far as I am able, to ensure that everybody knows what they will let themselves in for [in war]. They will become a criminal.'

Walter Fernau had reason to be grateful to the Russians because for a short period he was quartered with a Soviet family who were friendly and hospitable towards him. 'They even let me sleep together with the grandfather on the top of their oven,' he says today. But another NCO from his regiment, billeted with Russians nearby, was not so grateful to the civilians who gave him shelter, as Walter Fernau witnessed. 'All of a sudden I heard two salvoes from a sub-machine-gun firing out and I imagined it was partisans or something, so I went into the house with my sub-machine-gun. And then I saw that for no reason at all, this NCO had shot the two old Russians who lived in the house with his sub-machine-gun. I had a go at him, I said, "How can you do something like that?" Well, and then he said, and he'd certainly had too much to drink, "The only good Russian is a dead Russian!" I said, "But surely not these poor old people, you know!" But he just wouldn't go into it. Well, it was a sad business of course.'

Knowledge that Germans were committing atrocities in the East could provoke one of a number of responses within the army élite: officers could genuinely believe in the Nazi propaganda that they were fighting a nation of sub-humans who deserved all they got; or such knowledge could make officers more frightened of defeat and more desperate to keep fighting so that the crime could be hidden; more rarely, it could provoke a desire to see such crimes stopped and the chief criminal, Hitler, brought swiftly to account. Hans von Herwarth fell into the last group and was unique among all the German soldiers we talked to. Not only did he admit to knowing about the abuses being committed in the east, but he actually resolved, along with his friend Count Klaus Schenk von Stauffenberg, to do something about it.

Hans von Herwarth first learnt about the mass executions in the summer of 1942, when an officer who had personally witnessed the atrocities reported them to him. When he realized what was happening, he made a decision: 'We must get rid of Hitler. It confirmed my view that he was a devil of a person and that he had to be destroyed.' He met von Stauffenberg a year or so later: 'I met him when he was in hospital in Munich, and there was a burning fire, you know, a holy fire in this man. He said, "Well, I have to recover, I have something to do."' As von Herwarth says, 'There were quite a lot of people who were willing to kill Hitler, but there was no possibility to bring them into contact with him.' Von Stauffenberg, however, had both the opportunity and the will, being a staff officer at the Wolf's Lair.

On the morning of 20 July 1944 Karl Boehm-Tettelbach woke late in his bedroom at the Führer's headquarters near

Rastenburg in East Prussia. After working through the night he felt too groggy to attend the situation briefing with Hitler at midday. At 12.45, as he walked into his own office, there was the sound of a distant explosion. One of his colleagues rushed up and said, 'Did you hear that big boom?' 'Yes,' replied Boehm-Tettelbach, 'it's probably one of the deer.' The area around the Wolf's Lair was heavily mined and four or five times every night deer or rabbits in the forest would set off an explosion. This time, however, it was not a mine in the forest that had detonated, but a bomb in Hitler's own briefing room.

In the most famous act of resistance in the history of the Third Reich, a bomb placed by Count von Stauffenberg had exploded in an attempt to assassinate Hitler. Had the conference been held, as usual, in Hitler's command bunker with its concrete walls, instead of in the wooden hut to which it had been rescheduled, Hitler would probably have died in the explosion. As it was, the wooden walls of the hut exploded outwards and dissipated the force of the blast, allowing Hitler to escape with minor wounds.

Countless books have been written about the incident. Many, especially those written in the immediate post-war years, point to the 20 July plot as a glorious, albeit doomed, episode in German history. But that was not how it was perceived at the time. A study of letters sent back from frontline troops in the weeks immediately after the bomb plot shows a very different reaction. The censor's report, based on an examination of 45,000 letters, concludes: 'The treachery of the conspiratorial clique is rejected by all as the greatest crime against the German people.'[1] Obviously, knowing that letters were to be censored, it would have been foolhardy for any soldier to record anti-Hitler sentiments in his correspondence, but equally there was no obligation to condemn the bomb plot either. The letters point to an overwhelming feeling of betrayal. After all, the German officers who had conspired against Hitler had broken their oath.

Hans von Herwarth has little sympathy for those officers who accuse him of breaking his oath to Hitler and who used this as a reason not to join in the bomb plot: 'That's a very cheap excuse,' he says. 'Hitler broke his oath twenty times, fifty times, he broke his oath to Germany.'

I asked Karl Boehm-Tettelbach what he would have said to von Stauffenberg had he been approached. 'I would have said, "I am going to report to Hitler that you want to kill him."' More than fifty years later he still appears angry about von Stauffenberg's actions. 'I don't approve,' he says simply. He objects to the 20 July bomb for a variety of reasons: von Stauffenberg broke his oath of allegiance to Hitler ('Nobody approached me', he says, 'because they knew that I wouldn't break my oath'); simply killing Hitler would have accomplished little ('Himmler must be replaced, Göring must be replaced and many, many other people, because just blowing up Hitler is nuts'); and, crucially, von Stauffenberg did not sacrifice himself in order to ensure that Hitler was killed ('That's what the Palestinians do now').

After the bomb went off and failed to kill Hitler, the Nazi revenge was swift and brutal. Some seven thousand people were arrested and by April 1945 five thousand of them had been executed. Anyone who had even been approached to take part in the conspiracy was executed; it was no defence to say that one had refused to take part. At breakfast, the day after the bomb exploded, Karl Boehm-Tettelbach witnessed the Nazis' revenge as he sat next to a shaking army colonel. 'He was so nervous, I said, "What's wrong with you? You're so nervous!" His hand was trembling and coffee was spilling and he said, "I just don't, I can't say." And at that moment, during breakfast at 9 o'clock, two SS men came and said, "Colonel, please come along." And by that night he was dead, because he did not participate but he was approached by von Stauffenberg.' Hans von Herwarth was lucky. Even under torture, those who knew he had supported the bomb plot did not give his name. As he says today, 'I owe my life to them.'

We know that knowledge of atrocities in the east played a part in motivating the bomb plotters. Equally, we know from recent academic research that soldiers on the Eastern Front generally knew of the atrocities. What is less certain is how much the ordinary population of Germany knew in the final years of the war.

What we do know is that German society changed fundamentally during the war. Previously it had been a country whose government *preached* the values of racism: now it was a country that *benefited* from racism. As Professor Geyer says, 'Within Germany about 30 per cent of the industrial and agricultural labour force was foreign – forced labour, POWs, or even concentration camp inmates that were parcelled out basically on the principle of expendable labour.' And the disturbing conclusion historians such as Professor Geyer come to about the racist state Germany had become is that 'the Germans not only experienced it but by and large liked it'. The arrival of a huge class of people in Germany who were by definition inferior to the lowest German was plainly of benefit. At the very least, it enabled Germans to feel that they were superior and that the Nazi propaganda was correct – they were a 'master race'. The lowly German worker could become a foreman; the housewife could have servants. Society had changed in a profoundly racist way. This is the background against which one must judge the statements of Germans on the home front that they knew nothing of what was happening in the east. For not only did every German experience the racial propaganda of the Nazis, but almost all of them experienced the consequences of racism in the form of the 'sub-human' workers who were everywhere. How hard it must be in such an environment not to feel superior, not to think that these people are less than oneself. When Polish workers shuffled by in their rags, how could the Germans not feel superior? After 1945 it was hard for Germans to express openly such feelings of superiority, especially once detailed knowledge of the Holocaust became commonplace. The vocabulary of racism was denied to those on the home front, just as it was denied to the soldiers who had fought the enemy.

It is not too fanciful to imagine that the same Germans who benefited from living in a racist state would fear what life would be like once the slaves regained their freedom. If Germany fell, surely the oppressed would seek revenge on their oppressors? Anyone who benefits from a crime seeks to avoid the moment of reckoning.

If fear of eventual judgement for participating in a racist slave state played any part in the decision of ordinary Germans to follow the regime until the end, there remains a crucial question to answer – how many ordinary Germans knew during the war that the Jews were being exterminated? If one takes at face value the evidence from the many interviews we filmed with German civilians of the period, the answer is clear – none. When asked what she thought was happening to the Jews, Gabriele Winckler, a secretary, gave a typical reply: 'People always told us they were going to Madagascar or somewhere, some barren country. God knows what rubbish they talked, and then I really didn't think much more about it all.' Alternatively, our interviewees would say that they thought the Jews were being deported east to work. Johannes Zahn, a financial expert, says, 'I knew that the Jews were being put into work camps, but I didn't know that they were being systematically killed. But I do have to say honestly that if I had known about it then, I wouldn't have done anything about it...nobody in their right mind runs straight into the machine-guns.'

Our interviewees often expressed great indignation at relatively minor injustices meted out by the Nazis, such as forcing German Jews to wear yellow stars prior to their deportation. 'Terrible! Terrible!' says Erna Kranz, then a young woman living in Munich. 'In the street parallel to us we had a Baroness Brancka who was married to a baron, but was a Jewish shopkeeper's daughter from Hamburg...and she had to wear the Jewish star. I was sorry about that, it was so terrible because this woman was such a nice woman, that's what you felt. But really, just like today when you walk away from people in need, you can't help everywhere, it was the same then. You said what can we do? You couldn't do anything, could you? We were forced to do nothing and accept that a single person who wasn't at fault could be persecuted.' A lesson learned from such testimony is that the small injustice in front of one's nose can have a greater impact than a much larger injustice that occurs out of sight – even if that larger injustice is suspected. Thus the Nazi plan to transport the Jews *away* from Germany was an inspired act of evil.

The more we posed the question, 'When did you know about the extermination camps?' to our interviewees, the more it became clear that the question invited a black-and-white answer – either the interviewees knew during the war or they didn't – when it seemed the true answer must be in shades of grey. Professor Geyer believes there were at least three levels of recognition among the ordinary German population concerning the fate of the Jews. The first level was the simple one of 'visual' knowledge. It was clear that the Jews were no longer there. 'Neighbours were no longer neighbours,' as Professor Geyer puts it. 'They definitely knew and somehow acquiesced to the fact that their Jewish neighbours would no longer be present.' Every German would have recognized the fate of the German Jews at this level. At the other extreme, specific knowledge of the extermination camps must have been confined to relatively few people. None of the extermination camps operated within the pre-war boundaries of Germany, and even among the higher levels of the Nazi hierarchy there existed a euphemistic language to describe what was actually taking place in them (the code word 'evacuation', for example, used in Eichmann's memorandum of the Wannsee Conference). Those with the second level of recognition knew that something 'bad' was happening to the Jews. This is the most interesting level of knowledge and the one that is hardest to quantify. Once the Jews had disappeared from the towns and villages, it was possible for ordinary Germans not to think about what was happening to them. But if they *did* think about it, surely it must have been obvious that the Jews were going to a terrible fate? Jews had been public victims of Nazi persecution since the boycott of 1933. Hitler had announced in 1939 that a world war would mean the 'annihilation' of Jews in Europe. Knowledge of atrocities in the east, even if not specific knowledge of anti-Semitic actions, must have been widespread back on German soil if one accepts that the vast majority of German Army units were involved. The majority of Germans who thought about it even for a moment must have realized that, at the least, 'something bad' was happening to the Jews.

A Nazi report (by the SD, the intelligence branch of the SS run by Reinhard Heydrich) from Franconia in southern Germany, dated December 1942, demonstrates that the Nazis themselves were concerned about the effect on the population of knowledge about the killing of Jews in the east: 'One of the strongest causes of unease among those attached to the Church and in the rural population is at the present time formed by news from Russia in which shooting and extermination of the Jews is spoken about. The news frequently leaves great anxiety, care and worry in those sections of the population. According to widely held opinion in the rural population, it is not at all certain that we will win the war, and if the Jews come again to Germany, they will exact dreadful revenge upon us.'[2]

But there was only sporadic resistance within Germany to Nazi persecution of the Jews. One of the most famous acts was conducted by Hans and Sophie Scholl, both students at the University of Munich, who produced leaflets during the war calling for German youth to 'rise up immediately' to build a 'new, spiritual Europe'. They called the treatment of the Jews and the killing of the Polish intelligentsia 'the most terrible crime against human dignity'. They were both denounced, tortured and then executed. Sophie Scholl confided to another prisoner that she thought her execution would be the sign for thousands of other Germans to question the actions of the Nazis. Significantly, on the day of her execution, 22 February 1943, the students of Munich University demonstrated their loyalty to the Nazi regime. As the historian Ian Kershaw argues, 'Not only was resistance to Hitler carried out – inevitably one might say – without active support from the mass of the people, but even passive support was largely lacking for those risking everything to overthrow the system.'[3]

The citizens of Germany had only to walk as far as their local cinema to see one more reason not to support brave individuals like Sophie and Hans Scholl and to keep on fighting. The Nazi newsreels showed in graphic terms how the country was fighting a life and death struggle against the Red Army – the enemy they all feared most. Fear at what would happen to Germany if the hated Bolsheviks triumphed was a powerful incentive to support the war and, in doing so, to support the Nazi leadership.

'What did the German soldier fight for and, one has to ask, against what?' says Graf von Kielmansegg, a German staff officer. 'For me this is the decisive reason: all those who had been in Russia at least knew what Germany could expect if Bolshevism came to Germany...If it had only been England and France, we would have stopped earlier in a simplified manner. Not against Russia.' As Hermann Teschemacher, who served on the Eastern Front, puts it: 'We told ourselves that there's a storm over Asia and it will come over Germany, and then brutal extermination, mistreatment and killings would follow, we knew that. So we defended ourselves to the end and remained loyal to the oath...The worst would have been if Bolshevism stormed over Germany – then the whole of Europe would be lost. But first and foremost we thought about ourselves and our families and that is why we defended ourselves to the end.'

In the summer of 1944 in an attempt to prevent Bolshevism 'storming over Germany', Hitler would suffer his greatest military setback of the war, a defeat that would feed his nihilism still further. This defeat was not the successful Allied invasion of France on D-Day, 6 June 1944, but the less-publicized Soviet attack that began on 22 June against Hitler's Army Group Centre in Belorussia. There is scarcely a greater measure of the extent to which the Eastern Front has been ignored in the consciousness of the general public in Britain and the USA than the comparison between Operation Overlord in France and Operation Bagration in the Soviet Union: the former is famous in Western popular culture, whilst knowledge of the latter is mostly confined to historians. Yet the Germans possessed just over 30 divisions in the West (excluding Italy) to meet the Allied invasion of Europe, whilst they fielded more than five times as many – 165 divisions – on the Eastern Front. And Operation Bagration would eliminate, on the German side, more than three times as many divisions as the Allies landed on D-Day. (It was Stalin who named the offensive Operation Bagration – after a military hero in the fight against Napoleon in 1812; like Stalin, Bagration was of Georgian origin.)

'The Belorussian operation was a classic,' says Makhmud

Gareev, who as a young Red Army officer took part in the offensive. 'Everything was well thought through.' Stalin demonstrated how far he had come from the incompetent leader who had so catastrophically presided over the disasters of 1941 by the way he listened to the deeply held views of Konstantin Rokossovsky, commander of the 1st Belorussian Front, about the tactics that should be adopted in the operation. Rokossovsky believed that the Red Army should attack Army Group Centre in two equally strong strikes, from the south and from the north. Stalin, aware of the accepted theory that dictated that forces should not be split, told Rokossovsky to leave the room and 'think it over'. When the military commander returned, he repeated his view that there should be two strikes. Eventually Stalin let him have his way – no doubt aware that Rokossovsky must be committed to his plan since he knew the fate he would suffer if he was wrong; as a junior officer, Rokossovsky had been imprisoned and tortured during the purges of the 1930s.

The preparations for Operation Bagration also illustrated the extent to which the Red Army had developed the art of deceiving their enemy about their true intentions. The sophisticated Soviet deception (*maskirovka*) plan was evident from the highest level, where knowledge of the aims of the operation was restricted to a handful of senior officers, to the lowest, where individual units of the Red Army hid under camouflage during the day and moved only at night, observing the strictest radio silence. In other areas of the front line far from the designated point of attack (most notably the area of the 3rd Ukrainian Front to the south) Soviet forces would be moved into the area during the day in full view of German reconnaissance aircraft, and then secretly moved out again at night – only to be transported openly in again the next day. The Red Army intended to deceive the Germans both about the point of the intended attack and the size of the Soviet force.

None the less, not even the Red Army could completely conceal the build-up during May and June 1944 of the 1.4 million soldiers who were about to take part in Operation Bagration. Whilst the intelligence gathered by the German Army Command (OKH) did lead them, falsely, to believe that the Soviets were planning an attack in the south towards the Balkans, by the end of May some units within Army Group Centre believed correctly that the main offensive would be directed against them. Hitler was not convinced. He ordered Army Group Centre to stand firm and, if attacked, to concentrate their defence around key Feste Plätze or fortified towns. In a directive of 8 March that year Hitler had stated that these Feste Plätze would 'fulfil the function of fortresses in former historical times. They will ensure that the enemy does not occupy these areas of decisive operational importance. They will allow themselves to be surrounded, thereby holding down the largest possible numbers of enemy forces, and establishing conditions favourable for counter attacks.'[4]

The discontent felt by Army Group Centre at such orders from the Führer is evident from these words, written by the commander of the German 9th Army, General Jordan, in June 1944: 'Ninth Army stands on the eve of another great battle, unpredictable in extent and duration...the Army believes that, even under the present conditions, it would be possible to stop the enemy offensive, but not under the present directives which require an absolutely rigid defence...The Army considers the orders establishing "Feste Plätze" particularly dangerous. The Army therefore looks ahead to the coming battle with bitterness, knowing that it is bound by orders to tactical measures which it cannot in good conscience accept as correct and which in our earlier victorious campaigns were the causes of the enemy defeats...'[5]

'In 1944 we were advancing like the Germans used to advance in 1941,' says Veniamin Fyodorov, a Red Army soldier who took part in the initial assault of Operation Bagration on 22 June 1944, three years to the day since the German invasion. 'The German behaviour in their fortified areas was stupid…Our shelling broke them down. Huge amounts of shells flew towards them and you couldn't hear anything; only this – booming! The fortified area could be smashed completely. It was death…The Germans held the ground to the last man – they were all doomed to death.'

Heinz Fiedler was one of the German soldiers of the 9th Army ordered to hold the Fester Platz of Bobruisk in the face of the Soviet advance. Previous battle experience had made him cynical about such 'nonsensical' orders from the High Command: 'I remember once that one position had definitely to be taken back again, and the second lieutenant had refused to attack once more because more than half of his men had already died. And then they did attack, and they were all just sacrificed. They attacked again and again until the very last one died, and that of course makes you wonder. But those were the men of the General Staff. They had their little flags and they put them on the map and then they say, "This absolutely has to be restored, no matter what the sacrifices are."'

Harsh as Heinz Fiedler's past experience of the war had been, it was as nothing compared to life inside the besieged Feste Plätze: 'Everywhere dead bodies were lying – dead bodies, wounded people, people screaming. You didn't have any feeling for warmth or coldness or light or darkness or thirst or hunger. You didn't need to go to the toilet. I can't explain it. It's such a tension you're under…We were encircled, and in front of us were Russian tanks dug into the ground so that all you could see were their round turrets. They were shooting like mad. They must have had so much ammunition it was incredible. And from our back you heard [from the Germans], "We don't have any fuel, we don't have any ammunition left." And that's what you heard all the time…You have to think of the psychological burden on the individuals. I did not get married on purpose because – well, a widow with children will have difficulties in finding a new man when they already have limited means. But those who were married and who had two or three little children at home on the one hand, and on the other hand to fulfil this order [to stand fast] as an integral part of the unit – this psychological burden you cannot measure.' Heinz Fiedler admits he felt 'abandoned' and 'betrayed' by the High Command of the Army: 'Those in the Führer Headquarters have easy talking – it's easy to be clever when you're there, that's what you're thinking…On the other hand you had this obedience that nowadays we are reproached with as being the obedience of carcasses, but the way the German Wehrmacht was you will never ever find again. You will never find such an Army again in this world.'

The Soviet 65th Army threatened to engulf not just the German forces holding out in Bobruisk but also other German units to the east. General Jordan of the German 9th Army, of which Heinz Fiedler's unit was part, raged at his superiors' stupidity: 'HQ 9th Army is fully aware of the disastrous consequences of all these orders,' says the 9th Army war diary. 'It is a bitter pill to swallow, though, when one feels that behind these Army Group instructions, which so utterly ignore one's own pressing suggestions, and behind the answers given by the Field Marshal and his Chief of Staff, one can see no sign of a commander showing any purposeful will to do his utmost, but just the execution of orders whose basis has long since been overtaken by events.'[6]

Hitler, unhappy about the way General Jordan had deployed the 20th Panzer division during the battle and no doubt classing him as a typical 'cowardly wretch', relieved him of his command and appointed General Nikolaus von Vormann to take control of what remained of the 9th Army. But a change of command could not change the bare facts – which were that the Führer's own policy of Feste Platz had proved disastrous. In Bobruisk the defenders were hindered by German troops, who had retreated into the town seeking refuge, leaving their heavy weapons behind. Permission was finally granted to attempt a break-out – but one division was still ordered to stay behind and fight to the last. 'Then the last command arrived,' says Heinz Fiedler. 'Destroy vehicles, shoot horses, take as much hand ammunition and rations with you as you can carry. Every man for himself – go on and rescue yourself!'

Few of those who attempted to break through the encirclement managed to reach the safety of the new German line further to the west. Most were either killed by strafing from Soviet warplanes or by the Red Army on the ground in the kind of slaughter reminiscent of the massive German encirclements of 1941. 'We tried to break out but we were getting fired on and then there was panic,' says Heinz Fiedler. 'There was a private, a young boy, who sat by a birch tree with his intestines streaming from his stomach, crying "Shoot me!" and everybody just ran past him. I had to stop but I could not shoot him. And then a young second lieutenant from the sappers came and gave him the *coup de grâce* with a pistol to his temple. And that's when I had to cry bitterly. I thought if his mother knew how her boy ended...instead she gets a letter from the squadron saying, "Your son fell on the field of honour for Great Germany."'

Heinz Fiedler was one of the handful who made it through the Red Army lines, but the mighty 9th Army was all but eliminated. In total Army Group Centre completely lost 17 divisions, with another 50 suffering losses of 50 per cent.

Fear and hatred of Bolshevism had been at the core of Nazi ideology since the days of the Räterepublik in Munich in 1919. How much greater that fear and hatred were when there seemed the likelihood that the hated Bolsheviks would soon be on German soil. So great was the perceived danger that hundreds of thousands of non-Germans joined the fight against the Red Army. Contrary to popular belief, recruits did not have to be German to be ideologically committed members of Himmler's SS. Jacques Leroy was a young Belgian who had been impressed with the 'nice behaviour' of the occupying German forces and who resolved to join the Waffen-SS because he 'wanted to fight Communism and Bolshevism'. We asked him if he was not, therefore, a traitor. 'What is a traitor?' he angrily replied. 'What is a traitor, sir? Can you be a traitor at the age of sixteen? I didn't wear a Belgian uniform. You are a traitor when you fight ideas which are not those of Europe, which are not popular. When you take on ideas from abroad, you are a traitor. The word traitor never once came into my mind...I was fighting Communism.'

More than fifty years after the end of the war, Jacques Leroy is still openly racist. Even today he retains many of the views that his colleagues in the Waffen-SS held so dear. 'The difference between the people whom you call *Übermenschen* [superior races] and the ones whom you call *Untermenschen* [inferior races] is that the people who are the *Übermenschen* are the white race. That's why at the moment so many foreigners want to come to white race countries...In those days we were proud to belong to the white race.'

Jacques Leroy fought in some of the bloodiest battles on the Eastern Front, motivated by his racism and his hatred of Communism. At the battle of Teklino on 14 January 1945 his Waffen-SS unit came upon more than three Soviet regiments hidden in a forest. The SS attacked and lost 60 per cent of their men. At one point Leroy saw a Russian kneeling behind a birch tree and then suddenly he felt 'an electric shock' through his body. He dropped his rifle and 'at that moment I saw blood dripping on to the snow. I was bleeding, it was my eye which had been hit by a bullet.' Leroy's injuries cost him an eye and an arm, but after a few weeks in hospital, he pleaded to rejoin the SS, and was allowed to do so: 'Of course I had lost an arm and an eye but you know, when you're very young, one isn't affected by troubles in the same way that an older person might be.' When we asked why he wanted to rejoin the SS he replied, 'So as not to fall into mediocrity and to stay with my comrades...I don't like mediocrity, I don't like doing nothing, being idle and not having any aim in life...otherwise, what is your life for? Life is not about watching television all the time! You have to think, you have to see, you must have a goal.'

The Waffen-SS soldiers who fought the Russians for every step of territory as they advanced into the Reich included Bernd Linn, who was to take part in an engagement that in many ways symbolizes both the bravery and the futility of the Nazi armed resistance – the Battle of Halbe, fought on 29 April 1945, just days before the end of the war. Linn's unit was ordered to 'break through regardless of losses' – a futile order given that everyone knew that the war was lost.

'There was the sound of gunfire from every side,' says Linn, talking of the 'Hell of Halbe'. In the heart of the battle he came across a German tiger tank, damaged so that it was unable to move and yet still firing its machine-gun. 'Behind it was a lieutenant with a leg missing, but he wasn't dead yet. I went to him and said, "Is there something that you want?" And the lieutenant said, "Yes, please put my leg next to me." I wanted to take him with us in the vehicle and he said, "We have been ordered to break through regardless of losses. Please put my leg next to me."' As the men fell dead, German Red Cross nurses took up arms. Bernd Linn handed one a bazooka. 'Then the Russians shouted, "Surrender!" "Certainly not!" I said, "We're breaking through."' We pressed Linn to say why he fought on till the last. The nearest he came to making us understand was when he said that as a committed Nazi he thought it was simply his fate.

Conditioned as they were by Nazi propaganda about 'sub-human' Russians and the barbaric atrocities the Communists were allegedly capable of committing as they came west, the German troops' resistance is perhaps not so surprising. After all, what alternative did they have? Only surrender to a group who, they had been told, would treat them appallingly, and to whom the Germans had already done terrible things themselves. Since every soldier had been told from the beginning of hostilities against Russia that this was a war like no other, now, to surrender must be to experience a suffering as a Prisoner of War like no other. But it was more than fear which kept the Germans fighting in the east – hope also played a part. The dream that Britain, the United States and France would ask Germany to join them in a crusade against Communism was one that persisted in the face of all evidence to the contrary and the Allies' continued insistence on unconditional surrender.

Yet these cannot be the only reasons why German soldiers continued fighting to the end. In Italy, the country that opted out of the war in 1943, German troops continued fighting fiercely until the official surrender in May 1945. Facing their so-called 'honourable' adversaries – the Americans and the British – they could have deserted in droves if they had wished. And lest one imagines that desertion was considered 'un-German', it is worth remembering that one estimate is that as many as a million German soldiers deserted during World War I. Yet this didn't happen, even in Italy, during World War II.

The Nazis were born out of World War I and the pain of what they saw as a shameful defeat: one cannot overestimate the German desire not to see a repetition of November 1918. The German soldiers in Italy, just as much as the German soldiers fighting the ideological enemy in the east, were vividly aware of the circumstances of defeat in 1918. The Nazi élite themselves had an overwhelming desire not to relive these circumstances. Indeed, it is not too extreme to imagine that the decision to proceed with the Holocaust might have been partly inspired by a desire to ensure that Jews were not able to 'profit' from World War II as they had 'profited' from World War I. Ludicrous as these beliefs about the Jews were, they were clearly held by many Nazis and were, almost unbelievably, occasionally expressed to us even today. The German Army may not have been able to prevent the Allies advancing, may not even have been able to prevent them defeating Germany, but what *was* in their power was to ensure that the manner of their defeat in no way resembled the humiliation of World War I. This time German soldiers would not be surprised to hear the announcement of the surrender.

As the war drew to a close, Hitler remained a crucial presence in the German soldier's mind. During the last months Walter Fernau became a National Socialist Guidance Officer (NSFO) and gave propaganda speeches to soldiers in Germany, telling them why they should fight on. 'It was my task to address the troop at the company level, no bigger, to call on them to see it through,' he says. 'This accordion player appeared before the troop and then songs were sung, seamen shanties, and this created a wonderful atmosphere. And then I said, "Men, we haven't come together just to sing songs here. I have to tell you something about this entire situation in which we find ourselves. If we take a look at the military situation as it is at the moment, then we know that the Americans or the English are at our border. We know that the Russians are marching towards Berlin and we know that in the south the Americans have passed Rome. And furthermore, masses of planes are flying day and night over our country and dropping bombs on our cities. And none of us knows at this moment whether his family has already fallen victim or if his house is standing. If we are to judge the overall situation now, then I can only express it in simple soldier's language: 'It's all shit!' But in exactly the same way that we judge the military situation, so too must our Führer see it as the supreme commander. Perhaps he knows that it is even worse than we know today. But perhaps he knows that it is better. And he still demands of us today, however, that we continue to do our duty, that is, some of us must perhaps even be prepared to die or to be heavily wounded. And he can only demand that of us if he can expect a good end to the war." And then I said to the soldiers, "Do you want to chuck your rifles in the corner today and go home? And then when the war is over and Hitler comes and says, 'Well, you've thrown away your weapons! I wanted to find a good ending!' We do not want to expose ourselves to this reproach."' His view of Hitler at the time was simple. 'For us the Führer was, let us say, an idol.' This leads Walter Fernau to give a simple answer to the question – why did German soldiers desert in droves in World War I yet fight to the end in World War II? 'In the First World War there was no Hitler.'

The fact that German soldiers continued fighting to the end, though tragic in terms of human loss, may have had one positive benefit, according to Hans von Herwarth: 'The new *Dolchstosslegende* (stab-in-the-back legend) would otherwise have come true...Many of the women in Germany had lost their sons or their brothers and they couldn't imagine that all this was in vain, that they were killed for the wrong reason, they couldn't believe it.' If Hitler had been assassinated in 1944 and peace had immediately followed, in later years it would have been possible to argue that Germany would not necessarily have lost the war if she had fought on. Counterfactual history is by definition unprovable and the speculation would have been intense. In that last year of the war would the Western Allies have finally turned on the Russians? Would the Germans have developed their 'wonder weapons', including the V1 and V2 rockets, to a point where they could have made a real difference? The debate would still be raging, especially in ultra-right-wing circles. Ironically, the fight to the end may have prevented another Hitler being born from this war, albeit a new Hitler justly burdened with the legacy of the Holocaust.

Yet the benefits to Germany of peace in 1944 would have been immense, not just in terms of soldiers spared from death at the hands of the enemy, but in terms of German civilians who would have been saved from death at the hands of the Nazis. In that last year of the war, Nazi terror inside Germany spiralled out of control. One shocking case from the Würzburg archive illustrates how the Nazis turned on ordinary Germans as the war seemed lost.[7] Karl Weiglein, a farmer in Zellingen, a village a few kilometres from Würzburg, was fifty-nine years old in 1945 when he was called up to fight in the Volkssturm, the local defence force. He was assigned to a company led by a local teacher, Alfons Schmiedel, a fanatical Nazi who also led the local Hitler Youth. On 25 March, at about two o'clock in the afternoon, the whole battalion lined up for a roll-call in the village square and listened to a short speech from Dr Mühl-Kühner, the battalion commander, who said that with the war coming closer, regulations would be tighter and anyone who didn't obey orders would be shot. A group in the first battalion, including Karl Weiglein, replied 'Oh-oho!' Around the same time some anti-tank obstacles were removed from a nearby road, and a false rumour went around that Kurt Weiglein had something to do with it. On Tuesday 27 March the Nazis blew up a bridge connecting Zellingen with the neighbouring village of Retzbach in order to prevent the advance of American troops. Weiglein, whose house was near the bridge, said to one of his neighbours, 'Those idiots who have done this, Schmiedel and Mühl-Kühner, ought to be hanged!' Schmiedel overheard the remark and reported it to Mühl-Kühner.

The next evening the Fliegendes Standgericht (Flying Court Martial) of Major Erwin Helm arrived in Karlstadt. These courts had been formed to enforce discipline in the face of Germany's imminent defeat and had the legal powers of a formal court martial. The one headed by Major Helm was particularly notorious and referred to by locals as a 'lynching unit'. Major Helm was well known for his brutality and sadism; he had been overheard saying to a seventeen-year-old boy, 'Have you already chosen the twig you want to hang from?' On another occasion he had said to his officers, 'Look at this chap's neck, it's really tempting!'

Major Helm and Mühl-Kühner decided to execute Karl Weiglein as an example to others. He was promptly fetched from the police station in Zellingen and the Flying Court Martial convened at midnight. Helm ordered one of his lieutenants, Engelbert Michalsky, to chair the proceedings. Two local farmers, Anton Seubert and Theodor Wittmann, were brought in as 'assessors'. Walter Fernau, who by now was another of Helm's lieutenants, was ordered to act as prosecutor: 'Helm said, "You can take over the prosecution. It's a very straightforward case. I'll get the execution squad together."' He had written the death sentence before the trial even started. But then there was a hitch. The two local farmers, Seubert and Wittmann, refused to sentence Karl Weiglein to death.[8] Helm solved the problem by dismissing them, later threatening them with a court martial themselves. Karl Weiglein was found guilty, and Walter Fernau knew that the death sentence was the only possible outcome: 'Even if you now think I am a brutal dog,' he says, 'I really cannot say to you that at the time I thought that it was too harsh…The judicial authority decides that this is the case with a flying court martial, and I cannot then say, "Wouldn't it be better to give him three or six months in prison?" That would almost have been like saying to the soldiers, "Now all of you here commit some sort of crime, come up before the Flying Court Martial...you will spend six months locked up and in that time the war will be over and the others will die and you won't." Do you understand it then? Even today some people, lots of people, will confirm that such situations demand harsh measures, even though it's not to my taste. But I cannot make the laws.' Crucially, Walter Fernau talks of a link between the horrors he had seen in the east and his own attitude to the work of the Flying Courts Martial. 'I saw so many deaths of my own comrades in the war that you do get a rather thick skin as a result...Shooting people and seeing them fall too, that is terrible. But over time one becomes accustomed to it. If you are in Russia and see the Russians running about and coming towards you and then they come closer and then maybe they have attached their bayonets, well, then you shoot one after the other and are delighted when they drop. Dreadful! Can anyone understand that today, one being happy when another falls?'

At 1.30 a.m. Karl Weiglein was taken out to the pear tree Helm had selected for the hanging. He was made to wear a sign around his neck which read: 'Sentenced to death because of sabotage and destruction of fighting strength.' The pear tree was only 5 metres from Weiglein's home and he called out to his wife, 'Oh Dora, Dora, they are hanging me!' She opened the kitchen window and shouted at Helm and the others, 'Leave my husband alone! He hasn't done anything to you!' Michalsky shouted back, 'Shut up and close the window!' Her husband was hanged in front of her by Helm with the assistance of his lance-corporal. Even Walter Fernau, hardened as he was by his experiences in the east, was upset by the circumstances of Karl Weiglein's execution: 'One can describe it as shame...It's terrible for a woman like that to witness her own husband, to whom she has been married for maybe forty years or more, being hanged in front of their door.' The body was left hanging at the tree for three days until Easter Sunday, guarded by two soldiers.

After the war, and on reflection, Walter Fernau expressed his sorrow at what had happened: 'I spoke about it in my last statement, that I was so terribly sorry, but in such an event where people are simply executed it really is too banal afterwards to say, "I am sorry" or "I regret it." You can do that if you knock the mirror off a car; you can say, "I am sorry" then "What does it cost?" But not when a person is dead. And then I ask, what can be done at all? And that is the big question, which is still open today, what can I do?'

Many of the perpetrators of this killing escaped conviction. Of those who were punished, Major Helm was given a life sentence by an East German court in 1953, but since the East German secret service, the Stasi, wanted him to work for them in West Germany, he was released after three years. Walter Fernau was sentenced to six years in prison for his part in the court martial, and served more than five.

Such horrific tales of oppression in Germany are not uncommon in the final days of the war. In Penzberg, in the foothills of the German Alps, local inhabitants defended their coal mines against destruction from Hitler's scorched earth policy. The US Army was only a day away, but a Nazi execution squad was dispatched from Munich and coldly shot the leaders of the opposition. They then drew up a list of those considered 'politically unreliable' and had them hanged.

In the face of such terror the majority conformed. Johannes Zahn, for example, says, 'I personally reproach Hitler greatly, after it was clear that the war could not be won, for not immediately saying, "OK, I give up, I will make peace, I will withdraw, I admit that I'm weaker." He should have done this, but unfortunately he did not have the greatness of character.' Men like Zahn were not the sort to resist, purely for pragmatic reasons: 'When there is a clique like

Stalin's or Hitler's, when they are in power, they have all the means at their disposal and are determined to use these means of power ruthlessly. Everyone says, "There's no point. I won't risk anything," because anybody who risks anything will be killed. We saw that with the July affair. Even the people who were trained to kill and to exercise violence weren't able to do it, so how could a harmless civilian sitting in his chocolate shop selling sweets, how can he fight against something like that?' Zahn operated a simple policy of self-preservation: 'Fight them? I wouldn't have risked it. I put my tea-cosy over the telephone so as to survive these times. That's what the majority decided, that was their plan: shut up and see that nothing happens to you.' When, during an interview with one German who 'went along' with the regime, I questioned such sentiments and asked why there had been so much compliance, he angrily replied, with an element of justification, 'It's easy for you, isn't it? You've never been tested.'

In the last months of the war Karl Boehm-Tettelbach left Berlin and was ordered north to Neustadt-Flensberg. On the way he and his fellow officers stopped to meet Himmler. This was to be Boehm-Tettelbach's last meeting with the SS chief and, despite the Reich crumbling around him, Himmler could scarcely have been more charming: 'Himmler saw that I was really hungry and frozen and he wanted me to have tea and warm up a little bit, and then noticed that I was in my summer underwear, in just my short shirt, and he didn't like that and he said: "Now look here, you are going to Flensberg. In Flensberg there is an SS supply store and there you get a shirt and underwear for colder days." I went there when I arrived and with Himmler's signature out of his notebook they gave me three shirts and three SS underwear shirts…There is still one shirt which my American daughter wears when it's really very, very cold. That's from Himmler.'

Boehm-Tettelbach's anecdote demonstrates how even in the last moments of the war, with the knowledge that he would be known to history as one of the creators of the Holocaust, Himmler was still able to project the image of a senior officer who had polite concern for the welfare of his fellow Germans.

The leading Nazis thus held on to real power until the very end. Yet Hitler's own physical condition deteriorated severely over the last two years of the war: his left arm shook as a result of the July 1944 attack, and he felt dizzy and sick for hours at a time. His personal physician, Dr Morrell, filled him full of quack remedies; Albert Speer, the Nazi Armaments Minister, had the impression that Hitler was burning out. Despite all this, Hitler was still obeyed by his loyal entourage. In Hugh Trevor-Roper's words, 'Hitler still remained, in the universal chaos he had caused, the sole master whose orders were implicitly obeyed.'[9]

On 16 April 1945 Stalin ordered the final assault on Berlin. He was careful to organize the attack so that no single general could snatch all the credit. Marshal Zhukov and Marshal Konev, the commander of the 1st Ukrainian Front, were *jointly* charged with the task of conquering the capital of the Reich. 'Stalin encouraged an intrigue – scheming,' says Makhmud Gareev. 'When they were drawing the demarcation line between the two fronts in Berlin, Stalin crossed this demarcation line out and said, "Whoever comes to Berlin first, well, let him take Berlin." This created friction…You can only guess Stalin was doing it so that no one gets stuck up and thinks that he was the particular general who took Berlin…At the same time he had already begun to think what would happen after the war if Zhukov's authority grew too big.'

While Stalin was acting in a way that demonstrated his true character, so was Hitler. As his forces crumbled around him under the battering of attacks from both East and West, Hitler decided that the German people had demonstrated that they were unfit for his leadership. His vengeance would not be confined to Jews and other 'sub-humans' but would extend to all of Germany. In a Führer Order of 19 March he ordered the destruction inside Germany of anything 'that the enemy could use for the continuation of the struggle'. This command, which has come to be known as the Nero Order (*Nero-Befehl*), called for the same scorched earth tactics to be used on German soil as had been practised in the retreat from Moscow – and for them to be used at a time when defeat was inevitable. Albert Speer, the Nazi Armaments Minister, managed to minimize the effect of the order by insisting that its implementation be coordinated through his ministry, but the wording of the Nero Order itself is unequivocal. Hitler summed up his feelings at a military situation conference on 18 April when he said, 'If the German people lose the war, then they will have proved themselves unworthy of me.'[10]

As Hitler sat in the bunker of the Reichschancellery and raged at the failure of the Germans to rise to the genius of their Führer, both Zhukov and Konev felt the consequences of Stalin's imposition of a 'race to Berlin'. Stalin now issued a map with a demarcation line through the city which left Konev 100 metres west of the Reichstag, the parliament building, which was the trophy that both Marshals sought. The armies of Zhukov and Konev, already engaged in fierce fighting street by street with the Germans, became entangled with each other at the imprecise boundaries between their sectors. Chuikov's 8th Guards from Zhukov's 1st Belorussian Front ran into Luchinskii's infantry from Konev's 1st Ukrainian Front.

Anatoly Mereshko served with Chuikov in the battle for Berlin as part of Zhukov's 1st Belorussian Front, and witnessed first-hand the desperate rivalry that flourished after Stalin had set his generals at each other's throats: 'Once Chuikov sent me to a particular suburb [of Berlin] to find out whose tanks were there. I got into my car with machine gunners, rode up there and talked to the people in the tanks. One said, "I am from the Belorussian Front," another "I am from the Ukrainian front." "Who came here first?" I asked. "I don't know," they replied. I asked the civilians, "Whose tanks got here first?" They just said, "Russian tanks." It was difficult enough for a military man to tell the difference between the tanks. So when I came back I reported that Zhukov's tanks got there first and Konev's tanks came later. So the celebration fireworks in Moscow were in his name...At that time it was a custom to arrange fireworks in Moscow with the announcement saying that "in honour of such-and-such army capturing this suburb of Berlin there had to be fireworks".' Only on 28 April did Stalin finally authorize a Stavka directive that confirmed Zhukov could take the centre of Berlin himself.

On 30 April 1945, just before 3.30 p.m., as Soviet soldiers approached the Reichstag, Hitler killed himself. Only with his death did his power over the Nazi Party come to an end. Ultimately, Hitler's own hatred had turned on the Germans he ruled and, like a fire, had ended by consuming itself. Born of crisis and hatred they had died in crisis and hatred.

As Hitler shot himself in his bunker on 30 April, the Red Army celebrated – including units stationed in the east German town of Demmin. The victory in Berlin had not satisfied the Soviet soldiers' desire for revenge, and they wanted every German to pay for the sins of the Nazis. One of the innocent Germans who suffered their vengeance was Waltraud Reski, then an eleven-year-old Demmin schoolgirl. As Berlin fell, she and her family heard this terrible news: 'Demmin was to burn for three days...And the women were fair game for three days too – free to be abused.' Waltraud's own mother was raped many times by Soviet soldiers. 'All the women were disguised, but you can always see whether a woman has a good figure, and somehow they found my mother again and again and treated her terribly. And she never really recovered…It's impossible to imagine what it is like to be raped 10 or 20 times a day, so that one's hardly human any more…Both my sister, who is four years younger than me, and I, tried to shield our mother and screamed…This feeling of helplessness and cruelty – even today I am unable to find words for it.'

Such was the desperation of the citizens of Demmin that hundreds ran down to the rivers that surround the town. 'I kept seeing women holding children by the hand. And they were running down towards the water…and many had tied themselves together and I was wondering: why are they doing that?…I could hear it – there is a sort of splashing sound when a person jumps into the water – and so I kept asking: "Why are they jumping into the water?" And my grandmother said: "They are so unhappy, they want to take their own lives."…And the sight of those who had gone into the water the previous night, those terrible sights, those bodies, reddish-blue and swollen. I didn't often look because I didn't want it to be true.' Her own mother, distraught at having just been raped once more, grabbed Waltraud and her sister and ran towards the river. 'And my grandmother kept saying, "Please don't do this! What are you doing? What am I supposed to tell your husband when he comes back from the war and you've gone?" And somehow she then became calmer.'

Several thousand townspeople committed suicide in Demmin during the Red Army's rampage. The exact number of Germans raped or killed in acts of revenge in the final months of the war, and in its immediate aftermath, will never be known. It is a figure certainly – at least – in the hundreds of thousands. Although some Soviet soldiers were later court-martialled for a small proportion of these offences, there is evidence that those in authority were capable of turning a blind eye to their actions. When Stalin was told how some

Red Army soldiers were treating German refugees, he is reported to have said: 'We lecture our soldiers too much; let them have some initiative.'[11]

The vengeance exacted by the Red Army on the people of Demmin, perpetrated in the last hours of the war, is an appalling – if not unexpected – end for a war that had begun nearly four years before with the unleashing of such terrible hatred by the Nazis on the Soviet Union. Now this hatred was rebounding on Germany. 'This must never happen again,' says Waltraud Reski. 'Not just the fighting against each other, but also this idea of the enemy not being human.'

It was the Nazis who had brought this destruction upon Germany. In their twelve-year reign they had demonstrated just what human beings can do if they take the brute beasts of the animal kingdom as their role models and are inspired by words like, 'Close your hearts to pity. Act brutally'.[12] For all time the story of the Nazis will act as a terrible warning.

Shortly after Hitler's death, at the formal German surrender, Karl Boehm-Tettelbach observed the signing of the document that meant that Germany had lost her second world war in less than thirty years. These were the thoughts that went through his mind: 'I had to raise the question, "Was it worth it, to start a war with all these losses on all sides; the Russian side, the German side, the American and English and French?"...I said to myself, "You've got the wrong profession. From now on, think of something else. And don't think of being a soldier again."'

After the war Karl Boehm-Tettelbach ran the Nuremberg office of the American airline Pan Am.

NOTES

CHAPTER ONE

1 Laffin, John, *Hitler Warned Us* (Brassey's, 1995), p.31

2 *Ibid.*, p.33

3 Noakes, J. and Pridham, G. (eds), *Nazism: A Documentary Reader 1919–45* (University of Exeter Press, 1984), Vol.2, p.572

4 Kershaw, Ian, *Hitler* (Longman, 1991), p.33

5 Bundesarchive Lichterfelde, file R43, I/2696

6 Hamann, Brigitte, *Hitler's Wein* (R. Piper GmbH, München, 1996)

7 Bayrisches Hauptstaatsarchiv, Abt IV, p.3071

8 Fest, Joachim, *The Face of the Third Reich* (Penguin Books, 1972), p.211

9 *Ibid.*, p.208

10 *Ibid.*, p.115

11 *Marktbreiter Wochenblatt,* 26 October 1923, Bayrisches Hauptstaatsarchiv, Microfiche 1, Akt. Minn73725

12 Zentrum für Antisemitismusforschung, Technische Universität Berlin (pamphlet originally published by Dr Heinrich Budor, Leipzig)

13 Noakes and Pridham (eds.), Vol.1, p.35

14 *Hitler's Table Talk* (Introduction by Trevor-Roper, Hugh) (Oxford University Press Paperback, 1988), p.39

15 Meissner, Otto, *Staatssekretär* (Hoffmann und Campe Verlag, 1950), p.240

16 Bessel, Richard, *The Rise of the NSDAP and the Myth of Nazi Propaganda*, Wiener Library Bulletin, (1980), Vol.23, no.51/51

17   von Papen, Franz, *Der Wahrheit eine Gasse* (Paul List Verlag, Munich, 1952), p.249

18   Note made on 2 December 1932 by Lutz Graf von Schwerin-Kroszigk, Reichs Finance Minister, quoted in 'Preparations for the military emergency under Papen' by Wolfram Pyta, Militärgeschichtliche Mitteilungen MGM51 (1992), p.141

CHAPTER TWO

1   Noakes and Pridham (eds.), p.169–70

2   These facts about Blomberg are quoted in Fest, Joachim, *Hitler* (Harcourt Brace Jovanovich, 1974), p.453

3   Speer, Albert, *Inside the Third Reich* (Orion, 1995), p.84

4   *Ibid.*, pp.194–5

5   Kershaw, Ian, 'Working Towards the Führer', *Contemporary European History*, Vol.2, Issue 2 (Cambridge University Press, 1993), pp.103–18

6   *Gone with the Wind*: for more on the reasons for Goebbels' obsession with this film see *Selling Politics* (BBC Worldwide, 1992) by the present author

7   Professor Robert Gellately. What follows is based on an extensive BBC interview at the Würzburg archives with Professor Gellately. See also his book *The Gestapo and German Society* (Oxford University Press, 1991)

8   Gellately, Robert, *The Gestapo and German Society*, pp.55–6

9   The Children's 'Euthanasia' Programme: this chronology is based on documents in Noakes and Pridham, Vol.3, and on Professor Noakes's advice to us for the section of the script of episode two of the television series *The Nazis: A Warning from History*, which dealt with the workings of the Chancellery and the child euthanasia policy

CHAPTER THREE

1   Trevor-Roper, p.15

2   *Ibid.*, p.24

3   Noakes and Pridham, Vol.2, p.263

4   Wistrich, Robert S., *Who's Who in Nazi Germany* (Routledge, 1995), p.202

5   Trevor-Roper, p.635
6   Noakes and Pridham, Vol.3, p.615
7   *Ibid.*, Vol.3, p.614
8   Ribbentrop, Joachim von, *The Ribbentrop Memoirs* (London, 1954), p.41
9   Wistrich, p.202
10 *Ibid.*, p.202
11 Noakes and Pridham, Vol.2, p.278
12 Memo from Hitler, August 1936. *Ibid.*, Vol.2, p.281
13 *Ibid.*, Vol.3, p.680
14 *Ibid.*, Vol.3, p.680
15 Taylor, A.J.P., *The Origins of the Second World War* (Hamish Hamilton, London, 1961), Ch.2
16 Noakes and Pridham, Vol.3, p.696
17 *Ibid.*, p.688
18 Fritsch was forced...See Fest, *Hitler*, p.543
19 *Ibid.*, p.544
20 Noakes and Pridham, Vol.3, p.739
21 Fest, *Hitler*, p.546
22 Fest, Joachim (ed.), *Himmler's Secret Speeches* (Propyläen Verlag, Germany, 1974), p.49
23 Cooper, Duff, *Old Men Forget* (Rupert Hart-Davis, 1953)
24 Noakes and Pridham, Vol.3, p.739
25 Author's interview with Hans Otto Meissner, 1991

CHAPTER FOUR

1   Trevor-Roper, p.19; 1 August 1941
2   Browning, Christopher, *The Path to Genocide* (Cambridge University Press, 1992)
3   Personal correspondence, Greiser to Himmler, 21 November 1942 (Berlin Document Centre)
4   Noakes and Pridham, Vol.3, p.938
5   *Ibid.*, p.940
6   *Ibid.*, p.954
7   Public statement, June 1942; Institut für Zeitgeschichte, DokI–176, p.29
8   Noakes and Pridham, Vol.3, p.949

9   *Ibid.*, p.949
10 Browning, p.13
11 Noakes and Pridham, Vol.3, p.965
12 Letter, 19 January 1943 (Berlin Document Centre, BDC, SS-HOI/4701)
13 Dobroszycki, Lucjan (ed.), *Chronicle of the Łódź Ghetto 1941–44* (Yale University Press, 1985), p.37
14 Browning, p.36. See also this book (pp.28–56) for a detailed description of the decision-making process that led to the establishment of factories in the Łódź ghetto.
15 *Ibid.*, p.37

CHAPTER FIVE

1   Cecil, Robert, *Hitler's Decision to Invade the Soviet Union* (Davis-Poynter, 1975), p.167
2   Cecil, p.15, from Rauschning, H., *Hitler Speaks* (Thornton Butterworth, 1939), p.140
3   Leach, Barry, *German Strategy Against Russia 1939–41* (Oxford University Press, 1973), p.14
4   Salisbury, H.E, *Marshall Zhukov's Greatest Battles* (Harper & Row, 1969), p.154
5   Halder, *Spruchkammeraussage,* 20 September 1948, IfZ ZS 240/6, pp.23–4
6   Burdick, Charles and Jacobsen, Hans Adolf (eds), *The Halder War Diary 1939–42* (Greenhill, 1988), pp.220–1
7   *Ibid.*, p.446
8   Letter from Franz Halder to Luise von Benda, 3 July 1941; BA-MA, N 124/5: Colonel J. Rohowsky (rtd) papers; private property Luise Jodl, née v. Benda
9   Suny, Ronald Grigor, 'Stalin and Stalinism 1930–53', Kershaw, Ian and Lewin, Moshe, *Stalinism and Nazism* (Cambridge University Press, 1997), p.30
10 *Ibid.*, p.49
11 Talbott, Strobe (ed.), *Khrushchev Remembers* (Deutsch, 1971), p.307
12 *Trotsky Moyazhizn,* Vol.2, pp.213–14, quoted in Volkogonov,

Dmitri, Stalin: Triumph and Tragedy (Weidenfeld & Nicholson, 1991), p.57

13 Lewin, Moshe, 'Stalin in the Mirror of the Other', Kershaw and Lewin, p.109

14 Kershaw and Lewin, p.124

15 A.A.Yepischev, as quoted in Volkogonov, p.279

16 Reuth, Ralph (ed.), Goebbels' Diaries (Munich, 1990), Vol.3, p.198; 10 July 1937

17 With the notable exception of the Röhm Putsch of 1934, though that was directed at the Nazis' own SA – the brownshirts – and not the German Army. Ironically, Stalin, when he heard of the Röhm Putsch, remarked how much he approved of it

18 Bullock, Alan, Hitler and Stalin, Parallel Lives (HarperCollins, 1991), p.731

19 Quoted in Fest, Hitler, p.644

20 See Streit, Christian, 'The German Army and the Policies of Genocide' in Hirschfeld. In Streit's view, 'Statements by troop commanders that they had not passed it [the Commissar Order] on or had forbidden its execution prove to be wrong in most cases. Only in one instance do sources verify that a divisional commander ignored the order.'(p.8)

21 Froehlich, Elke, 'Joseph Goebbels und sein Tagebuch', Vierteljahrshefte für Zeitgeschichte, 35 (1987)

22 Voenno-istoricheskii Zhurnal, 9 (1987), p.49, quoted in Volkogonov, p.37

23 Volkogonov, p.369

24 Overy, p.74

25 Erickson, John, The Soviet High Command (Weidenfeld & Nicholson, 1983), p.574

26 Bullock, p.768

27 Barros, James and Grefor, Richard, Double Deception: Stalin, Hitler and the Invasion of Russia (Northern Illinois University Press, 1995).

28 Sudoplatov, Pavel, Special Tasks (Warner Books, 1995), pp.145–7

29   Volkogonov, p.413

30   But note that one estimate is that 600,000 Soviet POWs were handed over during the war to Heydrich's Einsatzkommandos under his instructions of 17 July 1941, giving 'guidelines for the cleansing of camps for Soviet POWs'. These went further than the Commissar Order and called for the 'liquidation' not just of suspected commissars, party and state officials, but also of 'intellectuals' in the camps. See Streit, Christian, 'The German Army and the Policies of Genocide' in Hirschfeld. (Also note that the figure of 600,000 is the subject of dispute.)

31   Minutes of a meeting of civilian and military officials, 2 May 1941. *Nuremberg Trial Files*, Vol.31, p.84, Document 2718-PS.

32   *Ibid.*, Vol.36, pp.135–57

33   Quoted in Aly, Gotz, *Final Solution,* (Arnold, 199) p.201; Reuth (ed.), Vol.4, 1645

34   Deutsch, Harold C. and Showalter, Dennis E., (eds), *What If? Strategic Alternatives of WWII*, (Emperor's Press, Chicago, 1997)

35   Quoted in Overy, Richard, *Russia's War* (Allen Lane, 1998), p.94

36   Bullock, p.811

37   *Voenno-istoricheskii Zhurnal*, 10, (1991), pp.335–41

CHAPTER SIX

1   The question of just how many civilians died is controversial. See Overy, p.288. This estimate comes from detailed consultation with Professor John Erickson

2   Quoted in Fest, *Hitler*, p.655

3   Quoted in *Ibid.* p.654

4   Goebbels also recorded... Reuth (ed.); 20 and 21 March 1942.

5   Trevor-Roper, p.38; 23 September 1941

6   *Ibid.*, p. 69; 17 October 1941

7   Mulligan, Timothy Patrick, *The Politics of Illusion and Empire* (Praeger, 1988), p.11, from notes by Dr Werner Koeppen, 19 September 1941.

8   Quoted in Dallin, Alexander, *German Rule in Russia 1941–1945* (2nd edition, Macmillan, London, 1981), p.163

9   Koch speech, 5 March 1943, quoted in Mulligan, p.68

10   Quoted in Wistrich, p.142

11   Trevor-Roper, p.319; 19 February 1942

12   *Ibid.*, pp.587–9; 22 July 1942

13   Bormann to Rosenberg, 23 July 1942, Document NO-1878, quoted in Dallin, p.457

14   For a full history of this row see Dallin, pp.454–8

15   See Streit, Christian, 'Partisans-Resistance-Prisoners of War', in Wieczynski, J. (ed.), *Operation Barbarossa* (Salt Lake City, 1993)

16   Bullock, p.824

17   Armstrong, pp.21–7

18   Estimates provided by Colonel David Glantz. See Grenkevich, Leonid, *The Soviet Partisan Movement 1941–44*, ed. Glantz, David (Frank Cass, 1999)

19   Timoshenko claimed when interviewed that, when possible, if there was a secure route through to Red Army lines, he would send German prisoners back. This should be treated with scepticism. For a partisan unit operating behind enemy lines, it must almost always have been easier just to kill the German POWs as he describes.

20   Quoted in Mulligan, p.137

21   NKGB report 17 March 1945, Minsk Central Archive.

22   Ukrainian Interior Ministry Procurator's Report sent to 1st Party Secretary of Ukraine, 15 February 1949. Central State Archive, Kiev.

23   Kosyk, Wolodymyr, *The Third Reich and Ukraine* (Peter Lang, 1993), p.621

24   *Ibid.*, p.554

25   Quoted in Mulligan, p.139

26   Quoted in *Ibid.*, p.139

27   Quoted in *Ibid.*, p.142

28   Report (sent 3 January 1944) to Army Group Centre about Operation Otto begun in December 1943. (Source BA-MA, RH 19 II/242, Anlagen KTB HG Mitte, 1.1.–24.9.44; Banden-bekämpfung, 01/44–03/44)

29   Quoted in Mulligan, p.143

CHAPTER SEVEN

1   Overy, p.160

2   Quoted in Cooper, *The German Army, 1933–1945*, p.443

3   Keegan, John (ed.), *The Times Atlas of the Second World War* (Times Books, 1989), p.104

4   Warlimont, Gen. Walter, *Inside Hitler's Headquarters, 1939–45* (Presido Press, 1964; first published Bernard & Graege Verlag, 1962), pp.303–6

5   Statistics quoted in Beevor, Antony, *Stalingrad* (Viking Press, 1998), p.415

CHAPTER EIGHT

1   Klee, Ernst, Dressen, Willi, and Riess, Volker, *Those Were The Days* (Hamish Hamilton, 1991; first published by S.Fischer Verlag GmbH 1988), p.293

2   Burrin, Philipp, *Hitler and the Jews* (Edward Arnold, 1994), p.38

3   Noakes and Pridham, Vol.3, p.1200

4   *Ibid.*, p.1075

5   Noakes and Pridham, Vol.3, p.1091

6   Klee, Dressen and Riess, p.27

7   *Ibid.*, p.28

8   *Ibid.*, p.31

9   *Ibid.*, p.90

10   *Ibid.*, p.90

11   *Ibid.*, p.96

12   *Ibid.*, p.51

13   Quoted in Aly, Goetz, 'Jewish Resettlement', in Herbert (ed.), *Extermination Policies*, p. 71.

14   Quoted in Christopher Browning, *The Origins of the Final Solution: The Evolution of Nazi Jewish Policy September 1939 – March 1942* (William Heinemann 2004), p. 318.

15   From Burmeister's testimony of 24 January 1961, Bundesarchiv Ludwigsburg, 303 AR-Z 69/59, p.3.

16   *Hitler's Table Talk 1941–1944* (Phoenix Press 2000)

17   Quoted in Longerich, Peter, *The Unwritten Order* (Tempus 2001), p.78

18   Weinberg, Gerhard, 'The Allies and the Holocaust', in Neufeld, Michael J., and Berenbaum, Michael (eds.), *Allies and the Holocaust in the Bombing of Auschwitz* (St Martin's Press, New York 2000), p.20

19   Noakes and Pridham (eds.), Vol.3, p.1126.

20   Quoted in Longerich, Unwritten, p. 92.

CHAPTER NINE

1   Kershaw, Ian, *The Hitler Myth* (Oxford University Press, 1989), p.218

2   Kershaw, Ian, *The Persecution of the Jews and German Popular Opinion in the Third Reich* (Yearbook of Leo Baeck Institute 1981, Vol.26), p.284

3   Kershaw, Ian, *The Nazi Dictatorship*, p.177

4   Quoted in Adair, Paul, *Hitler's Greatest Defeat* (Arms and Armour Press, 1994), p.66

5   General der Infanterie Hans Jordan, quoted in Ziemke, Earl, *Stalingrad to Berlin: The German Defeat in the East* (US Army Historical Series, Office of the Chief of Military History, Washington DC, 1987), p.316

6   Adair, p.117

7   This file was originally selected for us by Professor Gellately and then the research was completed by BBC Assistant Producer Detlef Siebert

8   Walter Fernau still disputes the assessors' version of what they said happened inside the courtroom. It was, after all, the assessors' evidence that helped convict him for participating in the court martial at his own trial after the war

9   Trevor-Roper, Hugh, *The Last Days of Hitler* (Macmillan, 1947)

10   Hauner, Milan, *Hilter – A Chronology of His Life and Time* (Macmillan Press, 1983)

11   Quoted in Overy, p. 261

12   Noakes and Pridham, Vol.3, p.743

NOTES ON EYE WITNESSES

KIRA PAVLOVNA ALLILUYEVA-POLITKOVSKAYA
Born in 1922, she was Stalin's niece, the daughter of Pavel
Alliluyev, who was the brother of Stalin's second wife,
Nadezhda Alliluyeva. After the suspected poisoning of her
father in the Kremlin before the war, she and her mother were
later arrested and she spent five and a half years in forced exile.

DR FRITZ ARLT
Joined the Hitler Youth in 1929 at the age of seventeen, and
became a Nazi Storm Trooper in 1932. He gained a PhD in
1936. Between 1939 and 1940 he was head of the
Department for Population Affairs and Welfare at the
Internal Affairs Office of the Government General. In 1940
he became head of the Reich office for the Consolidation of
German Nationhood in charge of the administration of the
resettlement policy. In 1943 he transferred to the Waffen-SS.

RUDI BAMBER
Born into a Jewish family in Nuremberg in 1920, he was educated in a mixed school until 1936. In 1933 his parents became
the caretakers of the B'nai Brith Lodge premises in
Nuremberg; from 1935 they ran a Jewish café and guest
house in the city. His father, who had won the Iron Cross
during World War I, was murdered by Storm Troopers on
Kristallnacht. In July 1939 Rudi Bamber managed to escape
from Germany.

ZBIGNIEW BAZARNIK

Aged fourteen at the start of the war, he worked as a handyman and assistant electrician at Hans Frank's estate at Krzeszowice outside Krakow from May 1941.

BERNHARD BECHLER

Born in 1911, between autumn 1940 and spring 1942 he was ADC to General Eugen Müller (General for 'special duties') who was in charge of the drafting and interpretation of the infamous Commissar Order. From March 1942 he was a captain in the 3rd Infantry Division within the 6th Army. He was captured at Stalingrad on 28 January 1943.

CARLHEINZ BEHNKE

Born in 1922, he joined the Hitler Youth in 1933 and volunteered for the Waffen SS in 1940. He fought from the beginning of the Barbarossa campaign, first as a private in Artillery Regiment 5 of the SS-Panzer Division Wiking and subsequently as a junior officer in an SS Police Grenadier Division.

GÜNTHER VON BELOW

Born in 1905, he entered the Reichswehr in 1925. He was Quartermaster of 4 Corps in the French campaign and subsequently a senior officer within the 6th Army at Stalingrad. From 1943 to 1955 he was a Soviet POW.

GERDA BERNHARDT

The sister of Manfred Bernhardt, a mentally disabled boy murdered at Aplerbeck psychiatric hospital in Dortmund during the Nazi's Children's 'Euthanasia' Programme. Only in 1989 did the whole truth about the killings at Aplerbeck become known.

MAYA IANOVNA BERZINA

Born in 1910. Her father was a close collaborator of Lenin's and one of his first ambassadors. In 1938 her father was shot dead in the purges because he was a 'suspect' Lithuanian. She experienced the panic in Moscow in October 1941, and with her husband and young child fled by boat from Moscow's southern port.

CHARLES BLEEKER-KOHLSAAT

Born in 1928 into a wealthy ethnic German family in Posen, in a part of Poland that had been German before World War I. He later became a member of the Hitler Youth and witnessed the resettlement of the incoming ethnic Germans.

KARL BOEHM-TETTELBACH

Born in 1910, he joined the Luftwaffe before the Nazis came to power and trained secretly as a pilot in Russia. He was adjutant to Field-Marshal von Blomberg during the Fritsch/Blomberg crisis of 1938. During the war he served at the Führer's headquarters in East Prussia, the Wolf's Lair; he was present in the compound at the time of the 20 July 1944 assassination attempt on Hitler.

ALEKSEY BRIS

Born in 1922 in the Ukraine. He worked as an interpreter for the Germans in Gorokhov during their occupation of the Ukraine. In 1942, after witnessing the mistreatment of his fellow countrymen at the hands of the Germans, he joined the UPA – the Ukrainian Nationalist Partisans.

PROFESSOR MIECZYSLAW BROZEK

As a young assistant professor in classical philology at the Jagellonian University in Krakow, he was arrested in November 1939 along with other academics as part of the Nazi plan to deprive Poland of intelligent people. He was imprisoned in various concentration camps, including Dachau. He and the surviving professors were released as the result of international pressure at the end of 1940.

FYODOR VASILIEVICH BUBENCHIKOV

Born in 1916, he first saw action in the war as a commander of a penal battalion at the Battle of Kursk. He subsequently participated in Operation Bagration and was wounded at Danzig in early 1945.

ADOLF BUCHNER

Born in 1923 in Munich, he later trained in agriculture at Marktoberdorf. He was arrested in 1942 after being denounced for listening to foreign broadcasts. In February 1944 he was called into the SS-Pionierbataillon Dresden for 'probation at the front'. He participated in 'cleansing' villages near Leningrad.

ALBERT LVOVICH BURKOVSKI

Born in 1928 in Stalingrad, when the fighting started he was left alone in the city after his grandmother had been killed. He was adopted by the Soviet 13th Radimeev Division and personally killed Germans at close range on the Mamaev Kurgan.

PAUL EGGERT

Coming as he did from a broken home, Paul Eggert was forcibly sterilized by the Nazis when he was eleven. He later spent three months in the children's ward of Aplerbeck psychiatric hospital where he witnessed the 'disappearance' of many of the children.

IRMA EIGI

An ethnic German from Estonia, she (at the age of seventeen) and her family arrived in the Warthegau in late 1939 as part of the first group of Baltic Germans to be resettled in 'Germany' under the terms of the secret protocol to the Nazi–Soviet Pact.

JOSEF FELDER

Born in 1900, he was a Social Democrat MP by the time Hitler became Chancellor in January 1933. After the Nazis came to power he was arrested and sent to Dachau. Released after eighteen months in the camp, he had to remove himself from politics for the duration of the Nazi rule of Germany.

WALTER FERNAU

Born in 1920 in Melsungen. As a member of the 14 Panzerjäger-Kompanie of his regiment, he took part in Operation Barbarossa and was wounded during the retreat from Moscow. He became a lieutenant in 1944, and in the spring of 1945 he joined Major Helm's unit which was charged with assembling scattered soldiers and later with 'Flying Courts Martial'. He became Helm's adjutant and was appointed NSFO (National Socialist Guidance Officer). In many of the Flying Courts Martial he acted as prosecutor.

HEINZ FIEDLER

Born in 1922, he was drafted into the Reiter-Regiment 10 in Torgau and trained as a radio operator. In the summer of 1944 he fought against the Red Army during their Bagration offensive and escaped from the fortified place of Bobruisk.

ESTERA FRENKIEL

Born into a Jewish family in Łódź she, along with other Lodz Jews, was forced by the Nazis to move into the designated 'ghetto' area of the city in the spring of 1940. She managed to get a job as a secretary working in the ghetto administration and was thus able to meet Hans Biebow, the Nazi who was the ghetto manager. When the ghetto was closed she and her mother were transported to Ravensbrück concentration camp.

VENIAMIN POLIKARPOVICH FYODOROV

Born in 1924, he served as a private with the 77th Guards Infantry Regiment of the Red Army during Operation Bagration.

MARK LAZAREVICH GALLAY

Born in 1914, from 1936 he worked as a Soviet test pilot at the Central Aerodynamic Institute. During the late 1930s he witnessed the effect of the purges on Soviet military aviation.

MAKHMUD AKHMEDOVICH GAREEV

Born in 1923 of Tatar nationality, he served more than fifty years in the Red Army, finishing his service as Deputy Chief of the General Staff of the USSR Armed Forces. In 1942 he was a captain, commanding the 3rd Battalion of the 120 Infantry Brigade, and by 1944 he was a major, the Operations Officer in the Headquarters of 45 Infantry Corps.

INNA VLADIMIROVNA GAVRILCHENKO

Born in 1926, she lived through the German occupation of Kharkov, witnessing her own father's death from starvation in May 1942.

IVAN IVANOVICH GOLOKOLENKO

Born in 1921, he volunteered to fight in the war in June 1941. In the autumn of 1942, as a lieutenant in the 19th Tank Brigade of the 26th Tank Corps, he participated in the Soviet Operation Uranus.

JUOZAS GRAMAUSKAS

Born in 1920, he lived in the village of Butrimonys in Lithuania. In September 1941 he witnessed the massacre of women and children by units of the Lithuanian Army acting on German orders.

PETER VON DER GROEBEN

Born in 1903, he was a senior German military officer during the war. In 1943–4 he was Chief of Operations of Army Group Centre, and he finished the conflict as Major General of the 3rd Cavalry Division.

ANATOLY MARKOVICH GUREVICH

Born in 1916, he was Head of Soviet Military Counter-intelligence in France and Belgium during World War II. During 1940 he learnt of the German intention to invade the Soviet Union and passed on the information to Moscow. At the end of 1942 he was arrested by the Gestapo. After the war he was accused by the NKVD and imprisoned for twelve years. He was 'rehabilitated' in 1991.

BRUNO HÄHNEL

Born in 1911, he joined the youth wing of the Storm Troopers in 1927 before working as a regional leader of the Hitler Youth in Westphalia until 1945.

HANS VON HERWARTH

Born in 1904, he joined the German diplomatic corps in 1929. From 1931 to 1939 he worked in the German embassy in Moscow and witnessed the signing of the Nazi–Soviet Pact. From 1939 to 1945 he served in the Wehrmacht.

GERHARD HINDENLANG

Born in 1916, he began the Barbarossa campaign as a lieutenant with the 71st Infantry Division. By January 1943 he was a battalion commander at Stalingrad. From 1943 to 1950 he was a prisoner of war. He is a recipient of the German Cross in Gold, one of the highest awards in the German Army.

WOLFGANG HORN

Born in 1920, he was a junior NCO with the 10th Panzer Division, commanding a six-man gun crew. He took part in Army Group Centre's advance to Moscow and his unit reached to within 30 kilometres of the Russian capital.

FRANZ JAGEMANN

Born in 1917 into a German family (but with a Polish father). He served as a 'supply translator' from July to October 1940 in the Warthegau.

ANNA JEZIORKOWSKA

Born in 1929 into a Polish family in Posen, she and her family were brutally evicted from their flat in November 1939 and transported in animal freight wagons to the General Government.

TAMARA BATYRBEKOVNA KALMYKOVA

Born in 1925, she participated in the defence of Stalingrad as a communications officer with the Soviet 64th Army and was wounded in November 1942.

WALTER KAMMERLING

Born into a Jewish family in Vienna in 1923; as a fifteen-year-old he witnessed the Anschluss and the mistreatment of Jews on the streets of Vienna. He managed to leave Austria in October 1938.

VLADIMIR KRISTAPOVICH KANTOVSKI

Born in 1923, he was sentenced to ten years' hard labour in 1941 for distributing leaflets protesting at the arrest of one of his schoolteachers. In 1942 he volunteered for a penal battalion and served in the 54th Penal Company. He was severely wounded during his first attack. In 1944 he was arrested again and sentenced to six more years in the camps.

JOHANN-ADOLF GRAF VON KIELMANSEGG

Born in 1906, he joined the German Army in 1926. In 1939 he became a member of the General Staff.

EMIL KLEIN

Born in 1905, he participated in the march through Munich during the Beer Hall *Putsch* and was later decorated with the Nazi 'blood order'. He joined the Storm Troopers in the early 1920s and became a Nazi propaganda speaker after 1925.

ERNA KRANZ

Born into a middle class Bavarian family, as a teenager she participated in the Night of the Amazons Pageant in Munich in 1938.

MARIA THERESIA KRAUS

Born in 1920, she is a former neighbour of Ilse Sonja Totzke who died in a Nazi concentration camp after being the victim of denunciations. One of the denunciations attacking Miss Totzke (in the Würzburg archives) is signed by Resi Kraus.

VALENTINA DMITRIEVNA KRUTOVA

Born in 1931, she was eleven years old when the Germans advanced on Stalingrad. Trapped within the German lines she, her younger sister and elder brother were lucky to survive after the death of their grandmother.

EVDOKIYA FYODOROVNA KUVAKOVA

Born in 1939, she was just four years old when the NKVD deported her and her family to Siberia as part of the punishment relocation of the Kalmyks.

JACQUES LEROY

Born in 1924 in the French-speaking part of Belgium, he joined the Waffen SS after the fall of France. He rejoined his unit after losing an arm and an eye and was decorated with the Knight's Cross on 20 April 1945 for his bravery in the defence of Nazi Germany.

EUGENE LEVINÉ

Born in 1916, he is the son of the Jewish Räterepublik politician Eugene Leviné who was executed in 1919. He later joined the German Communist Party and escaped from Germany in 1933.

BERND LINN

As a boy, growing up in Bavaria in the 1920s, he witnessed the arrival of the so-called 'eastern Jews'. He later joined the Waffen SS and fought on the Eastern Front during the war.

DR GÜNTER LOHSE

He joined the German Foreign Office and the Nazi Party in the 1930s. He witnessed the consequences of Hitler's chaotic method of government.

RIVA LOSANSKAYA

Born in 1918, she is one of only sixteen Jewish survivors from the massacres at the village of Butrimonys in Lithuania.

MARIA MAUTH

Born in 1924, she served in the Reich Labour Service during the war.

WALTER MAUTH

Born in 1923, he served as a lance corporal in a heavy machine gun company of the 30th Infantry Division. During 1943 and 1944 he participated in the German 'scorched earth' retreat.

HUBERT MENZEL

Born in 1908, he joined the German Army in 1927. From April to October 1941 he participated in the planning and then the direction of Operation Barbarossa as a major in the Operations Department of OKH (Army High Command). In November 1942 he was appointed Chief of Operations (Ia) of the 16th Panzer Division in Stalingrad. From 1943 to 1955 he was a POW in Russia.

ANATOLY GRIGORIEVICH MERESHKO
Born in 1922, he was a committed member of the Communist Party and as a young officer fought against the Germans' Operation Blue and subsequently in the defence of Stalingrad. From then until the end of the war he was an officer 'for special tasks' in Chuikov's Headquarters. After the war he rose to become Deputy Military Commander of the Warsaw Pact.

ALEKSANDR ANDREEVICH MIKHAILOVSKI
Born in 1921. During an anti-partisan sweep that encompassed their village of Maksimovka in Belorussia, he and his deaf and dumb brother were made to walk down a road that the Germans suspected was mined.

STEPAN ANASTASEVICH MIKOYAN
Born in 1921, he was the eldest son of Politburo member Anastas Mikoyan. He grew up in the Kremlin compound, playing with Stalin's own children, and went to flying school with Stalin's son Vasilij. He served as a pilot during the war.

ANNA MIREK
Twenty-seven years old at the start of the war, she worked as a cook at Hans Frank's estate at Krzeszowice outside Krakow.

SUREN GAREGINOVICH MIRZOYAN
Born in 1923, from May 1942 he served as a private in a reconnaissance patrol with the 33rd Guards Rifle Division in the Soviet 62nd Army. He fought in the Caucasus, the Kalach area and at Stalingrad, and ended the war in the Ukraine.

GERHARD MÜNCH

Born in 1915, in 1941 he was adjutant of the 194th Infantry Regiment with the 71st Infantry Division. In 1942 his was the first German battalion to reach the Volga in Stalingrad. He was flown out of the Stalingrad encirclement on 22 January 1943. After the war he became a general in the West German Army.

NADEZHDA VASILIEVNA NEFYODOVA

Born in 1927, she was fourteen years old when the Germans over-ran her village of Usyazha, 50 kilometres east of Minsk in Belorussia. She and her family were trapped between the Germans (who killed her brother) and the Soviet partisans (who killed her sister).

VLADIMIR TIMOFEEVICH OGRYZKO

Born in 1917, by 1939 he was a junior officer with the NKVD Moscow Division. During the Moscow panic of October 1941, he commanded a secret police unit that helped restore order. In the winter of 1941 he also served alongside the backmarker divisions on the Moscow front as part of the 1st NKVD Division.

ROMUALD PILACZYNSKI

Born in 1927 into a middle-class Polish family in Bydgoszcz, in what became part of Albert Forster's domain after the Nazi redrawing of Polish boundaries. His family were reclassified as 'third category' Germans.

OTTO PIRKHAM

Austrian diplomat who witnessed the meeting of Hitler and the Austrian Chancellor Kurt von Schuschnigg on 12 February 1938 at the Berghof.

NIKOLAY VASILIEVICH PONOMARIEV

Born in 1916, he was a communications officer in the General Staff Headquarters before the war, becoming Stalin's own personal telegraphist from July 1941 until the end of the war.

ZINAIDA GRIGORIEVNA PYTKINA

Born in 1921, she took part in the Stalingrad battle as a nurse with the 88th Tank Brigade. In 1943 she was selected to join SMERSH ('Death to Spies') as a lieutenant and counter-intelligence officer working alongside the Headquarters of the 54th Tank Brigade within the 3rd Tank Army.

RÜDIGER VON REICHERT

Born in 1917, he joined the Wehrmacht in 1936 and by 1941 was a battery commander in the 268th Infantry Division, 4th Army, Army Group Centre. By the end of the war he was a major on the General Staff. After the war he went on to become a general in the West German Army.

WALTRAUD RESKI

Born in 1934, she was eleven years old when the Red Army set fire to her home town of Demmin in East Germany in 1945. Her mother was repeatedly raped by Soviet soldiers.

ANATOLY IVANOVICH REVA

Born in 1935, he was six years old when the Germans occupied the eastern Ukrainian city of Kharkov. With his father dead and his mother in hospital he roamed the streets before being placed in an orphanage, where he nearly died of starvation.

DR HERBERT RICHTER

Born in 1899, he fought as a German soldier during World War I. In 1924 he joined the German Diplomatic Corps, and later served in Rome, Bombay and Colombo.

DR JUTTA RÜDIGER

From 1937 to 1945 she was Reich Leader of the League of German Girls (the BDM). As a child she witnessed the French occupation of the Ruhr.

WALTER SCHAEFER-KEHNERT

Born in 1918, he was an artillery officer with the 11th Panzer Division fighting in Kiev, Uman, Vyazma and Moscow. His unit was sent to France in May 1944.

ALBERT SCHNEIDER

Born in 1923, he was a mechanic with the 201st Assault Gun Battalion, fighting through Minsk, Borisov, Smolensk and Orsha to within 30 kilometres of Moscow. In 1942 he was transferred to the 101st Artillery Battalion and deployed near Stalingrad.

MANFRED FREIHERR VON SCHRÖDER

Born in 1914, he joined the Nazi Party in November 1933. In 1938 he entered the German Foreign Office. From 1937 to 1938 he was a member of the SS Cavalry Unit and, from May 1942 to August 1943, served in the Wehrmacht on the Eastern Front.

SUSI SEITZ

Born in 1923, she was not quite fifteen when she stood cheering in the crowd that welcomed Hitler into the Austrian town of Linz in March 1938. She went on to become a leading member of the Austrian Hitler Youth.

GEORGY VALERIEVICH SEMENYAK

Born in 1921, he was a scout with the 204th Division within the 11th Mechanized Corps. He began the war in Belorussia and was taken prisoner by the Germans on 6 July 1941 near Minsk. He was one of the few Soviet prisoners captured so early in the war to survive German captivity. After the war, and throughout his working life, he suffered discrimination within the Soviet state because he had been taken prisoner.

MELETI SEMENYUK

Born in 1912, he lived in a small hamlet near Gorokhov in the Ukraine. During the war he joined the UPA (the Ukrainian Nationalist Partisans) fighting both the Germans and the Soviet partisans.

VIERA SILKINAITE

A native of Kaunas in Lithuania, at the age of sixteen she witnessed the murder of Lithuanian Jews in the 'garage' killing in Kaunas in the early days of the German occupation.

FRIDOLIN VON SPAUN

Born in 1900, he volunteered to fight in the right-wing Bavarian Freikorps Oberland after World War I and saw action with the Freikorps in Poland. After Hitler came to power he worked to promote Nazi propaganda in Germany.

REINHARD SPITZY

Born in Austria, he joined the SS and the staff of Joachim von Ribbentrop in the 1930s. During the war he served in German intelligence.

OACHIM STEMPEL

Born in 1920, in 1941 he was a lieutenant with the 108th Panzer Grenadier Regiment within the 14th Panzer Division. He was caught within the Stalingrad encirclement, where his own father (a general and a divisional commander) committed suicide. From 1943 to 1949 he was a POW in the Soviet Union.

VIKTOR ADOLFOVICH STRAZDOVSKI

Born in 1923, he volunteered for the Red Army in 1941. As a private in the 52nd Infantry Regiment, 18th Division, 32nd

Army, he fought at the Battle of Vyazma and subsequently at Stalingrad and Kursk.

FYODOR DAVIDOVICH SVERDLOV

Born in 1921, he commanded an infantry company with the 19th Infantry Brigade, 49th Army. In the winter of 1941 he and his men fought in the area of Kubinki during the defence of Moscow.

ARNON TAMIR

Born in 1917 in Stuttgart, he went on to be active in the Jewish Youth Movement. In 1938 he was one of a large number of Jews deported to Poland by the Nazis, but subsequently managed to escape to Palestine.

WILHELM TER-NEDDEN

Born in 1904, he joined the Nazi Party in 1937. From the summer of 1941 he was Deputy Head of Economic Staff East. He also worked in Rosenberg's Ministry for the Occupied Eastern Territories. During the German occupation of the Ukraine, he witnessed the acrimonious relationship between Rosenberg and Koch.

HERMANN TESCHEMACHER

Active in right-wing politics in the 1920s, he later joined the Nazi Party. During the war he fought on the Eastern Front.

WOLFGANG TEUBERT

Joined the Nazi Storm Troopers in the east of Germany during the late 1920s. During the war he served in the German Army on the Eastern Front.

MIKHAIL IVANOVICH TIMOSHENKO

Born in 1909, he took part in the Finnish war with the 44th Ukrainian Division. In June 1941 he and his NKVD comrades fruitlessly tried to resist the initial German assault on the Soviet border. Later in 1941 he was the political commissar of a partisan unit behind the German lines.

WALTER TRAPHÖNER
Born in 1908, he served as a private (subsequently lance corporal) with an SS cavalry regiment operating in the rear of Army Group Centre. He was wounded in December 1942 and sent back to Germany.

IVAN STEPANOVICH TRESKOVSKI
Born in 1928, he lived in Usyazha, 50 kilometres east of Minsk in Belorussia. Like his fellow villager, Nadezhda Vasilievna Nefyodova, he experienced the brutality of both the Germans and the Soviet partisans.

PROFESSOR STANISLAW URBANCZYK
An academic at the Jagellonian University, Krakow, he was imprisoned by the Nazis at Sachsenhausen concentration camp. He was released after fourteen months, at Christmas 1940.

BORIS VLADIMIROVICH VITMAN
Born in 1920, he served as an intelligence officer at the Headquarters of 6th Army on the south-western front. He fought in the ill-fated Kharkov advance of May 1942 and was taken prisoner by the Germans during the Barvenkovo encirclement.

HELMUT WALZ
Born in 1922, he was a private with the 305th Infantry Division and fought hand-to-hand with Red Army soldiers in Stalingrad in October 1942. He was severely wounded on 17 October and spent the rest of the war in hospital.

SAMUEL WILLENBERG

Born in 1923 into a Jewish family in Poland, in 1942 he was sent to the Nazi death camp at Treblinka. In 1943 he managed to escape and, after a series of adventures, eventually joined the Polish underground and fought against the Nazis.

GABRIELE WINCKLER

She was a secretary in Germany during the 1930s.

PROFESSOR JOHANNES ZAHN

Born in 1907, he gained a PhD in Law in 1929. From 1933 to 1934 he worked at the Central Association of German Banks and in 1935 became Managing Director of the German Institute of Banking. From 1939 to 1945 he served in the Wehrmacht; during this period he was also German administrator of English and American banks in Belgium.

PETRAS ZELIONKA

Born in 1917 into a poor Lithuanian peasant family, in 1941 he joined the 3rd/13th Lithuanian Auxiliary Police Battalion. As a ghetto guard he witnessed killings in the 7th Fort in Kaunas and later murdered victims himself in numerous other actions. In 1948 the Soviets sentenced him to twenty-five years in Siberia.

EUGEN ZIELKE

An ethnic German from Łódź in Poland whose father ran a food shop. In 1940, when he was in his early 20s, he benefited from trade with the Jews who were imprisoned in the Łódź ghetto.

ACKNOWLEDGEMENTS

There are many people I need to thank.

Michael Jackson and Mark Thompson, successive Directors of BBC Television, made possible both television series – *Nazis: A Warning from History* and *War of the Century*. Without their support these projects would never have happened.

Many academics also contributed to this work, but I have to start by singling one out in particular. Professor Sir Ian Kershaw was the series historical and script consultant on both *Nazis: A Warning from History* and *War of the Century*. He is the most exceptionally gifted scholar and he was of immense help. His contribution to this project cannot be overestimated, nor can my gratitude to him. Other academics were also extremely helpful; Professor Christopher Browning, Professor Robert Service, Professor John Erickson, Colonel David Glantz, Professor Vladimir Naumov, Dr Krill Anderson, Colonel Yuri Gorkov, Dr Sergey Sluch, Dr Svetlana Argasceva, Professor Alexander Chubarian, Nikita Petrov, Professor Aleksei Litvin, Dr Sergei Kot, Dr Yuri Shapoval, Dr Volker Riess, Dr Christian Gerlach, Andrej Angrick and Peter Klein.

I was also lucky to lead one of the most talented production teams in television across both series. Tilman Remme was the Associate Producer on the *Nazis* series, Detlef Siebert the Associate Producer on *War of the Century*. Both are journalists of exceptional gifts. The dedicated Assistant Producers were

Sally Ann Kleibal, Sue McConachy, Corinna Stuermer, Martina Balazova, Tomasz Lasica and Alexandra Umminger. In Germany, Marita Krauss, Friederike Albat, Stuart Russell, Manfred Oldenburg, Marcel Joos and Frank Stucke also did important research for us. In Russia, Elena Yakovleva, Maria Keder, Elena Smolina, Stanislav Remizov, Eric Shur, Valeri Azarianc, Anya Narinskaya, Maria Razumovskaya, Maria Mikushova, Valentina Galzanova, Teodor Matveev and Viktor Belyakov all made an essential contribution, as did Roksolyana and Taras Shumeiko in the Ukraine. In Poland Wanda Koscia did a fine job for us, and in Lithuania excellent work was completed by Saulius Berzinis and Alicija Zakauskaite.

The ever cheerful camera team of Martin Patmore, Brian Biffin (alternating with Richard Manton) criss-crossed Europe and the former Soviet Union with me and put up both with my many foibles as a director and hotels in the East which lacked every conceivable amenity. Katherine Manners and Adrian Wood were outstanding as film researchers, as was Joanne King with picture research. Venita Singh Warner, Laura Davey, Harriet Rowe and Kate Gorst gave terrific support as Production Assistants as did, successively, first Stephanie Harvey and then Tanya Batchelor as my own assistants. Ann Cattini (ably supported by Shirley Escott when Ann was away on maternity leave) was the unit manager. I was fortunate that Ann worked with me for some ten years or so. Her management abilities are, in my experience, second to none, and she made a huge creative contribution to both these television series. I owe her more than I can ever repay.

John Kennedy did a terrific job with the graphics across both series and the film editors Jamie Hay and Alan Lygo both made a vital contribution. At BBC Books Sheila Ableman, Anna Ottewill and Martha Caute were always encouraging. Andrew Nurnberg remained a still point in all the various storms.

I need also to thank my co-producers. In America

A&E/the History Channel and in Germany NDR. Without their support neither series could have been realised as they were.

Most of all, of course, I thank our many interviewees whose names are recorded in the eye witness section of this book. Their memories are priceless.

This book is dedicated to my daughter and two sons with their father's love.

LR

INDEX

Alliluyev, Kira 153–4
Aly, Götz 135
Amann, Max 34
Anfilov, Professor Viktor 166, 179
anti-Semitism
  in Austria 100–1
  and the extermination camps 325
  in Germany 17–20, 291–3
  Hitler's views 21–2, 66, 69, 72,
    291–2, 293, 294, 310, 337
  Kristallnacht 70–2, 292–3
  Nazi 24, 31–2, 44, 65–72, 291–6
  see also Jews
Aplerbeck hospital 74–7
Arlt, Dr Fritz 130, 134–6
Auschwitz 19, 287, 291, 315,
  324–5
Austria, Anschluss (unification)
  with 90, 91, 96–102, 104

Bamber, Rudi 66, 70–1, 292, 293
Bazarnik, Zbigniew 134
Bechler, Bernhard 159–61, 167,
  276, 277, 278, 280
Behnke, Carlheinz 229–30
Belorussia
  Operation Bagration 339–44
  partisan war 221–4
Below, Günther von 254, 283
Bełżec 315, 317, 322, 324
Benda, Luise von 147
Beria, Lavrenti 151, 176–80, 191,
  192
Berlin Wall 7

Bernhardt, Gerda 74, 75
Bernhardt, Manfred 74–5, 76, 77
Berzina, Maya 190
Bessel, Dr Richard 38, 40
Biebow, Hans 138–40
Bitzel, Uwe 76–7
Blaskowitz, Colonel-General
  Johannes 116–17
Bleeker-Kohlsaat, Charles 119–20
Blomberg, General von 50–1, 55,
  90, 92–6
Bock, Field Marshal von 158
Boehm-Tettelbach, Karl 51, 55–6,
  68, 69, 92, 93, 94, 95, 108–9,
  329, 354–5
  and the formal German surrender
    359
  and the plot to kill Hitler (1944)
    331–2, 333–4
Bormann, Martin 73, 207–9
Bouhler, Philipp 72, 73, 74, 77,
  295
Brandt, Dr Karl 73–4
Brauchitsch, Walter von 147, 160,
  199, 202
Brest-Litovsk, Treaty of 175–6,
  179
Bris, Aleksey 203–4, 209–10, 211,
  219, 224–5
Britain
  and Hitler's foreign policy objec-
    tives 79–80, 83–6
  and the Hitler's invasion of the
    Soviet Union 143–4, 145–6,

156, 163, 171, 198
and the Munich Agreement 103
and the outbreak of war 106,
    107, 108, 109
Browning, Professor Christopher
    17, 132, 139
Brozek, Mieczyslaw 115–16
Brückner, Wilhelm 73
Brüning, Heinrich 37, 39, 81
Buchner, Adolf 215–16
Bukharin, N.I. 149
Burkovski, Albert 250, 253–4, 262
Butrimonys, killing of Jews in
    298–303, 308–9

Canaris, Admiral Wilhelm 107–8
Chamberlain, Neville 103
Chełmno gas vans 314–15, 317,
    324
Children's 'Euthanasia' Programme
    73–7
Chuikov, Vasily 254–6, 257, 262,
    263, 356
Communists in Germany 16, 32,
    37, 39, 42, 43
    interrogation and imprisonment
    47–9
    and the Nazi rise to power 37,
    39, 42, 43
concentration camps 46, 47, 48–9,
    115, 135–6
Czechoslovakia, German invasion
    of 91, 102–6, 108

Dachau 46, 47, 48, 49, 89
Dalton, Hugh 171
Darwinism, and Hitler 34–6, 73,
    104, 108
Demmin, Red Army rampage in
    357–9
democracy 10
    in Germany 16, 26, 33, 37
    and the Nazi Party 38–9
Dietrich, Otto 52, 188–9
Drexler, Anton 21, 23

Eden, Anthony 84
Edward VIII, King 92, 93
Eggert, Paul 75–6
Eichmann, Adolf 101, 294, 321,
    337
Eigi, Irma 120–2
Einsatzgruppen 114, 161, 173–4
    killing of Jews in Lithuania
    296–309
Eisner, Kurt 16
Engel, Major 116–17
ethnic Germans
    and the Nazi administration of
        Poland 118–36, 137–8
    in the Sudetenland 102–3
extermination camps 48–9, 324–5
    Auschwitz 19, 287, 291, 315,
        324–5
    German people and knowledge of
        336–8
    Treblinka 287–91, 324

Felder, Josef 43, 46–7
Fernau, Walter 330–1, 348–9,
    351–3
Fest, Joachim 98
Fiedler, Heinz 342–3, 344
Filippov, Lieutenant-Colonel 275–6
Finland, Soviet war with 155–6
former Nazis, attitudes of 9–12
Forster, Albert 117, 125, 126–7,
    129–30
France
    burning of Paris synagogues 316
    and the Madagascar Plan 294–5
    Nazi defeat of 146, 158
    occupation of the Ruhr 25–6
    and the outbreak of war 106,
        107, 108, 109
    and Polish Jews 132, 141
Frank, Hans 14, 111, 117, 130–2,
    133–5, 141, 211, 295–6,
    318–19
Frenkiel, Estera 136, 137, 139–40,
    323–4
Frick, Wilhelm 43

Fritsch, German Army commander 90, 93–4, 95, 99

Fuchs, Dora 139

Fyodorov, Veniamin 341–2

Gallay, Mark 150–2

Gareev, Makhmud 240, 241–2, 269, 340, 355

Gavrilchenko, Inna 212–13

Gehlen, Colonel Reinhard 227

Gellately, Professor Robert 59, 61, 62

German people
and the benefits of racism 334–5
and the final stages of the war 350–3
knowledge of the extermination of the Jews 335–9
and the Nazi state 56–65, 77–8

German Workers' Party (later Nazi Party) 21, 22–4

Gestapo 58–65

Goebbels, Josef 14, 30, 35, 55–6, 70, 72, 92, 109, 152, 329
and the Jews 312–13, 318, 320
and Operation Barbarossa 161, 172, 184, 199
on Ribbentrop 85

Golokolenko, Ivan 270–2, 273–5, 276

Goncharov, Efim 222, 223–4

Göring, Hermann 24, 26, 43, 49, 55, 85, 88, 90, 94, 95, 207, 329
and Austria 98–9
and the Battle of Stalingrad 276–7
and Czechoslovakia 104
and the Jews 310
and Poland 131–2, 133

Gottberg, Curt von 228

Graf von Kielmansegg, Johann-Adolf 49–50, 81

Gramauskas, Juozas 302–3

Greiser, Arthur 111–12, 117, 125–9, 130, 131, 136, 137–8, 139, 295, 314

Groeben, Peter von der 202, 229, 230

Gruhn, Erna 94

Grynszpan, Herschel 70–2

Guderian, General Heinz 168–9, 198–9

Gurevich, Anatoly 162

Gutterer, Leopold 312

Hácha, Emil 104–5

Haerter, Ernst Erich 207

Hähnel, Bruno 30–1, 36, 43

Halder, Franz 147–8, 159, 198, 217, 250–1, 254

Hamann, Dr Brigitte 21–2

Hefelmann, Dr Hans 74

Helm, Major Erwin 351, 352, 353

Herwarth, Hans von 107, 331, 333, 334

Hess, Rudolf 163

Heydrich, Reinhard 65, 114, 161, 296, 310–11, 312, 316, 337
and the Wansee conference 319–23

Himmler, Heinrich 9, 50, 56, 65, 100, 101–2, 160–1
and the final stages of the war 354–5
and the Jews 293–4, 310, 312, 316, 319, 320–1, 323
and the partisan war 230–1
and Poland 118, 125, 129, 130, 131–3, 135

Hindenburg, Paul 37, 39, 40, 41, 42, 43, 50, 51

Hindenlang, Gerhard 281–2

Hitler, Adolf
and anti-Semitism 21–2, 66, 69, 72, 291–2, 293, 294, 310, 337
appointment as Chancellor 39–44, 51
and the Armed Forces 50–1, 329–30
Army officers' plot to kill (1944) 331–4
and the Battle of Stalingrad 249,

250–1, 254, 265, 276–7,
277–8, 281, 282–3
and Blitzkrieg 146
and Blomberg's resignation 94,
95–6
and Britain 79–80, 83–6, 143–4
and the Children's 'Euthanasia'
Programme 73–7
daily routine 52–3
and the deportation of the Jews
310, 311, 313–14, 316–19, 323
early history 21–3
and the final stages of the war
348–50, 353–4, 355–6
foreign policy 79–80, 82–4, 90–4,
96–102
former Nazis' attitudes to 9, 10–12
and the Nazi leadership 328–9
and the Nazi Party 21, 23–4, 29,
32–6, 37–40
and Nazi rule in Germany 46,
54–6, 72–3
and Operation Bagration 341,
343–4
and Operation Barbarossa 147–8,
154–5, 156–9, 160, 163, 164,
166–7, 171, 182–4, 198–9,
201–2, 209, 234, 270, 275, 325
and Operation Blue 241–2
personality 11–12, 14, 32–3
and Poland 106–9, 112, 116–17,
117–18, 126, 129–30, 132–3,
141–2
Putsch trial and imprisonment
26–9
rearmament programme 50, 51,
80–2, 83, 86–7, 88–90
rise to power 13–15
and the Soviet Union 144–5, 146,
147–8, 222
and Stalin 148–9, 153–4, 195,
218
and the Storm Troopers 49–50
suicide 357
and the Ukraine 203–7, 208, 210,
226, 227

and the USA 197–8, 318
and 'working towards the Fuhrer'
53–4, 73, 112
'Hitler over Germany' presidential
campaign 37–8
Holocaust 49, 143, 180, 294, 325,
348
Horn, Wolfgang 168, 169, 187–8,
199, 215
Hossbach Memorandum 90–4
Huxley, Aldous 33

inflation in Germany 26, 29
Italy 98, 327–8, 347–8

Jagemann, Franz 124, 124–5
Jäger Report 309
Japan 166, 170, 198
Jews 287–325
'Aryanization' programme 67–9
Austrian 100–1, 294
and the Chelmno gas vans
314–15, 317, 324
deportation to the East 310–14,
316–19, 321–2
'eastern' 19–20
Einsatzgruppen killings of 173–4,
296–309
German 17–19, 69–70, 311–12,
312–17
German people and knowledge of
the extermination of the Jews
335–9
and the Gestapo 60, 62–3
and the Jäger Report 309
Łódź ghetto 118, 136–41, 293,
314–15, 323–4
Madagascar Plan 294–5
and Nazi rule in Germany 49,
65–72
Nuremberg Laws 67
in Poland 112, 113–14, 116, 118,
132, 134, 136–42
Soviet 174, 312, 316
and Treblinka 287–91
in the Ukraine 209, 214, 239

and the Wannsee conference
319–23, 337
see also anti-Semitism
Jeziorkowska, Anna 111, 122–4,
130
Jodl, General Alfred von 21, 96,
147, 156, 158, 188

Kalmykova, Tamara 247, 263–4,
265
Kammerling, Walter 100–1
Kantovski, Vladimir 242–6
Kasprzyk, Stefan 124
Kershaw, Ian 338
Kershaw, Professor Ian 53, 54
Kharkov 211–14
offensive (1942) 234–41, 248,
250
Khrushchev, Nikita 149–50
Kielmansegg, Graf von 338–9
Kiev, German capture of 184–5,
188
Klein, Emil 26–7
Koch, Erich 205–7, 209, 210, 214,
218, 227
Konev, Marshal 355, 356
Kranz, Erna 56–8, 71, 336
Kraus, Maria 62–3
Krüger, Friedrich-Wilhelm 131
Krutova, Valentina 250, 252–3,
284
Krutova, Yuri 252, 253, 284

Lammers, Hans-Heinrich 72
Landau, Felix 303–4
Lange, Captain Herbert 314–15
Lashuk, Vladimir 222–3
League of Nations 83, 84, 90, 104
Lebensraum (living space) 83, 91,
144
Lenin, V.I. 148, 149, 172, 175–6
Leningrad, siege of 188, 224
Leroy, Jacques 345–6
Leviné, Eugene 17–19, 44
Linn, Bernd 19–20, 26, 329, 346–7
List, Field Marshal 251

Lithuania, persecution of Jews in
297–309
Łódź ghetto 118, 136–41, 293,
314–15, 323–4
Lohse, Dr Günter 45–6, 72, 79
Losanskaya, Riva 298–301, 308–9
Lubbe, Marinus van der 46
Ludenfdorff, General 27

Madagascar Plan 294–5
Malenkov 193
Marder, Dr Karl 139
Mauth, Maria 172–3
Mauth, Walter 320
Mayr, Captain 21
Mein Kampf (Hitler) 11, 14, 21–2,
28, 82–3, 90
Meissner, Otto 39–40, 73
Mengele, Dr Josef 324
Menzel, Hubert 144, 158, 185
Mereshko, Anatoly 246–8, 254–5,
256, 259, 263, 274, 284, 356–7
Mering, Professor 290
Merkulov, V.N. 162, 163
Michalsky, Engelbert 351, 352
Mikhailovski, Aleksandr 227–8
Mikoyan, Anastas 192
Mikoyan, Stepan 149, 170, 171–2
Mirek, Anna 133–4
Mirzoyan, Suren 265–6, 284
Molotov, Vyacheslav 117, 156–7,
192
Morrell, Dr Theodor 104–5, 355
Moscow, Battle of 185, 189–94,
195–7, 198–9, 200
Moses, Wilhelm 113–14
Mühl-Kühner, Dr 350, 351
Müller, General 160
Müller, Heinrich 64–5, 322
Münch, Gerhard 248, 260, 261,
276, 278–9, 281
Munich
'Night of the Amazons' 57
Putsch 26–8
Räterepublik 16–17
Munich Agreement 103, 105

Mussolini, Benito 45, 98, 103, 105, 157, 327–8

Naumov, Professor Vladimir 176
Navasinskas, Alfonsas 301–2
Nazi Party 29–32
  economic policy 54–5, 80–1, 86–9, 207
  general election results 15, 36, 37, 38, 40–1, 46
  Gestapo 58–65
  and Hitler 21, 23–4, 29, 32–6, 37–40
  origins 21, 22–4
  policies 24
  propaganda 37–8, 40–1, 45
  rise to power 14–15, 37–44
  rule in Germany 45–78
  symbols 24–5
  see also Storm Troopers
Nefyodova, Nadezha 221–4
Neithardt, Georg 28
Nero Order 356
Neurath, Baron Konstantin von 90, 94, 95
Niebel, Dr Theo 76
'Night of the Long Knives' 41, 50, 89
Nuremberg Trials 91, 159, 329

Ogryzko, Vladimir 192–3, 200, 227
Operation Barbarossa 116, 142–94
  Battle of Moscow 185, 189–94, 195–7, 198–9, 200
  Battle of Vyazma 186–9
  and 'criminal' orders 158–61
  fall of Kiev 184–5, 188
  German scorched earth retreat 320
  and the Jews 325
  and Operation Blue 241, 248–9, 269
  partisan war 218–32
  and Red Army officers 170–1
  and Soviet prisoners of war
    180–2, 184, 188, 189
  and Stalin's 'cruel' policy 200–1
  in the Ukraine 202–14, 224–6
  see also Stalingrad

Palfinger, Alexander 139
Papen, Franz von 39, 41, 42, 43, 96–7
Paul, Prince 167
Paulus, Friedrich 254, 265, 275, 279, 281–4
Pawelczak-Grocholska, Danuta 127–8
Pfaller, Alois 31–2, 36, 37, 44, 47–8, 49
Philip, Prince of Hesse 98
Pilacynski, Romuald 126–7
Pirkham, Dr Otto 97
'Planspiel Otto' (army war-game) 42–3
Pol Pot 114
Poland 13, 111–42
  division of 117
  Germanization of 118–36, 295–6
  intelligentsia 114–16, 133
  Jews in 112, 113–14, 116, 118, 132, 134, 136–42
  Lodz ghetto 118, 136–41, 293, 314–15, 323–4
  Nazi invasion of 106–9
Ponomariev, Nikolay 185, 189–90
Pronin, V.S. 192
Pytkina, Zinaida 266–9

Rademacher, Franz 294–5
Rath, Ernst von 70
Rathenau, Walter 17
Ravensbrück 62, 324
Reichert, Rüdiger von 166, 168, 180, 197, 202, 210–11
Reichstag Fire Decree 46
Reski, Waltraud 357–8, 359
Reva, Anatoly 213–14
Ribbentrop, Joachim von 83–6, 92, 93–4, 95, 98, 104, 106, 109, 117, 145, 329

Richter, Herbert 15–16, 32–3, 79, 83, 85
Riefenstahl, Leni 45
Röhm, Ernst 23, 49, 50, 51
Rokossovksy, Konstantin 340
Roosevelt, Franklin D. 318
Rosenberg, Alfred 162, 204, 205–7, 208–9, 227, 311, 313
Rüdiger, Jutta 25, 36, 37, 97

Sankovich, Petr 222, 223–4
Schacht, Hjalmar 41–2, 54–5, 67, 80–1, 86–9, 90
Schaefer-Kehnert, Walter 173, 183, 186–7, 188, 196–7, 211, 214–15
Schcherbakov, Comrade 191
Schenk, Herr 225–6
Schleicher, General von 41, 42, 43, 50
Schmiedel, Alfons 350
Schneider, Albert 169–70, 216, 217–18
Scholl, Hans and Sophie 338
Schröder, Kurt von 43
Schröder, Manfred Freiherr von 48, 82, 85, 102, 103, 104–5, 106
Schuschnigg, Kurt von 96–7
Schwartz, Professor Meier 72
Seifert, Gustav 34–5
Seitz, Susi 99, 100, 101
Semenyak, Georgy 170–1, 181
Semenyuk, Meleti 210, 224
Sengenhof, Dr Weiner 76
Seubert, Anton 351
Seyss-Inquart, Arthur 97
Silkinaite, Viera 297–8
Simon, Sir John 84
SMERSH 266–9
Sorge, Richard 162
Soviet Union
  Einsatzgruppen 114
  and final days of war 355, 356–9
  German fear and hatred of Bolshevism 338–9, 344–7
  and Hitler 144–5

Non-Aggression Pact with Germany 106–8, 117, 145, 156–7, 163–4, 175
  Operation Bagration 339–44
  and Poland 117, 118
  SMERSH 266–9
  see also Operation Barbarossa; Stalin, Josef; Stalingrad
Spaun, Fridolin von 20, 32
SPD (German Socialist Party) 37, 43
Speer, Albert 12, 52–3, 72, 355, 356
Spitzy, Reinhard 84–5, 86, 94, 96, 99, 105
SS (Schutzstaffeln) 50, 101
  in Poland 113, 114, 116, 124, 130–1, 135
Stahlecker, Dr Walther 296–7
Stalin, Josef 53, 148–54, 245–6
  and the Battle of Moscow 189–93, 195
  and the Battle of Stalingrad 250, 255, 265, 269
  and the final days of the war 355
  and Japan 198
  and the Kharkov offensive 234, 241
  and the Nazi–Soviet pact 106–7, 108, 163–4, 175
  and Operation Bagration 340
  and Operation Barbarossa 162–7, 170–2, 174–80, 185, 200–1, 202, 233–4
  and Operation Uranus 273–4
  and order 227 242, 244, 247
  and the partisan war 218–19, 220–1, 222, 224
  and Poland 120
  purging of the Red Army 150–3
Stalingrad 232, 249–65, 269, 275, 276–85, 327
  and Operation Blue 241–2, 247–9, 254
  and Operation Ring 280
  and Operation Uranus 269–76
  and Operation Winter Tempest 277

women soldiers in the Red Army 263–4, 265
Stamenov, Ivan 176–7
Stauffenberg, Count Klaus Schenk von 322–4, 331
Stauffenberg, Count von 51
Stempel, Joachim 237–8, 240, 241, 248, 249, 251–2, 259–60, 261, 279–80, 283–4
Storm Troopers 25, 30, 32, 42, 46, 49–50
  and Jews 44, 65, 66–7, 69, 70–2
  in Poland 124
Strasser, Gregor 41, 50
Strazdovski, Viktor 186, 188
Streicher, Julius 14
Sudaplatov, Pavel 176–9
Sverdlov, Fyodor 197

Tamir, Arnon 65, 66, 67–8, 69, 292
Taylor, A.J.P. 91–2
Ter-Nedden, Dr Wilhelm 206–7
Teschemacher, Hermann 339
Teubert, Wolfgang 30
Theresienstadt 322
Thomas, General 157
Timoshenko, Mikhail 155–6, 219–21, 240
Todt, Fritz 197
Totzke, Ilse Sonja 61–3
Traphöner, Walter 174
Treblinka 287–91, 324
Treskovski, Ivan 220, 221
Trevor-Roper, Hugh 355
Triumph of the Will 45
Trotsky, L. 149, 150
Tupolev, Andrei Nikolaevich 152

Ukraine
  contraception issue 207–9
  fall of Kiev 184–5, 188
  German invasion of 202–14
  Kharkov 211–14, 224–41, 248, 250
  partisan war 224–6

unemployment, in Germany 36, 37, 39, 81
United States, and the Second World War 197–8, 318
Urbanczyk, Stanislaw 115

Vasilevskii 269, 270
Versailles peace treaty 10, 25, 31, 33, 39, 58, 80, 83, 89
  and Poland 106, 108–9, 118, 119
Vitman, Boris 234–5, 236–7, 238–40
Volkogonov, Dimitri 179
Vormann, General Nikolaus von 343–4
Vyazma, Battle of 186–9

Walz, Helmut 257–8, 266
Wannsee conference 319–23, 337
War of the Century 7–8, 12
Weiglein, Karl 350–3
Wiedemann, Fritz 52
Willenberg, Samuel 287–8, 289, 290–1, 309, 324
Winckler, Gabriele 37, 325
Wirth, Captain Christian 315
Wittmann, Theodor 351
'working towards the Fuhrer' 53–4, 73, 112
World War I 9, 10, 15–16, 18, 21, 55, 81, 146, 175–6, 312, 347–8, 349
Würzburg archive 58–65

Zahn, Johannes 42, 68, 80, 82–3, 86–7, 335, 352, 353–4
Zeitler, Kurt 251
Zelionka, Petras 304–8
Zhukov, Marshal Georgy 146, 164, 166, 170, 171–2, 179–80, 185, 234, 355, 356, 357
  and the Battle of Moscow 189
  and Operation Uranus 269, 270, 271
Zielke, Eugen 137, 138
Zinoviev, G.Y. 149

PICTURE CREDITS